WHAT TO
        DO
     ABOUT
EVERYTHING

WHAT TO DO ABOUT

A MANUAL FOR DOMESTIC LIFE

EVERYTHING

BARBARA TONER

hardie grant books

MELBOURNE · LONDON

Published in 2011 by Hardie Grant Books

Hardie Grant Books (Australia)
85 High Street
Prahran, Victoria 3181
www.hardiegrant.com.au

Hardie Grant Books (UK)
Dudley House, North Suite
34–35 Southampton Street
London WC2E 7HF
www.hardiegrant.co.uk

National Library of Australia Cataloguing-in-Publication entry
Toner, Barbara, 1948–
What to do about everything: a manual for domestic life / Barbara Toner.
9781740667111 (pbk.)
Home economics—Miscellanea
Life skills—Handbooks, manuals, etc.
640

Cover design by Vivien Sung
Text design by Vivien Sung
Typesetting by Megan Ellis
Typeset in Hoefler Text 10.75/15.5 pt
Printed in China by 1010 Printing International Limited

10 9 8 7 6 5 4 3 2 1

CONTENTS

Why households need managing, in my opinion

Domestic life is tricky. It's miles trickier than it was when the average household contained a man and a woman who were married to each other and whose ideal family consisted of a boy and a girl, born in that order, two years apart. Everyone in that household knew their place. They mightn't have liked it, but they knew it. Husbands provided, wives kept house, children were seen but not heard. If they were well off, they had a family house, a family car, a family holiday and a TV that never showed anything more dangerous than *Hawaii Five-O*. If they weren't well off, they lived within their means. There was no identity theft, no interactive online games with killing, no speed-dating, no easy credit leading to massive debt, no IVF, no cold calling, no global warming, no homosexuality you could properly acknowledge, and not much divorce. Smoking, butter and sugar were good for you. Life was slower and less cluttered. Exactly how boring, fulfilling or healthy it was remains a matter for personal reflection, but in complicated times it's easy to look back fondly on the simplicity of clearly drawn lines and uninformed innocence.

There's no longer any such thing as an average household. Couples don't always marry; couples don't always have children; couples aren't always heterosexual; couples often separate; parents are often single; people are often single; people marry a lot; families extend horizontally as well as vertically; mothers go out to work; fathers stay at home; both mothers and fathers go out to work.

Being able to choose the style and content of our home life is a wonderful thing because choice in general is a wonderful thing – only a very lazy person would deny it. But does it necessarily lead to efficiency, happiness, fulfilment and harmony? No.

Today's households depend for smooth running on complex structures that require endless decision-making. Aside from who should do what and when, which are truly simple questions only for people living alone, there's the seriously vexed question of how things must be done so no one feels cheated, stupid or negligent.

Our principles are on a constant collision course with necessity. We want to be free from debt, but borrowing is critical to home-owning and sometimes to eating. We want to save the planet, but we have to be able to drive, fly and buy cheap imports. We don't want to be wasteful, but we can't afford to collapse from botulism. In household terms, choice translates into an endless quest for perfect outcomes. Information on how to achieve them is at our fingertips but who has the time and energy to hunt it down? It's a nightmare for the perfectionist control-freak and probably not much better for the rest of you.

My family hates not knowing what to do; we hate thinking we aren't doing properly what we've elected to do; and we hate the thought that we've spent money on someone or something that was terrible value, if not a complete waste of time. Our several households, which are dotted about Australia and the United Kingdom, reflect the usual combinations (married, single, divorced, remarried, full nests, empty nests, transient and settled) but wherever we live and whatever our status, we're oddly assailed by exactly the same domestic dilemmas. Some are big, like dealing with debt, bad health and housing; some are trivial, like how to cure a hangover, master a pedicure or get rid of ants. And all of them require answers which mostly and annoyingly aren't a simple matter of common sense.

About ten years ago, my husband bought me an illustrated name thing in a frame from the newsagent because he thought it described me. It said: 'Gladys, from *Gladiolus* the flower, is the living dynamo of her family and job.' It may have been ironic and/or made no sense, but you take your inspiration where you find it and it was in the spirit of this name thing that I decided to tackle the fundamentals of 21st-century household management. If the answers were out there, I would find them.

I made a list of everything I could remember that had ever, could ever, or should ever have challenged me in the broad domestic arena. For solutions I drew first on the murky well of my personal experience and, where it could be relied on, the experience of family and friends. When I drew a blank, which was mostly, I consulted experts ranging from academics attached to government-funded studies to high-powered actuaries, relationship experts, and the man who runs our local booze shop. Most of them were endlessly patient. To plug the gaps, I consulted thousands of websites from the ridiculous to the 'must be right because a world authority wrote it' and did my best to sort the rubbish from the spot-on. (I've listed those I considered most useful up the back of the book, under, curiously, a section called Useful websites)

My aim was to discover first, how best a household dilemma could be addressed; second, how it could be addressed cost-effectively; and third, whether this entailed any damage to the environment that I could reasonably, responsibly – and, let's face it, easily – avoid. This book is the result. I don't expect you to agree with everything in it. Everything turns out to be open to dispute, whether it's food science or how to change a car tyre. (If you want to engage in the debate or add to the body of information, you're more then welcome. The website is whattodoabouteverything. com.) But here's the encouraging thing.

What I learnt changed my life, because, Householder, it turns out that even if answers aren't definitive, they simplify matters, whether it's how long to freeze meat or what to do if you get arrested. I hope that by sticking them all in a single book, I'll save household time and energy and contribute to household harmony. I know I've left out great wads of critical matter and included stuff of interest mainly to me. I know I've given cursory treatment to some subjects and over-loving attention to others. But in calling this book 'What to do about everything', I mean what to do about everything I can think of right now. The sieve has been my own curiosity and self-interest, which, I can only hope, more or less accord with yours.

PART I

THE HAPPY
HOUSEHOLD

I MARRIED MY HUSBAND when I was a teenager and I have remained married to him even though he calls me Gladys when my name is Barbara. To begin with, he called me Gladioli because I was Australian and he was English and he thought it was funny. Then he turned it into Gladys, which was even less so. I don't like the name Gladys, but in all the years I've known him he's almost never used it in anger, which is significant because we are a volatile and, in many respects, mismatched couple.

When I ask myself how it can be that we're still together despite our yawning differences and clashing similarities, I see that our natures complement each other – actually, less our natures than our strengths and weaknesses – and this has enabled us, with varying degrees of success, to negotiate the treacherous waters of domestic routine as well as the thunderbolts of family life.

Our household is just like any other in this respect. With or without the presence of significant others, all any of us wants from home is a haven in which we feel safe, at liberty to be ourselves and, in spite of that, welcome. We want a place as free from anxiety as possible, in which basic creature comforts are constant, and angry shouting is kept to a minimum. So the first question that must be addressed concerns the likelihood of attaining this.

Household harmony, it turns out, is contingent not only on efficient management, which begins with sensible use of the household's strengths, but on the way in which household members relate to each other. Even in one-person households, where moods expelled into the air can turn into separate entities and fight each other. Even in households where the only other member is a pet. What counts is how many people you live with, their stage of life, their expectations and, most importantly, the combination of their dispositions. Forget love, forget romance, forget friendship: a household is an arrangement of types, and a happy household is a well-arranged household.

1

UNDERSTANDING THE HOUSEHOLD

A happy arrangement isn't, for the most part, the natural outcome of love, passion or even affection. It's achieved with a modicum of self-awareness and a capacity for compromise whoever the household members are, and households may now include any of the following: a single person who has never been married; a single person who is divorced or widowed; a single person with children from one or more relationships; two or more people who are not related and not sleeping together; two or more people of whom some are related or some are sleeping together; two or more people who are brothers and sisters; a couple without children; a couple with children; a couple with children from more than this relationship; a couple with adult children; a couple whose adult children have left home; a couple whose relationship is so on/off that the household doubles as a single person's with a second person's clothes in the wardrobe. One restless lifetime can include any number of arrangements, but even if yours so far hasn't, regardless of where you are now, next year it will be different, if only because we all move on. Not only do people's needs and expectations change with age and circumstances but household members come and go and with them the balance of strengths and weaknesses which have been holding it all together.

Every addition, every departure, every change in circumstance requires a clear appraisal of the needs of the household's members: where and how they coincide and where and how they clash. It also requires a clear appraisal of temperaments and values, because a successful household is only the sum of its properly functioning parts, however disparate these might be. Unless the parts acknowledge their own and each other's peculiarities, there will be no easy rising to the challenges of domestic life, and, really, who needs the rising to be difficult? For a household to be well arranged, everyone needs to understand each other. Insight is the key. Insight plus acceptance. All you need to do is recognise who does what best, plus how and why, so that arguing can be kept to a minimum.

First up, Householder, know yourself. Know what you want and what you value, what you must have and what you can do without; know your strengths and weaknesses in the domestic arena, especially how you react to conflict, your preferred style of communication, your sensitivities and your blind spots. Acknowledge what you have in common with other household members as well as what you don't, and then decide not only what your priorities are but also how best you, as a sensible/crazy person, can manage among others on the sensible/crazy spectrum.

The fact that my husband and I remain married is living proof of this necessity. He struggles with change; I thrive on it. He likes his possessions to have their proper place and for that place to be as sacrosanct as the altar in St Peter's which means I now fret more about his possessions than I do about my own. I call him obsessive; he calls himself neat. I regard myself as restless; he thinks I'm reckless. Whatever we are, our quirks of nature are at the heart of our modus operandi. They serve us in good stead even when we are as full of loathing for each other as only couples as long-standing as we are can be. They settle who does what as a matter of course when speaking is just not possible. He mops a surface; I call the bank.

Knowing anything for certain, let alone yourself, is, I agree, no snack. But most of us are capable of at least a small degree of self-awareness. If you're not and your best friends won't tell you, go online and take a test to determine your personality type. You can scoff, especially if you are remembering the tests you've taken at work that meant nothing and got you nowhere. But the point about your personality type is that it affects all aspects of your life: how you approach it, how you make the decisions you do, how you implement the decisions you've made, how you respond to the outcomes of the actions you've taken, as well as how you go about explaining all of the above. Even if you know nothing else about yourself, at least sort out where you are with regard to conflict, communication and order, because, no two ways about it, these are of prime concern in a household.

Conflict is at the heart of all household disruption whether it's with someone or something in it or something or someone outside it. How you resolve it depends entirely on your personality type. You may, for instance be an 'I must avoid confrontation at all costs' type, or an 'I'm going to put a stop to this with one short, sharp observation' type, or maybe a 'We're going to thrash this out until both of us understand exactly what it is I'm upset about' type. And you can convey this in any number of ways that can be misunderstood by those who aren't the same as you because their behaviour patterns are just not yours. For example, one of you may argue from the gut, another from logic. The positions can be so diametrically opposed that there would seem to be no meeting point.

What helps is spotting the pattern. A gut arguer will always be a gut arguer, and a logic person will always be a logic person. It's a fundamental difference that can be overcome with listening. Not easy, I know, especially when it comes to The Argument That Never Goes Away.

This is a feature of all households in which a relationship is attempting to be permanent. How it's tackled is a make-or-break matter, regardless of its content. It can be about money, sex, in-laws, distribution of labour, how you speak to each other under stress, the mess in the kitchen or something I can't even begin to imagine. You'll know it by its life cycle. It crops up; it causes misery; it goes away; it crops up. The fact that it goes away is a testament to the good will that exists in your household. The fact that it comes back again proves that the fundamental difference that stokes it has yet to be properly acknowledged. I'm not saying that acknowledging the difference will banish the argument; only that acknowledging it – and not in a 'Here we go again' way, thanks very much – will lessen the misery because the reason for it is clear. Less misery is what we are hoping to achieve, and you will manage this by talking to each other nicely in moments of crisis. This brings us to how we talk to each other.

·············· COMMUNICATION AND ·············· THE HOUSEHOLDER

You may convey your ideas and emotions easily, openly and honestly, or you may be silent, secretive and prone to brooding. Maybe you are frank, honest and direct, and people think you're abrasive. Maybe you think quickly on your feet, and people mistake you for a bully. Maybe you need time in private to form an opinion and to recover from the shock of hearing what other people think, so maybe those people imagine you are withholding and unemotional. Maybe your response to conflict is so emotional that people stop hearing what you're saying because all they can hear is how you are saying it. I'm guessing.

You can, whatever the case, save yourself hours, even years, of bitter experience by taking a good hard look at your household's communication styles. Who needs what, how badly, and how are they going about getting it? Who's saying what, do they mean it and how hurtful are they actually trying to be? Are the needs of one household member at odds with another's, or is everyone after the same thing but just asking differently?

It will be your ability to recognise and adapt to each other's finer feelings that will dictate the tenor of your existence. First, though, spot the finer feeling. Some are so fine they look like no feeling at all. You need to be aware of that. When it comes to problem-solving, a logic person can trample all over the sensitivities of a gut person. Those who favour logic find it very difficult to concede a point to the person working by instinct, but, Householder, try.

········ ORDER AND THE HOUSEHOLDER ········

Some householders are sticklers for a right time and place for everything, because they need that degree of order in their lives just to function. Others need less order in their lives, because they like to think they have order in their heads.

People living alone are free spirits when it comes to order, not just in the degree of it but in the manner by which it's achieved. Their households can be pigsties or exhibition pieces depending on their whim. The rest of us must bend to the tempering influence of others. Over the years I have learnt, first, not to leave my mess anywhere that could in our house be called public, and, second, not to leave for the airport with anything less than four hours to spare. Whether I would have become this person in the fullness of time anyway I don't know. I'm just observing that compromise is the easiest solution to different attitudes to order, as the alternative is too noisy and stressful to endure for more than a year. Ditto should one of you be always punctual and another not.

Knowing who does what and why can't possibly avoid all arguments. People are just too irritating. But knowing that your approach to given situations is always going to be different, and that the argument isn't personal, will help. According to Carl Jung, differences between individuals are simply that – different ways of seeing things. People are just different and their differences can be easily recognised. This may be hard to swallow when one of you is aiming a plate at the other's head, but it's helpful long-term in the cold light of day and, more importantly, it's central to compromise.

2

HOUSE RULES

WELCOME

Compromise doesn't come easily to many people. This is why we have sulking and/or yelling, then, eventually, rules. If you want a successfully managed household, which is to say one that engenders minimal tension and maximum efficiency, you need to agree on essentials, most notably what works best for the good of the whole regardless of the conflicting interests of the whole's constituents.

In most households without children, rules go unspoken, but everyone knows what they are because they are based on a general expectation of order plus fair play. For example, my husband accepts that when I cook, cutlery and dishes and pots and pans will be used and rendered dirty. This causes him pain. He says pretty well every day, 'Did you have to use every pot in the house?' I don't allow this to upset me because I know he is in charge of cleaning up and so entitled. Should he not be around, and should I have to clear up, the mess causes me pain.

The trouble with unspoken rules is that one or some members of the household can pretend, once they've been broken, that they didn't know what they were. Then you have grounds for conflict, with everyone falling over each other's personality types: fast-thinking, verbal analysers annihilating sensitive ponderers, and so on. Therefore, rules are best said out loud in front of all concerned in such a way that the household doesn't turn on the person who appears to be making them. I don't know how you do this without looking like a meeting of the Communist Party's Household Management Committee. My preference would be for casually if a problem hasn't actually arisen, and, if it has, then firmly in the case of children, or over a bottle of wine in the case of adults. Just the one, though. It's during the second bottle that people get argumentative and silly, no question.

In the event of there being no spoken acknowledgement of rules of any sort and everyone relying on everyone else's good will and the good will being in short supply, I've taken advice and prepared some guidelines. They may be useful should arbitration be required.

Contrary to general expectations, most people living on their own are happy and not lonely or prone to feelings of isolation, even though a large percentage of them are aged over sixty-five. In the UK and Australia, elderly women are the largest group of single-person householders, as baby-booming husbands kick the bucket before their wives. Numerically, they're most closely rivalled by middle-aged men whose marriages have failed. Prominent among the rest are the stereotypes as seen on TV: the comparatively affluent young men and women who haven't found love, prefer their own company or are delaying the commitment to a relationship usually required by childbirth.

Despite the vast differences in personal situations, the rules for all occupants of single-person households are the same, which is to say largely nonexistent, but the following ought really to be adhered to:

○ Live within your means. It's hard having no one to share your expenses, especially when costs are so rapidly escalating and money is in such short supply, but there it is. Without someone else to watch your spending, you must watch it yourself. It may go right against your spendthrift grain, but uncontrolled debt is terrifying even if you're lucky enough to know a person who, if called upon in an emergency, could relieve you of it.

○ Avoid slovenliness. It leads to degeneracy and so no visitors. You need visitors, so wash up more than once a week, dust, clean the bathroom – especially the loo – and put newspapers out to recycle.

○ Temper any inclination to fussiness, because it will surely lead to obsessive and/or compulsive behaviour, which you won't notice but others will.

○ Eat properly. Snacking isn't a proper diet. Not even nuts.

○ Get out of the house or people will assume you're a freak. Soon you'll be suspected of crimes you didn't commit. Also, if people get used to not seeing you, your absence won't be noticed in the event of a fire, fall or flood. Should you hate going out (and I know most of you don't), make a point of phoning at least one person a day to ask this person about themselves. A tendency to self-centredness is unavoidable when you live by yourself.

○ Look in the mirror. Check yourself for a dirty face, clothes on inside-out, matted hair at the back of your head and anything else a housemate may notice before allowing you to appear in public.

.... LIVING WITH YOUR PARENTS ....

This is infinitely more appealing than it used to be, because baby-boomer parents make very accommodating housemates and moving out is ridiculously expensive. The drawback is that your parents will want to know far more about your personal life than you may like, and their expectations of you won't be those of a flatmate. You will remain a child in their eyes even though you are forty-two and responsible for a classroom of children or the company payroll. You will have no real say in the kitchen and you will suffer a protracted adolescence: parents laying down the law bring out the worst in everyone. Fair play counts, of course it does, but it will always be skewed, however affectionately, because the roof you are under is owned by your elders and betters, and you will want to rebel. So:

- Pay board. This confirms your adult status in the household. The amount (not to be confused with market-value rent) should cover at least a little more than your expenses. You may be out for most meals and use electricity only for light and hot water and to charge your phone and computer, but think of your saving. Board won't necessarily buy you an equal say, but contributing to the best of your ability will indicate respect and, believe me, parents are very big on respect from adult children.

- Notify parents should you be coming home early, late, or not at all or you will be accused of treating the place like a hotel. Parents are creatures of habit and like to eat at the same time every night and know how many people will be at the meal table. Also, they will start calling hospitals, the police and your mobile phone ten minutes after your anticipated arrival.

- If you can't keep your room tidy, at least close the door. Make an effort to confine your mess to your room, as your parents will have reached that point in their lives where another adult's mess is unacceptable, especially if it includes cables and shoes.

- Always return used items to the place your parents keep them or they'll be phoning you at work and making you come home to find them.

- Try not to talk to your parents as if they are morons. It's true that they look moronic, but this is because they haven't heard what you said or were so lost in thought when you spoke that they are taking time to digest the meaning and import of your remark. You may know a great deal more than they do about some things, but by and large they know a great deal more than you about everything else.

● Keep the noise down. You will almost certainly be observing different hours, so respect theirs before expecting them to respect yours (unless you are a firefighter, doctor or other emergency worker).

● Talk to them. Not all the time or about stuff you consider none of their business, but at least about the bits of your life that are amusing, interesting and if necessary alarming, so they have something to discuss when you're not home.

● Reach an agreement about having sex with others in your bedroom, which will never be far enough away from your parents for comfort. Under no circumstances should they be made aware that you are having it.

·············· LIVING WITH HOUSEMATES ··············

Housemates may or may not be friends or even people known to each other before living together. They are individuals who, while residing under one roof, have sole responsibility for themselves but equal responsibility for the running of the house. The running may be a little or a lot, and it's as well you appreciate just how much before you move in. Before committing yourself, take a good hard look at the cleanliness of the communal areas, the size of your bedroom, the available hanging space, the laundry facilities, the condition of the fridge, the locks on doors – internal and well as external – traffic through the bathroom/s, attitudes to sharing food, plus arrangements for rent- and bill-paying. All are indicators of the household's living standards and the degree to which they might coincide with your own. Walk around the place and sniff. Smells need to be congenial. Be alert to the smell of damp, old clothes, mouldy food, cigarettes, people and takeaways.

You don't actually have to like your housemates, because you don't need to see them if you can lock your door and arrange your comings and goings to avoid theirs. Indeed, liking may be a luxury you can't afford if there's nothing else on offer. On the other hand, there are some people that you simply can't and shouldn't have to live with. Should you have vague feelings of foreboding, listen to them. Ask yourself pertinent questions. Not only 'Is this person a psychopath?' but also 'Why does the house feel peculiar and how come when her mouth smiles her eyes don't?' Logical thinkers need to touch base with their instinct. You need to be comfortable, both physically and mentally. Once you've decided to move in:

- Agree on an out clause. Whether it's to kick someone out or to take off yourself, insist on a period of grace during which you see how well the arrangement is working.

- Get everything in writing: most significantly, what the rent is, when it's due, who pays the utility bills and how they are paid. Pay rent by direct debit. Rent comes before dining out in a hard-pressed monthly budget, and arguing over money is cheap. We hate cheap.

- Agree on chores: who cleans communal areas and when.

- Be nice. Overly assertive isn't attractive in a newcomer or towards newcomers. Once you've moved in, try to get the measure of your housemates before you judge them. They will certainly be weird in one way or another, because their parents aren't your parents and their habits won't always be yours, but they'll think you are weird as well.

- If something bugs you, like people taking without asking food you have bought or cooked, people wandering uninvited into your bedroom, non-resident boyfriends or girlfriends of housemates overstaying their welcome, or people using all the hot water or your clothes, say so.

- If saying so gets you nowhere, take stock. Is the cause of the conflict based on different attitudes to order and fair play or to different methods of communication? How bad is it really? If the answer is very, attempt to negotiate, but if there is no possible compromise, weigh giving in against checking out. If you give in, don't sulk. Sulking makes you miserable. Store the incident as information.

- Have sex with a housemate only if you appreciate that it can lead to regret so enormous that one of you has to move out.

· LIVING WITH BOYFRIENDS/GIRLFRIENDS ·

Moving in with your boyfriend or girlfriend is somewhere between sleeping with your housemate and marriage. It's much more complicated than anyone ever wants it to be, because there's always the unresolved issue of the timeframe. Before moving so much as a decent coffee maker out of your own place and into another's, ask yourself how long the shelf life is of this particular arrangement and whether you're agreed on that. Don't hope for a gorgeous outcome. Gorgeous outcomes take hard work.

I agree that not all marriages, either formal or de facto, last a lifetime – the average first marriage in the UK is reckoned to last eleven years – but a wedding does entail a commitment to stay together until it becomes intolerable. Moving in with someone you're sleeping with entails a commitment to stay together as long as it's convenient. This clearly is infinitely more casual than a marriage, but ending it can feel just as awful as a divorce for at least one of you, and the ground rules are vague. If you have moved in simply to save time travelling between each other's places, you need to ask yourself the following questions:

- ⦿ Whose home are you living in? If one of you is moving into a place the other already owns or rents, does it remain fundamentally their place? Whose pictures go on the walls? Whose books go on the shelves? Who's holding the reins here, and is this acceptable in terms of home-making?

- ⦿ If one of you has a mortgage on the house or flat, should the other be charged rent and thereby become a lodger? Then, are you mainly a lodger or mainly a boyfriend/girlfriend?

- ⦿ If one of you earns a vast amount more than the other, should the household expenses be shared equally?

- ⦿ How much independence is acceptable in this arrangement? Are your expectations of what it's offering the same?

·········· LIVING IN A RELATIONSHIP TILL ·········· DEATH PARTS YOU

A married relationship, with or without the vows, with or without children, with or without pets, has in its favour an intention of long-term stability. This is a big plus, but it doesn't guarantee untrammelled happiness. Even the most successful marriages turn out to be a fine balance between levels of misery and satisfaction simply because the two people in them are different. This important ratio, as estimated by me, ought never to be less than 55 per cent satisfaction to 45 per cent misery over a sustained period, though there will be rare days when 100 per cent misery or 100 per cent contentment can occur.

Far be it from me to tell you how to have a happy relationship, but you might like to know that research has identified characteristics of a healthy marriage as reported by people who are in them. They include: a mutual long-term view of the relationship; perseverance in times of trouble; acknowledgement of couple and individual needs; shared values and history; respectful methods of communication; humour; the ability to compromise; fighting fair; enjoyment of each other's company; physical and psychological intimacy strengthened through overcoming difficulties; feelings of friendship; and regular expressions of affection.

Conversely, research shows that unhappiness in marriages is caused by: lack of time together; lack of understanding; differing as opposed to different values; different goals and expectations; lack of communication; working full-time; housework; and lack of financial security. Your household may suffer from none or all of these. The point is that a beady eye must be kept on one's own wellbeing compared with the wellbeing of one's partner, always bearing in mind that the partner's method of expressing anything in the way of satisfaction or misery may not be yours, or may not exist at all. Common sense is required as well as empathy. If you are miserable, and your partner is equally miserable, are you looking at arrangement failure or total failure? Maybe all that's required are more realistic expectations. In which case:

◉ Respect each other's differences, especially if you see them as weaknesses. If, under pressure, one of you is short-tempered and the other sulks, or one of you always shouts and the other always stalks out, there's not much point in hoping it will be otherwise. Have therapy if you like but in my experience people revert to type so anticipate. Stay calm. Avoid pressure. No, seriously. When you can, avoid it.

◉ Respect each other's strengths. If one is better at money/cooking/car maintenance/speaking sensitively to the children or any other thing, then give the job to them. If neither of you is much good at it, or both of you are good at it, or both of you enjoy it, or both of you hate it, then share.

◉ Don't compete over who's more exhausted. Neither of you deserves more rest than the other, the exception being pregnant women and new mothers. If one of you is genuinely more tired, then you are either spending more than your fair share of time at work, on the tiles or on domestic matters, so take a look at your time management (see Chapter 4). This must be properly addressed in the interests of fair play.

● Don't compete full stop.

● Don't argue over money – preferably not over sex, religion or politics either – but especially not over money. How you organise your finances (see Chapter 13) will be a matter for you, but reach an agreement from the outset in the full understanding that what comes into the household should serve the household needs first and individuals' needs second. There's nothing worse than the sense of injustice caused by a tightwad about the place.

LIVING WITH CHILDREN

People with children may be couples who have had children together; couples who have had children with other people with whom these children now live, or with whom they share custody; or couples who have had children with each other as well as with other people, all or some of whom live under the one roof. Sole parents may have all their children living with them all the time, or they may share custody. Each of these households will have specific requirements related to time and emotion management. But the relationship and ratio of parents to children in any household ought not to affect the basic rules. In households containing children they should be very basic, and there should be as few as possible:

● Always enforce the rules you have made, even if it's in the middle of the night and you haven't slept for three months.

● Those worth enforcing include no lying, no stealing, no being where you're not supposed to be, no physical violence, and a little bit of respect if you don't mind, please.

These are probably enough. I can't speak for your household. Just don't make a rod for your back. Tidying any mess they make in areas of the house used by others should start the minute they can walk. A civil tongue in their heads should start the minute they can talk. But an untidy room isn't a capital offence. Nor is arguing a fair case, provided it doesn't come with insults. And nor, at least not in my book, and no matter how ill advised, is leaving the house in funny clothes or getting body parts pierced or tattooed.

Acceptable behaviour changes according to the age and needs of the child, so adapt rules sensibly. Not eating between meals may be a good rule one year for one child but may not necessarily be a good rule all the time or for all children. They change from one week to the next, so it's wise not to write them off too early as psychopaths or pint-sized. Give them a chance to grow out of it.

·········· LIVING WITH ADULT CHILDREN ··········

Adult children may want to return to live with their parents, or they may never leave their parents' household in the first place. This can happen for a variety of reasons, the most obvious of which is lack of money caused by low income, debt or job loss. Other reasons may be illness, pregnancy or studying. These all count as enforced dependency, which is different from not leaving home because you don't want to or you can't be fagged, and it embraces a completely different set of temperaments. How happy either arrangement is will depend not just on how well everyone gets on, but on the blend of expectations and values, and this can be lumpy across different generations under the one roof.

There is huge pleasure to be had by parents from the company of their adult children, but accommodating them also requires difficult compromises. Adult children can test their parents' tolerance to such a limit that the ensuing conflict may act as a prompt to them ultimately leaving. This phenomenon has been identified as fouling the nest. Even adult children who would die rather than foul their nest need to assert themselves from time to time to demonstrate the status to which they feel their years entitle them. For parents, children of any age asserting themselves can be taxing beyond belief.

The success of this household will depend on the good will of everyone involved, on children appreciating the benevolence of their parents and on parents not rubbing their children's noses in it. Rules will depend primarily on mutual respect but also on how everyone is occupied during the day and how this affects the child–parent dynamic. Does the working mother of working children insist on doing all the shopping, cooking and cleaning? Does the working father with a working wife and working children maintain responsibility for the car, the bills and neighbourhood watch? Sorry to resort to stereotypes, but curiously most households do. Rules for parents as opposed to rules for their adult children are as follows:

> ● **Trust your children.** Unless you have a very good reason not to, assume they can make their own decisions and that they won't be placing themselves in risky or ill-advised situations just for the hell of it. Even if they do, trust

them to get themselves out of it. You raised them so you should have properly equipped them.

⊙ Don't overstep the mark when it comes to interest in their work (calling their boss), friends (inviting yourself on their outings) or love life (flirting or arguing with their dates).

⊙ You aren't their best friend; you are their parent. There is a difference, and, although it's an increasingly narrow one, it's there for life.

⊙ Try not to nag. Agree on the rules and if they aren't respected negotiate a settlement which involves them leaving home so they can please themselves.

⊙ Having agreed they may live at home, either set a time limit or decide this is a great arrangement all round and enjoy it.

·········· LIVING WITH ELDERLY PARENTS ··········

However cosy the idea may seem of a grandparent living in the bosom of the family and imparting infinite wisdom to small children who grow up to write a book about them, the reality is, well, less cosy. Because it's not the norm, there's far too much obligation and far too much guilt. Elderly parents mostly move in with their adult children in a crisis, when they have become ill or had a fall and are unable to stay in their own home. It isn't usually planned and it becomes long-term or permanent only when it's acknowledged that the parent is too frail to live on their own again and the idea of a nursing home is untenable.

It's a cruel fact that sometimes 'untenable' is a luxury. The two prime requirements of any household wanting to accommodate a frail, elderly parent are space and the support of the other household members. Money, to a certain extent, is also an issue. Almost no one has a granny flat. Adult children whose own adult children have left home may have a spare room, but ideally there needs to be enough space for everyone to enjoy some privacy without feeling unacceptably crowded.

There's no denying the disruption to the household. The adult child and their partner may overnight be thrust into the role of carers, which can entail 24-hour alertness and anxiety. For this, good will large enough to fill several spare rooms must be available from the partner whose elderly relative this isn't. Most elderly parents are only too aware of their situation. Not only are they giving up their own home, but they will also be in some degree of discomfort owing to the crisis and torn between relief that they are now in safe and loving hands and guilt for the trouble they believe they are causing.

Should you be in a position to care for an elderly parent (that is, you have the space and the support of other household members), then you may as well know that you will be tested, no matter how much you love your parents or in-laws, and they will be tested as well. To survive the test:

- Once the crisis has passed, discuss the options with your elderly parent. They may not want to live with you for the rest of their life. They might want all avenues for everyone's future contentment to be explored.

- Don't presume.

- Don't patronise.

- Don't ignore.

- Get help in the event of an elderly parent's extreme dependence.

- Take time out.

·········· LIVING WITH IN-LAWS ··········

The fact of the matter is that in-laws are aliens. Sometimes they are loving, at other times they are strange but acceptable and at other times still they are the enemy. Usually they are capable of being all three sooner or later. You can be lucky. You may find you have so much in common with the family you marry into or that marries into you that living comfortably under the one roof is the only way to live. But mostly, tolerance and holding your tongue are required for any such arrangement to succeed.

The catch with in-laws isn't just that you have been raised differently and so have come to expect different things of normal behaviour; there is also the exquisite tension that exists between those of you who think you have first claim on the person common to you. You have to be very grown-up about it. Should you be a parent-in-law, you must step back and acknowledge that your child has created a unit of their own into which you must be invited, and that you have no automatic rights once you are inside it. Should you be a child-in-law, you need to know that your partner's parents don't actually wish you ill; they just want the best for their offspring and it's very hard for them to accept that you are it. Remember the following:

- Different doesn't automatically mean barking.

- Asking the person common to you to choose between you is criminal, no matter how disguised the request.

- Under no circumstances should you gang up against an in-law.

- The person common to both should allow the parties on either side to form their own relationship without intervention, as the intervention will almost certainly end in tears.

·············· LIVING WITH PETS ··············

Two in five UK and two in three Australian households include at least one animal. Therefore, a great many of you will know that a wise household doesn't take on the responsibility lightly. Not only will a pet require accommodating, for instance in a human bed, but someone will be called upon to feed, love, exercise, groom and care for this pet – in sickness and in health, for richer, for poorer – as well as clean up after it. The willingness of this person to make the sacrifice should be established well in advance. The commitment may be for ten or more years for a dog, and for twelve or more years for a cat.

Actually, there's no point in getting a pet, goldfish aside, unless everyone in the house wants it and not just the person who says they'll do all the work. This may even apply to goldfish. Goldfish live for many years even after they have thrown themselves repeatedly from the tank in order to seek a better life elsewhere; they require a tank, sometimes a pump for the tank, water to be changed and fish food to be remembered. They're not so easy. Not everyone wants a goldfish, and if you haven't bought it, why should you be the one to scrape it from the wall? Children can't be expected to look after a pet on any occasion other than the one that suits them. So, if you don't have a pet but are thinking of getting one, ask yourself who really wants it and why.

Consider the following. They aren't rules, just a series of questions you should ask yourself before you even think of going to the pound or pet shop.

- Who wants this pet? Is it you, your boyfriend, your wife, your children, your flatmate? Is it everyone but you, or everyone but your husband? Tell the truth here, because if someone you live with doesn't want an animal about the place, forget it. If everyone wants it, then why? For company, for fun, to replace a baby? Is a pet really the answer?

○ What kind of pet? Let's just consider cats and dogs. A cat, for instance, might do okay in a twelfth-floor flat, but a labrador in a twelfth-floor flat is a stupid idea. There are working dogs, lap dogs, dogs for children, guard dogs and cats. There are pedigrees, pretty ones, abandoned ones and ugly ones. Don't buy for looks. Buy for suitability. Dogs need exercise – the larger the dog, the greater the need. Cats can exercise themselves. A dog needs access to the outside world, if only to relieve itself, but a cat can manage without. Some cats don't mind being left all day; most dogs hate it.

○ How much mess, smell, hair and noise can you stand? Kitty litter in my experience spreads all over the kitchen. Its smell can travel into every corner of a largish house. Ditto the smell of a damp dog. Dogs and cats that shed hair shed it everywhere, and always into their owners' food. Factor in to your purchase the household tolerance for smells and hair.

○ Do you have time to see to a pet's needs? Not just buying it food, exercising it, dealing with its bad behaviour and getting it vaccinated, but also grooming it, loving it, finding someone to care for it when you're away and looking for it when it does a runner.

○ Can you afford it? While a goldfish isn't a big expense, dogs and cats require proper and regular diets as well as proper and regular health care, and vets aren't cheap.

If you must have a pet, do your research and don't decide after a year or two that you're over it and maybe your mother would like it, because she wouldn't.

3

ADDING CHILDREN TO THE HOUSEHOLD

Adding children to the household is the biggest decision of several lifetimes – yours as well as any you might help create. Some of us make it without a flicker of uncertainty or a scintilla of trouble, but for everyone else deciding what to do about having children involves some element of tussle: not just when, how and with whom to have them, but whether we want them at all. Should you be looking for clarity on the matter, you might begin by asking yourself the following:

- Do I want to have children ever?

- Do I want to have children in my current circumstances?

The questions require hard-headed answers, regardless of the condition of your heart.

Do I want children ever?

We have children to keep the gene pool going, to till the family land, to see what they look like, to prove our love for the other parent, but mostly we want them because we want what they entail – which is to say, family life. If we aren't up for family life and all its implications, then we won't be wanting and nor should we be having children and the fact that more and more of us are opting to be childless is a good thing, not only for global warming but for personal autonomy.

You might not want to have children for any of the following reasons:

- lack or absence of parental instinct;

- unwillingness to compromise a career that doesn't allow time for child-raising;

- a preference for life as it's currently lived, without the responsibility of raising children;

- a reluctance to bring children into a world whose future is uncertain;

- a general ambivalence about parenthood, connected to any or all of the above.

They are all fine reasons for elective childlessness, as we now know it to be called, and it is excellent to act on them. It is less excellent, on the basis of your own concerns, however, to decide on behalf of the person with whom you want to spend the rest of your life. If you have strong feelings about having or not having children, these should be declared openly and honestly because, like it or not, they will be central to the future of most long-term relationships. Confirm what you want and if it isn't what your significant other wants, then you may need to reconsider whether the arrangement you are contemplating or have embarked upon really is right for you.

Do I want children in my current circumstances?

The optimum time to have children, from a practical point of view, can be any of the following:

- when your body is best able to give birth;

- when you just can't wait any longer;

- when you are in a relationship which has proved itself to be enduring and all you need to complete your circle of love is a child;

- when your career can stand an absence or has come to a standstill;

- when you have a house, or when you have just about enough money to fund an extended household.

What's important for you won't necessarily be what's important for your neighbour, or even your best friend. In any case, it's just about impossible to arrange the order of events in our lives, because, on the sliding-doors principle, anything can happen at any time to sabotage our best-laid plans. On the other hand, since we are considering current circumstances you might want to focus on where you are emotionally, financially and physically.

EMOTIONAL CIRCUMSTANCES

It's true that babies are born into all kinds of situations, ranging from hideous to solid as a rock. It's also true that there's no predicting the ultimate outcome of any baby's upbringing. But we know for a fact that a stable situation is ideal and that stability is best assured when everyone is getting on with each other, so you want, very broadly speaking, harmony between you and your partner, even when there is no expectation that you will live together after the birth. No one expects untrammelled sweetness and light; what's required in the first instance – and, ultimately, for the long haul – is a level of understanding and co-operation that will see both parents through what can be a period of great upheaval entailing unexpected troughs among the unparalleled highs.

BIOLOGICAL CIRCUMSTANCES

There is much to be said for having children early, which is to say in your twenties: you conceive more easily; you have more energy; your body copes better; and you will still be relatively young when your children are adults. On the other hand, there are undeniable merits in later parenthood: your situation is likely to be more stable; your finances will probably be better; your career will be established; your life will be established; children will keep you young.

There are endless facts and figures concerning fertility, with which every woman interested in having children is no doubt already familiar, so I'm confining myself to brief summary. The broad picture is this:

- seventeen in twenty couples conceive naturally within a year of trying;

- nineteen in twenty couples conceive within two years;

- couples who haven't conceived within three years have about a one in four chance of conceiving the following year.

The odds in favour of your conceiving naturally are generally very high, but the older you get, the shorter they become, whether you are male or female. Your personal fertility may bear no resemblance to the average – we all know couples who had their first babies in their forties and went on to have another without any trouble at all, defying the odds as we have come to appreciate them – but taking the odds into account is part of the planning process.

What you need to bear in mind, if you are considering introducing children to the household, is that, while planning is excellent, more important is knowing this is what you want and that any baby of yours will be loved more than any other baby in human history – even when he or she is 29, still living at home and expecting their laundry to be done, no questions asked.

Going it alone

Ideally, babies are the result of a happy and loving relationship, but this isn't always available and the time may come when you feel you can't leave parenthood any later.

If you are in a position to plan single parenthood, your starting points are capacity and commitment. When it comes to providing stability, the buck will end with you: you will ultimately be the provider of physical and emotional comfort, and you may be the sole provider. This is plainly daunting, but plenty of single parents who haven't had the benefit of planning meet the challenge brilliantly. One in five Australian children under the age of 15 ends up being raised in a single-parent household for some of their lives, and while it may not always be desirable it's by no means an automatic handicap.

A solid support network is, however, critical. It can be provided by family, friends who are as good as family, paid help, reasonable employers and reliable child-care facilities. Hugely helpful, if not always achievable, is a proper agreement with the other parent concerning their proposed involvement: the degree of financial support you can expect and the degree of access they can expect. It's always wise to consult a solicitor about everyone's rights and obligations.

FERTILITY - THE FIGURES

Age plays a significant factor in fertility, like it or not. Three in four women aged 30 conceive naturally and have a baby within a year of trying. This reduces to three in five women who are aged 38 or 39, although 85 per cent of women aged 38 or 39 will conceive naturally within two years of trying. The odds continue to decline. Over the age of 45, the chances of conceiving naturally fall to minimal.

The decreasing fertility of men as they age is less noticeable because it's less discussed, and everyone remembers Charlie Chaplin, who became a father at 153. A man of 35, however, is reckoned to have half the chance of making a woman pregnant as he had at 25. A study reported in the 2004 issue of the American Journal of Gynaecology found male fertility dropped by 11 per cent each year because ageing sperm (I'm sorry – it's not a good word picture) decreases in volume and motility (ability to move towards the egg). It's also worth noting that the risk of miscarriage and birth abnormalities increases with the age of parents.

None of this is a reason to despair, merely to plan if you can or to act if you must. If you are in a position to plan, consider how many children you want and work backwards, bearing in mind that a third baby planned for when you are 42 may not be as easy to achieve as a first baby at 35.

Financial implications

Your current circumstances should include at the very least enough money to shelter, feed and clothe a newly extended household, but especially the baby, knowing that this obligation can last for more years than you could possibly imagine.

The chief consideration is the impact of a baby on your household's income and expenditure – specifically, a decrease in one and an increase in the other. To console yourself, factor in tax breaks, child allowances and parental leave payments. It's true that child-raising can be a vast expense, but it's a vast expense that is somehow met in households of all sorts by a simple rearrangement of expectations. Look at your current circumstances, compare them to circumstances which include a baby and decide what you might ditch to make ends meet.

REDUCED INCOME

The arrival of a child might involve any of the following:

- paid time away from work (parental leave) with no disruption to a career;

- longer absence from work, and a reduced income;

- return to work on a part-time basis after an absence which may or may not have been paid;

- loss of an income because one parent decides to give up work completely to care for the child.

More than likely, the income of the primary carer (usually the mother) will take a substantial hit. Current estimates are that the arrival of one child can reduce a mother's lifetime earnings by 30 per cent and the arrival of three by 50 per cent. But so what! Help is at hand.

FINANCIAL HELP FOR PARENTS

Governments offer all kinds of financial assistance to parents. What is available changes yearly, so you need to check what's current. In Australia, contact the Family Assistance Office (online, or in person at Centrelink and Medicare branches) for current information on tax rebates, child-care benefits and the 'Baby Bonus'. In the UK, to check for entitlements such as tax credits and job grants, contact the Tax Credits Helpline and your local Jobcentre or apply online.

Parental leave

Both Australia and the UK have legislation covering paid parental leave (PPL). In Australia a federal government scheme that took effect in January 2011 entitles the main carer (a paid worker with a taxable income of no more than $150,000) to eighteen weeks' paid parental leave at the current minimum wage. This will be on top of any PPL already negotiated, but there is no guarantee that employer-provided PPL will continue now the government scheme is in place. For further information, contact the Family Assistance Office.

In the UK, a year's unpaid maternity leave can be taken regardless of the length of employment, and the employer must reinstate, on the employee's return to work, the same benefits he or she received previously. Maternity pay (SMP) is mandatory if an employee has worked twenty-six consecutive weeks for the employer, has left work to have the baby and has been earning more than the statutory minimum. For the full range of conditions and entitlements, and current amounts, contact HM Revenue and Customs. Get the paperwork, read it and concentrate. Entitlements are entitlements, not hand-outs.

INCREASED EXPENDITURE

Adding a child to the household will involve both immediate and ongoing costs. On average, according to a UK report, the first year of a child's life costs parents something like £8000 (which is, roughly speaking, $15,000 Australian) but I pass this on with no great conviction – your costs might be nothing like that.

Expenses can range from moving house and buying a bigger car (in other words, hundreds of thousands) to using everything your sister had and buying only disposable nappies and a breast pump (hundreds, max). There may be medical and hospital bills if you have your baby in the private system, and immediate child-care costs if you're planning an immediate return to work. There are hidden extras like heating, washing and transport, but some expenditure will be reduced (you'll go out and eat out less).

A baby's needs in the first few months of life are minimal and so short-term that over-investing is daft: you don't have to buy everything and you don't have to buy everything new, though if you're planning more than one baby you might want to spend more than the minimum on essentials you're likely to re-use (stroller, etc.). What you can or choose to spend will be up to you, of course, but there is a limit to what you absolutely must have.

Essentials for a baby

Your most expensive purchases in the first instance will be a baby car seat or capsule, which will cost new around $280 in Australia and £120 plus in the UK, and is compulsory in both countries; and a pram and/or stroller of some sort (anywhere from $200–300 to $1700+ for top-of-the-range in Australia, and upwards of £200 in the UK). Shopping online, having found the model you want in a shop, can reduce costs hugely. You might end up buying these items new, because you need to be sure the car restraint meets safety standards and because other parents can be curiously loath to get rid of their prams. On the other hand, you might consider hiring both car seat and pram: websites in both Australia and the UK will direct you (google 'hiring baby equipment'). Given the pricing, this is less viable in the UK, where the cost of a baby capsule is around £50 a month compared to $99 for six months in Australia.

Other than that, you need to budget for the following for the first few months:

● Basic baby clothing – enough for a couple of changes a day and large enough for a baby to grow into. There's not much mileage in newborn sizes.

● Nappies to the tune of eight changes a day. Buying re-usable (cloth) makes sense if your plan is to have more than one child. Today's re-usables are streets ahead of the old and, on balance, kinder to the environment despite the extra washing, but many mothers believe that disposables are kinder to a baby's skin. I'd say suck it and see if it weren't so off-putting.

● Baby wipes.

● Somewhere to sleep that isn't your bed (even though the baby may spend the night with you for many years).

● Bedding – no pillows required.

● A nappy-changing table (not essential but a back-saver) and mat (not essential but a laundry saver).

● Nursing bra and breast pads if you plan to breastfeed; bottles and sterilising kit if you're not.

● A bath (not essential but useful for a very short while).

● A rocker (extremely handy for short-term amusement, but again not essential).

● A mobile over the rocker, cot and/or changing table – your first step to raising a genius.

Later in the first year you'll need a high chair, a new car seat, maybe a larger cot, possibly a blender in which to purée fresh food, and more clothes. Toys will arrive from family and friends, but let's not pretend you won't go crazy with your first offspring. Just keep the soft toys to a minimum, because apart from one or two they're of minimal interest to anyone other than the people who give them. If you assume that no one will give you anything and you buy a combination of new and secondhand equipment, your total initial outlay can be less than $1000 in Australia and £600 in the UK. That may sound like skimping, but babies need love not lavish.

CHILD CARE

If both parents decide to go back to work after the birth of a child, then satisfactory child-care arrangements will be at the heart of everyone's wellbeing and central to the arrangement working. Despite a huge amount of lip-service being paid by politicians to the needs of working parents, the situation remains fraught for many in both Australia and the UK, where the options are similar. In Australia, costs as well as regulations vary from state to state, so check with your government's community services; approved and registered care may qualify for government assistance. In England, child care is regulated by the Office for Standards in Education, Children's Services and Skills (Ofsted); in Wales it is the responsibility of the Care and Social Services Inspectorate. Both can provide information on standards of care.

What governs your options, apart from availability (which is always limited), is the age of your child, the number of hours of care you need, whether these will be regular, and what you can afford. But broadly full-time care can cost anything from $500 to $1000 per week in Australia and £150 to £500 a week in the UK. Your choices will be:

- Care by a relative in your home or theirs. Frankly, nice work if you can get it.

- Care in your own home by a nanny, au pair, mother's help or babysitter, which is ideal for children under the age of 2 because it offers continuity and familiarity in an environment which is largely controlled by the parents. Bear in mind that of the four, only nannies are properly qualified (so inevitably much more expensive) although both mother's helps and baby-sitters may be very experienced. Au pairs should only be employed to care for very young children if a parent is working from home. The main drawback for all four is that they are rarely able to provide substitute care at short notice should they fall ill.

- Care in someone else's home (family day care), which is undertaken by a child-minder registered with a local or government authority. It's ideal for pre-schoolers, as well as for school-age children after school and in holidays, and is cheaper than in-home care. There are strict rules governing this form of care, which has the value of consistency and a home environment as well as interaction with other children. There is usually no back-up provision if the carer is ill, however.

- Care in council-run or private day care centres, which has the advantages of properly trained staff in properly regulated surroundings, as well as consistency of routine, environment and faces. Carers falling ill is not a catastrophe for the working parent. Day centres have notoriously long waiting lists, so it's wise to get your name on the lists of those you like as early as possible.

● Before- and after-school care and school holiday care. Apart from live-in help or child-minders, care is usually provided in primary schools by education authorities or private organisations. The dilemma for working parents is deciding when a child is old enough to stay at home unsupervised: children over 12 are famously unhappy about attending programs they regard as too young for them. Finding a carer to oversee three or four children in a single house is a reasonable alternative.

LONG-TERM COSTS

The total cost of raising a child over a lifetime is supposed to be more than $500,000 in Australia and just under £200,000 in the UK. Maybe it is, but I don't trust the maths. Nor does a paper from Australian Policy Online called *Measuring the Real Cost of Children* (2009), which decided that, given the altered patterns of household spending once children are added, the real 'cost' is at most an additional $1300 per annum. I'm not sure I'd go along with that either. There is positively no doubt that children can cost you a fortune in food, clothes, gifts, recreation, education, child care, additional housing and transport requirements, but who's to say what you might have spent on yourself if you'd no children.

A detailed breakdown of the cost of raising children is available from sources such as the AMP.NATSEM (National Centre for Social and Economic Modelling) income and wealth reports in Australia, and in the UK from the annual report of Liverpool Victoria Insurance (LV), and, while these may have no impact on your decision to have children, they make fascinating reading.

···················· HAVING A BABY ····················

Once you've decided that your circumstances, whatever they may be, are right, you need to get yourself into shape. I'm addressing both parents here, since having a baby requires input from both even if the paternal contribution does seem kind of slight in the first instance. Addressing your physical fitness is not only in your interests, it's in the best interests of the baby and this is how it will be from now on. The baby's best interests come first.

There are loads of helpful websites, but Dr Debra Kennedy of Mothersafe at the Royal Hospital for Women in Sydney recommends caution when scouring the internet. Steer clear of anything sounding remotely hysterical, or confirm it with your doctor. In the meantime, parents-to-be should be alert to the following and assume that the advice applies to both unless it's a physical impossibility.

- Even if you aren't planning to become pregnant at once, come off the pill and use some other form of contraception while your menstrual cycle returns to normal.

- If you're overweight or underweight, get your body mass index (BMI) to between 20 and 25, or at any rate under 30 (see Chapter 22).

- Follow a balanced diet (see Chapter 9).

- Reduce your alcohol intake to the recommended levels for men and women (no more than two units a day for women and three units a day for men – see Chapter 12).

- Reduce your coffee intake (no more than a couple of strong cups a day).

- Stop smoking and/or using recreational drugs of any sort.

- Talk to your doctor about any medicines you take regularly and whether these may have unwanted effects on you or your baby. This includes alternative medicines.

- Take a daily pregnancy vitamin pill that includes folic acid (to reduce the chances of birth defects). Have blood tests (both of you) to confirm you've had German measles (rubella) and chickenpox, both of which can cause birth defects if contracted by the mother during pregnancy. If you haven't had it, you can be vaccinated.

- Arrange tests for thyroid function, diabetes, HIV, hepatitis and any sexually transmitted disease.

- Get vaccinated against flu. There's growing evidence that pregnant women are more than usually vulnerable.

- Men should restrict heat to the genital area (overheating is said to affect sperm production). So, out go the tight pants and hot baths.

For further information on conception, pregnancy and childbirth, see the list of resources at the back of the book.

Conception

Statistics suggest that if you have sex three times a week, even if your menstrual cycle is irregular, you will conceive. Sperm released on ejaculation survive for seven days in critical areas of the woman's body, and an egg released at ovulation will survive for twelve to twenty-four hours in the fallopian tube, so it stands to reason that they will sooner or later locate each other. It may take months or years, but eventually, on the balance of probabilities, they'll get there.

LEARNING YOUR FERTILE TIMES

Knowing when you are fertile can reduce the time it takes to become pregnant but really, don't get obsessive about it: obsessing leads to stress, and stress might cause such discord between you and your partner that you stop having sex and/or wanting a baby, ever. Women are fertile for the three or four days before they ovulate and possibly for a couple of days after. For those with regular cycles, this is generally about twelve days from the onset of your last period or ten to sixteen days before the start of your next one.

Charting your ovulation patterns, and/or your menstrual cycle and body temperature, and studying cervical changes during your cycle are all helpful to calculate when you're fertile.

Ovulation kits

These track hormone changes that relate to ovulation and are probably the simplest way to predict your fertile times. The kits are available from pharmacies and all that's required of you is a sample of saliva or urine, depending on the kit you buy.

You would normally test yourself (according to the manufacturer's instructions) on approximately day 11 of your cycle, but if you don't have regular periods you can get a clearer idea of the best days for testing by using any of the following methods.

Menstrual cycle (ovulation) calendar

This requires you to keep a record over several periods (at least eight months is recommended), so you can identify the pattern of your menstrual cycle, day 1 being the first day of your period and the last day being the one before your next period begins. At the end of the eight months, you subtract 18 from the number of days in your shortest cycle and 11 from the number of days in the longest cycle and the result will be the days in which you could be fertile. Let's assume your shortest cycle is 28 days and your longest is 42. Take 18 from 28, which makes 20, and 11 from 42 which makes 31. Therefore, according to this method, you might be fertile between day 20 and day 31. Calendar templates and instructions are available online, or you can go the old-fashioned way and keep a journal.

Temperature chart

If you already have a chart on the go, you might as well record your core body temperature (BBT) too, as it's another indicator. Your temperature drops before ovulation, then rises afterwards and stays up until your next period. This is a hindsight method, which is why it's best used over time and why it helps to see if it coincides with your fertile days as revealed by the menstrual cycle calendar. If you use it on its own, the chances are that you'll spot the temperature rise too late for conception.

Cervical indicators

Results are revealed more immediately by the state of the cervix. Therefore you should get to grips with how it looks and feels from one day to the next, even if you are squeamish. Typically, at the beginning of the cycle, when oestrogen levels are low and sperm stand next to no chance of surviving, very little cervical mucus is produced. As the cycle progresses and oestrogen levels rise, it increases in volume and its consistency changes (at peak fertility, it most resembles egg white). The position and condition of your cervix also changes during your cycle, though all you really need to know is that before ovulation the cervix is firm and dry, and easy to locate by feel; as ovulation approaches, it softens and rises into the vagina until it is difficult to reach.

DO POSITIONS DURING SEX MAKE A DIFFERENCE?

The general consensus is that apart from standing up (when gravity will prevail), most positions do equally well for conceiving. Allowing the woman to relax with a pillow under her bottom for twenty minutes afterwards is also supposed to help. This would seem to be the right time to have a smoke, but it isn't because we now know there is no right time to have a smoke.

Alternatives to natural conception

The alternative methods are artificial insemination, IVF (in-vitro fertilisation, possibly with donor sperm or eggs, and/or fresh or frozen sperm or eggs), and surrogacy or adoption. Each is subject to legislation that varies from country to country (and from state to state in Australia). Each has its pluses and minuses, and these are best discussed with your doctor and/or a counsellor. You might be considering them because you don't want to have sex with the other proposed biological parent, or are having difficulties conceiving naturally. Those in the former group might consider DIY insemination but it's also important to consult a GP about its implications. If you are in the latter group, you're no doubt already seeking medical advice.

Whatever the case, it makes sense to research the facts and issues thoroughly so that you understand your odds of conceiving, and the likely effects on both your body and your wallet. You will already have accepted its effects on your future circumstances.

FREEZING EGGS AND SPERM

Should your current circumstances not be optimal in your view and should you be determined to have a baby, you might consider freezing your eggs or your sperm.

Eggs can be frozen and stored for up to ten years, though the outcome, frankly, isn't brilliant. There are concerns not just about the poor success rate (at best 6 per cent) or the cost (about $12,000 in Australia and around £5000 in the UK), but there's uncertainty as to the long-term health and development implications for babies conceived in this way. The Human Fertilisation and Embryology Authority suggests the use of frozen sperm isn't that reliable either. The better bet, it seems, is to store fertilised eggs, which are more likely to survive. This, of course, complicates the planning should you be unattached, and the process isn't always altogether lovely, but if conceiving naturally seems unlikely or impossible then it's worth considering.

Pregnancy

You can suspect you are pregnant and reach for the testing kit in the event of any of the following:

- missed, or much lighter than usual, period;

- nausea or vomiting (any time of day);

- aversion to certain food or drink;

- unusual constipation;

- unusual fatigue.

The minute you know you are pregnant, book an appointment with your GP, who will arrange your antenatal care. This varies from place to place, according to who's running the health system, but the procedure is broadly similar in Australia and the UK.

You may choose to have the baby within the private health system, in which case you will be referred to an obstetrician. You may have a preferred hospital, in which case you will have to choose an obstetrician who attends there, or you may have a preferred obstetrician. Should you be using the public health system, your choice will be determined by what's available in your area and by your state of health, your personal circumstances and your general preferences for types of care. There is less intervention in births overseen by midwives, but you may feel safer within a hospital environment with a doctor in charge or it may be essential given your medical history. The Australian College of Midwives lists the following public system options, which are comparable to the choices available in the UK:

- Public hospital maternity clinic, where your care will be supervised by doctors or midwives. If you have complications, you may be referred to a specialist clinic.

- Midwives' clinic attached to a public hospital. Care is usually more personal than at the maternity clinic.

- Midwifery group practice, which will allocate you a midwife who will oversee your antenatal, birth and postnatal care.

- 'Shared care' program in which your GP oversees most of the pregnancy but you visit a hospital for assessments and hospital staff care for you during the birth.

- Early discharge program, which provides midwife supervision at home for women who want to go home within forty-eight hours of the birth (seventy-two hours if the birth was by caesarean section).

- Birthing centre – increasingly popular for their non-medical environment and emphasis on minimal intervention (birthing pools are usually available, but epidurals are not). The labour and birth are overseen by a midwife; should there be any complications, you will be transferred to another part of the hospital for specialist care.

- Home birth, which should be approved in principle by your GP (who will consider your health and general circumstances) and is supervised by midwives. While it's less popular in Australia than in the UK, women's satisfaction rates are extremely high. Doctors advise that home births are suitable only for women judged to be very low-risk.

Wherever you have the baby, your pregnancy will require regular monitoring. You will be offered between seven and fourteen antenatal appointments during which your blood pressure will be tested and the baby's heartbeat and size will be checked. You will also be offered ultrasounds (possibly three – one at six to eight weeks, one at eleven to thirteen weeks and another at twenty weeks), which can confirm the baby's gender (should you want to know), due dates, multiple pregnancies, the risk of Down's syndrome, and the health of the baby's organs.

Prenatal classes can be invaluable for first-time parents. Ask around for the best in your area, but if you draw a blank your doctor, hospital or midwife will be able to advise you. In the UK, the NHS offers classes free of charge.

MORNING SICKNESS

This is a misnomer. If you do experience nausea, it may be in the morning; it may last all day; it can last six weeks, twelve weeks, sixteen weeks or forty weeks. It is only of medical concern if excessive vomiting causes you to dehydrate, or leads to extreme weight loss. Anti-nausea tablets can be prescribed. Otherwise try the following:

- Eat dry toast or a dry biscuit before you get out of bed. Eat little but often during the day.

- If your job keeps you inside, take breaks. Get fresh air.

- Eat an orange or drink ginger tea (made with freshly sliced ginger). Each seems to have anti-nausea properties.

- Avoid stomach-turning smells – if this is impossible, overwhelm the pong by slicing a lemon into a dish to release a subtle citric vapour.

EMERGENCIES

Seek advice from your midwife, GP or antenatal clinic at once if:

- you suffer severe abdominal pain, or bleeding from the vagina (apart from streaking in the last two weeks);

- you suffer severe and sudden headache;
- after twenty-four weeks, your baby fails to move more than ten times in the twelve-hour period 9 am–9 pm.

Seek help within twenty-four hours if:

- you produce a watery discharge from your vagina (a sign your waters may have broken);
- you have pain or burning on urinating, or there is blood in your urine;
- you produce a coloured, smelly, itchy discharge.

Birth plans

Birth plans aren't compulsory but can be useful, especially during a first pregnancy when the idea of being able to exercise control over looming unknown circumstances is immensely comforting. To this end, you record in writing how you'd like your labour and the birth to proceed. Neither may go according to any plan you've even vaguely considered, but registering your preferences with everyone who might be involved makes sense for those occasions when they do.

Central to your preferences will be how you regard birth: as a natural event where the mother is primarily in control, or as a medical event where the hospital is primarily in control. Were Jung about, he'd say neither is right, neither is wrong, merely different; so, Householder, it really helps here to know yourself even if circumstances ultimately overwhelm your ideal. You will probably want to set out the amount of pain relief, the amount of medical intervention, and the circumstances in which you will agree to either. You should also include the kind of pain relief you'd like (and in what order), what kind of interventions you would rather avoid, who you wish to be present at the birth, whether you want accompanying music or other sounds, and so on. If you think you'd like someone on hand at the birth (other than, or as well as, your partner or your mother) for both emotional and practical support, you might consider employing a doula – a trained, non-medical birth attendant whose assistance can be invaluable. As with any consultant or adviser, ask around for recommendations and check the credentials of anyone you're considering.

PAIN RELIEF

There are women who claim to feel no pain during childbirth. I don't know who they are, but everyone says they're out there somewhere and possibly they have cast-iron vaginas, I don't know. The rest of us feel pain ranging from quite bad to 'I just need to be unconscious now'. Happily, there is a variety of drugs available to help us, but also on offer are the power of the mind and stoicism (which I grant are less reliable). None is necessarily better morally or ethically than the other but there is a case for using the power of your mind first, resorting to stoicism next, then yelling for drugs if you have to. Many women like to give vent to their pain with noise. This can be screaming or swearing, which require no tuition and are freely available to all.

Epidurals

An epidural is a regional anaesthetic which provides the most effective form of pain relief during labour. It's administered through a fine tube inserted into the small of your back. Most hospitals use low-dose epidurals. They can be administered at any time during the labour but, since it takes twenty minutes to set up and a further twenty to take effect, not when birth is imminent.

You can't have an epidural in a birthing centre, at home, or indeed with any midwife-supervised birth, but then you probably wouldn't be wanting one. There are small inconveniences attached to them. Epidurals can extend the second stage of labour (the pushing stage); they may cause headaches; they may make your baby drowsy and there is a raised likelihood of forceps or ventouse (vacuum extractor) being required to aid delivery. Discuss the situation fully with your doctor or midwife in advance, so you are as well informed as you need to be.

Opiates (e.g. diamorphine, pethidine, meptid)

Their effect is more to relax you than to relieve pain. They have no effect on the speed of labour and you can, for instance, climb in and out of a birth pool while under their influence. On the other hand, they might make you feel a bit sick, drowsy or dizzy, and they cross the placenta so your baby can also presumably be feeling a bit sick, drowsy or dizzy, especially if the drug is given within two hours of delivery and this drowsiness in the baby can last a couple of days after the birth.

Gas and air (also known as Entonox)

This is of limited use in pain control but can take the edge off your contractions. The heady mix of half oxygen, half nitrous oxide is inhaled through a mask or mouthpiece attached to a cylinder. It can make you feel a bit nauseous, but has no ill effects on the baby.

TENS machines

A TENS (short for transcutaneous electrical nerve stimulation) machine consists of a small box that emits pulses of electrical energy through sticky pads attached to your back. No one knows exactly how it works, but it's thought that the pulses stimulate the production of endorphins, the body's natural stress-relievers. If you're planning a home birth with minimal pain relief, you can hire a machine and practise with it before labour begins. (In Australia the rental is about $60; in the UK, about £22.95).

Mind over matter

Although the mind would seem to be a puny thing compared to, say, an opiate, this turns out not to be true for all women. For them, something kicks in which doesn't necessarily override the pain but makes it acceptable. There are various techniques that help, which include:

- relaxation, through focused breathing (taught in antenatal classes or accessible online) and commercial programs such as Hypnobirthing (not, strictly speaking self-hypnosis, but along those lines) which offer classes and CDs/DVDs;

- acupuncture or acupressure;

- yoga, which prepares both mind and body (antenatal classes are available).

Labour

Signs that you are in labour aren't always easy to identify. Braxton Hicks contractions (when your abdomen tightens and releases), for instance, can begin months before the birth. Strongest indications of labour include:

- regular contractions lasting more than thirty seconds and which are growing stronger and more frequent;

- 'waters breaking' (the bursting of the amniotic sac surrounding the baby, and release of the amniotic fluid from your vagina), which can be a trickle or a flood;

- feeling ill to the point of vomiting.

Other possible signs, though not necessarily proof that labour has started:

- **Loss of the protective mucous plug from the cervix, otherwise called 'a show'. It may be pink owing to bloodstaining, so don't confuse it with bleeding, which should be reported immediately.**

- **Lower-back pain that feels like period pain.**

Some of these signs can occur during labour as well as beforehand, and in some women they never occur spontaneously.

Once it does begin, there is no knowing how long the first stage of labour will last. Technically speaking, it is until the cervix is fully dilated (to 10 centimetres), but it can stop and start over a period of days. Most hospitals advise you to head for the labour ward (or birth centre) when you are having a contraction every five minutes but much will depend on your previous birthing history and your doctor's or midwife's preference.

Giving birth

The second stage of labour – the birth itself – is usually quicker than the first, but it can last two or three hours if you are less than lucky. Its overriding feature is the urge to push, which would seem a straightforward matter were the midwife or obstetrician not taking their cues from some other part of the planet and asking you to control it. The third stage is the delivery of the placenta, which occurs about twenty minutes after the birth of the baby.

It's important to be mentally flexible during the birth. It really doesn't matter how little intervention you specify in your birth plan, your baby won't have read it and may arrive too quickly, too slowly, more painfully or even less painfully than anticipated.

CAESAREAN BIRTHS

There are elective caesareans and emergency caesareans. Elective caesareans are agreed in advance of labour for a variety of physical and medical reasons, such as the baby being in an awkward position or the mother being in poor health or carrying more than one baby.

Emergency caesareans are performed when a vaginal delivery is failing to progress for some reason, or mother and/or baby are in distress. They are usually carried out under epidural anaesthetic so that the mother is conscious and alert.

Either way they consitute major abdominal surgery and require a longer recovery time than vaginal delivery, so doctors generally agree that they should not be undertaken lightly – to suit a timetable, say, or to avoid pain. 'Lightly', however, seems to be open to interpretation: a study of more than 1000 obstetricians in Australia in 2009 found that one in four elective caesareans were performed at the mother's request, for no good medical reason.

WATER BIRTHS

Birth centres and some labour wards offer water births; you can hire a pool for a home birth (and some midwives supply them). While being in water won't necessarily relieve pain, being relaxed and semi-buoyant will. And your birthing partner can hop into the pool with you, which you may or may not find helpful.

What next?

Once the baby is born, provided you are both well, you can leave hospital or the birth centre within hours.

Your only obligation to anyone other than yourself and your extended household is to the state, which needs to be made aware of your baby's arrival. This is compulsory: it is done via the Registry of Births, Deaths and Marriages in Australia where you have sixty days to get your application in (forms can be found on the websites). A birth certificate can be obtained at the same time. In England and Wales, your point of contact is the General Register Office and you have forty-two days' grace.

····· THE NEWLY EXTENDED HOUSEHOLD ·····

For the most part, having a baby entails astonishing euphoria and joy even when the baby wasn't as carefully planned as you might once have imagined. There's no escaping stressful times, however, for reasons which may include fatigue that is beyond the worst jetlag and goes on far longer; never-before-encountered demands on your physical and mental stamina; feelings of isolation (which may not be an issue if hunkering down suits your temperament); conflict as household priorities are rearranged. It may help to know that these experiences are the lot of new parents everywhere (except those freaks who are never fazed by anything).

Fatigue

There is positively no question that new mothers will be tired even before proper sleep deprivation kicks in, owing to the nine months of carrying a new life and the physical demands of giving it birth. They will be more tired than anyone else in the household, even if there are other members who would appreciate some decent sleep so they can stay awake during their stressful day jobs. Therefore they should grab sleep whenever they can and not feel compelled to deal with stupid household matters like the council not taking away the garbage.

Rearranged priorities

The arrival of a first child in particular will require a radical shift in the household's priorities because, let's face it, a baby's basic needs (food, sleep, comfort) have to be met and this will almost certainly be at the expense of someone else's needs or wants. Unless both parents have self-discipline verging on madness, not only will sleep patterns be altered, but meal patterns will be altered, time spent in attentive adult conversation will be altered, the distribution of labour will be altered, sex lives will be altered, and the look of the house will be altered.

Survival in such circumstances requires acceptance; resistance is counter-productive and, frankly, useless. A household that is extended by a small, helpless and sometimes outrageously demanding creature will never be the same again – and nor should it be. What's required is a rough routine that takes account of rearranged priorities and into which the usual demands of the household can be fitted so that no one is resentful and everyone is nice to each other. Even when you think you've hit rock-bottom, chisel away: we all have reserves of patience and stamina we'd rather not have to draw upon, but now's the time. Dig deep and know you aren't alone.

Stepchildren

Given the likelihood of blended families (around one in five are) in today's households, it's possible that yours will be extended by stepchildren. A range of attitudes are required of the non-biological parent, which can be confusing at best and a source of conflict at worst. The following may help:

- Don't expect or assume immediate closeness with your stepchild/ren.

- Children will react differently to the situation according to their age and temperament, so don't expect the same response from all.

○ Stepchildren from different families may not have the same values or expectations, so all need respecting – or, anyway, addressing.

○ Don't hope or expect to replace the non-resident biological parent. Your role is separate and different, even though it will almost certainly be loving and giving, not to mention mutually rewarding.

○ Discuss any problems with the biological parent. If they appear unsolvable, remove yourself physically from the moment, even if these moments turn out to be many.

○ Respect the biological parent's relationship with their child and encourage them to have time on their own.

○ Present a united front with the biological parent on matters of discipline, but avoid ganging up.

○ Allow the child time and space to get to know, like and (maybe, maybe not) love you.

○ Get professional help if needed.

PART 2

ORGANISING TIME AND SPACE

MANAGING YOUR TIME and space is central to household organisation and comfort, even if it does sound more clinical than cosy and cosy is what we like best in a home. Some of you will have been born super-organised, and what follows will be a statement of the blindingly obvious or annoyingly laborious. Others of you may have achieved organisation from necessity born of heartache; for you, what follows might be moderately interesting. But if your household can never manage anything on time or find anything in a hurry, then you are just going to have strategies rammed down your throat because you need help.

Happily, organisation can be learnt, and by adopting even some of the suggestions outlined here, you will see the joy there is to be had in order. I know step-by-step explanations look and are time-consuming, but you didn't get where you are today by taking your time. You've never had enough of it, which is why your life will be immeasurably improved by managing it. Freeing yourself from clutter will give you more space to think. I don't know why; it just does. First, however, you may need to take a minute to explain to yourself that this is acceptable information. It may look unpalatable, but if you can absorb it, it will be for your own good and the good of others.

4

TIME MANAGEMENT

Time management is not cramming as much as possible into twenty-four hours. It's deciding what you want to achieve in the next day, week, month, year or lifetime, acknowledging the steps required to achieve it, calculating how long they ought to take, then arranging your life to accomplish it. It requires decisive thinking, determination and focus, as well as lists.

I know you don't regard yourself as a list person. I know you regard the list person as a pain-in-the-neck stickler for order, and you may be right. But maybe you are relegating yourself to the dustbin of household chaos. How, I hear you whimper, will you find time to make lists when you don't even have time to clean your teeth? In the room in your brain called Need is where. We all need lists. When the list is your friend, you have a companion for life. This is a friendly exercise.

Its point is to enable you to control your circumstances; to change your modus operandi from reacting to acting, and your natural state from drifting to efficient. Such simple adjustments are pivotal to minimising stress, and that's our aim. It's lack of control that sends you to bed with your heart pounding and your breathing erratic, so in the interests of a good night's sleep, ask yourself the following:

- Do I rarely manage to do everything I need to do in a single day, and do I go to bed fretful?

- Am I mostly running late or, anyway, running?

- Do I ever leave the house in clothes that need to be washed or mended when this is not how I want to leave the house?

- Does dinner often involve a last-minute dash to the shops?

- Do I spend far too long doing things I hate?

- Does stuff I like doing get shoved to the backburner?

- Is my day at the mercy of other people's needs and whims?

If you didn't answer yes to at least one of the above, then you are the perfect person and I hope one day to meet you and stare at you. Just about everyone else, certainly every household, can benefit from a little planning, even households consisting of people who really don't need to worry about anyone other than themselves. It's true that you will have fewer activities that absolutely must be done compared with a household containing children or an invalid. But all that gives you is more time to procrastinate, obfuscate and any other '-ate' that prevents you getting on with the things you know you should do or have always said you are longing to do.

The very least you will learn here is how to construct a framework into which you can arrange your household's time. You can ignore, adjust, abbreviate or abide by it according to your whim, but even if you do nothing else you should familiarise yourself with the essentials and these include a weekly timetable, a calendar, a personal diary and a reporter's notebook. The timetable is your master plan. Use the calendar for everything that crops up occasionally but regularly, or irregularly but often, like bill payments, holidays and birthdays, and use the diary to note social, medical, recreational and professional events. The notebook is for your daily to-do list.

Getting the process up and running requires a little effort. Okay, a lot of effort. And if you're not a list lover, you won't want to make it. You'll think, 'Who can be fagged?' But if the least you grasp is the broad intention, then progress will have been made.

THE WEEKLY TIMETABLE

Part 1 – the contents of your day

Your first step is to compare what you have with what you want. In consultation with other members of the household, should there be any, draw up a calendar for your week as it's currently lived. Block out hours of work and sleep. Fill in every activity you can recall that involves the household's members.

Now compile a list of everything you would like to have included in that timetable but haven't. Stick everything in: everything you know you have to do or think you might want to do.

Ask yourself why you are neglecting your second list and whether everything in your first is absolutely critical or taking longer than it should. Remove from the first (your existing calendar) anything that can be dumped without serious consequences and note the things that can't be removed but which could probably be managed more efficiently. With both lists, the what-you-have and the what-you-want lists, in front of you, compile a third, which is the basis of your master plan. It should include everything that must be done and everything that you really should or want to do but currently don't.

Break large tasks from the calendar like 'get ready for work' or 'housework' into their component parts and estimate roughly how long each takes. Factor in travel and preparation time. For instance, going shopping includes the time it takes to get to and from the shops. Cleaning the bathroom doesn't just involve squirting stuff all over the shower and wiping it off, but finding the squirting stuff, looking for the mop and filling the bucket to wash the floor.

Here's an example of the kind of list we are discussing:

EVERY DAY

Task	Time
Get up	1 hour (seriously, some people take ages)
Get children up	10 minutes
Shower/shave/dry hair	30 minutes
Get dressed	10 minutes
Make sure children are dressed	5 minutes
Unload dishwasher	10 minutes

Task	Time
Get breakfast	10 minutes
Eat breakfast	10 minutes
Put on a light wash or dark wash depending on the state of the laundry basket	5 minutes
Make packed lunch/es	10 minutes
Decide what food is required for the evening meal and what you might need to buy that day	5 minutes
Make bed/s	5 minutes
Tidy kitchen and living room	5 minutes
Brush teeth/put on make-up	10 minutes
Take children to school or childcare	30 minutes
Travel to work	40 minutes
Travel home from work	40 minutes
Collect children from school or child care	30 minutes
Shop for day	20 minutes
Prepare evening meal for children	30 minutes
Check children's satchels for uneaten lunch and undelivered notes	5 minutes
Oversee homework	30 minutes
Play with children	30 minutes
Bath/shower children	30 minutes
Read to children	20 minutes
Put children to bed	30 minutes
Prepare evening meal for self	30 minutes
Eat evening meal	30 minutes
Talk to other household members in a relaxed manner	30 minutes
Load dishwasher	10 minutes
Unload washing machine and put stuff in dryer or on the line	15 minutes
Put clean clothes away	10 minutes
Tidy bedroom and bathroom	10 minutes
Exercise	30 minutes
Watch TV	2 hours
Read the paper	30 minutes
Choose clothes for self for the next day and make sure they are wearable	5 minutes

Task	Time
Ditto clothes for children including any sports kit	10 minutes
Plan the next day – check weekly timetable	10 minutes
Shower/cleanse/moisturise	15 minutes
Get ready for bed	10 minutes

EVERY WEEK

Task	Time
Arrange flowers or chuck them out	10 minutes
Vacuum house	1 hour
Wash car	1 hour
Buy petrol	10 minutes
Iron	1 hour
Dust and polish furniture	30 minutes
Wash all tiled floors	30 minutes
Clean bathroom/s	30 minutes
Clean kitchen	30 minutes
Tidy cupboards	30 minutes
Change the beds	30 minutes
Wax legs, do nails	1 hour
Shop for week	1 hour
Pay bills	1 hour
Water the garden	30 minutes
Mow the lawn	1 hour
Family activities	3 hours
Own activities	2 hours
Put the garbage out	10 minutes
Telephone family members/friends	30 minutes
Visit family members/friends	6 hours
Buy clothes for children/self	1 hour
Buy non-supermarket household items	1 hour
Clean windows	1 hour
Arrange children's social life and extra-curricular activities	30 minutes

Task	Time
Decide on meals for the week	10 minutes
Meditate/pray/go to church	1 hour

Part 2 – prioritising the contents of your day

This is the important bit. You must now arrange your list according to each activity's importance; in other words, prioritise. Even if you haven't made a list already, make a small one now. The first rule of time management is to swap the question from 'How will I fit this in?' to 'How important is this to me?' You could use as a guide the much-admired urgent/important quadrant invented by Stephen Covey, author of *The Seven Habits of Highly Effective People* (and US Father of the Year in 2003, which may or may not endear him to you). It rates tasks as:

1. urgent and important;

2. important but not urgent;

3. urgent but not important;

4. not urgent and not important.

Covey's theory is that we devote so much time to what we think is urgent that we lose sight of what is important. In other words, we waste too much time in quadrants three and four. Urgent activities are those demanding immediate attention. Important activities, according to Covey, are those that lead towards our desired outcome, in this case efficiency, leading to stress reduction.

Clearly, top of your list must be tasks that are both urgent and important, like feeding yourself and getting yourself to and from work. Next will be the important but not urgent tasks. How you define these is plainly a value judgement you make for yourself, but they could include the laundry, time for yourself or time with the children. Urgent but not important activities probably won't appear on your list, because they are by and large unforeseeable – neighbours dropping in, phone calls, looking for lost items and so on. But some unimportant and non-urgent activities, like mucking about on the internet, will be included because they are fun and you might do them every day just for the heck of it. Efficient time managers call this time-wasting, but it is only if you're neglecting something you must do or want to do more. So, beginning with what you regard as urgent and important, modify your list.

Make a time for when each task should be done (day and hour). Put initials alongside the tasks due to be tackled by each household member, including children (who can certainly put their toys away). The aim is a fair share for everyone according to availability and ability. There's no point in getting a lousy cook to make dinner or a person who gags at the smell of bleach to clean the loo.

Look hard at the list. Is one person getting more than their fair share of attention? Is anyone missing out? Is everyone getting up early enough or going to bed too late?

Now make a timetable with each day of the week divided into twenty-four hours. Block out sleeping and working hours. Fill in everything that *must* be done each day from your list, then find time for the optional extras according to their urgency and importance. This is your master plan.

From this you can extract a daily plan to which you will add activities or tasks transferred from your personal diary (or diaries) and yearly calendar. Copy it into your reporter's notebook, which you will carry with you at all times. Information critical to other household members should be transferred to post-its and stuck on the fridge.

Making the timetable work

Whether you've drawn up a master plan or not, a to-do list at the beginning of every day is critical. If you're serious about improving your time management, here are a few further points to consider:

- When working out who should do what and when, keep expectations within the bounds of reasonableness and kindness. Take into account everyone's peak performance times. Bear in mind that some of us are more effective in the morning, others in the evening. And take into account the time it takes different personality types to accomplish anything. Not all of us are multi-taskers.

- On the subject of multi-tasking: it's not always so smart. You can do too much at the same time. I once collected the children from school with a sock in my hair because I unloaded the dryer while I was talking on the phone.

- Should you be managing time with other household members, know when to cut your losses. Abandon problems that can't be solved without endless arguments, even if you are a chronic fixer or interventionist.

● Don't procrastinate. If you have an unappealing task allotted for a certain time, do it. Decide how long it should take, set the clock and finish it.

● On the other hand, if a task is long and arduous, take breaks. Painting a room doesn't have to be knocked off in half an hour. You'll start cutting corners if you rush to finish.

● Focus on the achievable – never allot more than three non-urgent chores to a day.

● Cluster like activities together: make all your calls, answer all your emails, collect dirty washing from all rooms, and so on.

● Say no to people whose claims on your time are excessive, unwarranted or unwelcome (neither urgent nor important). You may have to welcome some unwelcome claims out of the goodness of your heart, but you don't have to be at the world's beck and call just because you have a generous nature. This is what you say: 'No'. You say it in whatever way sounds best coming out of your mouth.

● Say no to yourself. You don't have to check for bargains online if you seriously have nothing clean to wear the next day. Remove yourself from the area of temptation.

● Ignore distractions for as long as possible. The phone doesn't always have to be answered.

● Use the rule of double-thinking and double-touching. If you pass something twice (a form to be filled in, a large object to be moved) or you remember twice that you should do something (call the dentist), deal with it.

● Utilise small amounts of time. If you have half an hour to spare, find a job that takes ten minutes and do it.

● Stick to your timetable but know it is a living thing. It will be added to and subtracted from every day, several times a day, as the household diary changes or a new task makes itself urgent. Tweak it when you have to, but, by and large, stick to it and keep it up to date so everyone knows where they stand.

● Give it time to work. Someone has calculated that it takes twenty-one days to form a habit. Who knows who it was? I think the same person said, 'If you fail to plan, you plan to fail.'

HOUSEHOLD TYPES AND TIME MANAGEMENT

Clearly, how you approach organisation of any sort will depend on your personality type. There is an argument that says there are only two that count – male and female on the Mars–Venus principle – but this is stupid. My husband and I once did a test that identified gender orientation according to personality traits. I was highly masculine and he was feminine. We could be freaks, but I don't think so. On the other hand, it helps to be aware of two extreme attitudes to time management, because both can muck everything up.

Control freaks

These are super-organised people who appear to be across all aspects of their lives, including where the TV controls live and in which direction they should point. Most of us are too lazy to care, and so we are grateful to anyone who does because they get things done even if it is mostly to their own satisfaction, which might not be ours. Sadly, some of them are bordering on crazy and others of them are always crabby because no one is as interested in order as they are. This can create massive tension in a household, which is precisely what we're aiming to reduce. Sit down with the control freak and produce a piece of paper, because this will reassure them. Make a very short list of no-go areas over which they can have no definitive say, and another very short list over which they have complete control. Use different-coloured pens for clarity.

Slackers

Slacking applies to anyone who stays out of the house or in bed when other members of the household are snowed under by activities that are urgent and important. Some people are chronic slackers, others occasional. Everyone is allowed an occasional slack. Sit down with the chronic slacker and produce a piece of paper. Force them to remain seated. On this paper draw up a very short list of responsibilities which are exclusively theirs and which will have an impact on their comfort should they remain ignored. After that, it's removal of privileges, and after that, it's removal from the household. No one likes a dyed-in-the-wool slacker.

TIME MANAGEMENT IN A CRISIS

Time management is immaterial when your life is overwhelmed by circumstance: if for instance your child care goes pear-shaped, there's a crisis at work and a pipe bursts in the bathroom. No amount of organisation can plan for the bolt out of the blue. Plan B is always useful, but most of us have a Plan B for one crisis at a time, not multiple meltdowns. We have a network of friends and family and people we pay to save us. In a massive system failure, don't panic. Get help, if necessary paid and from strangers, and take time out to restore calm, your own if no one else's.

Clearly, how you divide your non-critical time is a matter for you. Just be aware that organising it is using it properly. If you don't have time to do the things you want to do, make time or you'll be on your death bed regretting. When you tell yourself you don't have enough time for something you think you want to do, you're actually telling yourself it isn't nearly as important as you're saying it is.

Our days are full of goals that can be achieved more easily if they're recognised for what they are. I'm not suggesting you become a slave to routine; the last thing anyone wants is to become obsessive. But manage your time effectively so you can spend it happily is all I'm saying.

5
_____

SPACE MANAGEMENT
_____

Space management is the flip side of time management. You can't have one without the other. If you don't know where anything is, everything you do will take twice or twenty times as long. Professional organisers suggest that if you can't lay your hands on the thing you are looking for within thirty seconds, you have a problem. They don't mean a memory problem, or male-pattern blindness of the where-do-we-keep-the-bread variety. They mean a failure of organisation. That's why it pays to take stock, which is all space management is: stocktaking. Stocktaking and efficient storage.

It doesn't matter how much or how little space you have; if your stock can't be stored in an orderly manner anywhere, then you have too much stock. And most of us have. Nine in ten households in Australia include at least one room the householders call cluttered; one in two have three rooms they wouldn't invite the public into, owing to the mess. Fair enough, you may think. Your home is to do in as you will. But here's the thing: we need much less stuff than we like to own, which is all to do with how we see ourselves. This is the opinion of every declutter expert I consulted.

We like to own stuff either because we don't want to be the kind of people who run out of towels or sheets in the event of a global warming disaster or the whole family arriving or because we want to be the kind of people who own a lot. It's pathetic, really. Especially when you consider that in 2004, just as an example, Australians spent $10.5 billion on unused items. This makes us the kind of people who buy indiscriminately and dump stuff wherever, regardless of its relevance.

The reason this is weird as well as profligate is that clutter is deeply depressing. It signifies lack of control and causes us to feel overwhelmed by our surroundings. Two in five Australians say it makes them feel anxious or guilty. One in five say it's a serious cause of household conflict. One in eight opt to move house in order to solve the problem.

But you don't have to move. Unless you live in truly overcrowded conditions, you can manage. Maybe you are overcrowded; maybe you aren't. To test for overcrowding, compare your household space to the extremely generous standard provided by the Canadian National Occupancy Standard, which says that:

- No more than two people should share a bedroom.

- A household of one unattached individual may reasonably occupy a bed-sit (that is, have no bedroom).

- Parents or couples may share a bedroom.

- Children under five years of age of different sexes may share a bedroom.

- Children of five years of age or above of the opposite sex should not share a bedroom.

- Children under eighteen years of age and of the same sex may share a bedroom.

- Single household members of eighteen years or above should have a separate bedroom.

For most of us, clutter is not an occupancy issue; it's a possession issue, so upping sticks to get away from it is bonkers. It's called running away, entailing unnecessary expense and stress. You run away and your stuff goes with you. You think you have more space so you get more stuff and before you know it you have to move again but by now you are very poor owing to so much moving and you are on tranquilisers and no one comes to stay so what's the point of all the sheets? You just need to have less stuff, and the only time this isn't true is when the stuff is living and breathing and called children and your name is The Old Woman Who Lived in a Shoe.

WHAT IS CLUTTER?

Clutter is the indoor equivalent of the common or garden weed: not necessarily useless, just not where you want it, or not wanted at all. It's stuff that gets in the way so you can't move around it easily or comfortably, or stuff so jumbled you can't find what's buried within it. It can also be stuff that has no use, provides no visual satisfaction, is only there because it always has been and actually gets on your nerves if you think about it. It can be stuff you've bought that you thought you needed but can never find, stuff you used to need or have never really needed, stuff you've inherited and can't part with, or stuff you've been given that you feel obliged to keep. All households have it to a degree, but degree is the key.

HOUSEHOLD ATTITUDES TO CLUTTER

Some households are hugely tolerant of mess. Or maybe one member of the household is. You need to consider if this is you and whether everyone shares your threshold. Maybe you can walk into any room of your house and smile with satisfaction because it is exactly as you like it even though it's piled with junk willy-nilly, because willy and nilly are the cornerstones of your personal philosophy. Maybe everyone who lives with you likes it like that as well, and good for you. But for sane people this won't be the case, and it's more than likely that you, with your willy and nilly, will be living with sane people and driving them mad.

Sane people don't want to live in a space that looks like a permanent garage or car-boot sale in which nothing can be found because it's under something else that couldn't be found last week. They prefer everything to have a proper place and for everyone they live with to know what that proper place is, so any item at any time can be found and made to serve the purpose for which it was acquired. Forget mess threshold: consider clutter limit. Who needs their surroundings to mirror the fruitlessness of their existence? Who needs to be so overcome by objects they can't think straight?

UNAVOIDABLE PERIODS OF MAXIMUM CLUTTER

There are times, of course, when it can't be helped. Clutter is mostly containable, but there are occasions in all our lives when it appears not to be. The challenge is to acknowledge both the occasion and the mess and allocate time to deal with it before it becomes entrenched. Mostly these occasions involve crises of one sort or another when the time required is wretchedly short: the birth of a baby, the death of a parent, any new arrival, moving house or changing jobs. Suddenly the rooms are filled with items that either weren't required before or occupied a space that wasn't the one they are in now. You deal with it the same way you deal with chronic clutter, which is to say methodically, and, because both time and energy may be short, you tackle it in short bursts.

It may help to know that space, however limited, can be made to fit just about any circumstance, because there are tricks based entirely on common sense that will make it so. Most of them are used by professional organisers whom you can pay to come into your life if you really can't fix it yourself, but none of them are hard, so try them. Take it slowly, don't go at it like a bull at a gate, and be realistic. The aim is to find a proper place for everything so that once an item has been used, it can be returned to that proper place and no one need ever say again, 'How come we don't have any scissors?' Even if you have just moved in and there are fifty-two unopened boxes on your living-room floor.

···················· **HOW TO DECLUTTER** ····················

There are two general rules you need to absorb before you throw yourself into a major prune: everything should have its own place and the place should be obvious; any system created must be one that can be maintained. Your aim at the end of a declutter is to know where everything is. That's everything, from your last phone bill to the extra scourers. As an exercise, make a rough inventory of areas you consider most cluttered – your wardrobe or the toy cupboard. See what you've got; see what can go. It will both relieve and appal you, even if you get sick of writing it all down halfway through.

The advice that follows has, for the most part, been supplied by people who manage clutter for a living and have seen everything. Some of their suggestions sound a little excessive, but that's me. I haven't included their various recommendations for storing items with fancy labels, mainly because I know I would never attempt a fancy label in a month of Sundays. And I left out the tip for giving everyone their own net bag for light and dark laundry so the bags can be returned fresh from the dryer to be folded by their respective owners, because it just seemed unlikely. On the other hand, there is nothing like common sense when it is spelt out for you to make you realise it's all pretty simple once you get down to it.

Getting started

○ Start with something easy, like a drawer or a small cupboard. You need a fast and impressive result for encouragement.

○ To tackle something huge, like a room, set aside a fixed time, no more than two to three hours. Don't leave it open-ended or you'll never finish and matters will only become worse. Tackle the room section by section. If you're having trouble, make it a two- or even a three-step process. Aim to have it looking different at the end of each step.

○ Involve all household members in the clear-out, including children. Knowing where things should be won't stop them asking you to find them, but appreciating that there is a place for everything establishes good habits.

○ Allow for personality types. Some people will always be messier than others; they may have very orderly brains. Untidiness is not the same as cluttered.

○ If clutter keeps appearing, take a look at your consumer tendencies. If you buy on impulse stuff you don't need or even especially want, stop wandering around shops. Before any random purchase, ask yourself, 'Why am I buying this and where will it go?'

○ Apply the 'one in, one out' rule. If you buy a new item for the house, you need to pass on a similar older item. This applies to clothing, toys, books, old tools, jewellery, kitchen appliances: anything.

○ Know things will get worse before they get better, so take into account that the job isn't just about throwing things out. It also includes putting back, and putting back in some kind of order.

○ On a cheerier note, an area might look cluttered, but if you can find what you are looking for and it's not weighing you down emotionally, then it isn't an issue.

How to cull

Take everything out of whatever it is you are sorting – wardrobe, cupboard, toy box, pantry, kitchen or bathroom cabinet – give the now vacant space a thorough clean, then divide its contents into piles. One is for rubbish, one is to sell or give away, one is to keep where it is and the last is to be put somewhere else in the house.

When deciding what to keep, ask yourself: 'Do I need this? Do I need this many? Does it work? Does it fit? Do I own it? Will I ever need to wear it again? Will it ever come back into fashion? Am I saving it for my children? Who am I kidding?' Be ruthless. Note your immediate response. Any hesitation over whether to keep or ditch would suggest you ditch. You could also ask yourself: 'Do I love it?' Loving it counts. If something forms part of your history then it has value.

You aren't morally obliged to keep unwanted gifts. You can pass them on to someone who might like or need them more. You can give them to charity, sell them or just sling them. Slinging them is a bit harsh if they haven't gone mouldy.

How to store

The point of space management is to create areas in which you can live comfortably. Not only do you need designated places for everyday items but also you need places to store the things not immediately in use. If there's no room on the premises, you might consider renting a storage space or building a shed. Claim items you have stored only as required: anything not required after twelve months should be looked at very carefully. Do you need it? Really?

⊙ Use all available space on the premises. Under the bed, the tops of built-ins and quirky little spaces under the stairs are excellent for storage. Strange-shaped gaps can take strange-shaped objects.

⊙ Drawers are incredibly effective storage spaces. If you're planning a new kitchen or bedroom, opt for as many drawers as possible, with varying depths.

⊙ Look at how you fold or stack and ask yourself if it's appropriate for the storage space. Think sheets and towels – do they actually fit comfortably into the linen cupboard? Try folding differently, or possibly rolling.

⊙ Use stacking effectively in food cupboards and wardrobes; if shelves are big, buy a divider so you can double the surface space. Space for air is wasted space.

⊙ Store like with like, if necessary in a labelled basket or box. The most common space management problem is unlike items jumbled together.

○ Avoid piles, especially with paper work.

○ If you have more towels than your family actually uses (three for each person), store the extras until the others wear out.

Maintaining an uncluttered space

Once achieved, maintain control of the order by daily tidying as a matter of course. Pack things away neatly once they've been used. Don't just shove stuff in drawers.

○ If you're too tired to sort paperwork at the end of a day, make a time each week to file bank statements, bills, notes from school and so on.

○ Never walk out of a room without taking something with you to return to another room.

○ The average home needs two proper clear-outs per year. Chuck out or pass on items that you never use or are broken beyond repair. Go through every room in the house and make a point of culling; charities are usually grateful for clothes and bric-a-brac.

○ Don't accept cast-off anything if you can't store it.

·········· MANAGING SPECIFIC SPACES ··········
Paperwork

It's possible to cut down hugely on paperwork by banking, receiving bills and paying accounts online. If you can go paperless, do, but you still need to address, one way or another, all paperwork as it comes into the house. This means either destroying, recycling or filing it. Destroy by burning or shredding anything that contains personal information that could be used for identity fraud (see Chapter 16), recycle all junk mail, flyers, envelopes, newspapers, etc. and file the rest.

If your house doesn't have a designated office or study, use a filing cabinet in a bedroom or at the very least a drawer in the kitchen. You need folders for all important documents: insurance, car, house, banking, health, hobbies, receipts. Tax requires you to keep bills and bank statements for five years post-submission, so these papers need a place. It also helps to have folders for paperwork requiring urgent attention, paperwork that needs to be dealt with in the near future and paperwork that should be stored. It sounds like an awful lot of folders, but they clear your head space. Just be careful that the In tray (or immediate attention folder) doesn't become the Stay There Forever tray.

To cut down on paper, save only the pages containing critical information (say, the first page of bills). Sort folders twice a year and junk stuff you don't need. Be especially callous with the bits of paper you keep because you think they might be handy one day – holiday brochures, exercise regimes and so on. All that info is readily accessible if you really want it.

Kitchen

First cast your eyes swiftly and coldly over its long-standing inhabitants and chuck out any chipped or cracked china plus any pots and pans with broken handles, dings and unacceptably dense coatings of burnt fat. Keep them if you love them, but really, do you? Audit your plastic containers. Lose anything that doesn't have a lid.

Move directly to the utensil drawer. Empty the contents into a large container and return them to the drawer only if you need them. Should you find seven potato peelers, four can openers, twelve blunt knives, four cake slicers, three broken garlic crushers and four sets of plastic egg poachers, ask yourself: 'Why?' I mean it. Why?

Three times a year, sort your food cupboard. Check the sell-by dates on cans and sauce jars. Check for stuff exposed to ants or moths. Empty ancient packets of buckwheat flour, polenta, lentils or anything else you may have been storing for several years on the off-chance you will be caught in a siege. Wash the containers. Replace according to use. Arrange cupboards according to type. Everything needs to be accessible.

Keep work surfaces as clear as possible. They can be quickly overtaken by cumbersome appliances. Juicers, food mixers, breadmakers, rice cookers and deep fryers should all be housed in drawers or cupboards. The least used should be housed furthest away. The never used should be given away.

Bedrooms

To maximise space, put away clothes seasonally. Only have out what you need for each season. Store the rest (see Chapter 8). When you get out your new season's clothes, put the hangers in backwards on the rod; when you've worn a piece of clothing, hang it up facing the front. At the end of the season, you'll know what you haven't worn, and those items can be stored elsewhere until you are ready to get rid of them. (This isn't something I would do but I can see how it might work, so in an ideal world and only if you have that kind of brain.)

Use proper hangers – wooden or padded. They cost a bit, so ask for some for Christmas. Leave out the hangers for clothes you have worn that day so you'll remember to re-hang them at night. If things aren't hung because it's too much trouble, stack them, either flat or rolled. If there aren't enough shelves in built-ins, buy storage systems that fit inside them. Use suitcases for storage under the bed and clear plastic boxes for shoes; use a tie hanger for belts and scarves.

Compartmentalise large drawers so fancy bras are separate from sports bras and business socks from sports socks. The idea is to be able to find what you want without looking.

Toys

To encourage children to put their toys away when they've finished using them, give them easy and obvious places to store them. Bear in mind that small children use two hands to put things away, so they don't have a hand left to hold open a lid. Use containers without lids. Store items in related groups like games, puzzles, books, paints and lego.

Note favourite toys and activities. Put anything that's out of favour away and re-introduce it next time you need a distraction. In the same vein, keep toys within reach to a manageable number. It reduces the size of the mess should everything be out at once and encourages maximum usage.

Bathrooms

Bathrooms are where we go to maximise clutter and there's no excuse. The small cabinets, trays and shelves become repositories for everything to do with the upkeep of our bodies as well as bits of old candle. Not only do we constantly replace shampoos, cosmetics, body lotions, bath and shower gels, medicines, toothbrushes, toothpastes, cotton wool, cotton pads and cotton buds before we actually need to but people give us more of them as gifts. Everything gets put into the cabinet or onto a shelf, gets opened in an idle moment and there you are: one more half-used item taking up space, leaving a ring mark and hiding the medicines, which somehow get dispersed and disguised.

Remove everything from the shelves, trays and cupboards. It's a one-step process because you need to know exactly what is lurking in there. Get rid of anything that isn't being used. This includes the complimentary items from hotels and airlines you were saving for guests, because the guests won't want them. And it includes all the shampoos and conditioners that were almost finished but not quite and hung on to in case you finished the next one and were left with nothing.

Put the medicines into two plastic containers. Store them somewhere that meets the usual requirements of light and temperature: the least used items might go on a shelf in a bedroom cupboard; the most used onto a high shelf in the food cupboard in the kitchen. Arrange essential bathroom items into type, if necessary in plastic containers to avoid spillage and spreading.

These are the basics. You will note the reliance on plastic containers. You can't beat them for the sense of efficiency they engender in the user. You can see what's in them; they keep out ants; and when you wash them they have a suggestion of sterility that makes you trust you will never poison anyone again. The plastic container is to space management what the list is to time management. To incorporate the pair of them efficiently into your life, you need serious intention which, frankly, you may struggle to find. But you can find it, Householder, you can.

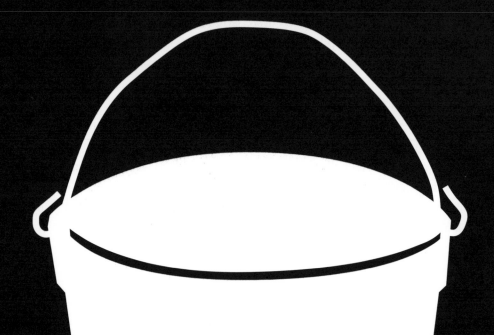

PART 3

HOUSEHOLD
CHORES

CHORE IS NOT a word that warms the cockles of your heart. It has few pleasant connotations, yet households run on them. Every day, every week, every year, a series of tasks must be done and someone has to do them, so it helps to know why and how. It goes without saying that you should neglect any your household doesn't consider necessary. This could be ironing. Actually, that's all it could be. I can't think of any others that are optional, unless it's darning, but even darning, now we're embracing thrift, is a skill to be mastered. The rest are connected to sustenance, hygiene and the house not falling down, all of which we need to stay alive.

The thing is to tackle what must be done as efficiently and speedily as possible so that our time and energy are properly used and household comfort is assured. It's important to approach the job at hand in a friendly manner. Wanting to chew off an arm rather than pick up a vacuum cleaner is not helpful. The choice is to live in squalor, which might work for some people but almost none, or be cleanish and organised. Cleanliness, regardless of its proximity to godliness, is critical to our mental and physical wellbeing. We already know the point of being organised, so it's in the spirit of organisation that I've divided chores into three: cleaning the house; doing the laundry; and caring for clothes. I appreciate that everything to do with food can be regarded as a chore, but sustenance is such a large part of household survival that I've dealt with it separately.

6

CLEANING

Two things to consider before you lift a finger are when it's best done and by whom. Proper timing plus a fair distribution of labour make life so much simpler. How often each room should be cleaned and the manner in which it's best cleaned are discussed throughout the chapter but when and by whom are open to negotiation.

WHEN

Any time, really depending on your household's timetable. Few chores outside meal preparation and school runs are time-specific. They're energy-specific so it makes sense to tackle them when you have time to sit down afterwards. Just factor in how long it's going to take. For instance, if you don't intend to put washing on the line, in which case it should be tackled in the morning, it can be done any time because it requires next to no energy . Cleaning, shopping, clothes-sorting and blocking the holes where the cockroaches come in should be done either as an emergency or fitted into a routine based on no more than three chores a day. Smaller, infrequent, less critical jobs, like drawer-tidying, you can do on the hop. For example, when the dishwasher is full, the cutlery drawer should be half-empty, so that's when you tidy it. If the drawer is never half-empty, you have too much in it. When the fridge is more or less empty before a weekly shop, clear a shelf. No matter how time stretched you are, or which hours of the day you allocate to them, don't eschew a routine for regular chores. It might suggest monotony, but actually it's a mark of accomplishment. It's a way of putting one foot after the other without having to weigh the pros and cons when the cons can so easily take precedence.

BY WHOM

Apart from breast-feeding, domestic duties are never gender-specific but here are three funny things: despite the number of women now in the labour force, they still spend nearly twice as much time on domestic responsibilities as the men they live with; in eight out of ten couple households, women usually or always do the laundry; and men are reckoned to spend a quarter of the time women do in activities generally described as child-raising. All the research points to working mothers functioning in a state of zombie-like exhaustion. There are several possible reasons for the imbalance: women in most households spend more time at home than men; more women work part-time than the men they live with (although, in Australia, half of all mothers with children under two work an average of twenty-four hours a week, so are seriously pushing themselves); and 90 per cent of all single-parent households are run by women. UK research shows that the most liberal distribution of domestic chores is found in households where the woman works full-time and earns more than her male partner, or has a partner who doesn't work outside the home. It's a horrible thought, so one that I am going to dismiss at once, that, in bearing the brunt of domestic responsibilities, women are simply conforming to expectations – their own and everyone else's. More likely they're better practised at multi-tasking and so get more things done. Who cares why? Is it fair and is it efficient? Can't be.

Assuming that you aren't employing a cleaner (if you are, see page 97), who does what will of course vary from household type to household type and according to the personalities within them, but your first concern is stress reduction so this means eliminating resentment and/or unwarranted martyrdom. You may live in a household where one member is perfectly happy assuming responsibility for endless thankless tasks. Or you may live in a household where neither is, in which case there is only one option: a list of jobs plus who will tackle them and when, with regard only to physical stamina and available time. I would urge you to embrace this solution happily and without moaning or lying about how much work you have to do elsewhere because it's in the household's best interests which means your own.

Cleaning is what most people mean by housework, and it's what we do to avoid the plague. Tidying is a different matter altogether. Tidying is what we do very quickly to make our place look clean even if it isn't. It's a chore that ought to be done daily, even if you only use your place for sleeping, but especially if you're pushed for space. If you have embraced the basic rules of space management, it won't be difficult. Everything in your home will have a proper place to which it can be returned, and that's all you have to do. Return it.

Since even this simple task can be put off indefinitely, make time for it. Give it ten to twenty minutes at the beginning of the day and ten to twenty minutes at the end. For example, in the morning, tidy the bedroom/s and the bathroom/s; in the evening, do the living room and the kitchen.

Morning tidy

It stands to reason that you don't leave your bedroom in the morning without making the bed. You get out of bed, you open a bedroom window if it isn't already open, you pull back the bed covers and you air the bed while you dress and have breakfast. Then you make it. An unmade bed is slovenly, and it's not hard to pull up a quilt or a sheet and blanket. A child of five can manage it. If you have a child of five, insist they manage it. Should you have a complicated bedding arrangement involving throws, then you will be tidy by nature and obsessive about design so your bedroom will be immaculate and you need no advice from me. If you're sloppy by nature and you still have a throw, what on earth are you doing? Ditch the throw.

Ditto hospital corners. If you are a hospital-corners person, you won't be an untidy person. You will be a person who likes everything done properly and whose education vis-à-vis the bed has been comprehensive.

Having made the bed, put away clothes into drawers, wardrobes or the laundry basket. If you've worn anything to bed, put it under the pillow or hang it behind the bedroom door. Check the room for extraneous items like water, glasses, newspapers, notepads, books, laptops, hand creams, animals, work documents, stray bodies, toys or bits of food, and either arrange them tidily or remove them. An untidy bedroom is the least restful room in the house.

THE HOSPITAL CORNER

If you want to be a hospital corner person but are unfamiliar with the technique, I'll try to explain it, but trust me when I tell you I have never read a comprehensible description. Mainly, you need someone to show you as my mother showed me. What follows is her technique. It can apply to the bottom sheet if it's flat and not fitted, as well as to the top sheet and blankets.

● Smooth the sheet or sheet and blankets over the bed so that there is an equal drop on either side and a good 40 cm (15 in) at the bottom of the bed.

● Stand at the bottom of the bed and in one swift movement lift the mattress and tuck in the overhang.

● Move to one side of the bed.

● Take hold of the edge of the sheet, or top sheet and blanket together, at a point 50 cm (20 in) from the bottom of the bed and lift it up onto the bed where it will form a point. This will leave a rough triangle of overhang 50 cm (20 in) along from the bottom of the bed.

● Tuck that overhang under the mattress, then allow the lifted portion to drop back down over the side of the bed.

● Tuck that in.

● Repeat on the other side.

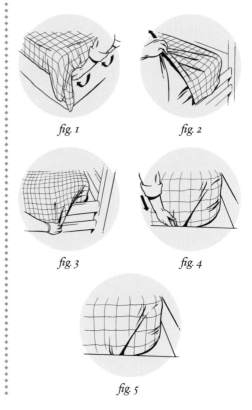

fig. 1

fig. 2

fig. 3

fig. 4

fig. 5

Then give the bathroom a once-over. At least pick towels up from the floor. It should be a household rule. Nothing makes a bathroom look smaller or smell damper.

Evening tidy

Before you put the lights out in the living room, pick up all the papers from the floor and put them into the recycling bin, the rubbish bin or the place where bills and important documents are kept. Put away toys, shoes, mugs, plates and sweet wrappers. Check for anything that might interest a rat, an ant, a cockroach or a fly. Remove any obvious dirt from the floor or the furniture. Sweep the kitchen floor and make sure all utensils and china and pots and pans are either washed, dried and put away or in the dishwasher. Check that the work surface is thoroughly clean and dry and that all the cupboard doors and drawers are closed. Should there be rooms in the house containing mess that is unavoidable, or too enormous to be tackled at the end of a long day, shut the door on it because you don't need to think about it until it can be properly dismantled.

·············· THE POINT OF CLEANING ··············

Before we even begin to consider how to clean, we need to ask ourselves what we're hoping to achieve. Specifically, how clean do we need to be? Plainly germs, rats and cockroaches will invade our property and/or it will begin to smell if we don't clean it. I can't say for sure that the household will collapse from dirt-induced illness, because there is a school of thought that argues we are better off with some dirt than no dirt and that no dirt is actually responsible for the rise in allergies. But no one has actually quantified the 'some' or specified the dirt. Do they mean dirt dirt, or dust dirt, or squalor, or what?

What we know for a fact is that households are a source of illness because kitchens, toilets, householders' hands, pets, telephones, taps, door knobs, toys, mops and dishcloths are rich breeding grounds for the pathogenic micro-organisms (germs) that will do us in given half a chance, and that carpets, bedding, clothes and pets harbour bugs and mites which, along with toxic household cleaning products, can cause allergic reactions, although it's hard to say when and why they will because their impact appears to be random.

Ill effects depend not only on the extent to which germs and allergens are allowed to flourish, but also on their type and the general robustness of the householder. Clearly, babies, the elderly and those with compromised immune systems are most at risk, but we can all fall victim. We can all feel off colour, get headaches, catch each other's colds and flu and puking bugs, yet mostly we never ask ourselves if maybe that particular germ came off the tea towel. This is because we don't like to imagine it was there in the first place. And maybe it wasn't, but a damp tea towel is said to harbour 30 trillion colonies of bacteria, which will linger if they aren't despatched with proper cleaning. I don't know who's counting and I don't know why the tea towel is more congenial for bacteria colonies than the dishcloth, which houses just the 10 million, but it stands to reason we'd better properly clean. The next question is how properly?

Good cleaning practice

The answer must be moderately. You don't need to go nuts. A cold is preferable to nuts any day in my book. But this is a matter of personal preference as well as the personal preference of other household members, should there be any. Occupiers of single-person households can be as insanely clean or repulsively messy as they choose because they have no one to please or place at risk other than themselves. Households containing more than one adult member owe each other's sensibilities respect. Probably, most respect should go to the person who cares so much about cleanliness that they are prepared to do whatever is necessary to achieve it, but this is shaky ground. Issues of fairness, privacy and offensiveness will soon be raised and may become household breakers. Compromise. Avoid petulance. Monitor your health. All households, but especially those containing children, need to observe at least the basic rules of hygiene. To reduce the risk of illness and allergic reactions, you need only adopt good practice. This means knowing where the risks are and cleaning, disinfecting, drying and airing as required, as well as shoring up your home against rats and cockroaches. It takes first awareness, then practice.

To assist householders such as ourselves, the Infection Control Nurses Association in the UK has produced a table of risk levels which is as comforting as it is surprising. Toilets, as you might expect, have a high germ presence but they have a low risk of spreading them. Cleaning cloths, sponges and mops which are semi-permanently damp have a high germ presence and a constant risk of spreading them. Hand- and food-contact surfaces, like kitchen worktops, taps and door handles, have a medium germ presence and constant risk of spreading them. Dirty clothes and bedding have a moderate to low germ presence and are a risk only to the person handling them. Floors and walls have an occasional germ presence and a low germ-spreading risk, which really, given the amount of food we eat off the floor, is a relief. I think we can rest just that little bit easier knowing that we are at greatest risk from damp kitchen cloths and dirty work surfaces, and so that is where we should concentrate our efforts.

Household germs

Germs can be either killed or removed. They are killed by disinfectant or a temperature of at least 60°C (140°F) maintained for a decent amount of time. They are removed by immersion in detergent and hot water. Wiping won't do it. Wiping is spreading. You need to clean with detergent and rinse with hot water. Then you need to dry. Germs survive in damp conditions, which is why the dishcloth, like the tea towel, is a problem. Wash the dishcloth in the dishwasher and dry it daily.

For myself, I prefer removing to killing. This may be the privilege of a comparatively healthy household, but you slather your house in antibacterial stuff and where does that leave your immune system? I say this in the face of contrary evidence. My late mother-in-law, who was a state-registered nurse, always added Dettol to her washing-up water. Tea tasted like Dettol. Sunday lunch tasted like Dettol. Her house smelt like Dettol. Her husband lived until he was ninety-five.

In times of epidemic, say of swine, chicken or any other flu, the antibacterial wipe or detergent comes into its own. It should be used on hands, door knobs, surfaces and taps, especially in households containing susceptible individuals including babies, pregnant women or people with underlying health issues.

Household allergies

The tendency to allergy is mostly inherited, but dust mites are responsible for much of the asthma, chronic rhinitis and eczema from which many of us suffer, so you need to clean to get rid of them, and that's easier said than done since they live everywhere: in carpets, mattresses, pillows, bedclothes and clothes.

Mites are trickier than germs and can never be fully eradicated. They dehydrate then come to life again in humid conditions, and that's a scary thought. What they prefer is to remain undisturbed in a humid environment, so the trick is to disturb them and to keep the humidity in your house to a minimum. This means a daily airing of all rooms and the treating of all mould. Anything wet, like fish tanks, should be removed from bedrooms. Extractor fans should always be used in bathrooms and kitchens.

If you are dealing with chronic allergy, you need to think again about having carpets throughout the house and especially in the bedroom/s. The mite loves a bedroom. Over 2 million dust mites live in the average person's bed. It helps to use anti–dust mite mattress covers and hypoallergenic bedding, but the truth is those pesky blighters will get wind of your breathing and sweating and they will track you down, so you have to wash your bedding regularly and dust the house regularly with a damp cloth (which you must then wash and dry). If your child is allergic, you need to keep soft toys to a minimum. You might try putting favourite toys into a plastic bag and into the freezer overnight, so the mites will get frostbite and die.

Should your household be comparatively allergy- and infection-free, good for you. But think of your visitors. You still need to air your house and you need to clean. Given the range of products on the market, we can now be cleaner than nature ever intended us to be, so we should at least be as clean as we need to be. This is clean enough to render high-risk areas as germ- and allergen-free as possible, and otherwise clean enough to look as if whoever lives in the place cares about it. You can achieve this by removing any visible signs of dirt or food as soon as they appear and by a weekly cleaning of the whole house. Dirty, just so you know, ought not to be confused with worn. All homes suffer from regular wear and tear or spillages on the sofa and stains on the paintwork. These are called signs of life.

·········· THE GREAT PRODUCT DEBATE ··········

How you keep your house clean is, of course, your call. You can't move for information on the matter. Central to the current debate is green versus traditional, which translates, according to your inclination, as expensive versus cheap, doesn't work versus works, personal health and the health of planet versus prove it. The loudest argument from those opposed to them is that green products aren't as effective as the chemical-based versions, and the usual reply from those who use them is that they work just as well once you appreciate they require longer contact with the surface to be cleaned and a little more elbow-grease. On the matter of cost, green adherents argue that you don't need to buy commercially produced chemical-free products; if you have access to hot water, rags, vinegar and bicarbonate of soda, the expense is minimal. And on the question of global and personal health, they suggest that subjecting either or both to toxins via cleaning is the great domestic folly of the last 100 years. Standard cleaners contain chlorine, which damages the ozone layer, and phosphates, whose build-up can have disastrous effects on waterways.

In search of a disinterested opinion but not really up for conducting a major scientific survey, I telephoned a professional cleaner on a number I chose at random from the telephone book. It was a local domestic and business cleaning service in regional New South Wales. The head of the firm told me he'd abandoned traditional commercial cleaning products in favour of green citrus-based products because the chemicals he'd used in the past had knocked him about too much. The only exceptions he made now were for the backs of badly encrusted ovens and roofs covered in mould. Green products don't have the abrasive qualities of traditional products, he said, and they take longer to work, but he no longer has headaches.

On the strength of this I phoned Nature's Organics, whose cleaning products are 99 per cent plant-based, to ask whether effectiveness had to be sacrificed for greenness. The son of the company's founder said the market is so competitive that there is no question of his products not performing at the same level as traditional products. His challenge is not to compromise on eco-friendliness. The aim of his company is to minimise its products' impact on the environment, not only through the use of plants – palm oil, coconut oil and soya as opposed to petro-chemicals – but also through the use of recyclable and recycled packaging. In the last fifteen years, the company's sales have increased by between 20 and 25 per cent per year, which suggests a growing concern about toxicity in the household that is only vaguely addressed by the major companies whose failure to list the components in their products is disconcerting. I telephoned Colgate Palmolive for their input but, after several weeks of failing to establish contact with an elusive spokesperson, gave up.

The problem with green products, it seems to me, is cost-effectiveness in fiscally challenged times. I went to the local supermarket to make some price comparisons. Taking the all-purpose cleanser as an example, I found green products on sale for roughly three times the cost of traditional, although the most expensive traditional very nearly matched the most expensive green. For the same price you could buy a box of bicarbonate of soda plus a bottle of cider vinegar. In terms of cost, DIY products win hands down. But do they work?

I consulted Betty, who cleans our house. She isn't a huge fan of any commercial products, green or traditional. She finds green products too greasy for her liking and she's been wary of chemical-based products ever since she discovered that a traditionally produced shower cleanser made her nose bleed. The critical ingredients in any successful cleaning operation, as far as she is concerned, are water, rags and elbow-grease. This is what she uses to clean windows, which gleam: three rags – one for washing, one for drying, one for polishing – water and elbow-grease. They cost next to nothing. They require, however, energy and they require time, the missing ingredients in most householders' lives. If it comes down to cheap and non-toxic versus fast and nose-bleeds, it would be no contest. But is it that simple?

I personally love the idea of DIY products. Who could fail to be charmed by their homely simplicity and their harking-back to our great-grandmothers baking the bread while they churned the butter and corned the beef? My concerns about ye olde harmless potions and remedies, however, are not just their effectiveness but, ironically, their toxicity. Generally speaking, their effectiveness depends on how many times you are prepared to repeat the simple process until it works, and their toxicity on exactly what it is you are using. Old and simple doesn't necessarily mean hazard-free. Mostly, the endless column inches devoted to DIY cleansers rarely step outside the benign soda/vinegar/lemon-juice triangle, but occasionally you come across recipes that include ammonia, turpentine, paraffin or borax, and how comfortably do these sit in a green household?

I would like to report that I have, in the interests of thrift, health and saving the planet, tried every suggested DIY cleaning process that I've ever encountered but, nope, I haven't, because my interest in cleaning runs mostly to talking about it. I can thoroughly commend the effectiveness of Gumption (the non-green but all-Australian cleaning paste whose ingredients are soap, water, silica and perfume) and I know for a fact that a basic three-parts-oil-to-one-part-vinegar furniture polish works, because my mother swore by it. I've used bicarbonate of soda to clean our toilets, which seems to work, but this may be because bicarb works on everything one way or the other, eventually.

This isn't to put you off. Should you, Householder, have the time and the inclination to take the DIY route, then your staples will be wine vinegar, lemon juice, bicarbonate of soda (for cleansing) and glycerine (for stain removal). Below are the claims made on their behalf:

- Both lemon juice and vinegar are highly effective disinfectants.

- White vinegar mixed with water will sort out glass and windows and also remove lime scale, mould and stains on furniture (gently applied).

- Bicarbonate of soda is an excellent all-purpose cleanser. Mixed with hot water until it fizzes, it will unblock drains. It can cut through grease of all sorts in bathrooms and kitchens. Mixed to a paste with white vinegar, it can clean grouting. It can also be used to clean shower curtains and remove stains from carpets (1 teaspoon soda to 1 cup water). An all-purpose cleanser can be made from ½ cup vinegar, ¼ cup bicarbonate of soda and 8 cups water, mixed in a spray bottle.

Other than that, I can vouch for sun being a great bleach. As is lemon juice. Salt is a fine stain remover. I have often admired its effectiveness on red wine after a spill has been absorbed first by kitchen towel. Tea-tree oil removes mould.

Everyone has a tip. Whatever you use – green, traditional, DIY – it's the manner in which you clean that will give you the results you need. What follows is a room-by-room guide based on advice from experts in both hemispheres.

············ CLEANING THE BATHROOM ············

For bathrooms, I consulted the head of household at the Observatory Hotel in Sydney. His job is to ensure that guests paying a fortune for their rooms don't recoil at scum on the bath and don't come down with hotel-bred infections that will reflect badly on the management. His methods didn't include green anything but were extremely thorough.

The hotel's bathrooms have marble walls and floors, on which the staff use a traditional chemical-based shower cleanser and an all-purpose cleanser, an anti-mould spray where necessary, plus a hard sponge, a normal sponge and dry rags. Their method is:

- Spray the shower cubicle from top to bottom with the shower cleanser. Leave for a few minutes.

- Turn the hot water tap on hard for five minutes, so the shower is thoroughly steamed.

- Open the shower door and allow the cubicle to dry for one minute.

- Wipe the cubicle and fittings from top to bottom with a hard sponge to remove any soapy residue. (Change sponges frequently.)

- Use the normal sponge to finish it off, then dry with a rag, possibly an old bath towel, which must be large and in good condition.

- Should there be any mould in the corners of the cubicle, treat it with an anti-mould spray left on for five to ten minutes.

- Use the same technique on the hand basin and the bath: cleanser, hot water, hard sponge, soft sponge, rag. The surfaces should be left immaculate: dry and clean to the touch, without the slightest suggestion of slipperiness.

- Clean the toilet with the all-purpose cleanser and a toilet brush which reaches under the neck of the toilet bowl. Spray the cleanser into the bowl, under the seat, on the seat and under the lid. Clean the bowl with the brush, the seat with sponges. Clean the nooks and crannies with a nail brush.

According to Betty, removing the various build-ups of soap and lime scale requires physical effort. She swears by the nailbrush, or an old toothbrush, and suggests that lime scale or mildew around taps can be removed with vinegar and an old toothbrush, followed by thorough rinsing and drying.

While you have the vinegar out, if you mix a solution of one part vinegar to four parts water you can apply it to your stained mirror with a sponge and wipe it off with crumpled newspaper.

The trick, in any case, is to clean the bathroom regularly, at least weekly, because once neglected it can degenerate quickly, and there is something tragic about dirt in a room designed to make us clean.

CLEANING THE KITCHEN

Of prime concern in the kitchen are the work surfaces, the cooking utensils and the cleaning equipment, because these are areas of maximum potential contamination. They must be kept constantly clean, which means cleaning immediately after use. The floor doesn't matter so much, but it stands to reason that you don't allow spilt food to congeal, crumbs to linger or puddles to gather.

To clean the work surface, use hot soapy water to wash and kitchen towel to dry before and after use, but especially when it has seen contact with raw meat, fish or poultry, which should never be allowed to come anywhere near other food. Chopping boards should be put into the dishwasher after use for a proper cleaning.

A dirty dishcloth as stated earlier can harbour 10 million germs, which is impressive. Either use disposables or wash the cloths daily. To kill the germs, put the cloths in a hot wash in the washing machine, or wash them in detergent and warm water, rinse them, then leave them in a disinfectant solution for twenty minutes. Stick washing-up brushes into the dishwasher.

Change tea towels when they are dirty or wet. Any damp cloths in the kitchen are dodgy. Mops are less so, but they do need proper rinsing, arguably disinfecting, and drying after use.

Stacking the dishwasher

Dishwasher-stacking says a lot about personality type and probably more than it should. Everyone has their method, except for those of us who don't and who annoy the living daylights out of those who do. The correct way, clearly, is to follow the manufacturer's instructions, but should you have lost them, the following might interest you. It's based on advice given to me by the Wolseley restaurant in London, which washes up after 1100 customers a day. This feat turns out to be in no way similar to washing up at home, because restaurants sluice crockery under a fierce jet, then load trays that pass through a washer that never stops. Its cycle is four minutes as opposed to the 104 minutes a domestic dishwasher can take. But basics apply:

- To save water, avoid the pre-rinse. Scrape off excess food.

- A dishwasher works by jetting water over the surface of dirty items to remove food particles, so make sure that the surfaces are properly exposed and that the spray arms can move freely.

- Don't allow plates to touch each other, and don't stack items on top of each other – this stops the detergent solution from washing effectively and can cause scratching.

- Load the most heavily soiled items in the lower basket.

- Plastic items can distort in a dishwasher.

- Never pack items too tightly. Glass or china can crack as the items expand on heating.

- Don't put crystal items into the dishwasher: it makes them go cloudy. Other glass items should be stacked in the top rack, where the water movement is gentler, and, like cups, they should be placed at an angle so that water can drain off. Alternate cups and glasses to avoid scratching.

- When loading cups or mugs, ensure that the handles face in the same direction to maximise the available space.

- Mix spoons, knives and forks in the basket. This maximises the exposure of the cutlery to the detergent solution.

- Never load the knives with the blade pointing up. Falling on them can be fatal.

- On the other hand, don't load cutlery so it falls through the basket. It will foul the mechanism and your load will come out dirty.

- Never put silver and stainless-steel cutlery in the same basket, because the metals react against each other.

Unloading is less fraught, but there is a technique:

- Empty the bottom basket first, so any water left on the items in the top basket doesn't drip onto the items below.

- Because cutlery can begin to rust in the hot, moist atmosphere of the drying cycle, get it out as quickly as possible after cycle completion, or open the door while drying.

It has nothing to do with dishwashing, but while at the Wolseley, I learnt the best way to clean copper. Coat it for three or four minutes in a paste of lemon juice, salt, flour, water and vinegar. Does anyone eat off copper?

Washing up by hand

If you prefer to wash up by hand – and you may like to know that 71 per cent of all UK households do as of 2008:

- Dirty dishes should be washed as soon as possible after eating – only leave until the morning in extreme circumstances.

- Don't soak and then put away: soak, wash, dry and then put away.

- To wash, use a proper detergent and rubber gloves, and make the water as hot as you can stand.

○ Change the water regularly during a hefty wash, but you don't need to rinse. Washing-up liquid left on china, cutlery or utensils won't hurt you.

○ Allow dishes and glasses to air dry, then put away.

○ Dry cutlery at once to avoid rusting.

○ Wash and dry any cloths or brushes that were used in the process (see page 89).

○ Put any damp or soiled tea towels into the wash.

Fridge

You need to clean your fridge every week to keep it free from bacteria. Remove all its contents and chuck any dodgy remains you've been saving for another meal in the interests of thrift. (See Chapter 10 for food storage times.) Take out the shelves and wash them in hot soapy water. Wash the inside of the fridge with a solution of $1/4$ cup bicarbonate of soda with 2 pints warm water, or if you prefer 1 cup vinegar to 3 cups water.

Oven

Most modern ovens are self-cleaning, but the walls and sides will still get splattered during roasting, the glass will certainly brown up and the shelves are always at risk, so it has to be addressed – not weekly, but when you have the energy or should you smell old food burning when you heat the oven. Your first step is to read the manufacturer's instructions. Unless they specifically tell you not to, you can apply a paste of 1 tablespoon bicarbonate of soda to 1 cup warm water to both the walls and the glass, leave it on for five minutes, then wipe it off. Should you feel safe only with hot soapy water, elbow-grease will be required but will almost certainly be as effective as any other form of cleaning. Certainly, hot soapy water and proper effort will clean the shelves, but the job will be made easier with an all-purpose cleanser, commercial or DIY, and once they are grime-free you will have a sense of satisfaction engendered by almost no other area of housework.

Stainless steel

Stainless steel is a mixed blessing in the kitchen. It scratches and marks easily and is notoriously hard to clean without causing streaks, but nothing beats it for its suggestion of sterility and professionalism. The most effective way to clean it, in my opinion, is with baby oil and paper towels. Apply the oil in small amounts and wipe down.

Garbage

Always line your kitchen bin with a bin liner and take bags out to the rubbish regularly, certainly daily even if not full. Wash both the kitchen bin and the rubbish bin often, because the longer they are left coated in bits of waste, the more likely they are to attract not only germs but pests.

PESTS

Your basic pests, attracted by crumbs and exposed food of any sort, or, to be fair, possibly warmth or water, are ants, cockroaches, weevils, moths, rats and mice. If you have a serious infestation, consult an expert, because household pests, while not necessarily disease carriers, can pose health problems for the allergic.

In moderate cases, your first step is to track the line of entry and either block it up to render access impossible or make it so uncongenial to the pest that it will never return. Gaps around hot water pipes and heating ducts are especially inviting so seal them. It's also critical to keep food on shelves in containers with tightly fitted, preferably screw-top, lids. If necessary you can stand those containers in a larger container of water, but this implies living with the varmints. Mostly you need to get rid of them.

Ants

If you find the nest outside, you can destroy it with boiling water. If they are inside the house, you can use commercial products strategically placed to poison them or you can sprinkle the affected area with cinnamon (which in my view constitutes a food crumb that might attract other insects), talcum powder or bicarbonate of soda. These are just suggestions which have worked for some people. The commercial poison, more broadly tested, works by having the ants do the dirty work: becoming contaminated and taking the horror back to the nest. This isn't my favourite interaction with animals but, really, I hate ants in my food.

Cockroaches

Cockroaches love heat and will seek out the warmth of ovens and fridge motors, so if you have them, that's where you should target them. Try a mixture of sugar and bicarbonate of soda in equal measures, and, if that fails, commercially sold baits. They are incredibly tenacious, however, and it might be wise to bring in an expert sooner rather than later.

Weevils

A weevil is one of several families of mostly small beetles that feed on plants and plant products, but I, wrongly, use the word to cover anything that gets into my food cupboard and breeds on a nasty sticky, silky thread thing. These can also be moths and book lice. There are hundreds of species, but five are killer-dillers, on earth solely to repulse the sensitive householder.

They arrive in your food cupboard via any grain, cereal or flour brought in from outside, or through the window or door as moths from next door, should your very annoying neighbours have allowed themselves to become infested. Once you have them in your cupboard, if everything is not in tightly sealed containers, you're in trouble. Even if you have tightly sealed containers you may still be in trouble should you have left an infested packet open and forgotten about it until the silky threads appear.

In that event, there's nothing for it. You have to empty your food cupboard and put all suspect items into plastic bags which should be removed at once from the premises. Every container needs to be washed in hot soapy water; the cupboard must be washed in hot soapy water; any surrounding areas that display the telltale sticky web should be washed in hot soapy water. Having rinsed everything and dried it, you could – if you wanted, but you don't have to – spray the cupboard with a weevil-specific pesticide, then restock. Restock with care, because prevention is infinitely preferable to the problem. While you can't guarantee that everything you bring into the house will be weevil-free, you can take steps to stop them developing and/or to contain the problem. Recommendations include putting all grains and flours into the freezer for four days before using and storing them in clear sealable bags so you can spot an infestation before it spreads. Slightly less conventional suggestions include putting nails or an open book of matches into the storage containers along with the grains, because weevils have a horror of both.

Rats and mice

Rats are bigger than mice and so scarier. Neither is poisonous but they both carry fleas and disease, rats probably more so than mice. They will enter your home through any available gaps, so fill as many as you can. A mouse only needs a gap of 5 millimetres (¼ inch). You know you have them when you see their droppings or scraps of the gnawed newspaper or cardboard they use for their nests, and you don't want to harbour a nest because the female mouse produces eight litters a year and each litter contains between four and seven baby mice. We are talking thirty babies minimum a year, and that's just the one mouse. This mouse will have been attracted by any edible refuse, so sweep up, wipe down and make sure the kitchen bin is tightly closed. Solutions are age-old and obvious: get a cat; set traps; bring in an expert.

·········· CLEANING THE LIVING ROOM ··········

The four processes involved in cleaning the living room are wiping, dusting, vacuuming and polishing. The basic equipment required is a bucket of water containing a mild detergent, a mop should the floors be timber, a feather duster, a paint brush, a rag, furniture polish, a long-handled broom and a vacuum cleaner.

The order in which you work is open to debate, but, having consulted Betty, I would opt for this:

○ Use the broom (wrapped in a cloth if you're squeamish) to remove cobwebs from the ceiling. Then use the paintbrush to remove dust and cobwebs from the corners of windows and skirting boards, as well as any other nooks and crannies.

○ Wipe the skirting boards, window frames and sills, plus doors and their architraves, with a damp rag.

- Use the feather duster to remove dust from all surfaces and light fittings.

- Vacuum the floor (even a timber one) and the upholstery.

- Wipe a timber floor with a damp cloth. (You can add methylated spirits to the water in which you submerge the mop if you want the floor to dry quickly and/or a wood specific detergent.)

- Polish the furniture using a commercial polish, or an oil-and-vinegar solution you've mixed yourself (three parts oil to one part vinegar).

- Clean the door knobs, either with an antibacterial cleanser or extra-hot soapy water.

Furniture

Check the manufacturer's instructions before cleaning furniture. Upholstery can be professionally cleaned as needed and spot-cleaned in the event of a spill or stain. Some stains will defeat you – it's just the way things are – but it's worth having a crack at tackling them. Try a straightforward detergent in cold water in the first instance, or a mixture of white vinegar, water and detergent then glycerine, or go directly to specially formulated upholstery cleaner and follow the directions on the can.

Loose covers can be either dry-cleaned or washed carefully in a washing machine, according to the manufacturer's instructions, and dried naturally, since any heat will almost certainly shrink them.

Scotchgard or similar

Scotchgard is a stain repellent that can be applied to carpets, upholstery or leather goods. Its manufacturer, 3M, claims that it defies liquid spills, helps eliminate stains and protects against re-soiling by providing an invisible shield. This, as you might imagine, is only achieved by a mighty powerful chemical and, sure enough, the main ingredient is PFBS (perfluorobutane sulfonate), which, in 2003, replaced an even more powerful chemical called PSOS (perfluorooctane sulfonate). The good news is that, according to a report published in 2005 by Australia's National Industrial Chemicals Notification and Assessment Scheme, PFBS poses few risks to humans. At least that's what I deduced from sentences like 'Potassium PFBS does not meet the approved criteria for classification as a substance toxic to reproduction, development and lactation'. It seems not to be a skin irritant, but it is an irritant to the eyes, which is a good reason for having it applied by a professional rather than yourself. That's if you choose to use it. And should you?

I've always been a sucker for the sales pitch. The idea of magic stain resistance is just too attractive to pass up. In my experience it's been well worth it on the sofas, and possibly on the carpets. I don't know about shoes, which is as unscientific a view as you can get. For confirmation, I consulted a cross-section of householders (numbering ten in all) and discovered that it was regarded as most helpful on furniture. But really, it's less a matter of opinion than one of perspective. Having it applied professionally was generally regarded as producing better results than applying it yourself, but either way it's an act of faith since no one can know for sure how clean their Scotchgarded carpets are compared with the carpets they might have had were they not Scotchgarded.

···················· CLEANING THE OFFICE ····················

Your house may not stretch to an office or study, but somewhere in your place there will be shelves lined with books and possibly box files and maybe a table or desk with a computer on it. You can ignore this space if you like, but eventually the keyboard will become clogged with debris, the screen will become splattered with grime, the shelves and files will become thick with dust and the books not only thick with dust but possibly also infested with insects.

Shelves

Every week, dust the edges of the shelves, the tops and spines of the books and the tops and spines of the box files, with a medium-size paintbrush. This is sturdier than a feather duster but less violent than a cloth with a fist inside it.

Periodically, in a well-ventilated room, remove everything from the shelves and vacuum them. Then, depending on the nature of the shelves, either polish them with a cloth and appropriate product, or take a damp cloth and wipe them down. While you are waiting for them to dry, dust the books and files all over. Never use anything damp on books. If any are especially dusty, give them a gentle shake before returning them to the shelves.

Computer

Not just the computer, obviously. You also need to clean the bits that go with it. For the most part, this is a job for the computer-owner alone. Anyone else tampering with the computer is asking for trouble. It calls for caution and delicacy, but don't let this put you off.

- Turn the computer off before cleaning.

- Don't spray anything directly onto the computer. If you need to apply anything damp to clean it, spray it first onto a soft cleaning cloth. Only use recommended products; otherwise, stick to water.

- You can buy a mini vacuum that plugs into the USB port to clean your keyboard. Otherwise, to shift embedded debris, aim a hair dryer at it or use cotton buds moistened in water.

- You should clean the CD-ROM port with a CD-ROM cleaner, and the CD-ROM tray with a damp cloth.

- Clean the computer screen with a damp cloth. If it's glass you can use an everyday glass cleaner.

····· GETTING SOMEONE ELSE TO CLEAN ····· YOUR HOUSE FOR YOU

It's very often essential. If all the above has been neglected for many months owing to illness, fatigue or lack of time, then someone must be paid handsomely for tackling it for you. In our household, knowing that the house is going to be thoroughly cleaned once a week by someone who is fast and efficient is a huge relief. When I was newly married, women who cared about other women were not expected to ask other women to clean their messy houses for them, no matter how much money they paid them. I never understood the politics and I'm not sure the concerns were ever relevant. There are, however, two questions you need to ask yourself for a little perspective on the matter:

- Can I afford a cleaner? It's easy enough to check the going rate. Phone an agency. Multiply the rate by the number of hours you think it takes to do your bathroom/s and kitchen, then add another half-hour per room.

- Do I need a cleaner? Central to this is how many hours you work outside the home, how much help you get from other household members, how good a cleaner you are yourself, how much you seriously hate cleaning, how tired you are and whether the money is better spent elsewhere.

While the notion that I might be heaping humiliation on the people cleaning my house always struck me as mad, there's no denying the relationship between the householder and any household employee is a delicate one. Some sensitivity on both sides is required. In over thirty years, we've employed ten cleaners and not one has ever suggested that she (all were women as it happens) felt exploited or down-trodden. Maybe one did. She arrived from an agency and told me at once that she never picked anything up from the floor as this was not what she was paid to do: she was paid to clean and not to pick up after people. Fair enough, I thought. Except that in a house with three children, I needed someone to pick things up from the floor, if only to toss them into the toy box before the floor was cleaned. We agreed to part company immediately. Other than that, our household has enjoyed fine and friendly terms with everyone we've employed over the years and we've always been impressed by and grateful for their efficiency. Because I've always worked from home, I've formed close relationships with them, but just as successful are the non-relationships based on the householder never being in. The cleaner comes in, does the work, gets paid and leaves. Whatever the arrangement, observe the following:

● Agree on the terms in a meeting beforehand. Communication problems matter less when there is an agency to intervene, but otherwise you need to assess at this stage any language or cultural or personality differences that may create difficulties for either or both of you.

● Terms should include pay, hours, exactly what both of you expect can be achieved in those hours and who supplies equipment and products.

● Be realistic about how much can be achieved in a set number of hours given the number of rooms you have and the state they are in. An experienced cleaner will know how long it takes to clean the space in question. He or she will factor in the number of items that need moving for a clean to be thorough.

● Never underpay. An agency will have a set rate, but if you have found your cleaner through a personally placed ad or word of mouth, make sure you know what the local going rate is and under no circumstances undercut it.

● If you leave the place like a pigsty, either pay the cleaner more to stay longer or expect less.

● There's 'pigsty' and there's 'disgusting'. No one should be expected to clean up a health-threatening mess created by able-bodied people.

- Agree on extras, like bed-making or changing beds, window-cleaning, oven-cleaning, fridge-cleaning, removing books from shelves and ironing.

- Agree on the kinds of products that will be used. Most professionals have a preferred method of cleaning which is best respected unless you have proper reasons for objecting.

- Say up-front if you have a particular way of cleaning any particular room or item.

- Let the cleaner do the job. Don't hang around watching and waiting for breakages.

- In the event of breakages, use your discretion. Accidents happen and in most cases the employer should wear the cost. If the broken item is valuable, it ought to be covered by your household insurance. Should there be an ongoing series of breakages, think hard about the suitability of the cleaner for the job.

- If the job is well done, say so.

Your tax and insurance obligations towards a cleaner

In Australia, legislation governing insurance for domestic cleaners varies from state to state, so you need to check it. In New South Wales at the time of writing, for instance, should you, as the householder/employer, pay more than $7500 in annual wages to domestic staff (or should you employ trainees or apprentices), then you must take out domestic workers compensation policy.

Generally speaking, unless he or she is a housekeeper you employ full- or part-time, your cleaner will be a casual contractor and so liable to meet his or her own tax obligations. Contractors aren't entitled to holiday, sick pay or any guarantee of ongoing employment. They may work for you on a regular basis, but neither you nor they have any obligations to maintain the arrangement. This means they aren't obliged to turn up every week and you aren't obliged to employ them every week, so at either party's convenience the arrangement can be skipped. Skipping can be harsh if your cleaner is depending on you for a regular income, and it can be very inconvenient for you if the cleaner chooses not to work when the house is a tip, so I would recommend a reasonably hard-and-fast agreement even though no one is contractually obliged to stick to it.

The situation is similar in the United Kingdom. If your cleaner is employed by an agency, the agency assumes the tax and insurance obligations. If you employ a non-agency cleaner and you pay them less than £110 a week (as of the tax year 2009–10), you don't have to deduct tax. Most non-agency cleaners are self-employed and so responsible for their own tax and insurance.

Finding a cleaner

This depends on the type of cleaner you want. Should you prefer a firm that comes in at the same time every week, does the business and leaves, then ask around and if at all possible go by recommendation. If the firm is a large one, it should be able to supply alternative cleaners in the event of regulars falling sick or going on holiday. The same is true, but not guaranteed, if you use an agency to broker a permanent arrangement between you and your cleaner. Most satisfactory, in my experience, has always been the cleaner recommended by a friend with whom you can make arrangements as needed. But should you not be in that happy position, advertise, interview and always ask for references (which you should take up), and agree a trial period.

7

LAUNDRY

Generally speaking, this means washing clothes, towels and bedding, drying them and maybe ironing them. It isn't the trickiest of life's domestic challenges. People have been banging wet laundry onto rocks and laying it out in the sun to dry since Eve was a rib. The very weird thing is how often it goes wrong. How can it be? How can the cleverest people on the planet still put perfectly nice clothes manufactured in distinct colours into a washing machine and pull out a pile of grey sludge? How can they shrink their cashmere? After all everyone has said? Plainly, it can't be said too often, so here it all is, one more time.

The mistake most of us make in terms of economy, time and the environment is that we wash too often. Clothes that don't smell or aren't obviously soiled, with the clear exception of underwear and socks, can be worn more than once. They can be worn all week if necessary, though by then the dust mites might be having a field day. I'm sorry if that disgusts you.

As a rule of thumb, towels and sheets should be washed at least weekly, but this can vary according to circumstances. Towels and bathmats used once or twice every day need to be dried between uses and, if this is impossible, they need to be changed more frequently. Owing to our capacity for shedding skin and perspiring at night, even clean-looking sheets need to be changed weekly. Allergy sufferers might benefit from a twice-weekly change, but this takes time and energy so a test run to check for significant improvement in the allergy is seriously advised.

There's machine-washing and there's hand-washing. Both carry risks to inoffensive fabrics going about their business, so it pays to understand the process, which is to say the way heat, pummelling, detergent and rinsing work to produce the perfectly laundered item.

The washing machine

Any washing machine is better than no washing machine, but there is a choice and it's not just between costly and cheap. There is also the choice of top loader or front loader. Australians tend to use top loaders; front loaders are favoured in the UK. So which works best? I consulted two Australian professional launderers. Both only ever use front loaders. The problem with the top loader, they say, is its poor mechanical action, which is to push and pull. There's very little movement in it and it won't necessarily push and pull in equal amounts. Its load is more often than not tangled at the end of the program. The action of front loaders takes the washing in opposite directions equally, and the load is rarely tangled.

Since most fabrics can be machine-washed, the very best favour you can do them, before you bung them into the drum, is to appreciate the way the machine works best and how it will work best for any particular item. Read the manual. Even if you can see from the control panel what's what, read the small print. It's all in the detail. For both front and top loaders:

⊙ Refer to the washing machine manual for temperature settings and extra-clever cycles. Usually, hot water should only be used on whites, and warm on coloureds. Some households only ever use a cold wash. Useless, say the professional launderers consulted above: all it does is shift surface dirt. They do, however, recommend beginning all washes with a quick rinse in cold water on the final rinse cycle, to get the dirt moving.

⊙ Use a high temperature (60°C, or 140°F) for sheets and towels to kill allergens and germs.

⊙ Always separate the load into whites, coloureds and coloureds that will almost certainly run.

● In the interests of the environment, run a full load. In the interests of your washing, don't stuff the machine to the brim. Washing needs room to move freely. Don't call a full laundry basket a natural load, because it may not be. Both washing and drying machines run most effectively on three-quarter loads.

● Your manual will advise on your machine's capacity in weight, but only a weird person will weigh every wash. You may like to know that a bath towel weighs about 0.5 kilograms (1½ pounds) and a heavy cotton king-size sheet 1.5 kilograms (just under 3 pounds).

● Wash items of different sizes in the same load. It allows them to move more freely in the machine. This ensures better washing and rinsing. Don't, however, load very heavy fabrics with very light ones, as the light ones will be crushed to death.

● Whether you use green or traditional detergents, don't exceed the recommended dose. It will cause foaming, which reduces efficiency and can prevent spinning. On the other hand, don't skimp. Using too little will result in a grey wash. If machine-washing wool, use wool-specific detergent only.

● If properly separated whites still emerge grey, chief suspects are not enough detergent or the water. Hard water (which is to say water with higher concentrations of calcium and magnesium) can cause whites to go yellow or grey. Even if the water in your area is considered soft, old pipes in the house can harden it. Try a water softener if all other boxes have been ticked.

● Fabric conditioner isn't obligatory. Manufacturers would like us to consider it in the same way we do hair conditioner. They suggest that it prevents laundry from becoming tangled, eases the burden of ironing, and smells nice. It can certainly be helpful in areas where the water is hard. On the other hand, you can use white vinegar, lemon or Epsom salts instead. They are cheaper and chemical-free.

● Close the door of the washing machine firmly or it won't start.

● Don't leave washing in the machine for any length of time once the program has finished. Slightly damp laundry left in a machine or basket can become smelly and eventually mouldy.

● Always mop up residual water in the machine at the end of the wash and leave the door open. It prevents smelly mould developing on the door seal.

Machine-washing clothes

Most garments are machine-washable. It would be a dreadful pain if they weren't. Machine-washing is more thorough than hand-washing, but, having said that, it's also harder on your clothes, especially clothes of poor quality that may have started life expecting nothing, not even a proper shape. Equally, expensive clothes of a sensitive nature may wilt and die if subjected to a washing machine's heat and pummelling, so check the care labels and remove from your wash anything that looks remotely frail. It will be made of silk, cashmere, the occasional synthetic and linen. This isn't to say that anything made of these must be hand-washed, just that they need proper respect.

LAUNDRY SYMBOLS

A wash tub without a bar indicates that machine washing and that normal (max) washing conditions may be used, such as a cotton wash.

A single bar beneath the tub indicates reduced (medium) washing and is suitable for synthetic washes.

A double underline beneath the tub indicates much reduced (minimum) washing conditions, and is designed specifically for machine washable wool products.

Garment must be hand-washed and in some instances the hand-washing cycle on the machine may be used.

Garment must not be washed in a domestic washing machine or by hand. Dryclean only

Can be ironed to maximum temperature of 110°C

Can be ironed to maximum temperature of 150°C

Can be ironed to maximum temperature of 200°C

Any bleach allowed

Only oxygen bleach/non-chlorine bleach allowed

Do not bleach

Maybe tumble dried with high heat setting

May be tumble dried with medium heat setting

May be tumble dried with low heat setting

Do not tumble dry

Indicates that the fabric should be drycleaned using tetrachloroethylene or hydrocarbons.

Indicates that the fabric should be drycleaned using hydrocarbons

Indicates that the garment is suitable for professional wet cleaning

Do not dryclean

You can machine-wash clothes on cycles from sensitive to rigorous, using temperatures from cold to very hot, but you really need to get these right if you don't want to ruin your wardrobe. Follow the washing machine manufacturer's instructions and use discretion. Be especially vigilant about separating coloureds from whites. If you are even slightly uncertain, run a cold wash on a gentle cycle, even if all it does is remove surface dirt; otherwise, hand-wash in the first instance to see what the colour does. Aside from that, all you really must do is:

○ Put machine-washable delicates, especially underwear, pantyhose (and socks, if you want to see a perfect pair ever again) into a net washing bag or a pillowcase, to protect them from tangling. Bra hooks can snag other garments; they can also get caught in the perforations of the washing machine or dryer cage.

○ Close all zips, hooks and eyes to prevent them shredding a nearby garment or being forced out of shape (even if they are in a net bag or pillowcase).

○ Check pockets for tissues – a single tissue can cover a whole load of garments in confetti, and garments may need another complete wash after you've picked the big pieces off.

○ Check all garments for marks or spillages. In the case of grease or coffee, spot-clean with soap, a DIY stain remover as listed below or a laundry solvent, depending on your attitude to chemicals.

○ When washing wool always use the wool cycle and always set to the maximum water level regardless of the size of the load.

Hand-washing clothes

Sometimes you hand-wash non-delicates because you aren't in a position to use a machine, but mostly you will be hand-washing delicates and these will be woollens and silks, both of which are natural fibres and can be safely washed provided they are uncomplicated by dodgy dyeing or unwashable finishes. The general rules are the same: slightly more demanding and time-consuming than machine-washing, but easily and successfully managed if you stick to the following:

SILK

◉ Before washing, check for colourfastness on a bit of the fabric that is invisible to the public gaze. Gently dab detergent onto it and rinse. If the colour of the water is anything other than slightly dirty or clear, forget washing.

◉ Check for stains. Silk is highly absorbent, so anything spilt on it will need extra care. Be wary of mopping the spill with water because it can leave a watermark. Wash the entire garment as soon as possible in a detergent designed for delicates, or, if you prefer, in baby shampoo. Perspiration stains can usually be removed by careful sponging with diluted vinegar. If in any doubt about a stain, get professional help.

◉ To wash, fill a basin with lukewarm water and add the appropriate detergent. Double-check the water temperature. It needs to be slightly cooler than skin temperature.

◉ Swirl and squeeze the garment gently in the water. If there is any obvious soiling, massage the area between your fingers carefully to remove it.

◉ Don't soak.

◉ Rinse twice in cold water. Add a splash of white vinegar to the first rinse, to neutralise residual detergent. It also prevents bacteria and mould growth.

◉ Remove excess moisture by rolling in a towel as you would a fajita and applying gentle pressure to it. Or, if you're brave enough, follow the advice of the professional launderer who says sticking the garment in the washing machine on a short spin cycle won't do it any harm.

◉ Place the garment on a plastic or padded hanger to dry. There's no reason for it not to hold its shape. Avoid wooden hangers, which may stain the fabric. Don't hang it in direct sunlight or on a radiator, because heat can cause the fabric to yellow.

◉ Never be tempted to tumble-dry silk. It causes far too much damage to the fabric fibres.

WOOL

Your main concern when washing wool is shrinking it. This is usually caused by exposure to heat. Your next concern is losing its shape. This is caused either by rough handling or incorrect drying. The steps for hand-washing wool are more or less the same as for hand-washing silk, although wool is usually a little more robust, and in my experience requires considerably more rinsing. So:

- Check for colourfastness and stains. If in doubt, get professional advice.

- Wash in a gentle detergent in lukewarm water. Knead the garment gently in the suds.

- Rinse in cold water and continue rinsing until there is absolutely no sign of detergent left in the garment. Again, a splash of white vinegar in an early rinse will neutralise any residue. Don't wring between rinses; gently squeeze water from the garment.

- You can use your washing machine's gentle rinse and spin cycle to rinse woollen garments placed in a pillowcase or garment bag. I personally wouldn't do this to cashmere.

- Never tumble-dry wool. The heat and tumbling motion will ruin it. If you are reluctant to commit your garment to the washing machine for any of its cycles, roll the washed garment in a towel. Sit on it, if necessary. You can then shape the garment on a new towel and dry it flat, which may take days. (A short burst on the gentle spin cycle is more appealing, but that's up to you.) An alternative, once you're confident you've removed all excess water which can pull the garment out of shape, is to thread it via its sleeves or armholes onto a pair of pantyhose whose ends you tie either to a clothesline or a shower rail.

Stain removal

There are loads of products that can remove old stains, new stains, protein stains, vegetable stains and stains prior to washing or post-washing, and there are endless books and websites especially devoted to them. The most important thing to know is that the sooner you deal with any stain the better, and you should forget hot water (except in the case of fat – see opposite). Flush first in cold. Also, in most cases, if you have no commercial products to hand or you despise them, the good old stand-bys are worth a shot. You treat, then you wash in detergent.

- Biro stains can be treated with methylated spirits, provided the damage is slight.

- Coffee and tea stains can be attacked with one part vinegar to two parts water.

- For wine, use salt or soda water or any carbonated water.

- Two quite different treatments recommended for fat stains are a thirty-minute soaking in water to which bicarbonate of soda has been added, or a soaking in warm water to which baby shampoo has been added.

- Curry usually needs bleach, but you could try one part vinegar to two parts water.

Anything drastic will need dry-cleaning, but check the price because the spotting agent required for the type of stain you've incurred might cost more than replacing the garment. Prevention is best. Wear an apron in the kitchen and use a napkin when you eat.

DRYING

There's tumble-drying and there's line-drying and, while tumble-drying has the distinct advantage of convenience, it isn't energy-efficient. Line-drying most certainly is, but it requires both a line and time for hanging. Also, overdrying on the line can make laundry infinitely crisper than we might like.

The tumble-dryer

There are two versions of tumble-dryer: the vented and the condenser. Vented tumble-dryers direct hot, damp air out of the house via a hose through a window or specially constructed vent; condensers gather condensation in a container which must be emptied after every use. Condensers can be sited anywhere in the house; vented are cheaper to buy and to run. Your choice will be governed by space, then expense. The programs on offer are the same.

Modern tumble-dryers are usually fitted with sensors which stop the machine when the load has reached the desired degree of dryness. This is very helpful. It doesn't mean you can cram everything in and let rip, however.

- First shake out the damp laundry. It gets rid of more wrinkles than you would imagine.

- Don't stuff the tumble-dryer. Three-quarters full is best. Overloading reduces the effectiveness of the tumbling action and also causes wrinkling and tangling.

- Don't load small items with heavy towels or any items together of significantly different weights. The drying will be uneven.

- If you want to dry a very small load, add a couple of hand towels to balance it.

- Don't put in anything that is dripping wet.

- Check the care labels: more items than you might think are damaged by the heat and action of a tumble-dryer, especially T-shirts and lingerie. If doubtful, dry only to slightly damp.

- Always allow the dryer to run through the cool-down program. It reduces heat in the load, which is critical for safety and the condition of the clothes.

- Overdrying causes wrinkling. Overheating causes shrinkage.

- Remove laundry when slightly damp if you intend ironing it.

- If you want to put laundry away without ironing, fold while warm.

For your edification, here is a list of garments and fabrics unsuitable for tumble-drying as listed by Hoover, who manufactured my dryer:

- underwear containing metal reinforcements;

- anything chemically impregnated;

- anything you've cleaned with a dry-cleaning solution;

- anything, in fact, not washed in water;

- anything plastic;

- anything rubber-backed;

- anything pleated, other than permanently pleated.

Line-drying

Should you be in a position to hang clothes on a line to dry, you need to know that how you hang counts, first in terms of speed of drying; second in terms of reducing creases and peg marks; and third in terms of keeping clothes in shape. Sheets and towels should be pegged so that the maximum amount of fabric is exposed to the wind and sun.

To prepare a sheet most easily for line-hanging involves two people; one can manage, just not as well. Take the sheet from the washing machine and shake it out. With a person at either end, fold it in half lengthwise, then fold it again in the same direction. Carry it to the line. Drape it over the line lengthwise. Then unfold it twice so that it hangs full-width, immaculately uncrumpled, for pegging.

For shape-sensitive items, use seams for pegging, as they are the strongest part of any garment and most likely to hide peg marks. Peg shirts upside-down on the side seams, or place them on a hanger and attach the hanger firmly to the line.

Shrinking disasters

Salvaging apparently ruined clothes is a challenge. The likelihood of success depends on the degree of ruin, and the chances that they will be returned entirely to their former glory are slim. But before you chuck out an only slightly ruined garment, you might like to know that a T-shirt that has shrunk can be steamed and reshaped, possibly by wearing it in the shower, and that although shrinkage in jumpers is usually permanent (and will only get worse with every treatment), there are a couple of remedies worth trying if the damage isn't severe and you love your jumper very much. You will know 'severe' by the tightness of the fibres as they cling to your flesh.

There's the Fullers Earth solution, as recommended by the authors of *Spotless*, which aims to relax the wool. Lower your jumper into a sink of hand-hot water to which you've added between 2 and 4 tablespoons (depending on the colour of the wool – more for lighter colours) of Fullers Earth. Knead the jumper gently and briefly, then leave it for fifteen minutes. Take it out, rinse, then dry.

I have three comments to make about this method, which I tried on what I imagined was my slightly shrunken Aran sweater. First, it wasn't easy finding Fullers Earth (a chemist finally remembered he had some out the back which he'd originally ordered for someone who was detoxing, which says something about the compound's catholic properties). Second, although this chemist was confident that it would work very effectively as a jumper stretcher, it didn't. Third, this was probably my fault and it may well work for you.

Spotless also recommends Epsom salts, used in a similar fashion, and I tried this as well. Probably the jumper was always beyond hope. Neither it nor I now feel remotely relaxed in the company of each other. On the other hand, a lecturer in textiles I consulted reminded me that in lands of frozen waste where populations live on blubber and herring, garments are knitted miles too big so they can be deliberately shrunk. What a shrunken jumper loses in size, it gains in density, so I've kept my now very dense Aran jumper in anticipation of my next trip to the tundra.

IRONING

There are people who iron and people who don't; people who see no need and people who can't imagine life without it. Our current household likes its items ironed, including sheets and pillowcases, though not underwear or tea towels. Currently my husband does the ironing. This is a generous act for which I am definitely grateful, though I would be more grateful if I thought my clothes were given as much attention as his. My T-shirts leave a lot to be desired on the shoulder seam, which is always wrinkled. Possibly this is because he sees no merit in ironing the T-shirt or because he thinks only he will look at my shoulders.

Our daughters, whose garments were always ironed throughout their childhood, almost never iron. They regard it as a terrible waste of time and they rarely look unkempt, so they either have excellent washing and folding skills or the beauty of their faces draws attention from their clothes.

If you iron at all, you might as well understand the principles of the perfect finish.

The iron

The modern iron is a steam/dry iron, which is to say it offers you an alternative: you can use it to steam the clothes as you iron or you can dry-iron as required by certain fabrics, such as acetate and nylon. The steam facility uses heated water, usually distilled, ejected as a fine spray from a small tank in the iron to dampen the fabric and ease wrinkles. It can be switched off or regulated according to the fabric you are pressing. Modern irons will also switch themselves off if unused for fifteen minutes, a major convenience for compulsive checkers who in the past had to come home after half an hour to see if the house had burnt down.

My greatest ironing horror is the jet of brown water spewing over the pristine garment stretched on the ironing board. This is usually rust and occurs when someone has failed to use distilled water in the reservoir, to empty the iron after use, or to clean it regularly using the iron's self-cleaning program. It can also occur if the iron is made of anything other than aluminium or stainless steel. Distilled water isn't imperative, but in its absence, regular cleaning is. In dire circumstances, you can clean your iron by one-quarter filling it with white vinegar and topping up with water, then heating it and using the steam program. This might stink your house out, but it will also sort out any residual rubbish in the iron.

If you melt any fabric onto your iron, warm the iron and gently remove the gunge with a spatula, then clean the surface by sprinkling salt either directly onto the ironing board or onto a tea towel, heating the iron to its highest setting and, with the steam turned off, ironing the salt.

How to iron

If you are a novice, begin with a simple exercise in visualising. Put up an ironing board, place the iron on it, and note the shape of the ironing board and the shape of the iron. The ironing board has a narrow end and a wide end, both of which can be used to divide the garment into ironable sections – especially the T-shirt, whose shoulders should be manoeuvred carefully into position over the narrow end. The iron has a pointed end and a flat surface. You need both bits.

Next look at the settings on the iron then at the clothes you need to iron. Begin with those requiring the lowest setting. Ironing delicates last will involve waiting for the iron to cool down.

Turn to the setting required by the fabric you are ironing. Lay the garment to be ironed on the ironing board and move the iron lightly and continuously over the garment, following the grain of the fabric (up and down or side to side). Lingering will lead to scorching; heavy-handedness will cause creases you spend the next five minutes ironing out. A spray bottle of water for extra dampening will help matters a lot.

The following might be useful:

⊙ Acetate should be ironed inside-out while slightly damp, using a cool, dry iron.

⊙ Acrylic should be ironed inside-out while dry.

⊙ Cotton is best ironed slightly damp on a high setting.

⊙ Hand-washed woollens mostly won't require ironing, but should they, turn the garment inside-out, set the iron to warm and use a damp cloth as protection.

IRONING TROUSERS

● Turn the trousers inside-out. Using the wide end of the board, iron the waistband, the pockets and the seams on both legs.

● Using the narrow end of the board, iron both the back and front of the trousers below the waistband but above the crotch. Negotiate pleats with the tip of the iron.

● Turn the trousers right side out. Lay them flat along the ironing board with one leg on top of the other, lining up any seams or pre-existing creases.

● Fold the top leg back and iron the bottom leg. Place a damp tea towel over the fabric to avoid shininess.

● Turn the trousers over and do the same with the other leg.

● Repeat the process, this time ironing the outsides of the legs.

● Hang the trousers up while warm.

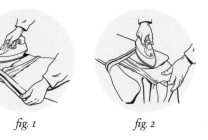

fig. 1   fig. 2

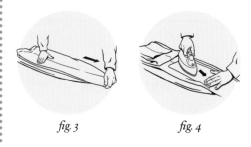

fig. 3   fig. 4

● Nylon and polyester should be ironed inside-out on a cold setting.

● Silk might or might not need ironing. If it does, iron it inside-out while it's still a little damp, using an ironing cloth to prevent shine and to protect the fabric. Use a dry iron on a very low temperature: the one that says silks (although launderers will tell you that silk is very resistant to heat and you can use a hot iron even though the silk setting is low).

The object of the exercise may be to remove wrinkles, but this is easier said than done if you iron the wrong bit first. Above and opposite is a suggested order of play on a pair of trousers and a shirt since either, poorly ironed, looks worse than if it hadn't been ironed at all.

IRONING A SHIRT

● Begin with the underside of the collar. Press from the outside towards the middle.

● Turn the collar over and press the other side as before.

● Slip a shoulder over the narrow end of the ironing board and iron half of the yolk, which is the bit of the back of the shirt above the seam, moving from the shoulder towards the middle.

● Turn the shirt around and slide the other shoulder over the end of the ironing board. Iron the other half of the yolk.

● Iron the cuffs, starting with the inside.

● Iron the sleeves, cuffs first. For each sleeve, take hold of the shirt at the top of the arm, and lay the sleeve flat on the board. Smooth it with your hand so that it's wrinkle-free, then iron from the top to the bottom, creating a crisp crease opposite the seam.

● Using the wide end of the board, iron the front parts of the shirt on the inside, taking care to negotiate buttons with the tip of the iron.

● Iron the lower half of the back, from the yolk to the bottom.

● Iron the collar again.

● Hold up the shirt, look for wayward wrinkles or missed spots, especially where the sleeves meets the shoulders, touch up, then hang up.

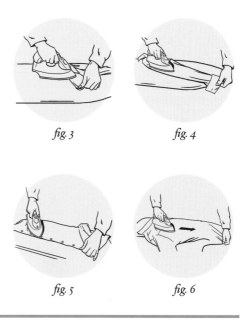

fig. 3   *fig. 4*

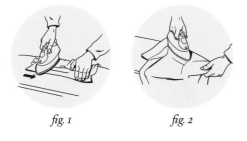

fig. 1   *fig. 2*

fig. 5   *fig. 6*

HOW TO FOLD A FITTED SHEET PRIOR TO IRONING

My husband was taught how to do this in a laundromat by a lady who managed it without once putting the sheet onto a flat surface. That's how easy it can become. He taught me in an hour, but not before we'd analysed each other's failings as thinking and feeling human beings. I hope you will be aided by the diagrams.

● Lay the sheet flat on a bed with the elasticised edges facing you.

● Slip your hands into the bottom two corners from the outside of the sheet, forming two points. Keep them there as you fold the sheet from bottom to top.

● Tuck the bottom two corners into the top two corners, leaving your hands inside the corners. You now have a sheet folded in half horizontally, with the bottom corners tucked into the top corners, making two points, each of which is draped over a hand. Lift the sheet in this manner from the bed.

● Straighten the fingers of each hand. Bring your hands together as if in prayer. Keeping the left hand straight, drop the right-hand corners over it, so all four corners are now balanced on your straightened left hand.

● Lay the sheet on the bed and carefully arrange it so that you have a sheet folded neatly into four.

● Now you can iron it. Or, if you can't be fagged, you can continue to smooth and fold into whatever size your shelves will take.

This may take a whole afternoon of practice and it's never going to be as flat as a flat sheet, but it won't be a crumpled mess either. On the other hand, you can take the sheet from the line or dryer, shake it, roll it and store it. Suit yourself.

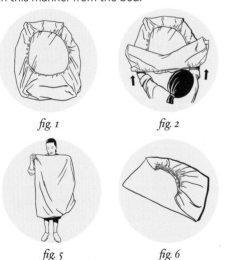

fig. 1   *fig. 2*

fig. 5   *fig. 6*

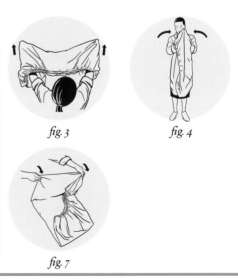

fig. 3   *fig. 4*

fig. 7

Ironing bed linen

You can't beat the sensation of freshly laundered sheets which only ironing can give. Ironing pillowcases and flat sheets is a snack. You just dampen them, and run the hot iron over the surface. The fitted sheet, however, can be nightmare (see box opposite).

Scorching disasters

Scorching is almost as final for a garment as shrinking (see page 111), but fabrics with any kind of pile can be rubbed down with a frayed toothbrush, then washed in a gentle detergent. The aim is to remove the damaged ends of the fibres. The scorched area can also be bleached. Soak a cloth in a diluted bleach solution, place it over the scorched area and press lightly with a warm iron. The heat from the iron will intensify the effect of the bleach.

The textile expert I spoke to says the problem with the toothbrush solution is that the garment will never look the same again in the scorched area, because the pile will be shorter. And the danger with the bleach solution, should the garment not be white, is that the scorched area will look bleached. On the other hand, shorter or bleached may be acceptable where scorched simply isn't.

Ways to avoid ironing

I accept that you don't have to iron, but avoiding it works better if you observe the above recommendations for washing and drying plus the following:

- Wrinkled clothes can be dampened slightly and returned to the dryer, or returned to the dryer with a damp tea towel. Set the dryer to the cool-down cycle and let it run its course – usually twelve or so minutes.

- Clothes can be steamed in the bathroom while you shower.

- You can dry dampened clothes with a hair-dryer set to warm, concentrating on the most wrinkled areas.

8
CLOTHES CARE AND MAINTENANCE

There are the looks you are born with and the looks you acquire, and central to the looks you acquire is how you dress. Even if you are permanently in uniform, what you wear suggests to the world what you are. Only suggests, I grant you, since no one can tell from the cut of your jacket whether you drink blood. On the other hand, how you dress is a matter of choice. If you go into the world in anything you've picked up from the floor, regardless of the dirt, the smell, the rips, the wrinkles, the lost buttons, or even its likelihood of fitting, then the world will notice and say, 'What a slob.' You might be a brilliant, stylish, charismatic, holy slob, but nonetheless, you will look like a slob so people will think you are a slob. The same goes for your children. Children by and large have the advantage of innocence and charm, but send them into the world looking unkempt and dirty and the world will see them as unkempt and dirty. You might tell yourself this doesn't matter, but it can go against you and them in certain critical social and professional circumstances. On top of that, who wants to smell?

There are exceptions. These are new mothers who are frankly too tired to notice what's on their shoulder or down their back and whose sense of smell is travelling on a different dimension. There are those whose daily work involves getting grubby, so clean clothes are a waste of time, but I would advocate that even they start the day not smelling. There are accident victims who have fallen down the escalators on the way to work. And there are people without ready access to washing machines, buttons or a needle and thread, which, let's be fair, Householder, means not you.

Looking and smelling like you couldn't give a toss from choice is, in my opinion, alienating in a very long-term kind of way, so in the interests of looking friendly at least, I would strongly recommend a wardrobe of clean, uncrumpled, more or less well-fitting clothes without buttons missing. Not only will you enter the fray with greater confidence your clothes will last longer, and, in straitened times, this is critical.

Quite possibly, you haven't in the past wanted your clothes to last longer. Long gone are the days when most wardrobes contained a few impeccably tailored items in sturdy fabrics designed to see the wearer out. Most by far now contain a sizeable chunk of disposable clothes which have cost next to nothing and which will last next to no time. Even if they've cost an arm and a leg, few have been built to last a lifetime because consumers no longer demand that. This makes the turnover constant and the inclination to lavish care on even cherished items minimal. But it's a folly. Replacing clothes is time-, money- and energy-consuming and very irritating if you hate shopping. Not only that: disposable clothes are becoming the world's fastest-growing waste product.

Sustainable clothing, well designed in natural fibres which – properly cared for – look good forever, must be the way of the future. But, having said that, not necessarily. The lecturer in textiles from whom I sought help pointed out that they can be a complete pain to care for. If householders have little time or inclination to care for their wardrobes, they're better off buying easy-care clothes which are usually blends of natural and unnatural fibres. They can be simply washed and require little or no ironing to look smart. I don't know why I hate the idea of them. Their unnatural shininess maybe.

Whatever you buy, keeping it clean is critical to making it last. Ingrained dirt acts as an abrasive and damages the fibres of any fabric, regardless of what it cost and where it came from. So launder carefully according to the previous chapter and use a clothes brush and a lint remover. These simple items can transform an otherwise scruffy appearance, and there is no excuse for a scruffy appearance, however poor or green we are.

AUDIT YOUR WARDROBE

Should the contents of your wardrobe be a cause for concern, there are clear steps that can be taken. The first is a sensible and ruthless audit during which you junk everything that is beyond wear or repair. It's a simple process. Put all your clothes onto the bed. Two beds. Three beds. However many it takes. Extract the clothes that you like, that fit, that are clean and that don't need mending, and put them back into the wardrobe on proper hangers which you have bought for the occasion. Where appropriate, neatly fold them and return them to drawers or onto shelves. With luck, this will take care of just about everything.

Divide the rest into piles:

- clothes you don't like or no longer suit the way you want to look;

- clothes you haven't worn for years because they don't fit but could be made wearable by a small adjustment either to your body or to the garment;

- clothes that are dirty, stained or smell a bit;

- clothes that need mending.

The clothes you don't like should be put into a pile to be given away or sold. Divide the clothes that need cleaning into clothes you can wash yourself and clothes for the dry-cleaner. Divide the clothes that need mending, including those that need altering (who are you kidding – it's easier to alter the garment than your body) into clothes you can mend or alter yourself, and clothes that need an expert.

This leaves you with three piles: clothes that will leave the house forever, clothes that will leave the house to be tended to by an expert and clothes to be attended to by yourself. To decide what goes where (apart from out of the house forever), you need to understand a few basic facts about cleaning and mending, including what is realistically within your scope to accomplish. What counts here is time, money and inclination, as well as what is actually appropriate.

For most people, time is of the essence. A professional clean might cost more money than sounds reasonable, but a poorly executed job will be a waste of time. On the other hand, you aren't an idiot and much of what follows is a matter of inclination rather than expertise. The critical question you must apply to your sorted soiled clothes is: wash or dry-clean? But first:

· SHOULD YOU EVER USE DRY-CLEANING? ·

There is an ongoing debate about the health risks of dry-cleaning. How much attention we pay to it depends more or less on how great our need is. For most of us, dry-cleaning is an essential service, and devoting time to finding an alternative is low priority. But if the chemicals used by the industry are as dangerous as they smell, then we'd be mad not to ask why we expose ourselves to them via items that come into direct contact with our skin. I asked, and as with anything contentious, the answer depended on the interests of the answerer.

In contention is the solvent used by the majority of dry-cleaners everywhere: perchloroethylene, otherwise called perc. It's been the subject of countless studies over the past twenty-five years, and some of them have given such serious cause for alarm that its use is being phased out in several US states and is under review in Europe. In Australia, while none of the states has banned its use, Willoughby City Council in New South Wales has proposed phasing it out on health and environmental grounds. Their reservations were spelt out in a report to the council's Cultural and Environmental Committee:

> Like many chlorinated hydrocarbons, perc is a central nervous system depressant, and inhaling its vapours (particularly in closed, poorly ventilated areas) can cause dizziness, headache, sleepiness, confusion, nausea, difficulty in speaking and walking, unconsciousness, and death.

> Perc has been classified by the International Agency for Research on Cancer as a Group 2A carcinogen, which means that it is 'probably carcinogenic to humans'. The main effects of exposure to perc in humans are neurological, liver, and kidney effects following acute (short-term) and chronic (long-term) inhalation exposure.

A further report to the council notes that the chances of getting cancer from exposure to perc are between 50 and 500 in 1 million, which might be smallish but who wants to be one of the 50 or 500 for the sake of only slightly offensive soiling? Even if other studies suggest that accountants are more likely to suffer an increased risk of cancer than dry-cleaners, the mere use of the words 'health' and 'hazard' in conjunction with 'consumer' is unnerving.

I put this to the Dry-Cleaning Institute of Australia, whose reply was that, used in modern machinery under properly controlled circumstances, perc poses no threat to the health of industry workers or consumers. They have seen no increase in the incidence of cancer within the industry, nor are they receiving an inordinate number of complaints from consumers who, as they point out, should never be exposed to it in any case. Their advice was that, should you smell the solvent in the shop or on your clothes when you take them from their packaging, then the machinery used on them is deficient or being wrongly operated. All traces of the solvent should be removed from items before leaving the shop. If they're not, you should complain to the shop and possibly to the local authority, and certainly refrain from using that shop again.

Environmental concerns about perc are less debatable. The industry readily concedes that, untreated, it is a serious contaminant but it would like us to know that the dangers have been acknowledged and are now minimised. While the Dry-Cleaning Institute believes that perc gets a worse press than it deserves and that it's no more toxic than nail varnish remover or household bleach, its days would appear to be numbered. Maybe in the trillions, but, nonetheless, numbered.

Alternatives are making an impact on the market. Among them are wet-cleaning (a water-based non-toxic system), hydrocarbon (a petroleum-based system) and Green-Earth (a liquid silicone). The view of the dry-cleaning industry is that GreenEarth probably doesn't clean as well as perc, but it does leave clothes looking brighter and feeling softer, which, speaking as a consumer, is no small accomplishment. Currently, however, alternatives to dry-cleaning exist only in small numbers and mostly for city dwellers, so, for peace of mind at least, remove your perc-treated clothes from their plastic wrapping and air them before putting them away or wearing them. You might prefer to shun the process completely, but it's a rare household that doesn't need to dry-clean sometimes. The question is: when and how often?

CAN DRY-CLEANING SHRINK YOUR CLOTHES?

The answer is yes, but rarely. You'll know from the lining if a garment has shrunk. If it's falling below the hemline, then the outer fabric has shrunk. Also, the side seams will show signs of puckering.

The thread used to sew the garments very rarely experiences any shrinkage. In the event of shrinking, return the garment to the dry-cleaner and discuss compensation.

When 'dry-clean only' means 'dry-clean only'

It's an acknowledged fact that clothing manufacturers often cover their backs by sticking 'Dry-clean only' labels onto garments. They feel safer advising the gentler cleaning process even when garments are 100 per cent cotton. As any professional launderer will tell you, there is a big difference between the ways water and perc relate to fabrics. If you immerse a garment in water, the fibres of the fabric swell and never entirely return to the way they were. Perc is inert. It doesn't penetrate the fibre; it removes dirt from its surface so the fibre doesn't change. Dry-cleaning certainly carries less risk of shrinking cotton and linen, but almost all cotton and linen can be hand-washed. There's no reason why you as a more or less competent person can't do it, given time and proper attention. You need to bear in mind the following:

- By and large cotton, linen, silk and wool can be washed, but check the finish of the fabric and the washability of any additional fabrics like ribbon or lace.

- The nature of the soiling (soiling might be an unpleasant word, but the dry-cleaning industry says a stain is only a stain once it's failed to be removed).

- Whether the item is hard to iron.

- Whether the item cost you a fortune or next to nothing (plainly, it's false economy to risk ruining an expensive garment, just as dry-cleaning is a ludicrous expense for a cheap garment)

The benefits of dry-cleaning, according to the industry, are the thoroughness and gentleness of the clean. Generally speaking, dry-cleaning is far more effective than washing at removing oil and grease marks. It's also advisable if your garment is potentially stained, and you haven't been able to treat the problem within twenty-four hours, or you don't know how to.

········· PUTTING YOUR CLOTHES AWAY ·········

This is where most clothes care comes unstuck. No matter how carefully you wash, iron or fold your clothes, if you then cram them randomly into wardrobes or onto shelves that are too crowded or too small, they will emerge looking worse than they did when you last wore them, and the whole laundry palaver will have been a waste of time and energy.

It helps to observe the following:

● Never cram clothes into too small a space, whether it's in drawers, on shelves or on a rod in a wardrobe. Clothes hate to be weighed down or squeezed to death.

● Never put away clothes that are even slightly damp. Damp clothes will wrinkle easily if stacked and, if stored for any length of time, will start to smell mouldy. It's worth airing your newly laundered, folded or ironed clothes overnight on a drying frame.

● Before putting clothes away, with or without laundering, do up all buttons and zips and remove anything from the pockets. It preserves their shape.

● Rummaging causes wrinkles. Put the clothes you wear most into the most accessible part of your wardrobe or drawers.

If you have too many clothes for the available space, you can either change the number of clothes you have or increase the space. You can, as advised in Chapter 5, store clean and properly folded clothes out of season in suitcases. If your shelves are too narrow to hold your clothes comfortably, address your manner of folding (see below).

Hanging or folding

With the exception of suits, jackets, most dresses, smart trousers and skirts, just about everything can be folded. Knitwear, for example, should never be anything else, according to manufacturers, although I personally prefer to hang anything delicate, like a cashmere cardigan, on a padded hanger. My issue with folding is that folded items are disturbed more than hung items, and this disturbance can be terminal when you can't find anything to wear and you need to try on every single thing in eight minutes. Since folding is an art, let's look at hanging first. Let's look at hangers.

HANGERS

Throw out anything in wire for a start. Wire hangers are a totally useless means of support and should only be used for transporting garments from the dry-cleaners. At worst, they can give clothes a very peculiar shape and, if they rust, a very peculiar colour. Plastic hangers also give minimal support but are preferable to wire. Mostly, you need wooden hangers, trouser and skirt hangers with special clips, fabric hangers or padded hangers.

Aside from choosing the proper hanger, you should also always use the straps stitched into garments for hanging purposes. Their function is to spread the garment's weight. Uneven distribution can cause distortion.

ROLLING

Before we get to folding, most underwear and socks can be rolled up. Rolling saves space. Don't stick socks into drawers unattached. Lay a pair one on top of the other. Roll from the toe to the top, then flick the top over the socks to hold the pair together.

FOLDING

When it comes to folding in its purist form, an issue arises as to the use of tissue paper, which prevents creasing. I like a pure form, but really who has the time? Who has the tissue paper? Who can be bothered rearranging the tissue paper around the stored item once it's been disturbed? By all means use it for long-term storage or long-haul travel, but for every day? I don't think so.

The first rule of folding is to stack items on like items. Stacking heavy clothes on top of light is laundry suicide. Have a T-shirt pile, a jumper pile, a jeans pile, a shorts pile and so on. To avoid creasing, which, unwelcome though it is, seems inevitable in the case of folding and stacking, you can observe the 'bundle principle' beloved of hardened travellers. This involves folding items inside each other. It's only suitable for very patient people who don't mind rebundling piles every time they grab a T-shirt.

That aside, you can fold in any way that makes sense, with two notable exceptions. Long trousers are always folded horizontally, with hem towards waist. Shorts are folded vertically. There are no other rules, but there are excellent techniques with regard to the shirt and the T-shirt. You need to know them if only to enjoy the sense of gratification when your stacked shelves are so neat they wouldn't disgrace a posh shop.

FOLDING A SHIRT

The following instructions on how to fold a shirt were passed on via a friend from a Gap salesman. Most people hang shirts, I appreciate that. But sooner or later you will want to fold one to pack into a suitcase. You can adapt the technique for jumpers.

● Button the shirt.

● Lay it flat, face-down, with both sleeves spread out horizontally from the garment.

● Fold the first sleeve back on itself in its entirety, across the body of shirt, then fold it from the middle (elbow) at 45° flat, so that the cuff to elbow is lying parallel to the side of the shirt and pointing to the bottom.

● Repeat with the other sleeve.

● On the left-hand side, simultaneously take hold of the shirt at the bottom outward edge and at the top shoulder crease and fold inwards, so that the outside edge is aligned to the mid-point of the collar and base, along the shirt's central spine. (Please don't say you didn't know a shirt had a spine.)

● Repeat with the right half, so that you have a neat rectangular parcel whose folds meet at the middle.

● You can now fold from the bottom up, either once or twice: once for jumpers and twice for shirts.

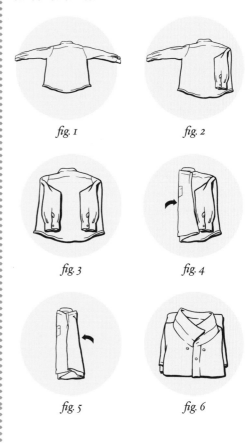

fig. 1   fig. 2

fig. 3   fig. 4

fig. 5   fig. 6

FOLDING A T-SHIRT

There's the conventional method and there's the three-pinch method, which I know sounds complicated but is so miraculous that you will want to perform it as a party trick.

CONVENTIONAL METHOD

● Place your T-shirt face-down on a flat surface with the bottom hem towards you.

● Smooth it until it is wrinkle-free.

● Fold it vertically from first the left and then the right, so that the two edges meet in the middle. Check at the neckline for the midline point.

● Fold the sleeves back towards the outside edges.

● From the bottom, fold horizontally, either once or twice, depending on the space in your shelves.

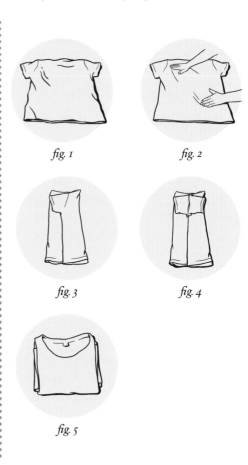

fig. 1   *fig. 2*

fig. 3   *fig. 4*

fig. 5

THREE-PINCH METHOD

Lay your exquisitely ironed T-shirt face-up on a flat surface with the neck to your right and the bottom hem to your left (unless you're left-handed, in which case you might want to reverse it).

● Starting at the seam furthest from you, trace an imaginary line towards you along the middle of the T-shirt with your left hand.

● Stop when you get to a spot parallel to halfway along the shoulder seam closest to you. Pinch the fabric (both layers) at this point with your left hand so you have it in a firm grasp.

● From that pinch, with your right hand, trace a straight line directly up to the point halfway along the shoulder seam closest to you. Pinch both layers of the fabric at that point with your right hand.

● With the fabric firmly in your grasp, take your right hand behind your left hand and pinch the fabric at the bottom of the T-shirt in a direct line from where you pinched the shoulder seam. You are now holding both the top and the bottom of the T-shirt in your right hand.

● Lift the T-shirt from the surface and bring your right hand back across your body. Your left hand is still grasping the T-shirt's midpoint, which is now to the left of your body.

● Shake the T-shirt, then lay it flat again, folding the left sleeve under as you do.

When you are experienced, you will be able to shake and flip the sleeve under in one swift movement. You won't have a perfect finish on the first go, and shop shelf perfection is elusive if your T-shirts have succumbed to too much washing, but it's still brilliant because the result is so unexpected. Performing the trick in public turns out to be unwise after the consumption of alcohol.

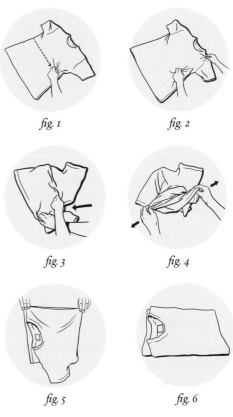

fig. 1

fig. 2

fig. 3

fig. 4

fig. 5

fig. 6

Seasonal storage

If you are putting away your summer or winter clothes until they are next needed, there are a few storage rules to follow:

- Don't put clothes away without cleaning them. Even if they look clean, there will be residual skin, perspiration and dust ingrained in the fabric, as well as almost invisible food spills, all of which will attract animals of some sort.

- Make sure that your clean clothes are 100 per cent dry before you store them. Damp causes mildew and mould.

- Be careful where you store. Don't expose your clothes to heat, light or damp. A suitcase under the bed is fine for most clothes.

- Don't cram your suitcase as full as possible. Fold carefully, avoiding large creases. Use tissue paper, if you have any, to separate garments. Put heavier stuff on the bottom.

- Avoid storing in plastic bags from the supermarket. Buy proper storage bags with hangers for suits and dresses, which you don't want to store flat.

- Don't use mothballs because they are toxic and you will smell demented all the following winter or summer. Try bay leaves or cedar balls.

- When you take your clothes out of storage, air them on a drying rack in front of an open window.

Moths

You probably think you don't have moths in your wardrobe, but if you find tiny, unexplained holes in your jumpers, then you do. Our lack of interest in clothes care and overfilling our wardrobes with cheap and only occasionally worn clothes has led to an increased problem. I'm talking secondhand clothes from charity shops as well as mass-produced viscose. We put these undervalued (because they cost so little) clothes away without cleaning them, they sit in the back of the wardrobe undisturbed for months at a time, and female moths come and lay between 70 and 100 eggs in them. Why wouldn't they? The solution is to:

- Keep your clothes, especially your woollens, clean.

- Keep your wardrobes and shelves clean – vacuum corners to remove any moths hiding in them.

- Check secondhand or vintage clothes for signs of moths before putting them in your wardrobe.

- Keep your wardrobes shut tight so moths can't enter.

- Chuck a couple of cedar balls or some lavender into the wardrobe, because moths don't like either. Neither will cure any existing moth problem, but they will deter any moths loitering and thinking about creating one.

- If you have an existing moth problem or are concerned that you might, you can stick cashmere in a plastic bag in a freezer with a temperature of between –18 and –25°C (0 and –13°F). Leave it there for four days and all moth eggs should be killed. You can store cashmere permanently in plastic bags in the freezer, but only if you are obsessive and have a huge freezer.

- Treat moth infestations with an insecticide or a commercial moth trap.

MENDING

If you own a sewing machine, I'm assuming you know how to use it, so this information isn't for you. It's for everyone who's never picked up a needle and thread in the whole of their lives because they've never seen the point when mending takes time and damaged clothes are easily, and often cheaply, replaced. Now, however, there is a point. There are two points. Saving money and saving the environment.

To extend the life of our clothes, we need simple mending in our repertoire of household skills, which is to say sewing on a button, hemming, repairing a minor rip and darning. These can be mastered by anyone. All you need is a basic sewing kit, which you can buy ready-made from a haberdasher or department store. But if you're in the shop you might as well assemble one yourself. You need needles (various), threads (various), a needle threader, buttons (various), a fabric tape-measure, a thread unpicker, small scissors and a darning mushroom. Less or more essential, depending on your skill and inclination, are hemming tape and/or hemming web, iron-on interfacing (to repair rips) and double-sided tape, all of which are perfectly legitimate mending tools.

Replacing a button

Buttons fall off, you lose them, you wear the garment without the button, it looks terrible. You put the garment back in your wardrobe, and every time you take it out to wear it you remember it doesn't have a button so you put it back again. Eventually it looks old or too small and you throw it away. This is called waste. Save the button. Even match the button by going to a button counter or a button shop, but replace the button. It takes less than five minutes, lo, a garment that was lost will be returned to the fold.

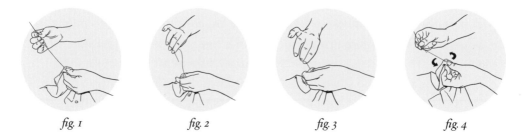

fig. 1   *fig. 2*   *fig. 3*   *fig. 4*

◉ Thread your needle.

◉ Double the thread and knot the end.

◉ Find the imprint of the original button, if possible the original holes. If there's no obvious sign of them, do up the other buttons on the garment and mark the spot under the missing button's buttonhole with a pin. In exactly this place, make two small securing stitches. You know how to do this. Place your non-needle hand under the garment so that you don't sew it to anything other than the button, then slide the needle into the fabric (running it parallel to the fabric, not down into it), then slide the needle out of the fabric. Easy. The distance covered should be no more than a needle tip.

◉ Hold the button over the needle and thread the needle through one of the holes. There may be two; there may be four. Any hole will do.

◉ Drop the button down the thread so that it lands over the stitches (in other words, the location of the original button).

◉ Make sure the button is in place. Insert the needle down into another hole in the button. Pull it through to the wrong side of the fabric.

- Line the needle up with another hole in the button and pull it through from the wrong side of fabric to right, through a hole in the button.

- Repeat the above two steps, moving around the pairs of holes three or four times, until the button is secure.

- Finally, insert the needle into a hole in the button, but not through the fabric. Pull it out between the button and the garment.

- Wind the thread two or three times around button, then insert the needle into the fabric beneath the button and pull the thread through.

- Make a couple of stitches in the fabric on the wrong side, beneath the button, then cut the thread.

Hemming

You may need to repair an existing hem or replace an existing hem with another. The repair is obviously simpler, because it involves no measuring, just a pinning-back of the hem into its original place, a pressing, then a stitching. Should the hemming be a major alteration or complicated by the delicacy of the fabric, don't hesitate to hand it over to a professional. Just don't ignore it, because a detached hem looks tacky.

If sewing seems far more trouble than it's worth, use a hemming tape. My local haberdasher offered the following: as a temporary measure, to hold up a dropped hem, use double-sided tape; for synthetic fabrics, use hemming web (the packet will have instructions); for cotton and wool, use iron-on hemming tape.

If you decide to sew, whether you're hemming a pair of trousers or a skirt, the procedure is the same.

- Pin the hem into place.

- Using giant stitches which you will later remove, sew the hem into place. This step is called basting, and it's worth including in the process because it helps you to adjust any puckering of the fabric.

- Iron the hem into place.

- Sew the hem, working from right to left if you're right-handed, and from left to right if you're not, using a hemming stitch (see page 134). When you reach the end, make two small stitches in the hem and cut the thread.

HEMMING STITCH

(As described by Helen Kinne in *Clothing and Health: An elementary textbook of home making*, published in 1916. It makes no concessions to left-handedness, which was presumably beaten out of the nicely brought-up girls for whom the advice was intended; should you be left-handed, adjust accordingly.)

Hold the cloth slanting over the fingers of the left hand, with thumb on top. Begin without a knot. Put the needle up through edge of hem and allow 25 mm [1 in] of end of thread to lie under the hem as you pull thread through. This end will be worked over and held securely. Now you are ready for the stitch. Point the needle which is in your right hand towards the left shoulder. The point of the needle is passed first through the cloth under the edge of the hem, with a tiny stitch which shows on the right side. The needle, at the same time, catches the edge of the hem. This makes a tiny slanting stitch on the right side. The next stitch is taken about 1 mm [$\frac{1}{16}$ in] from the first, in exactly the same way. As the thread carries from one stitch to the next, it makes a slanting line on the wrong, or hem, side but in the opposite direction from the stitch which shows on the right side. It slants like this: \

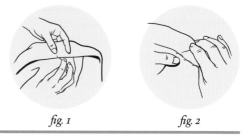

fig. 1   *fig. 2*

A word of warning: if you don't have a sewing machine and you want the hem of your jeans to look normal, have them altered professionally. Traditionally the hems of jeans are machine-sewn, and anything else looks stupid.

Repairs

Serious repairs, by which I mean holes or tears, need to be mended by a professional. But simple problems can be simply addressed. These are when: the garment is a child's so not going to last that long anyway; it's yours but old; it's yours and didn't cost much; it's yours, you're desperate and the rip is almost out of sight.

Iron-on interfacing can be very helpful. If you've ripped a shirt or dress, place the interfacing under the rip, line up the torn edges as best you can, tuck the thread out of sight, and iron. If this isn't possible or you have no interfacing, turn the garment inside out, line up both sides of the rip and stitch as neatly as you can. A darn might be required in the event of a hole.

ALTERING THE HEMLINE OF A SKIRT OR A PAIR OF TROUSERS WHICH AREN'T JEANS

- Use your stitch unpicker to remove the old hem.

- Decide how long you want the skirt or trousers to be. You may need someone to help you to pin them to the required length.

- Iron the new hem into place.

- Try the skirt or trousers on again to be sure the length is correct, then trim any excess fabric, leaving a proper hem allowance.

- Turn the raw edge of the fabric under.

- Using basting stitches to avoid puckering, stitch the hem into place.

- Hem as above.

Darning

I know, who darns? Why darn anything when a pair of socks costs less than six sausages? But great woollen socks and tights can become very precious. It's worth maintaining their life until you're emotionally prepared to end it. You've already invested in the darning needles, assorted darning wools and the darning mushroom, and, should you become proficient, you may tackle holes as described below in cardigans, jumpers, wedding dresses or anything.

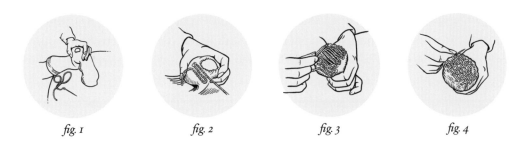

fig. 1   *fig. 2*   *fig. 3*   *fig. 4*

The first thing you need to know is that darning isn't stitching, even though you use running stitch. It's more like weaving, and the reason you weave is to keep the repair flat. In a sock or tights, a bumpy repair will rub against your shoe and hurt like stink.

- Place the sock or whatever over your darning mushroom.

- Begin by making several rows of running stitch above the hole, starting well to one side of the hole and ending well to the other side of the hole.

- Carry on until you get to the hole, then continue over the hole, making long stitches quite close together. They should look like very close-together guitar strings.

- When the hole has been covered one way, turn the garment around and weave the thread in the other direction, going in and out across the existing threads over the hole until the hole is completely covered.

It's easier done than said, honestly. Just think weaving: filling the hole with threads, going first one way then the other, with the thread in the second direction being woven in and out of the thread in the first direction.

Invisible mending

Very expensive or precious clothes should be sent to professional menders who might or might not call themselves invisible menders. Invisible mending is a broad term which, in my experience, can result in a mend that is invisible to the naked eye or in a tidy repair that anyone handy with a needle might have made.

Real invisible menders work magic. Theirs is a 200-year-old trade that involves, as the British Invisible Mending Service explains, 'taking individual threads from a hem, side seam or other concealed part of the garment of the same type and re-weaving them over the damaged area to make as near perfect repairs as is humanly possible'. It's time-consuming and incredibly skilful and ought not to be confused with patching. A true invisible mender can make a large hole in a checked garment disappear. Needless to say, this may make a large hole in your pocket but it's not as costly as replacing an expensive piece of clothing, and well worth the investment.

•••••••••••••••••••••••••••• SHOE CARE ••••••••••••••••••••••••••••

My husband's first bank manager told him that you can tell the calibre of a man by the shine of his shoes, which he noticed before the firmness of his handshake. As calibre indicators go, I'm not sure how reliable either is, but scuffed or dirty shoes are sad, and neglected shoes give up the ghost far sooner than those which have been cared for. So:

- Buy a shoe-cleaning kit that includes brushes, polishes and conditioner.

- Always use a wax polish.

- Polish your shoes regularly if they are leather, not just when they look scuffed. Good polish protects, conditions and shines the shoes.

- Get rid of surface dirt before you apply polish. Finish with a soft rag or a soft brush to raise a proper shine.

- Brush suede shoes with a suede brush (which usually has brass bristles) to rid them of dust and dirt and to restore the pile.

- Don't wear new shoes out in the rain. They haven't weathered.

- Let wet shoes dry naturally – don't put them in the oven or the tumble-dryer.

- Store shoes on shoe trees to maintain their shape.

- Don't put trainers in the washing machine. It causes the glue in the seams to melt. Clean them with an old toothbrush and dishwashing liquid.

- Use a shoe repairer. If the heels or soles of your shoes are wearing thin, replace them.

- Shoes that are too tight can be stretched widthwise but not lengthwise. You can buy your own shoe-stretcher, but shoe repairers have better equipment and know-how. A retired shoe repairer told me that when he played football as a young man he soaked his new football boots in water warming in his mother's copper for an hour, then put them on wet. They moulded to his feet and never caused a moment's discomfort. He didn't recommend the process for dress shoes, however.

- Smelly shoes are caused by sweat and bacteria growth and will be housing, for sure, smelly feet. This mightn't be your fault. Synthetics don't always let feet breathe. Synthetic insoles make matters worse. Take them out and replace them with leather ones. Sprinkle powder in your shoes, either talc or specially formulated foot-treatment powder, and wash your feet with an antibacterial soap.

PART 4

FEEDING THE HOUSEHOLD

WE ARE BETTER OFF nutritionally, financially, emotionally and probably ethically, if we eat most of our meals at home, around a table, in the company of people who love us, even if the loving comes and goes. There's clearly nothing wrong with eating alone in front of the telly, but it requires greater vigilance because we can quickly become sloppy. That's point one. Point two is that how we eat is not the same as what we eat.

What we eat depends on what's in the house. What's in the house depends on what we like, what we think we should eat and how committed we are to preparing things to eat, all of which will be influenced by our budget, our health, the time available, and how well household members receive what the designated cook puts in front of them.

It would be so much easier if we ate only to ward off starvation, but we also eat for pleasure and to maintain our health, neither of which are clearcut. When it comes to taste, members of the same household can describe with equal passion the same food as disgusting and delicious. When it comes to health, we know that if we eat too much of the wrong stuff it will make us sick. Obesity is worse for us than smoking. But which stuff is wrong and how much is too much can be debated more or less endlessly.

Our household consists of one person who loves to eat, will eat anything in any amount and has a minor weight problem that has become a minor heart problem, plus a second person who loves to cook, cooks more than is needed, is delighted that the food lover eats it, but doesn't eat that much herself so doesn't have a weight problem. This isn't to say food doesn't affect my health. It does: too much acid, not enough greens. But I struggle, Householder, as you do, to keep a sense of proportion.

The challenge is to eat sensibly. Sensible eating boils down to marrying what we like with what we need, so no one in the household goes hungry, everyone gets meals they like, no one eats too much or too little, no one dies of boredom or exhaustion from shopping and cooking before they die of obesity, the climate doesn't suffer, food isn't wasted and meals don't blow the household budget. It's a tall order, but can it be managed? Having examined the issues, I know it can.

9

EATING PROPERLY

To eat might be an instinct, but deciding what to eat has always been a worry. Who knows how many brave and hungry souls venturing from their caves died discovering that privet wasn't a staple? And still we're learning, even in – especially in – countries where food is plentiful and requires next to no effort to be rendered irresistible. For us, food is a problem not because of its toxicity, but because of the choices we make.

Perversely, we're disinclined to eat only what is good for us, and to eat what is bad for us only now and then. We take what's good for us and either strip it of its nutritional value or smother it in what's bad for us, then we eat it in quantities that can kill us. It's actually bonkers when the fundamental rules are simple: a balanced diet consists of three square meals a day with snacks mid-morning and mid-afternoon. A square meal is: a) nourishing; yet b) filling. Right? Definitely. But look to science for proper explanations of how and why, and you find mostly question marks and contradictions. What follows is an attempt to make sense of it all so that we can eat and be happy as well as healthy.

WHAT IS FILLING?

'Filling' is a difficult notion, because it's measured in comfort and not kilos, and many people never feel full, no matter how much they eat. But a general rule seems to be that if you feel full you've probably over-eaten and that people who never feel full, however much they eat, are eating more than they need.

This raises the question: What is a healthy appetite, and how come one person's can be so much greater than the annoying skinny person's next to them? Science has only the vaguest idea. What's healthy for a physically active teenage boy is clearly not healthy for a mostly sedentary elderly woman and nor, with luck, will the sedentary elderly woman want even slightly to eat the meals of a teenage boy. But take ten elderly women (or ten teenage boys) and, sure as eggs, they will have differing appetites. The reason might be any or all of the following:

- some are much bigger than the others;
- some expend more energy than the others;
- some eat more because they are bored, depressed or stressed;
- hormones are at play.

Points one to three are self explanatory. The jury is still out on the role of hormones. The main area of scientific interest is the appetite-regulating hormone peptide YY (PYY), which is released from the gut into the bloodstream and alerts the brain to food having been eaten. Studies suggest it registers this fact not only in centres controlling hunger but also in those registering pleasure (the orbitofrontal cortex, most specifically), and that people in whom the latter area showed most marked activity after eating ate less. This is only slightly helpful to the over-eater. The fact remains that what and how much we eat is our own responsibility, which brings us to the balanced diet and how we can best achieve it.

WHAT IS NOURISHING?

Our daily intake should include enough of everything we need to maintain bodily health. This means carbohydrates (for energy), protein (for growth, and the repair of muscles, tissues and organs) and fat. It's true. We do need some fat. Since carbs, proteins and fats (the macronutrients) are essential to life and wellbeing, it's important, I think, to know why we need each of them in the proportions we do.

Carbohydrates

The vogue for low-carb diets is completely out of kilter with all current medical thinking. All carbohydrates, with the exception of fibre (see page 146), are converted by the digestive system into glucose. Our bodies require glucose for energy, and we use energy for everything from breathing and thinking to walking and talking. The important distinction to be made is between starchy or complex carbohydrates and simple carbohydrates.

Generally speaking, complex carbs provide the energy our bodies need for fuel and simple carbs are regarded as having next to no nutritional value. But this isn't always the case. So when is a complex carb no better than a simple carb and when is a simple carb to be as valued as a complex carb?

COMPLEX CARBOHYDRATES

Complex carbs are found in foods such as cereals, pasta, rice and bread. Most dietary guidelines specify wholegrain (or brown, for the sake of the argument) bread, but few insist on wholegrain rice and pasta, and this is a thorn in the side of the Harvard School of Public Health (HSPH). They consider 'complex carbohydrate' an unhelpful term and suggest that identifying all cereals and grains as such ignores the fact that refined starches like white bread, white pasta and white rice behave like sugar: 'They add empty calories, have adverse metabolic effects, and increase the risks of diabetes and heart disease.'

In Australia, dietary guidelines from the National Health and Medical Research Council (NHMRC) recommend switching to wholegrain, but they aren't insistent. The UK Food Standards Agency (FSA) seems easy either way, perhaps on the grounds that any bread, cereal, rice, etc. is better than none. Maybe the argument could be settled by consulting the glycaemic index, which ranks foods according to their effect on our blood-sugar levels.

The release of glucose into cells from any carbohydrate is controlled by insulin secreted from the pancreas. The slower the release of glucose and hormones, the more stable and sustainable are our energy levels. The preference must be, whatever the food, for a slower, gentler change in the blood sugar. The more refined the carbohydrate, the faster the glucose is released into our bloodstream and the higher the GI (white bread scores 70, wholemeal 50). It must be said, though, that the glycaemic index, like everything else, has its proponents and its detractors and can confuse as easily as it clarifies. Stay with me.

SIMPLE CARBOHYDRATES

Sucrose, lactose and fructose are all simple carbohydrates. Of these, sucrose (a combination of glucose and fructose) – which is to say table sugar and the sugar we use in baking – is the carb best avoided. The rule for simple carbohydrates is to enjoy them in their most natural form, which means from a fruit (fructose), or a cow, sheep or goat (lactose). Most fruits contain simple carbohydrates, but they are usually high in fibre, which slows the digestion. Fructose and lactose are less speedily absorbed than sucrose and are delivered in packages infinitely more beneficial to our health: why, even the humble orange contains not only fibre but protein, potassium, selenium, magnesium, phosphorous and calcium as well as vitamins A, C and B plus folate and pantothenic acid. If you think you can't do without sucrose, you really need to know more about sugar.

The truth about sugar

The upside: even in its most refined form, sugar not only makes food taste sweeter, but it also has a useful function in the chemistry of cooking and preserving. The downside: we survived for aeons without it, but now we manufacture and refine it and eat it in such undue quantities that some regard it as a poison. Not everyone, of course. There's rarely a consensus in the science of food. Others argue that the only scientifically proven damage it does is to teeth.

A frequently quoted paper published by the Food and Agriculture Organization of the United Nations states quite categorically: 'While there is substantial data suggesting that high levels of dietary fat intake are associated with high levels of obesity, at present there is no reason to believe that high intake of simple sugar is associated with high levels of obesity.' Plainly the FAO is a reputable body and plainly they mean no one any harm and plainly sugar is less harmful than fat. But arguing that it doesn't contribute to our obesity problem, when ingesting vast quantities of empty calories can only mean storing those empty calories about our body as fat – the very fat that, when stored in abundance, can lead to all manner of diseases, if not kill us – has to be nuts. Well, it is to me, a simple householder.

Raw and unrefined sugar may not have been stripped entirely of all goodness, and fructose in fruit juice tastes healthy and has some health benefits, but sugar (even if it's called molasses) is sugar and the problem we have is quantity. We've developed such a taste for it that few foods are manufactured without it being added in some form or another, so we eat it even when we think we're not. Australia's NHMRC recommends a 'moderate intake', which isn't especially helpful. The Department for Environment, Food and Rural Affairs (DEFRA) in the UK suggests 50 grams (roughly twelve teaspoons) a day, which seems a lot but not when you consider there is sugar in just about everything. It's tragic, but there you are. Modify your sugar intake: retrain your tastebuds if you have to – and if you think you can't, you almost certainly have to.

Fibre

Fibre is a form of complex carbohydrate that doesn't convert into glucose. (Technically speaking, it's a non-starchy polysaccharide.) For the most part, fibre undergoes virtually no change in composition as it passes through the digestive system. This would seem to be a pointless exercise, except that our bodies need the roughage it provides, not only to avoid constipation but also for bulk (fibre is filling).

Naturally, there's not just one type of fibre, but two: one soluble, the other not. Fibre in the form of plant foods tends to combine both soluble and insoluble forms, though fruit and vegetables (peas and beans, for example) are mostly soluble. The extremely useful functions of soluble fibre are to lower cholesterol and control blood sugar. Insoluble fibre (found in wholegrain cereals, nuts, and fruit and vegetable skins) can hold up to fifteen times its weight in water, so that when it passes through the digestive system, it shifts everything in its path. (A word of advice: if you up your intake of insoluble fibre, increase your fluid intake or you'll face a logjam.)

Protein

Protein is a string of amino acids (helpful molecules sometimes described as the building blocks of life) and is essential for growth and body maintenance as well as the proper functioning of our metabolic and immune systems. If you don't eat enough, wounds won't heal, you'll lose muscle, grow weak and your skin will go all flabby. The problem won't be lack of meat, should you at this point be thinking of all the wan vegetarians you know; it will be a deficiency in amino acids. The nine amino acids required from protein (histidine, isoleucine, leucine, lysine, methionine, phenylalanine, threonine, tryptophane and valine, if you're interested) can all be found in meat (which is why meat is regarded as complete protein), but they're also in tofu, which is why it's a staple for most vegetarians. Other generous sources of protein are fish, poultry, beans, milk, cheese and eggs.

Despite protein being essential to life, we need almost none. You will in fact be staggered by just how little we need, though you won't be staggered to hear that this information causes chaos in dietary guidelines. The confusion, in my mind at least, stems from the minimum daily protein requirement recommended by the World Health Organization (WHO) and repeated wherever you care to look. It is 0.8 of your weight in kilos, the answer being expressed in grams: so if, say, you weigh 57 kilos (9 stone), you will need 45.6 grams (1.6 oz) of protein a day.

Forget your quarter-pounder with cheese, then, this would seem to mean. Even a plain steak is way off the need-to-eat graph, which fact, in my household at least, would be unacceptable. I sought clarification from a government body, whose representative refused to allow that body to be named, which just goes to show how controversial the whole thing is. She said that the WHO's ratios are not for interpretation by householders but for the benefit of health professionals who might, for instance, be setting up an intravenous drip. She advised looking at the servings recommended by other government bodies, as they were all the householder really needed to understand, which left me feeling both patronised and irritated, but after sulking for a while I consulted *The Merck Manual* (the world's best-selling medical manual), whose suggested daily intake – 185 grams (6.5 oz) of meat and beans for a 40-year-old man who engages in moderate physical activity, for instance – is miles more than recommended in Australian and UK dietary guidelines (see page 151).

The truth is that it's practically impossible to under-consume protein, because there are small amounts in just about everything we eat, from wholegrain foods and fruit and vegetables to the better-known sources. Over-consumption, of course, plays havoc with the liver and kidneys, and should the protein be mostly from meat and dairy there's also a risk of raised cholesterol levels. But unless you find it repulsive, appreciate its benefits, serve it judiciously and eat it with gusto.

Fats

Fats should account for between 20 and 30 per cent of our diet, depending on whom you ask. Either way, it sounds a lot and is slightly sick-making. But our bodies need it for energy and for the maintenance and repair of cell walls (which are composed substantially of fat), for insulation and to help us absorb fat-soluble vitamins, most notably A, D, K and E. To deprive our bodies of fat completely is possibly suicidal so don't. Instead, distinguish between the fats we need and the fats we don't, as well as the quantities we must have of each. The science of fat is probably very interesting for anyone interested in the relationship between the hydrogen atoms that determine fat's usefulness to humans, but I'm not going to dwell on it. I'm not sure I even care that saturated fats are saturated with hydrogen atoms and unsaturated fats are not and therefore contain fewer calories. It's enough to know for easy reference that fat which is solid at room temperature is called, well, fat; fat that is liquid at room temperature is called oil; and fat in the bloodstream is cholesterol. Here I will be confining myself to fats we choose to consume.

FATS IN DESCENDING ORDER OF USEFULNESS

Trans fats (or trans fatty acids) produced artificially are the devil in fat form. Do not eat them. If you are hooked on fast or junk food, this could be tricky, and even if you're not you need to scour labels, looking not just for trans fats but also for 'hydrogenated' oil or fat (which means vegetable oils to which hydrogen has been added for reasons such as extending shelf life). Trans fats not only raise the body's levels of LDL (bad cholesterol) but also lower the levels of HDL (good cholesterol) and increase the risk of coronary heart disease (see Chapter 22).

Saturated fats are usually solid at room temperature (butter, lard and so on) and are found in all manner of my husband's favourites: chicken skin, marbled steaks, sausages, cream and full-fat cheese. The general view is that saturated fats raise levels of bad cholesterol and contribute to heart disease, so we should eat less of them. You don't have to eat none of them: you may eat some. Obviously, you should especially eat less of them if you have concerns about your waist measurement or BMI, or your doctor has told you to lose weight (see Chapter 22).

Polyunsaturated fats, aka the 'good' fats, are also known as essential fatty acids (specifically omega 3 and omega 6). We need these fats in our diet because our bodies can't make enough of them. The main source of omega 3 is oily fish (salmon, tuna, mackerel, sardines) and the main source of omega 6 is oil (sunflower, safflower, soy, walnut and peanut oils, which also contain omega 3). We need more omega 6 than omega 3, but not nearly as much more as we currently consume. The Okinawans (as reported by *The Okinawan Program* written by Wilcox, Wilcox and Suzuki, 2001) consume omega 6 and omega 3 in a ratio of roughly four to one, and since they are the longest-living race in the world it's possible they have got it right. To redress the western diet's imbalance between omega 6 and omega 3, we should eat more oily fish, flaxseeds and walnuts.

Monounsaturated fats (so known because they have only one site for hydrogen) are admired and respected because of their ability to resist free radicals. A free radical, just to remind you, is, according to the *Gale Encyclopedia of Medicine*, 'an unstable molecule that causes oxidative damage by stealing electrons from surrounding molecules, thereby disrupting activity in the body's cells'. The damage caused to cells by abundant free radicals can lead to cancer, so they must be resisted. Important sources of monosaturated fat are avocados, almonds, olive oil and canola oil.

THE GOOD OIL?

Olive oil is the current fat du jour owing to its completely delicious taste, its resonance of the Mediterranean and, total bonus, its health-giving properties. Whether we should choose virgin (unrefined) olive oil or non-virgin is a matter of some discussion. Studies suggest that virgin varieties are higher in the antioxidant polyphenol and have a measurably better effect on levels of good cholesterol.

Canola oil (made from rapeseed) is more controversial. Those in favour point to its health benefits; those against say it's genetically modified rapeseed whose effects on humans are uncertain. Rapeseed was toxic to humans until Canadian farmers produced a strain with a greatly reduced content of erucic acid; they later renamed it canola (as in, Canadian oil). In the mid-1990s Monsanto, the world's leading producer of the herbicide glyphosate (Roundup), produced a Roundup-resistant strain of canola. This means it can be saturated in the stuff but all that will die are the nasty weeds around it. Should you choose to use canola oil, buy organic.

Balancing the diet

Exactly how much of each macronutrient we need for a balanced diet is under constant review. In fact it's under such constant review that the measuring of proteins, carbohydrates and fats is ever-changing. Most recently, out has gone the old view that half of our food intake should be from complex carbohydrates, a quarter from proteins and a quarter from fats. In has come 'food choice' as recommended by any number of bodies, including those whose advice I am going to float past you: Australia's NHMRC, which has a healthy-eating pie chart (it's a plate, actually); and the UK's FSA, which has produced the 'eatwell plate'. The HSPH was responsible for the original healthy eating pyramid, so I've referred to its recommendations as well.

Broadly speaking, all these are divided into proteins, carbohydrates and fats, although the words scarcely get a look-in. Instead ratios are explained in types of food (down to the last nut), which most certainly has the benefit of clarity. There are variations, however, which reflect the eating habits of each population but would seem to suggest some flexibility in the science.

(Eatwell, Food Standards Agency; www.eatwell. gov.uk, reproduced by permission)

The UK's eatwell plate (above) and The Australian Guide to Healthy Eating food plate illustrate respective governments' recommendations for sensible eating which are very sensible indeed.

(*Australian Guide to Healthy Eating*, Canberra, ACT, Department of Health and Aging, 2008; © Commonwealth of Australia, reproduced by permission)

Both the NHMRC and the FSA divide their plate into five. The NHMRC separates fruit from vegetables (presumably on the grounds that the sugar from simple carbohydrates is different from anything converted from complex ones). The FSA combines fruit and vegetables, with the fifth (tiny – eat sparingly) 'slice' for fatty and/or sugary foods such as butter, biscuits and sweets. The Australian plate's largest segment contains complex carbohydrates (bread, cereals, etc.), closely followed by vegetables and legumes; the smallest is for lean meat, fish and poultry, and other protein sources. Fatty and sugary foods, called extra and not included on the plate at all, are to be eaten no more than three times a day. On the UK version, equal billing (about one-third of the plate) is given to breads, cereals, etc., fruit and vegetables. Approximate equal value is also given to the smaller divisions containing meat and other non-dairy protein foods, and low-fat dairy.

Whether such guidelines will continue to reflect dietary science is anyone's guess. Potatoes come in and out of favour, as does red meat. Until she died a decade ago, my mother served her household meat and potatoes (plus peas or beans and carrots or pumpkin) every day of the week except Friday, when the meat was replaced by eggs or fish. My father had meat three times a day. My mother baked cakes on Saturdays and most evening meals included a dessert. My father's diet contained way more than the recommended measures of alcohol but he lived until he was 79 and my mother to 85. Maybe they took more exercise, maybe the quality of food was better, maybe the air was cleaner or maybe their diet was properly balanced. Certainly my mother never fried food, apart from the very occasional chip, or bought anything ready-made. More significantly, I think, they ate less – not less often, just less. It seems very likely to me that how much is on the plate is as central to our weight problem as what is on it.

Portion control

The UK guidelines are chary of being overly specific and you can see why. Diet control can go pear-shaped when, for instance, the need to reduce your intake of one thing translates into reducing everything, which becomes so upsetting that the reducers go back to eating too much of the thing they wanted to reduce in the first place. But let's assume that this won't happen, that you take from the suggestions no more than a general impression, you make whatever adjustments you need to your diet and then you move on.

The recommendations below are based on both Australian and UK government guidelines.

CEREALS AND GRAINS

Carbs give us energy, in case you skipped the above. Therefore the amount we burn is significant to the amount we need. Complex carbs also provide fibre and, depending on the package, a range of minerals (iron, calcium, thiamine) essential for good health. The NHMRC says women aged between nineteen and sixty need four to nine servings a day; men of the same age, from six to twelve (the ranges are governed by size and levels of activity). A single serving consists of any of the following:

- 2 slices of bread;

- 1 cup of porridge;

- 1 bread roll;

- 1 cup of breakfast cereal or ½ cup of muesli;

- 1 cup of cooked rice, pasta or noodles;

- 1 medium potato, ½ sweet potato or 1 medium parsnip (they may be vegetables but they're starchy, which is why they are grouped with breads and cereals).

FRUIT AND VEGETABLES

The current view is that we should eat more vegetables than fruit, probably twice as many. The NHMRC recommends five servings of vegetables per day and two of fruit for both men and women aged nineteen to sixty (and more for pregnant or breastfeeding women). This is so much more than the previously recommended five portions of either, which we've been struggling to manage, that many of us will be wondering how to fit them in. The only answer is to rethink our snacks and meals.

We are advised, in our daily intake of vegetables, to mix up colours on the plate, so try to include something green, something yellow and something red. Below are the portions recommended by the NHMRC from which we are to choose five vegetables and two pieces of fruit a day:

Vegetables

- ½ cup of vegetables, such as spinach, silverbeet, broccoli, cauliflower, brussels sprouts;

- 1 cup of lettuce or other salad greens; or ½ cup of broad beans, lentils, peas, green beans, zucchini (courgettes), mushrooms, capsicum, cucumber, sweetcorn, turnips, swedes, sprouts, celery, eggplants, etc.

To the first group, the FSA adds 4 heaped tablespoons of kale, spring greens or green beans. To the second it adds 1 medium-sized (or 7 cherry) tomatoes, plus tinned and frozen vegetables in roughly the same quantity as the fresh. It also notes that beans and pulses count only as one of the five portions, no matter how much of them you eat.

Fruit

- 2 or more small fruit (for example, 2 plums, mandarins or kiwi fruit; 3 apricots; 6 lychees; 7 strawberries; 14 cherries);

- 1 medium-sized fruit (apple, banana, pear, orange, nectarine);

- 1 slice large fruit (papaya, melon, pineapple); or 2 slices mango or ½ grapefruit;

- 1 tablespoon dried fruit (raisins, currants, sultanas, mixed fruit); 2 figs or 3 prunes.

As with vegetables, tinned and frozen fruit can be eaten in roughly the same quantity as fresh. One glass (150 ml/5 fl. oz) of 100 per cent juice (fruit or vegetable juice, or smoothie) counts as one portion, but you can only count one portion per day, however much you drink.

MEAT, FISH, POULTRY

Meat and fish are excellent sources of iron; meat is an excellent source of zinc; meat, poultry, fish, shellfish and eggs are fine sources of B12; fish, as you will recall, is a great source of omega-3 fats. Since iron, zinc, B12 and omega-3 fats all are essential nutrients, we would ditch meat, fish, eggs and poultry from our diets only under the most desperate of circumstances, and we should pay them due respect if we want a properly balanced diet – which, of course, we do. For instance, simply buying low-fat cuts isn't enough: the FSA points out that lean rump steak, grilled, contains half the fat of rump steak with the fat, and that fried, crumbed chicken breast contains nearly six times as much fat as grilled, skinless chicken breast. The NHMRC recommendation – a serve per person per day of any of the following – remains minute by most household standards:

- 65–100 g (3–4 oz) cooked meat or chicken;

- 80–120 g (3¼–4½ oz) cooked fish;

- 2 small eggs, or maybe ⅓ cup of cooked pulses (including baked beans) or ⅓ cup of peanuts or almonds.

EGGS

A further word on eggs. You actually can't go beyond an egg for a perfect nutritional package, despite concerns about their cholesterol content. Of course they contain cholesterol, but the cholesterol in eggs is infinitely less harmful than the cholesterol our body produces from eating too much saturated fat. The current thinking seems to be that you would have to eat so many to affect your cholesterol adversely that you can eat one for breakfast every day without fear of your heart congesting on the train. Clearly you don't substitute them for all other forms of protein, but you can appreciate the value they offer when they are an excellent source not only of protein but also of vitamins, minerals and iodine.

DAIRY

Milk, yoghurt and cheese are also fine sources of protein, but their specialist area is their calcium content, required especially by young bones as they form and old bones as they weaken. Calcium requires vitamin D to work most efficiently, and theoretically you should get enough of that from just five to fifteen minutes a day in the sun several times a week (though not between 10 am and 3 pm), unless you are an Inuit or a night worker who sleeps all day. There are, however, concerns that even in Australia, a growing number of us are deficient in vitamin D because we're exposing ourselves to less sunlight, either from fear of skin cancer or because we're spending too much time indoors at the computer. Should you be such a person, eat more eggs and fish.

How much dairy we need is a source of some argument – well, an argument among the bodies I chose for advice – but the general consensus is that since dairy products contain saturated fat as well as abundant goodness, low-fat versions are preferable. In Australia the NHMRC recommends two servings a day; in the US the HSPH, possibly reflecting its concern about obesity levels and the over-consumption of full-fat milk, recommends one or at the most two servings of dairy a day and these to be no-fat or low-fat versions. The FSA in the UK advises eating or drinking moderate amounts and sticking to the low-fat versions.

A serving, as recommended by the NHMRC, includes any of the following:

- 250 ml (8 fl. oz) of milk;
- 40 g (1½ oz) of cheese;
- 250 ml (8 fl. oz) of custard;
- ½ cup of evaporated milk;
- 200 g (7 oz) of yoghurt.

FATS AND OILS

A top-of-the-range estimate of how much fat we should eat each day is 35 per cent of our total energy intake, with no more than 11 per cent from saturated fat. Currently, we are hitting the top of the range and our intake of saturated fat is roughly 13 per cent, so all we really need to do is exchange saturated for unsaturated. HSPH actually rates healthy fats and oils highly in its recommended foods, on the basis that Americans get a third of their calories from fats and if only they chose them healthily their cholesterol would improve and their hearts would be less at risk (which sounds kind of fanciful to me). The high-protein 'total wellbeing diet' recommended by Australia's CSIRO, on the other hand, suggests we limit fats to 20 per cent of our total intake, or three units a day of added oils, which may be:

- 3 tablespoons of margarine;
- 3 teaspoons of curry paste in canola oil;
- 60 g (3 oz) of avocado;
- 20 g (1 oz) of nuts.

I'm sure there will be people who can confine themselves to these quantities, but I'm not one of them because I like butter on my toast and olive oil on just about everything.

Butter or margarine?

Should you be tossing up between margarine and butter, it might interest you to know that each tends to have the same fat content, but the fat in marg, once reviled for its high trans fat content, is generally unsaturated (a plus), whereas butter is saturated (a minus). You probably can't argue the case for butter on health grounds, even if you can for palate-pleasing reasons. Palate doesn't dictate a balanced diet, but it will inform the choices you make within it – so, if you like butter, have butter, just not a lot.

The truth about salt

As with saturated fats, we're advised to consume as little salt as possible, to lower our blood pressure and reduce our risk of strokes. We need some, but not much, to maintain normal fluid levels, healthy muscle function, stomach and nerve function, and proper acidity of the blood. The general view is that we eat at least 50 per cent more salt than we need and maybe up to nine times more. The most we should eat is 4–6 grams a day (depending on which government is issuing the guidelines).

Here is the difficulty: salt is composed of sodium and chloride, which are electrolytes. Electrolytes draw water to and from our cells, helping essential processes such as keeping the body's fluids in balance, transferring nutrients and flushing out waste products. But if our bodies become oversupplied with sodium, our kidneys attempt to secrete it by increasing their fluid volume and so we have water retention and before long we have a problem. Retained water puts pressure on the kidneys, which causes our blood pressure to rise; the higher our blood pressure, the greater the strain on our heart, arteries and brain, not to mention kidneys. Worst-case scenario? Heart attack, stroke, dementia, kidney disease.

So see you later, salt. It's easier said than done, because salt is added to just everything (around three-quarters of our salt intake is said to come from processed foods). The answer is adding less when cooking, less to the food on our plate, and a lot of label-reading. Not easy, but worth it.

In short...

- Food is a source of pleasure.

- It should be eaten in sensible quantities for your age, gender, height and activity levels.

- Cook it yourself as often as possible.

- Eat some of everything, but fry it only now and then.

- Don't pile your plate with protein.

- Eat more vegetables than fruit.

- Eat wholegrain carbs rather than refined carbs, but white pasta and rice are better than no pasta or rice.

- Eat most of your sugar in fruit, but having a cake once in a while won't kill you.

- Eat slowly. If you eat slowly you eat less and you might notice when you've had enough.

10

**BUYING
AND STORING
FOOD**

You remember the list, the list which will be your friend for life if only you could learn to love it. Well, here's where the learning starts in earnest because shopping for food is utterly inefficient if you do it on the hop – especially if your priorities are time, money, a balanced diet and saving the planet. You may think your potential for planet-saving, when it comes to food, is limited and much as you wish to help, your hands are tied. Maybe you'd commit yourself to self-sufficiency and growing your own eco-friendly crops in a different life, but you don't have a different life so what can you do? We can stop wasting food, for a start.

Food waste in developed nations is bordering, if not on the criminally negligent, then on the ridiculous. Australians throw away 3 million tonnes of food every year, which is equal to roughly a quarter of the edible food the nation produces. What's junked is worth more than $5 billion and accounts for one-fifth of every household's food bill. Sydney bins half the food it buys. Half! Who can afford it? In the UK, annual food waste amounts to 6.7 million tonnes and is worth £10.2 billion. Estimates suggest a third of all food bought in the UK is ditched: a quarter of it goes because its sell-by date has expired, but a tenth of it is still within the recommended time for consumption, which suggests that people either aren't reading labels or can't tell when food is off. Families with children throw out more than childless households do. The waste is as likely to be food that's been served but not eaten as food bought but not served, so we're either overestimating portions or we're dishing up food that won't or can't be eaten.

When did food get to be so unvalued? Research from the Waste and Resources Action program (WRAP) in the UK puts it down to:

- lack of planning when shopping, which leads to overbuying;

- lack of knowledge about food storage;

- lack of confidence in cooking available food in the house;

- lack of understanding about portion control.

The first rule of catering is to buy only what you need. There are two ways of going about this. Method One, my preferred option to date, is to make a scant list on the way out the door and pick up anything else I think I need when I see it on the shelves. All I can tell you is that I always buy far more than is on the list, spend a good deal more than I mean or want to, and at the end of every week I'm looking at yoghurt that wasn't eaten. I should stop buying yoghurt or I should plan better, which brings us to Method Two – beginning with a proper and thoughtful list. It sounds irritatingly prescriptive, but prescriptive turns out to be smart.

The proper shopping list

You can't just knock it off. It's an ongoing two-tier thing based on: 1) the staples which live in the freezer and food cupboard; and 2) your weekly menu, which takes into consideration not just what the household will be eating but also a proper estimation of how much they eat. You add staples to the list as you run out of them; you add fresh food to the list once you've worked out what you need. Some meals can be made from the staples, but most won't and the ideal is to use all your fresh food before the next shop, no matter how sad the fridge and fruit basket end up looking.

You need to sit down with a diary, or with the rest of the household if that's helpful, make a note of the number of meals in and who will be eating them, then roughly calculate the portions required. This takes less time than you might think, because the average household is a thing of routine and habit, and even though adventurous cooks might try new meals often, most household members don't have the time or energy for much innovation.

To decide how much of each per head you need, refer to the portion sizes outlined in the previous chapter or investigate nutrition websites for a portion calculator (see Useful Websites). You punch in what you want to eat, how many people want to eat it and whether they are adults or children, and up come portions. A household of two adults enquiring after a dinner of chicken with potatoes, broccoli and carrots will be told they need 280 grams (10 ounces) chicken, ten small potatoes, four florets of broccoli and 6 tablespoons of sliced carrots. This will give you a reasonable idea of how much to buy if you're hopeless at gauging it for yourself.

Most households function on a large weekly supermarket shop, with top-ups every few days depending on the time available and the urgency of the need. Lucky households might also manage trips to specialists like the greengrocer, the butcher, the fishmonger or even bulk stores selling grains or local produce, but this will be a matter of time, access and money.

Shopping for food by household type

Some households, in particular those consisting of sharers, single people and professional couples, limit their staples to a box or two of cereal, a jar of olives, and tomato sauce. In the fridge are pre-cooked meals, pre-packed salads, yoghurt and hummus. For them, cooking anything beyond toast and the occasional jacket potato is too big a pain to be contemplated and I can see that – but actually, should you belong to such a household, ask yourself this: how big can the pain really be, how much are you spending and how balanced is your diet? Not only that, but how consistently delicious is the food you're eating, and even when it is delicious, is this down to silly amounts of fat, salt and sugar, plus a load of additives that appear nowhere in daily dietary requirement lists but are somehow addictive? It's a long question, but ask yourself anyway.

Households containing families and domesticated people of all sorts will almost certainly have fuller food cupboards and a stronger inclination to shop for food they cook themselves. Ideally, a household will be stocked in line with the food groups described in the preceding chapter. That means cereals, fruit and vegetables (including pulses and legumes), dairy products, meat, poultry and fish (or vegetarian alternatives), fats including oils, as well as a few treats which have no nutritional value but whose total absence from our lives is unacceptable.

We get most of our food in the form of perishables that need to be bought weekly, unless we have a freezer so large the whole family could sleep in it. But we need to stock tinned and dried stuff too, in as much abundance as is prudent but not greedy.

Shopping for the basic food cupboard

Store-cupboard foods are called non-perishables: they're the things that don't go off out of the fridge or freezer, and with luck won't go off ever. A siege mentality is helpful when stocking the larder, so think of ingredients you'd need if we were warned not to venture from the house under any circumstances, not even to forage. (We're talking nourishing and filling.) I'm not suggesting you need all the below, just a decent selection.

grains: pasta (all sorts, all colours), rice, couscous, flour (all sorts, both colours), breakfast cereals.

seeds and nuts: sunflower seeds, pumpkin seeds, pine kernels, almonds, walnuts.

fish: tinned sardines, anchovies, tuna, salmon.

fruit and vegetables: tinned fruit in juice, dried fruits, tinned tomatoes.

pulses: tinned beans (all sorts), chickpeas.

fats and oil: olive oil, sunflower oil.

sugar: granulated, caster, soft brown.

syrups and spreads: golden syrup, honey, jam, peanut butter.

baking ingredients: baking powder, custard powder, vanilla essence.

*miscellaneou*s: curry powder/paste, coconut milk, organic stock powder.

herbs and spices: sea salt, black peppercorns, marjoram, oregano, bay leaves, cardamom, ginger, nutmeg, cinnamon, paprika (don't bother with dried basil and parsley – they taste like nothing and are much better bought fresh).

sauces: tomato, Worcestershire, soy, Asian fish, pesto.

beverages: tea (assorted), coffee, cocoa.

Buying for the freezer

What you buy for the freezer will clearly depend on the size of the freezer and this will be dictated mostly by the size of the household and the space available. Bulk-buying only makes sense if you think you will eat the contents within the next year. Multiple buying, on the other hand – four loaves of bread or free-range chickens when they are on special, can be both time- and money-saving. Should your freezer be a very small section of your fridge, used mainly for ice-cubes and ice-cream, try at least to make room for frozen peas, beans and summer berries, and enough frozen meat or fish for two meals (one grill and the other a dish that stretches, like a lasagne, fish pie or curry).

The fresh-food list

You can't beat freshness of product, but you can't guarantee it either, which is why it pays to know your shop and its delivery patterns. While city supermarkets get fresh food delivered daily, supermarkets in regional or outlying districts may not. If you generally do the bulk of your shopping in a single weekly hit, then buy some fresh vegetables but mostly frozen, because they're infinitely preferable to anything that's more than several days old. And freeze any meat that you aren't going to eat within three days.

Based on the requirements of the aforementioned balanced diet, your fresh-food list should include bread, fruit (for a week), vegetables (for a few days), eggs, meat/chicken/fish, and dairy (milk, yoghurt, cheese, butter, cream).

Getting value for money

This involves a small amount of flexibility (however prescriptive your shopping list) and an eagle eye, especially in supermarkets. A little research saves time, especially if you have a choice.

- Check in advance for specials, which will be advertised in the local paper, via your letterbox and online. If you have a choice of two stores, compare their offers: this week, on cheese, tinned tuna and cereal alone, I saved $7.20 without even trying (over a year, this adds up to $375 – which, in our household, is food eaten at home for a week).

- As you make your way along the aisles, check for reduced prices (look not just at the sale price but at the usual price too). Perishables are often marked down as they approach their sell-by date, or items may simply be offered at a knockdown price because the store has over-ordered.

- Should your store get deliveries every day, it pays to shop after 5 pm, when that day's stock needs shifting. Most foodstuffs won't degenerate too much during the course of a single day, so you'll lose nothing in the way of freshness.

- Should your store not receive daily deliveries, find out what's delivered on which days. Buying on delivery day means the food will be fresher (just as buying the day before may mean the food is cheaper).

- Buy local and seasonal (or at least not imported) wherever possible.

● Choose from the back of the shelf. Sell-by dates can vary in the same display, with the oldest items to the front.

● Stores that bake their bread and cakes inhouse will mark down towards late afternoon/early evening.

● Home-brand items are very often equal in quality to more expensive brands – but not always, so experiment. Home-brand organic products, if available, often represent excellent value.

● It pays to buy more discounted items than you immediately require, as long as the packaging is intact, any loose stuff doesn't look dilapidated, and you have the space to freeze or store them all. They may not have been on your list, but it is clever shopping.

● Don't, however, be seduced by the special that can't be frozen or is unlikely to be eaten. If your household only kind of likes hummus, don't buy the bulk offer on the basis that they ate it once. Harden your bargain-hunter's heart.

● Don't buy anything liquid (juice, milk) in a package which feels swollen. Swollen equals going or gone off.

● Buy in bulk. (This isn't to be confused with panic buying.) Buying oil or water or flour or even grains from bulk-food shops is certainly worth considering. If you have a favourite greengrocer, ask if they're interested in getting rid of produce nearing the end of its glory days. (A box of overripe tomatoes, for instance, can go a very long way, even if you just purée and freeze it.) Sometimes it makes sense to share bulky purchases (as in a side of beef or lamb, or a 10-kilo bag of dried beans) with other households.

● To avoid chilled or frozen food melting or defrosting before you get home, buy it last and carry it in an insulated bag.

········ UNDERSTANDING FOOD LABELS ········

Food labelling is now compulsory on everything except unpackaged meat, fruit and vegetables, and some deli items. The labels indicate ingredients, sell-by, best-by or use-by dates, and nutritional content, which means you can now know what weirdo additives or unhealthy quantities of salt and fat are on offer. And if you buy food that's past its use-by date, it's your lookout.

AUSTRALIAN FOOD LABELS

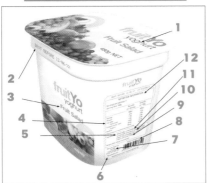

1 Name or description of the food
2 Date marking
3 Labels must tell the truth
4 Legibility requirements
5 Information for allergy sufferers
6 Directions for use and storage
7 Food recall information
8 Country of origin
9 Food additives
10 Percentage labelling
11 Ingredient list
12 Nutrition information panel

UK FOOD LABELS

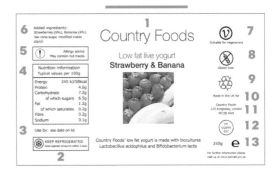

1 Product name or description
2 Instructions on storing or using the food
3 Date marking
4 Nutrition information
5 Allergy advice box
6 Ingredients listing
7 Suitable for vegetarians
8 Gluten free
9 Recycled material
10 Country of origin
11 Contact details
12 Health marking
13 Size

The labelling in Australia is currently tricky to decipher if you don't know what you're looking for, so take time to familiarise yourself with the tiny print and the nature of the information. What goes into one brand of a particular food isn't necessarily what goes into another, so compare products. Bear in mind that ingredients are listed in order of weight, so if first on the list is sugar, you're looking at a lot of sugar.

Ingredients

The basic rule for ingredients is 'The fewer the better'. Even a small carton of yoghurt might list eleven, including thickeners, flavours and food acid, and this is upsetting unless you know what the thickener, flavour or acid is or does. It's true that preservatives such as salt, vinegar and spices have been used for centuries to make meat, fruit and vegetables last longer, but time-honoured simple preservatives are known to us. The antioxidants, colours, emulsifiers, stabilisers, gelling agents, flavour enhancers and sweeteners in today's food are mainly not.

Without them the pre-packaged things we buy might look funny, possibly taste funny or go off before they've left the shop. They won't poison us, according to the regulatory bodies that scrutinise them for harmful side effects, but there are so many of them, and do we want to eat them? Personally, I hate the notion of swallowing 'foaming agents'. Keeping track is practically impossible when some are listed on labels as numbers not names, and others have more than one name. Monosodium glutamate, for instance, is 621 in Australia and E621 in the UK and is also called MSG, sodium glutamate or hydrolysed protein.

You can buy pocket guides to additive codes or find them listed online, and it makes sense to be fully informed. The least we need to know is: most suspect additives would have to be eaten in substantial quantities to do any harm to any but the allergy-prone; only a few are truly controversial and even they have their advocates:

○ *Monosodium glutamate*, or 621, is a chemically manufactured powder whose chief function is both to disguise unpleasant tastes and to boost flavour. It has long been under a cloud for possible adverse health effects (headaches, tingling), though no tests have proved conclusively that it is harmful to the population at large (despite concerns over its effects on rats subjected to overdoses). Additive 621 has its champions from a culinary point of view, but speaking as a headache-sufferer, I'm not one of them.

○ *Aspartame*, or 951 (sometimes sold under the brand name NutraSweet), is an artificial sweetener 200 times sweeter than sugar. It's found in all kinds of foods labelled 'diet'. People who want to lose weight substitute it for sugar, but there are doctors who argue that owing to the way aspartame is broken down in the body, the hope is a vain one. Weight loss aside, it remains controversial because it's said to increase the risk of certain cancers, and questions have been raised in the US about the licensing process. While neither allegation has been proven to the satisfaction of regulatory bodies, the fact remains that some people have poor reactions to it. According to NutraSweet and, incidentally the Australia New Zealand Food Standards Authority (whose endorsement is the same, word for word, as the manufacturer's), aspartame consists of amino acids, which 'are building blocks of protein and are found naturally in all protein-containing foods, including meats, grains and dairy products ... [and] are also common in many foods such as fruits, vegetables and their juices.' They conclude it is safe and, to be fair, it is less harmful to teeth than sugar.

○ *Nitrites and nitrates* (additive numbers 249–252 inclusive) are used as preservatives in cheese and in processed meats like salami and bacon. Once digested, nitrates convert to chemicals called nitrosamines, which are considered carcinogenic. They have been associated with gastrointestinal cancers, but found to be innocent of causing them. Go easy on the bacon, is all I can suggest.

• *Artificial food colourings* are increasingly a cause for concern. The UK has introduced a voluntary ban on the following: tartrazine (yellow), E102; quinoline (yellow), E104; sunset yellow (orange/yellow), E110; carmoisine (red), E122; ponceau (red), E124; allura (red), E129. Of concern are their links with allergies, asthma and hyperactivity in some children.

'Best before' and 'Use by' dates

Freshness is to a certain extent a quality judgement, but manufacturers of food with a shelf life of less than two years are required by law to make the judgement for you and it's in their interests to be as cautious as possible. In both Australia and the UK, date marking is indicated by 'Best before', 'Use by' and sometimes 'Sell by', and there is a difference, however slight it sounds. (If you intend to freeze food, you should do so before the best-before or use-by date.)

Best before means that the quality of the food will be fine until that date – in other words, it won't be stale and it probably won't poison you after the date either, even if the quality (colour, flavour, nutritional value) is no longer optimal. Shops are permitted to sell food beyond its best-before date, because at issue is quality and not safety. Yoghurt, cheese and butter, for example, have best-before dates, which means you can exercise your own judgement, within reason. The experts advise that if you are in any doubt, chuck it out, and clearly that's what most people do. You can inform your doubt, however, by employing your senses of taste and smell as well as the usual common sense, which should be guided by horror of unnecessary waste.

Use by is applied to highly perishable goods like meat, milk and fish, which deteriorate quickly and which can, after a comparatively short period of time, constitute a danger to health. Selling food beyond its use-by date is illegal, and should you choose to eat food beyond that date, it's at your peril.

OTHER DATE MARKS

You may sometimes also see a 'Sell by' or 'Display to' stamp on packaged goods. This is to do with stock control and is not a judgement on safety or quality, except in the case of eggs. It is against the law to sell eggs beyond their sell-by date.

Food with a shelf life of less than seven days, such as bread and other baked goods, may carry a 'Baked on', rather than 'Best before' date.

Nutrition information

This is a list of the energy, protein, carbohydrate (usually sugar), fibre, fat, salt (often referred to as sodium) and calcium content of any given product. Such information must be provided for most manufactured foods. (Exceptions include very small packages, and some unpackaged foods.) Energy is usually listed in terms of kilojoules (kJ) and sometimes in calories as well. (To convert kilojoules to calories, divide by 4.182.) Fat may be listed as trans, saturated, polyunsaturated and/or monosaturated (look for no trans and minimal saturated).

All these elements are listed by serving and per 100 grams, and also as a proportion of the recommended daily intake. It helps to know whether the level of any particular element is low, medium or high. In the UK this is signalled by a traffic-light system – green for low, amber for average, red for high. In Australia where the system remains annoyingly unclear:

- low *fat* = less than 3 grams of fat per 100 grams of product (no more than 1 gram saturated fat), and 'high' = more than 20 grams of fat per 100 grams;

- low *sugar* = less than 2 grams of sugar per 100 grams, and 'high' = more than 10 grams of sugar per 100 grams;

- low *salt* = 0.1 grams of sodium per 100 grams of product, and 'high' = 0.5 grams per 100 grams. (Every gram of salt contains 0.4 grams of sodium: to convert sodium to salt, multiply it by 2.5.) The FSA recommends no more than 6 grams salt (2.4 grams sodium) per day.

NON-SPECIFIC LABELS

'Reduced fat' and 'Low salt' can mean anything. Reduced from what? is the question. A label of '95 per cent fat free' means it contains 5 per cent fat.

Fruit 'juice', concentrated or not, must be 100 per cent pure fruit juice. A fruit 'drink' need only contain 5 per cent pure juice, so read the ingredients to see what constitutes the remaining 95 per cent. 'Fruit-flavoured' food means the item doesn't necessarily contain any fruit at all.

'No artificial colours' and 'No preservatives' may be true, but still check the sugar, fat and salt content, as in the end these are the killers.

You know in your heart what decent food is and there's no excuse not to buy it. There's no point in loading your trolley with junk (low in nutrients, high in additives, fat, sugar and salt) because it costs next to nothing. It's miles better to buy less and stretch it by adding less expensive food to the meal (a small amount of good-quality meat to be served with pasta). Cheap doesn't have to mean rubbish, obviously, but it can, so know what you're looking for not only in terms of basic quality but also in terms of its suitability for the meals you are planning.

Buying meat

You don't necessarily find the best meat in butcher shops or market stalls, but their huge advantage is the presence of a person to consult, and, with any luck, an enthusiast who loves their product and wants to talk about it. The quality of meat in a supermarket will depend on the quality of the store buyers and the skill of its butchers. Many supermarkets have meat counters where you might find a butcher or you might just find a shop assistant who doesn't know what you're talking about, in which case, be guided by your eyes and nose (licking isn't an option).

You want to know specifically:

- if the meat is free-range and/or organic (was the animal given antibiotics and hormones?);

- where it was sourced;

- what it was fed (grass or grain);

- how long it was hung (aged);

- the various cuts and how they can best be cooked.

You might not be fussed by any or all of these details, but they are the best indicators of quality and good butchers will be happy to advise you. Mine was. I found out that all his meat is locally sourced and free-range, bought from a wholesaler he trusts. He steers clear of organic, because among the demands of certification is keeping organic separate from anything non-organic at all times, which for him is impractical. He hangs his beef for two weeks and his lamb for between five and seven days. (Hanging increases the flavour and tenderises meat by breaking down the muscle fibres.)

CHOOSING MEAT

◉ The fat around the meat should be creamy-white; yellowish fat suggests age.

◉ The surface of the meat should be dry, even a little sticky, not wet.

◉ Too much gristle will make the meat tough. A thick layer of gristle between the fat and the meat suggests an old beast and probably a tough one. A thin layer is normal.

◉ Some fat is desirable. Fat equals flavour.

◉ The cheaper the cut, the longer it will take to cook, but it need be none the less delicious for that.

◉ Don't buy pre-packed meat if the package is swimming in blood or torn.

Beef

Beef comes from bullocks or heifers which haven't bred. Veal is from a calf, usually several months old; milk-fed veal is from an animal only a few weeks old. The most widely available beef is from yearlings (between eight and ten months old), which with luck have been aged properly after slaughter.

Purists look for grass-fed beef, on the basis that this is the natural food for cattle and that grass produces leaner meat than grain, and that growing grain for feed requires huge natural resources the world can ill afford. They argue to boot that grass-fed beef has a much lower ratio of omega 6 to omega 3 (3:1) compared to 20:1 in grain-fed (and you will recall from the previous chapter that the preferred ratio is around 4:1). The beef my butcher buys has usually been grain-fed for some of the time, anywhere between thirty and 100 days: the longer the grain-feeding, the heavier the marbling of fat and his customers won't buy anything too heavily marbled. Who cares, you might be thinking, when all you're making are rissoles? But a rissole can be a rissole or a great rissole, depending on the meat.

Cuts of beef

Buying meat is infinitely easier if you know which cut is best suited to which dish and how expensive it might be. In descending order of cost (as a general rule):

◉ *Fillet* (sometimes called tenderloin) is the leanest and most tender, as well as the most expensive, cut. It can be roasted in one piece or cut into steaks for grilling, barbecuing or pan-frying. Aficionados consider it has less flavour than ribs, rump and sirloin.

- *Rib roast* is arguably the finest beef. Rib eye can also be cut into steaks.

- *Rump* is lean and tender, though not as tender as fillet. It can be grilled, barbecued or pan-fried.

- *Sirloin* can be roasted or sliced into steaks. *T-Bone* and *porterhouse* steaks are part sirloin and part fillet (porterhouse contains larger section of fillet). All three are tender, lean and good for quick cooking, such as grilling or barbecuing.

- *Topside*, *top rump* and *silverside* can all be roasted, but (with the exception of top rump) are more tender after longer cooking such as slow- or pot-roasting. Silverside is also sold salted (corned): it should be simmered slowly.

- *Brisket* can be tough unless slow-cooked. It is usually sold boned and rolled, and is also often salted.

- *Chuck*, *round* and *blade* are ideal for casseroles, pies and any sort of stewing. Choose chuck, my butcher says, because with slow cooking it becomes flaky (rather than stringy).

- *Shin* (with or without the bone removed) can look unappetising, but cooked very slowly for a long time it produces a tender and full-bodied stew.

- *Mince* comes in various grades. The best and leanest is topside mince.

Lamb

Lamb is regarded as the most naturally free-range of meats. It's usually sold when the animal is between three and ten months old. 'Spring lamb' is closer to three than ten months old. Although meat from younger animals may be the more tender, it doesn't necessarily have the best flavour. Lamb becomes hogget (though usually still called lamb) when the first baby tooth falls out; it becomes mutton once the animal is over two years old.

There's relatively little demand for hogget in Australia and the UK, and even less for mutton (because, according to my butcher, most people don't know how to cook it), though both have good flavour and are tender when slow-cooked. Lamb should be hung for about a week, hogget and mutton for at least twice that time.

Cuts of lamb

● *Leg* is tender and usually roasted, for which it may be sold on the bone, or boned and butterflied. It is also available for grilling or barbecuing as steaks or cubed. The *shank* is often sold separately: it can be roasted, but benefits from long and slow cooking.

● *Loin* (a double loin is called a *saddle*) is the most tender cut and ideal for roasting or barbecuing in one piece, on the bone or boned and rolled. *Loin chops* or *noisettes* may be grilled, barbecued or pan-fried. *Backstrap* is a boneless cut that is good grilled or barbecued.

● *Shoulder*, on the bone or boned, is a cheaper yet, many argue, more delicious, roast. It is also sold as chops and cubed, for stewing. *Forequarter* (chops or roast) is from the upper shoulder and is more sinewy, so best slow-cooked.

● A *rack* (also, confusingly, called 'best end of neck' though it comes from below the shoulder) is a tender cut consisting of the first eight ribs. It may be sold in one piece for roasting, or separated into *cutlets* for grilling or pan-frying.

● *Fillet* (sometimes called tenderloin) is delicate in texture and flavour, and good for quick cooking, such as grilling and pan-frying.

● *Chump*, from above the leg, is mostly divided into chops for grilling but is occasionally sold in one piece for roasting.

● *Scrag* (middle neck) is usually sold as chops or thick slices, for stewing.

● *Breast* (sometimes called flap) is an inexpensive, fatty cut that may be boned and rolled for pot-roasting.

Pork

Best cooks reckon that the flesh of female pigs tastes infinitely better than flesh from hogs. Check this is what you are buying. And look for free-range and RSPCA-accredited pork.

Cuts of pork

● *Leg* is a tender cut for roasting, bone in or boned. It is also available as steaks, which can be grilled or pan-fried. The *hock* or *shank* is tender and delicious when slow-cooked; it is often sold pickled. (Cuts from the hind leg may be cured for ham.)

● *Loin* can be roasted, or divided into chops or cutlets for pan-frying or braising. (It also supplies back bacon.)

● *Fillet* (tenderloin) is tender and delicately flavoured, so ideal for quick cooking.

● *Belly* is a fatty cut that is commonly braised or slow-roasted. (It also supplies streaky bacon.) *Spare ribs*, which come from this section, are delicious marinated and then slow-roasted or barbecued.

Chicken (and eggs)

Nowhere are our consciences more likely to be tried than when we're buying chicken, since we now know that intensively farmed birds are raised in cramped misery to supply us with cheap, mostly flavourless meat. Chicken isn't what it used to be, unless you can buy organic or free-range from smallish farms. Local and organic is even better but not always feasible. Mass-produced birds will have been bleached to get rid of surface bacteria and even though this may be a harmless exercise, it can't do much for flavour and it does make you want to heave a little.

Good cooks argue that meat from a whole chicken has more flavour and is less dry (not to mention less expensive) than bits of it sold separately, despite the convenience of the bits. It's often worth buying a whole chicken and asking your butcher to cut it up for you. Any chicken, in bits or whole, should be purchased with the skin on (the fat from the skin doesn't enter the meat when cooking) and preferably on the bone, since the skin and the bone add flavour and moisture. When buying chicken, look for creamy-white, unblemished skin.

PRODUCTION METHODS

The Australian Chicken Meat Federation stresses that chickens *intensively farmed* for meat in Australia aren't raised in cages but in sheds (or barns). A typical shed, 150 metres long and 15 metres wide, will hold 40,000 chickens, and the most rudimentary maths suggests that's ten chooks to just over half a square metre. Their diet is 85–90 per cent grain, 7 per cent meat and bone meal, and 2 per cent tallow (fat). Corn-fed chickens, which have yellowish flesh, aren't necessarily superior: they are simply the result of a feed choice made by the farmer. It's a common misconception that chickens are fed hormones, but hormones have been banned internationally for forty years.

Free Range chickens account for less than 5 per cent of production in Australia. To be certified free-range (look for the stamp of the FREPA, Free Range Egg and Poultry Australia Ltd though their standards are surprisingly relaxed), chickens must be allowed access to an outside run for a part of each day once they are three weeks old. They must not be given antibiotics, but may be fed GM grain. Both conventionally raised and free-range chickens can have their beaks trimmed, though not in the case of free-range at a day old.

About half the free-range chickens in Australia are *organically farmed*. The additional rules that distinguish organic from free-range birds are that their feed must be mainly from certified organic ingredients and they may not be given artificial supplements or receive routine vaccination (except in the case of a national emergency); they have up to ten times the living space of conventionally farmed chickens. Unfortunately, organic chicken is expensive and can be hard to find outside the major cities. Also, it can look a little scraggy, but this is no doubt because we're used to the chemically enhanced plumpness of conventionally raised birds. Chickens may, however, be labelled organic without being certified. For certification, production must comply with standards of the National Standard for Organic and Bio-Dynamic Produce. In the UK, there are a load of organic certification bodies, whose standards vary: DEFRA's are pretty basic and comply to basic EU requirements; the Soil Association's are more stringent.

Eggs

Australians eat, on average, about 200 eggs per person per year, so this is big industry. Since few studies have proved conclusively that eggs produced one way are substantially more nutritious than any other, our decision to buy, say, barn-laid, free-range or organic eggs is informed primarily by our sense of justice. Few people, if any, could tell whether the eggs used in a cake were from a caged or organically raised hen. But the price variation is substantial: cage eggs can be had for half the price of free-range and about a quarter of the price of organic, which is probably why free-range supplies only 26 per cent of the market. The RSPCA accredits barn-laid, free-range and organic eggs, so, if you can't bear the thought of eggs from hens kept in cages, look for their logo. In the UK look for Soil Association certification.

Australia's many millions of cage-raised hens that lay eggs spend their lives in an allocated space per bird that is roughly the size of an A4 sheet of paper. They are unable to perch, but according to the Australian Egg Corporation they can turn, or stretch and flap their wings, despite widespread belief to the contrary. Whether a hen in such a confined space can possibly be producing her best work is a matter for speculation.

Barn-raised hens live in luxury by comparison. They have perches, nest boxes, litter to scratch in, and they can move about. Free-range layers have access to outside space (the recommended density is no more than 1000 per hectare) during the day, and shelter at night. Australia has no legal definition for the term 'free-range', and while voluntary standards have been set by FREPA and the RSPCA they are often abused. The largest suppliers of free-range eggs to supermarkets have such vast flocks that only some find their way out of the barn to enjoy the great outdoors. The Australian Egg Corporation's quality assurance scheme, Egg Corp Assured, has less rigorous standards but say they are guided by the latest science whatever the means of production.

Certified organic eggs must meet standards set by one of several accredited organisations, like Australian Certified Organic or Organic Growers of Australia, both offshoots of Biological Farmers of Australia (BFA). You can go online for a list of these organisations, but look for the proper logos (rather than pictures of happy hens) when buying. Hens whose eggs are certified organic must not only be free-range but fed only certified organic food; the production process will be free from artificial chemicals and antibiotics.

Organic food: the broad issues

Organic farming uses no artificial fertilisers, herbicides, pesticides, growth regulators, antibiotics, hormone stimulants, genetically modified organisms or intensive livestock systems, and this is at once appealing. What householders need to know is whether the benefits warrant the cost and whether some products, without question, should only be bought organic because what happens to them conventionally is just too awful to contemplate. The question that arises is who to believe. The growers? The suppliers? The certifiers? There are profound arguments in favour of organic products and equally vehement arguments against. There are studies that justify their expense and studies that condemn it; there is argument over what actually constitutes organic, the precise value of certification and the degree to which organic fights with sustainable. Where the science exists at all, it's either poor or confusing, and I'm going to spare you most of it.

PEACE OF MIND

I'm calling it peace of mind instead of 'health and nutrition' because, whatever our instincts tell us, no one has shown for sure that organically grown food is more nutritious than its conventionally grown equivalent, and we only assume this is so on the basis of common sense.

Ultimately, the argument isn't so much that food grown organically has extra health or nutritional benefits, but that food grown conventionally has substantially fewer. The suspicion is that, as well as being grown in depleted soil or soil that has been so enhanced chemically that it might as well be blotting paper, conventionally grown food is so subjected to synthetic chemicals that we have no real idea what we are eating or what damage is being done to our health in the long term. I would like to be able to inform you categorically that your health will improve if you eat only organic produce but I can't. On the other hand, knowing you are eating food produced with as little interference from chemicals as possible will almost certainly make you feel better.

ETHICS

Food that has been certified organic has been grown to standards that also govern animal welfare, which have a significant impact on how they are housed, fed and treated in general. The conditions enjoyed by conventionally farmed animals are well documented, so I won't distress you with further details here. Food grown organically is also considered less harmful to the environment, which would stand to reason. It is said, for example, to enhance the soil and control erosion.

Naturally, it's not as simple as that. A UK report for DEFRA in 2007 found that, while many organic products had lower ecological impacts than methods using fertilisers and pesticides, things weren't rosy across the board. Organically produced milk, tomatoes and chicken, for instance, were less energy-efficient: raising organic chickens required 25 per cent more energy than conventional methods. The Soil Association argues the benefits to animal welfare, soil condition and water use outweigh the problems and to many minds, they do. But there are widespread concerns about the viability of organic farming as it is currently practised.

Arguments against organic food are its cost and the reliability of the source.

COST

There is a danger, according to some environmentalists, that organic food will become a niche product for the rich. And it's true that, although costs come down as production volume increases and/or the market grows, organic food is expensive relative to non-organic. Organic growing is more time- and labour-intensive, and the farms are usually smaller, so the yield is smaller. The industry says increased costs are also a result of certification requirements which extend to transportation, storage, processing and packaging. In the end its value to you is personal, but with supermarkets showing a greater interest in home-brand organic food, shopping around makes a difference.

CAN YOU BE SURE IT'S ORGANIC?

Not entirely. In Australia, anyone can call his or her product organic and unless it's certified you have no way of knowing what it means. If you buy produce that's non-certified organic, know your supplier. Certified producers must tick boxes, but critics of the system say this is unreliable and counter-productive since, in order to comply, producers might have to ship organic materials across the country, which is costly both materially and to the environment and has been known to drive perfectly fine growers out of the market. Certified growers are audited every year, which includes a physical inspection. But contaminants can be carried (by insects or the wind or birds) from non-organic land to organic land, so how pure can any one plot be? It's the spirit of the thing, I suppose. Buying organic would seem to be one way of wishing the world well.

Buying fish

On the other hand, your concern about sustainability shouldn't be a reason to go easy on eating fish, because a balanced diet will include it at least twice a week and there are good supplies of non-endangered fish available all year round. Just buy seasonally (fish migrate and are more plentiful locally at different times of year) and, when you can, buy fresh from the sea (so not on a Monday, because fish in the shop on a Monday will usually have been caught the week before). Fishmongers are as valuable a source of information as butchers, so ask them for suggestions. They're also usually happy to do any boning, scaling and filleting for you.

WHAT TO LOOK FOR IN FRESH FISH

- The smell should be fresh and not overly fishy.

- The eyes should be clear, not cloudy.

- The gills should be red.

- The scales should be sparkling.

- Fish should look moist but not mushy or broken.

- The fish should be clean.

Also be aware that outsized fish will have less flavour than medium-sized ones. Ditch any shellfish with slightly open shells that don't close when you tap them (ditto any that don't open when cooked).

Buying fruit and vegetables

Make friends with your greengrocer. I know it's not easy when mostly you're buying from a supermarket or a shop that is almost the size of a supermarket, but it really helps. You can discuss which potatoes are best for what (baking, steaming, salads), what is meant by waxy and floury, what's newly in season, what's local. If you can shop at a farmers' or general produce market, talk to the stallholder.

Failing that, as with meat and fish, the quality of fruit and vegetables is more or less evident from their look, their colour, their texture and their smell. You won't necessarily be able to tell how sweet oranges are or how floury or crisp apples are, but you'll be able to gauge pretty accurately the freshness of produce for which freshness matters. Loose salad greens spoil quickly, so under- rather than over-buy. I don't actually see the merit in buying pre-washed leaves, when more often than not they haven't been properly dried and in next to no time your plastic bag of wild rocket melts to a mass of green gunge.

HANDLING FRUIT AND VEGETABLES

It's what proper cooks recommend and what you see experienced shoppers do in markets, so I'm going with it. But my greengrocer says fruit and vegetables should be handled as little as possible, which is why he'd rather we didn't press our thumbs into the top of avocados, for instance, to test for ripeness. Ten customers pressing that avocado aren't doing it any good. Should an avocado have a stalk, he advises, it should move freely if the fruit is ripe. He also says that you can tell if an apple is floury by giving it a quick tap: if it sounds hollow, it's floury. But ten people tapping that apple ...

Instead of mauling the produce on offer, opt for the following:

- fruit in season, which definitely tastes better;

- smaller apples, which taste better (according to my greengrocer);

- citrus fruits that feel tight and heavy in their skins;

- broccoli and cauliflower with tight florets and even colour;

On the other hand, avoid:

- anything spotted, which is likely to be insect-infested or old;

- overlarge root vegetables, which can be woody (smaller have a better flavour);

- potatoes that are sprouting or have any green patches;

- pre-packed trays of berries with juice in the bottom. (Turn the tray upside down and look for mould, or fruit that has turned to mush.)

Further advice from the greengrocer:

- The riper the banana, the higher its sugar content.

- Baby salad leaves, whether loose or pre-packed, don't much like being transported and stored.

- Buy a mix of ripe and less ripe fruit, so you'll have something in peak condition all week.

Buying dairy

MILK AND CREAM

The big milk debate is whether this is a high-fat food we should buy only in its reduced-fat versions to lower the risk of cardiovascular disease, or whether it has never been a high-fat food and actually those of us who have been drinking skimmed for years in order to feel virtuous have been paying a large price in terms of flavour.

There are dozens of milks in the dairy cabinet, catering for all intolerances, tastes, fears and allergies. Should you have any sensitivity, you will be familiar with them. Meanwhile, it might help to know that full-fat milk in a carton is usually around

3.8 per cent fat (3.9 per cent in the UK), low-fat is 1.5 per cent (the equivalent 'semi-skimmed' in the UK is 1.7 per cent) and reduced-fat is 2 per cent. (Low-fat milk isn't, as is popularly believed, milk with added water: it's milk that has had all the fat taken from it then replaced in quantities that match market specifications.) Given that a serving of regular peanut butter is 15 per cent fat, full-fat milk sounds positively slimming.

We have less room to negotiate with *cream*. Cream is fat that has been removed from milk (which is, in any case, simply an emulsion of water and fat droplets). You can, however, choose your fat content. The higher it is, the thicker the cream (the fat content of cream for whipping needs to be higher than 35 per cent). Buying cream is a treat so buy it only occasionally.

The question also arises as to the importance of organic versus non-organic dairy, especially when milk is served most commonly to children. Conventional intensive farming methods, including the artificial stimulation of growth and milk production, can place intolerable stress on the animals; organic methods are kinder, freer of chemicals and more likely to produce milk as nature intended it to be produced. But the usual arguments apply. Any organic website will inform you further.

CHEESE

Most people have a favourite cheese and mainly this is called cheddar, which is commonly sold in pre-packaged blocks. It's true, cheddar is a fine cheese, but there are many, many more. Whenever possible, taste cheese before you buy it: deli counters will usually be happy to oblige. The softer the cheese, the shorter the life, so buy what you know you'll eat within days and don't eat so much of it that your cholesterol levels shoot through the roof.

···················· STORING FOOD ····················

No food lasts forever. I would like to think this wasn't true, but it is, so you need to know how the stuff you've bought (or cooked) can be stored to maximum advantage. Failure to observe the rules may be fatal. It almost never is, but here's a salutary thought: about 5 million cases of food poisoning occur in Australia and 9 million in the UK each ear. They're plainly not always the fault of the householder, but it's estimated that about half are and of those most are a result of poor storage. You don't want to be responsible for that. On the other hand, you don't want to be wasteful, so you need to be informed.

The recommendations below came from scientists (I'm indebted especially to those who advise Food Science Australia) who have devoted a lot of time to deciding when food is dangerous and how it can be rendered not so. Some of the measures might seem overly fussy to those of us who don't mind scraping mould off jam, and maybe they are, but I would be failing you if I didn't describe best practice. The primary storage questions are where, how, and for how long. The choices are a cool storage cupboard (pantry, larder, whatever you call it), a fridge or a freezer. Generally speaking, food must be stored wrapped, or in airtight containers. There are exceptions, of course, but everything has its optimum requirements.

Health and safety recommendations usually conclude, 'When in doubt, chuck it out' and this is clearly sensible, but given the all-pervasive nature of doubt it's not necessarily helpful. The idea is to eliminate doubt and reduce waste. So, regardless of any food's maximum shelf, fridge or freezer life, your aim should be to use it. By all means have emergency rations, but you don't want them to be decrepit. In an emergency, eating might be your greatest pleasure.

The store cupboard

Mostly the goods you keep in your pantry are the 'non-perishables'. This can't be taken absolutely literally: while tinned foods have been sterilised during manufacture, then sealed to prevent contamination during storage, over time the quality of their contents will deteriorate. This may not be for four years beyond its best-before stamp but eventually. If you don't rotate, one day it will be 2020 and you'll find, rusting away, a tin of cannellini beans bought in 2006. So, every month or so, take everything out, check its best-before date, bring elderly stuff to the front and use it at an early opportunity. If you find jars and jars of ancient herbs, junk them because they will taste like nothing.

Once a tin has been opened, the contents should be treated as fresh and will be prone to contamination. Should you open any whose contents smell off, don't taste it, sling it immediately. Don't put a half-used tin of anything in the fridge, as its contents can absorb iron from the container and make you sick; not dead, but sick, and this is what we're trying to avoid. Transfer any leftovers into an airtight plastic container or a screwtop jar and then refrigerate and use within two days.

Mould on food is mostly not acceptable. It's OK on salami, other cured meats, blue cheese, hard cheese (not soft) and in tiny specks on fruit, but it's actually not a great idea to scoop it off jams because it might be producing mycotoxins. These, under the wrong conditions, will see us off.

There are other pantry items that are best refrigerated after opening. These include coffee, jam, peanut butter and dried yeast (check the labels). Others, like flour, rice and pasta, are best stored in airtight containers once the packet has been opened.

SHELF LIFE

There are survival guides that reckon low-moisture foods (like grains and dehydrated goods) stored in airtight containers at a stable temperature of 21°C (70°F) in a dark cupboard can last for up to thirty years, and maybe they can. You wouldn't knock them back if they were all that was on offer, but conventional wisdom is more conservative and best-before dates recommend no more than a year or two. Most items in the pantry have shelf lives of a year or two, properly stored (so not in their packaging but in airtight and insect-proof containers) or until their flavour runs out.

Following is the shelf life of some of the foods we tend to have in the store cupboard.

Common staples

- baking powder – 18 months;

- [packaged] cereals – 6 months unopened, within 2–3 once opened;

- grains – 12–24 months;

- gelatine – 18 months;

- honey – 12 months;

- oil – 12 months;

- pasta – 12 months;

- rice – forever;

- spices – up to 4 years or until they lose their flavour; whole spices last longer than ground;

- dried herbs – 1 to 3 years or until they lose their flavour;

- stock cubes – 12 months;

- sugar – indefinitely.

Certain foods require special mention:

● Some *dried fruits* (especially soft ones like apricots) can deteriorate after a few months (check for discolouration or mould). Once opened, they are best stored in airtight containers, not just to maintain freshness but also for protection from insects.

● *Flour* usually has a best-before date of a year from purchase, but once opened it's certainly safe for eight months in the pantry, up to a year in the fridge and longer, in a properly sealed bag, in the freezer.

● *Soft brown sugar* has a shorter life span than white because it's more likely to harden and become unmanageable. It's still fine to eat: blast it for 30 seconds in a microwave (or for a few minutes in a conventional oven at 250°C/480°F) to soften it.

● *Bread* should be stored in an airtight container, not in the fridge (where it will go stale faster).

● *Starchy vegetables* such as potatoes and sweet potatoes are also best stored in the food cupboard rather than the fridge, where the cold temperature will convert the starch to sugar. This can spoil the flavour but, more alarmingly, it can lead to them producing higher levels of a possibly carcinogenic chemical called acrylamide when cooked at high temperature. Throw out any potatoes that have green patches or are sprouting, as these signal the presence of toxic substances called glycoalkaloids (caused by exposure to light), which are not destroyed by cooking. Don't even think about eating anything green if you're pregnant or hoping to be, because there is a potential risk to unborn babies. The risk to everyone else is a case of illness so similar to gastroenteritis that potato poisoning will almost certainly be among the millions of food poisoning cases reported each year. That said, enjoy your potato: there is just about no finer food, in my opinion.

● *Onions* and *garlic* are best stored in the food cupboard, or hung in a cool dry place if bought with the leafy tops intact, which you have taken the time and trouble to plait.

The fridge

Refrigeration reduces the rate at which food deteriorates, specifically the rate at which germs in it multiply and/or the rate at which its structure collapses. Therefore you store in your fridge anything that has a use-by date, any meat you don't intend freezing, eggs, any leftovers, most desserts, dairy and deli items, and (in the crisper drawer) most vegetables with the exception of those mentioned above. Fruit stored in the fridge will last longer than fruit kept in a fruit bowl, but chilling fruit doesn't do much for flavour so anything to be eaten within twenty-four hours is best kept at room temperature.

A properly functioning fridge has a temperature between 0°C and 5°C (32°F and 41°F). The only way to check is to use a refrigerator thermometer (your mother may have managed without one, but she probably didn't keep as much food for as long, and anyway, this is why we have science). Overcrowding and constant opening and shutting of the fridge door rapidly reduces the temperature and what we think is a healthy climate for sensitive food may not be.

SOME BASIC RULES OF REFRIGERATION

◉ Food should be covered, to stop it drying out and to prevent the transfer of tastes and smells. Use foil, plastic wrap or plastic bags and containers.

◉ Keep raw and cooked food separate.

◉ Store raw meat, poultry and fish in the coldest part of fridge (this varies between models, so check), either in its own compartment or (covered) on a rack on a plate at the bottom of the fridge where it can't drip onto other food. If it's packaged in a tray covered in plastic wrap, leave it like that until you use it. Otherwise, wrap it in foil or greaseproof paper.

◉ You need good air circulation around every item, and nothing should touch the cold plate at the back of the fridge, so don't overfill. Keep the fridge clean, outside and inside, and don't leave spillages to congeal. Apart from health and safety concerns, a grubby fridge will work less efficiently.

FRIDGE LIFE

The length of time perishable goods can be stored in the fridge without deterioration is best indicated by the label. But since not all foods are labelled, the following information might be useful:

◉ There's nothing like the smell of *milk and cream* to let you know when they've had it. At the very least, milk should be good for a week (cream a little less), but both can last longer. Milk that is slightly soured can be used in all manner of biscuits, scones and bread. (Use it fairly swiftly, or it will become bitter.)

○ 'Real' *butter* (salted and unsalted) should last six to eight weeks in the fridge. Renowned Australian cook Stephanie Alexander advises against keeping it, once opened, in the butter compartment for more than a day or two because it goes rancid but I must admit this hasn't been my experience. Margarine can last up to six months.

○ *Cheese* lasts longer than milk, depending on the variety. It's best stored wrapped in greaseproof paper or a cloth. The softer the cheese, the shorter the life, and you'll know when it's off: ricotta, for example, smells and tastes sour; brie or camembert discolours and smells of ammonia (even then it won't kill you). Hard cheese can survive in a fridge for two or three months, and is edible even if it has some mould on it (just cut off the mouldy bit).

○ Fresh *meat* (by which I mean lamb, beef and pork) can survive happily in the coldest part of the fridge for three to five days, depending on its size. Large cuts (like roasting joints) will last for five days; steaks or chops, for between three and five. If it's pre-packed on a tray, three days will do (if you take the meat from its packaging, it may last longer). Food Science Australia recommends storing meat loosely wrapped, so air circulates but it doesn't dry out. Mince, sausages and offal have a storage time of two to three days. Leaner cuts last longer than fatty cuts, because fat goes rancid before meat does. Telltale signs of meat that's off are a bad smell and a slimy surface.

○ *Cured meats* such as bacon, ham and salami can last up to three weeks in the fridge. You can store whole, dried varieties, such as salami or Chinese sausages, in a cool place for a couple of weeks, but they should be refrigerated once cut.

○ *Chicken* and other poultry is less robust than red meat. Use whole birds within five days and portions within three days.

○ *Fish and seafood* should be used within two days. It's best to remove the original wrapping and rewrap in foil before refrigerating.

○ *Fruit* (pineapple and bananas excepted) lasts much longer when bought unripe and then refrigerated. Most fruits, especially berries, are best removed from their packaging and then stored in perforated plastic bags or on a covered plate. Depending on the variety, unripe avocados can be stored in the fridge for three to six weeks; ripe ones will last two or three days. (The knobbly-skinned Hass lasts longer than other varieties.) Avocados can be ripened at room temperature, and the same goes for mangoes, stone fruit and melons. To speed ripening, fruit can be placed in the fruit bowl with passionfruit, or enclosed in a paper bag with a banana or apple.

● *Vegetables* have varying storage requirements, but most are best kept in the crisper drawer. Leafy greens should be stored in perforated bags or wrapped in a tea towel: use loose leaves within a day or so. Buy tomatoes a little unripe and ripen them at room temperature, then store in the fridge, but (as with berries) chilling does their flavour no good at all, so they are best eaten as soon as they're ready. Removing the leafy tops from carrots, parsnips and beetroots extends their fridge life to several weeks.

EGGS

Eggs need special treatment because without it, especially when raw or undercooked, they can poison us. The most common culprit is salmonella, the cells of which may be present on egg shells or within eggs, and salmonella poisoning is horrible – chills, vomiting, headaches. Showing proper respect begins with buying eggs as fresh as possible (some farmers mark containers with the date the eggs were laid), and as long as possible before their use-by date. Keeping eggs in the fridge isn't a fashionable view, when so many cooks swear by letting them come to room temperature before use, and few supermarkets bother to refrigerate them, but safety and pragmatism are prime considerations in the household, like it or not. Eggs kept in the fridge (in their cartons to protect the porous shells from absorbing other food smells) at or below 5°C (41°F), for anything up to three weeks will be as fresh as eggs stored for a week at room temperature.

Other things to know about eggs:

● Raw eggs (and foods containing them, such as home-made mayonnaise) should be kept well away from ready-to-eat foods such as prepared salads or sandwiches. This applies when preparing food as well.

● Use only uncracked eggs. Don't wash dirty shells, as this removes the egg's natural protective coating.

● Test for freshness by placing a raw egg in a pan or bowl of water: fresh eggs sink; stale eggs stand on their end or float. (A weak shell or fine cracks can also cause the egg to float, but either way this is a poor egg.)

- To store cooked *leftovers*, cool them quickly, cover and refrigerate as soon as possible. Use within three to five days (according to many food experts, cooked rice should be eaten within twenty-four hours).

The freezer

There are those of us who freeze as a major storage alternative and have chest freezers full of sides of meat, fruits and cakes. The rest of us use our freezer compartments to store leftovers, foods we've bought or cooked in abundance, or have bought frozen.

Whatever the case, the important thing to appreciate is that frozen food has the same nutritional value as fresh, provided the freezer temperature is maintained at around -18°C (-0.4°F). This temperature inhibits the growth of microbes and slows the chemical changes that cause food to deteriorate. As with the fridge, it's important to keep the freezer temperature as constant as possible, so avoid leaving the door open for any length of time and avoid overloading.

Packaging is critical. Use heavy-duty foil, cling wrap, sealable plastic bags or plastic containers. The aim is to eliminate freezing air with the food which will lead to frost and possibly freezer burn. (This appears as brown or grey spots, which you can simply cut off: it's not dangerous, just ugly.)

SOME BASIC RULES OF FREEZING

These are similar to those of refrigeration.

- Foods intended for the freezer should be as fresh as possible; cooked food should be cooled as quickly as possible and put into the freezer warm, if necessary.

- Exclude as much air as possible. If you are storing food – a sauce, say – in sealable freezer bags, seal the bag to the tiniest hole, insert a drinking straw through the hole, suck out the air, then seal the bag completely. (Try not to choke on any food particles you extract with the air.) If this appals you, or if you freeze a lot, buy a vacuum sealing machine that extracts the air for you.

- If storing in containers, fill almost completely to reduce the amount of air, but leave a small space for expansion (otherwise the lid might be forced off and ruin everything).

- Meat or poultry can be frozen in its supermarket wrapping, but this packaging isn't strong enough for long-term freezer storage. Unless you're using the food within a month or so, rewrap it in foil or place it in a sealable plastic bag.

● Fat meat has a much shorter freezer life than lean.

● If wrapping individual portions of food, use heavy-duty foil or cling wrap, then stack the portions in a container and label it. (A one-litre container usually holds four to six average servings.)

● Labelling is important and should include both the date and the food, since one cut of meat can look very much like another when frozen.

● Fresh food that you've decided to freeze should be frozen before its use-by or best-before date.

In the event of a power cut, don't open the freezer door. Once the power is restored, check the food is still frozen. Melted ice-cream should be thrown away. Any meat or fish that was frozen raw and has just defrosted should be used immediately. Any that has completely defrosted should be thrown away, as should anything that has been contaminated by thawing meat or fish juices. Turn the temperature control up to maximum for twenty-four hours, then back to -18°C (-0.4°F). Bread and frozen vegetables can be refrozen.

FREEZER LIFE

Bear in mind that most frozen food will be safe for years, though not very appealing in terms of taste and texture after its optimum period. Food bought frozen will have a best-before label for guidance.

Available freezer-life charts give wildly differing times, presumably taking into account what is safe and what is edible. The following list of commonly frozen foods assumes a freezer temperature of -18°C (-0.4°F), and I'm steering towards the more conservative estimates on the basis that you probably don't want stuff hanging around forever anyway.

Raw meat and poultry

● beef (joints and steaks) – 12 months;

● lamb (joints and chops) – 12 months;

● pork (joints and chops, whole and pieces) – 9 months;

- chicken – 9 months;
- mince – 3 months;
- sausages – 2 months.

Fish

- whole non-oily fish – 6 months;
- whole oily fish, and all fish fillets, steaks and cutlets – 3 months;
- meat from molluscs (such as squid and mussels) – 3 months;
- crustaceans (other than prawns) – 3 months;
- prawns (cooked and peeled) – 5 months.

Fruit and vegetables

- melon (pieces) – 9 months;
- peaches, nectarines, plums – 6 months;
- strawberries and other berries – 24 months;
- beans, sprouts, carrots (blanched) – 12 months;
- broccoli, cauliflower – 9 months;
- uncooked potato chips or cakes – 1 month.

Cooked food

- soups and stews – 3 months;
- pasta dishes – 3 months;
- ham – 1–2 months (store Christmas leftovers in small portions);
- pies (sweet or savoury) – 3–4 months;
- bread in shop wrapping – about 1 month; properly wrapped (double layer of cling wrap and plastic bag) – up to 6 months;
- cakes – 2–4 months;
- biscuits – 6 months.

Foods with specific requirements

The quality of frozen *fish* depends entirely on how fresh it is when it's frozen. Commercially frozen fish will not only be cheaper than most home-frozen ones, but it will be better processed (commercially harvested fish is frozen immediately after catching). Any fresh seafood should be scaled, gutted and completely clean before freezing. Fillets and cutlets are easier to freeze than whole fish: wrap them individually so you can defrost only what you require. (Having said that, small fillets can be cooked from frozen if it's at a high temperature.) Large pieces or whole fish should be thawed in the fridge for twenty-four hours, or quickly under running water.

Because *milk* expands when frozen, make sure the packaging is secure. (If it isn't, decant the milk into a container which allows enough room for expansion.) Defrost milk in the fridge.

You can't freeze whole *eggs* in their shells, but you can freeze them whole slightly beaten, or the whites and (slightly beaten) yolks separately. To avoid freezer damage to yolks, which can make them a disappointing addition to cakes, either sweeten or salt them with a pinch of sugar or salt before freezing (label them sweet or savoury, to avoid despair, which is infinitely worse than disappointment). They're fine frozen for 3 months.

STORING HOT FOOD

There is some argument about whether cooked food needs to be completely cool before it can be stored in the fridge or freezer. The argument for not doing so is that anything hot placed in an appliance designed to cool or freeze will reduce its effectiveness, which makes sense. But bacteria multiplies most rapidly in food that has been kept for any length of time at 5°C–60°C (41°F–140°F), so you don't want yours hanging around in the danger zone any longer than need be. The solution, it's suggested, is to cool the food only until steam stops rising and then place it directly in the fridge or freezer. Modern fridges can tolerate some heat without collapsing on you.

Should this go right against your grain, a compromise is to cool your food as quickly as possible by transferring it to the container in which it's going to be stored and standing that, lid off, in a sink of iced water. The longest you should let food cool is for an hour, then whack it in the fridge (uncovered, to minimise condensation if it's still warm) and wrap or cover it once it's properly cool.

According to the British Cheese Board, the only *cheese* really worth freezing is Stilton (wrap it in foil or cling wrap). Hard and semi-hard cheeses can freeze well: they tend to lose their texture and become crumbly, but they still taste okay, so if you have a glut or are going away and have a big chunk you'd like to save, who cares about crumbly? (Use it for cooking.) Hard cheeses like parmesan and cheddar are best grated before freezing, and stored in sealable bags or airtight containers; use from frozen. Soft varieties like cottage and cream cheese are not suitable for freezing. Other cheeses can be frozen for up to 3 months.

DEFROSTING

The safest way to defrost food is slowly, which is to say in the fridge (for twenty-four hours). Food thawed in this way can survive in the fridge for another two days before having to be eaten, because it remains chilled. If you thaw food by running it under cold water (never hot) or defrosting it in a microwave, it should be eaten at once.

REFREEZING FOOD

You can freeze food that has been frozen and then cooked. And you can refreeze food that has thawed slowly and then kept refrigerated because you can't use it immediately. It won't kill you, despite common advice to the contrary, but the quality will be pretty awful owing to the moisture lost, so why bother?

FREEZING HOME-MADE PIES

This is as simple as it gets. Bake them, cool them, wrap them securely and then place them, wrapped, in a plastic bag and freeze for up to four months. When you want to eat one, thaw it in the fridge and heat at 160°C (325°F) for 20 minutes. If it was frozen uncooked, you don't need to thaw it: bake at 220°C (425°F) for 15 minutes, then lower the temperature to 190°C (375°F) and bake for 30–40 minutes.

Home-made pizzas can also be frozen uncooked. Bake from frozen, for about 15 minutes at 190°C (375°F). Don't freeze custard or cream pies.

11

WHAT
TO DO ABOUT
COOKING

The trouble with cooking is that it so easily becomes a chore and a bore that the meal as an occasion can become meaningless. This does no favours to anyone, least of all the cook whose food is eaten unnoticed and unappreciated. And it's actually crazy when households that eat in front of the telly are just as likely to be watching professional cooks smacking their lips over something in filo with a splash of verjuice.

Food, as seen on TV and in exquisitely produced cookbooks, food in our heads, is one of life's great pleasures, and in the last fifty years our fascination for regional cuisines has made it even more so. What don't we know about food from distant places and how it looks in foreign shops chock-full of pigs' heads? My mother grappled with pasta; the tagines, burritos, wontons and kormas which would have meant nothing to her aren't even exotic anymore. They're available ready-made from supermarkets or takeaways that are open until the small hours seven days a week. We're blessed, you might think, when takeaways were once fish and chips or nothing. Why wouldn't a tired and hungry person pick something up on the way home from work as a matter of course, rather than cook from scratch? Two reasons, really: cost and content.

If you're tempted to justify your ready-made meal on the basis of cost, telling yourself that actually it's very cheap given the number of ingredients, ask yourself how come? How come it costs so little when the price also includes packaging, transport and labour? Maybe it does taste delicious, but it almost certainly tastes delicious because it's full of sugar, salt, fat and 'flavours', and this much sugar, salt, fat and 'flavour' on a regular basis is something we may one day live to regret. I'm not saying never buy in – we'd go nuts if there were never any respite from the daily grind, and some takeaway food is brilliant. Just make it a treat: don't go for cheap, go for great and go for now and again. If it's not a treat, it's not worth the money.

What's worth the money is the food we dream of cooking ourselves. All we have to do is get it out of our heads and onto the table via our own very capable hands. When it comes to health, the best way to control what goes into our stomachs is to prepare it ourselves.

There are people who reckon they can't cook and you might be one of them, but cooking isn't like singing. You don't have to be gifted or creative to produce edible food. God gave us recipes and that's all you have to do – follow them. If you truly can't be fagged, this chapter isn't for you. Go back to the section on shopping and understanding labels. For everyone else the simple truth is this: if your household likes the few things you've mastered, you can cook just about anything. The cook's dictum should be: never despair. There are tragedies and sometimes dishes bearing no resemblance to anything we anticipated. Mostly, though, there are triumphs and here's the thing: just about everything savoury is fine on toast and anything sweet can be topped with ice-cream.

I'm not going to tell you how to cook. For that, you can browse the bookshops and pick up a cookbook by any one of the hundred brilliant chefs whose recipes appeal to you. My aim is to address a few cooking fundamentals that have challenged me, like the best equipment, conversion tables, poaching an egg so it sits in a packet, eating more vegetables that aren't potatoes, and sharpening knives. Cooking is infinitely easier with basic facts at your fingertips and proper utensils within easy reach.

HEALTHY COOKING

You don't have to abandon sugar, salt and fat completely. TV chefs tend to use them liberally, because cooking would be bereft without them. The rest of us need to use them sparingly if our health is at risk, in moderation otherwise and in abundance when the occasion calls for them. It doesn't take much to rein them in without sacrificing flavour. It's all in the choices we make, the first of which is how to cook what we feel like eating.

Generally, we steam, boil, grill, fry, bake, poach, braise, roast or barbecue our food. Some people do things in pits as well. I don't know why. By and large, as a very general rule, all cooking compromises the nutritional value of food to a certain extent (except in the case of tomatoes), so least cooked, least compromised. The methods below are ranked according to the favour they find with nutritionists:

- *Steaming*, where food is put on a rack and cooked over boiling water in a covered pan, is regarded as the healthiest form of cooking because nothing nutritional is lost in the cooking liquid.

- *Boiling*, when food is steeped in lots of liquid (which is then discarded) was once regarded as healthy, but turns out to be less so, owing to the loss of vitamins and minerals thrown out with the cooking water. Generally speaking, it doesn't do much for flavour either. (This doesn't apply to foods such as soups, when the nutritious liquid is retained and flavourings are added.)

- *Stewing* involves cooking meat and/or vegetables in a liquid (often frying them gently first), with flavourings such as herbs and spices. A distinction is sometimes made between stewing and *braising*, a stew being cooked on top of the stove and a braise cooked in the oven. Both methods are nutrient- and flavour-friendly.

- *Poaching* means cooking food gently in relatively little liquid (usually water or stock) in the oven or on the stove.

- *Roasting* means cooking in an oven, using little fat (preferably oil), for which reason it's a comparatively healthy cooking method. When roasting meat, any juices from the joint are often used for basting, since roasting can have a drying effect, and saved for gravy, or jus as it currently likes to call itself.

● *Grilling* (sometimes called griddling) involves food being cooked directly over or under heat. This is also a comparatively healthy cooking method, since it requires no fat and any fat in the food itself melts away. There is, though, a risk that blackened or burnt food can produce carcinogens (proving yet again just how delicious carcinogens can be), so avoid overcooking. *Barbecuing* is really just another word for grilling, though traditionally outdoors.

● *Shallow-frying (sautéeing)* refers to quick cooking in a minimum amount of fat (often, and preferably, oil) in a frying pan. *Stir-frying* is similar, but the food is cooked over a higher heat and even less fat is required. These are by far the healthiest ways to fry food, especially if olive oil is used, inflicting least damage to nutrients and colour.

KITCHEN BASICS

There are charts in all kinds of cookbooks that list what you must absolutely have in your kitchen and provide conversions of alien oven temperatures or measurements. But you can never find them when you need them, so here they are again, in one place.

THE TRUTH ABOUT COOKING WITH OLIVE OIL

There are two bones of contention when it comes to cooking with olive oil. One is that it loses its nutritional value when heated; the other is that heat converts the otherwise unsaturated fat into a saturated fat by hydrogenating it. The science I have chosen to believe contradicts both these theories. According to the Olive Oil Source website (which I grant may have a vested interest), heating has no effect on the health qualities of olive oil, only on its flavour, because overheating causes oxidisation. As for it being converted to an unhealthy fat when cooked, the website quotes an oil chemist Dr A Kiritsakis, who has found that all oils oxidise and hydrogenate minimally when repeatedly heated to high temperatures, but that olive oil is less resistant to the process than others. There you are, then.

Equipment

My kitchen equipment reflects my affection for baking as well as the usual getting-food-onto-the-table, so what's essential for me may not be for you. On the other hand, if you want to be prepared for all kinds of cooking, the basics (as discerned from my own kitchen), are:

- two thick-based frying pans (one large, one small);

- a wok for stir-frying;

- a set of stainless-steel, copper-bottomed saucepans, including a steamer;

- two baking trays (one large, one medium) for roasting;

- large ceramic oven-to-table dishes for lasagne, fish pie, etc.;

- assorted cake tins (ideally made of aluminised stainless steel);

- cast-iron, enamel-coated casserole with lid;

- range of fluted flan trays;

- heatproof pudding bowls;

- copper bowl for beating egg whites (I actually don't have one but they're recommended for best outcome);

- glass measuring jug;

- assorted mixing bowls (plastic, metal, glass) of various sizes;

- food strainers (sieve and colander);

- assorted knives – a serrated knife, a 25-cm (10-in) chef's knife, an 18-cm (7-in) paring knife – of the best quality you can afford;

- a steel for honing knives;

- a very large fork to go with the carving knife;

- a pronged carving tray;

- a vegetable peeler;

- a grater;

- a whisk;

- a rolling pin;

- tongs;

- wooden spoons of various sizes;

- a ladle and one or more slotted spoons; other large spoons for transferring food from one thing to another;

- a potato masher;

- a fish slice;

- measuring scales;

- a tin opener;

- a food processor;

- an electric beater.

Pots and pans

It's worth lashing out on saucepans and other cookware, because they will stay with you for life and a rubbishy pan can ruin an otherwise perfectly cooked meal. When choosing saucepans, frying pans, baking trays and other cookware, there are a few things to consider in addition to size, weight and colour, like what they're made of and why one material is better than another. I scrimped on a non-stick baking tray, which burnt the bottom of my Christmas turkey: it took me ages to realise the problem was the tool, not the workman or my oven. Similarly, a saucepan with a heavy, reinforced (you can tell by looking at it) base, is recommended, to reduce the likelihood of food sticking or burning.

Reactive/non-reactive

Some recipes specify non-reactive saucepans: this is because certain metals react chemically to specific ingredients (especially those with a high fat or high acid content) and the reaction will affect both the taste and colour of whatever you're cooking. Reactive metals are iron, non-stainless steel, copper, cast iron and aluminium. (The Food Standard Agency suggests we avoid cooking anything highly acidic, like tomatoes or rhubarb, in aluminium pans because the food can acquire an aluminium taint which will affect flavour. But they also advise that the risk of absorbing aluminium into our diets via cooking in aluminium pans is minimal.) Stainless steel is non-reactive, as, obviously enough, is anything ceramic.

The problem is that neither ceramic nor stainless steel are the best conductors of heat – they respond slowly to changes of temperature and may develop hot spots. Copper is the best heat conductor; iron and aluminium are also good. So, look for a compromise, in other words, a combination of great heat conduction and non-reactiveness: copper-bottomed stainless steel; stainless steel with a base that's fortified with aluminium (which also extends up the sides, with luck); or iron or aluminium lined with enamel. They may be pricey, but they're a fine household investment.

Non-stick

Who hasn't stared at a non-stick pan and wondered if some non-stick poison has just attached itself to the bacon? The answer is that it almost certainly hasn't, but it's worth bearing in mind that, if heated to an astonishingly high temperature, non-stick coatings can release toxic particles and gases, including trifluoroacetic acid (TFA), which may trigger chills, fever, headaches and other flu symptoms.

The Australian Consumer's Association road-tested non-stick frying pans in 2004 and decided that, although the danger exists, the temperature has to be around 500°C/930°F, which is unlikely to happen in the domestic kitchen. They also noted that TFA has not been shown to have harmful long-term effects or that non-stick cooking poses a safety risk. If heated to 'extremely high' temperatures means burnt beyond recognition, you will probably have tossed out the wrecked food, so breathe easy. Similarly, don't panic should you think you have inadvertently ingested particles of non-stick stuff – they go in, they go out. But should your pan be chipped I'd get a new one: it's not the non-stick surface itself that makes you unwell, but what it emits when subjected to those extremely high temperatures.

Knives

As with pans, buy the best you can afford (go to a cookware shop and get advice). Professionals reckon you only need three knives for everyday use, provided they're good ones. Your main considerations (price aside) are the thickness of the blade, the weight of the knife and the size of the handle. Very simply, blades range from thick and sturdy to fine and super-sharp. The weight is actually less important than the 'weighting': longer knives should be equally balanced between blade and handle; shorter knives require more weight in the handle, for finer control. All handles should fit comfortably in your hand so you can use them easily – so try a few for size.

Sharpening knives

Some good-quality knives rarely need sharpening, but when they do your best bet is to take them to a knife-sharpener, because it's a serious skill. Honing, on the other hand, you can easily manage with a steel at home and it's worth a few swipes up and down every time you use the knife. To use a steel, hold it with the tip pointing down. Rest the knife blade against it at an angle of about 20° (the blunter the knife, the greater the angle). Swipe the knife down the steel and flick your wrist as the blade passes the end of the steel, turning the blade over to bring the cutting edge back up the steel towards you. Professionals apparently sharpen their knives up rather than down the steel, but in our household this would lead to arm loss.

Microwave ovens

You need to make up your own mind about using a piece of equipment that cooks foods by altering the magnetic polarity of their atoms, when nice conventional cooking heats foods by friction Who cares what it means? Some people swear by microwaves, others think they emit death rays. My view is that every home should have one, even if it's just to reheat meals, warm milk and melt chocolate or butter.

Simplicity of reheating is one of the joys of the microwave. The other is that is uses up to 70 per cent less energy than a conventional oven. This should count for more, but in fact it seems to count for less because 'microwave' seems to war in our imaginations with 'green' (which is a bummer for the inventors who had such high hopes for it). After forty years on the market, it has just never become the anticipated alternative to conventional cooking, but, that said, roughly nine in ten UK and three in four Australian households own one.

Many people use their microwave far more comprehensively than I do: they steam vegetables and rice and fish in it, bake lasagne and shepherd's pie, and cook puddings. Food Science Australia says food cooked in a microwave is as nutritious as food cooked any other way; in terms of vitamin leaching, it is preferable to boiling and as good as steaming. I don't know anyone who's successfully used theirs to cook meat from scratch, but according to manufacturers, the failure of meat to brown is a sign that the cooking is gentler than other methods.

Reheating in the microwave

There are rules for reheating in general (see page 208) and a special caveat for reheating in microwaves, even if it is one of the appliance's strengths. The results can be uneven if you don't stir the food halfway through the process and/or leave it to stand after cooking and before serving. The larger the portion, the greater the vigilance required: food heated to just-about-warm in the middle is an invitation to bacteria. On the other hand, it's undoubtedly healthier to reheat food quickly in a microwave than to keep it warm for hours in a conventional oven.

What are the risks?

I have no qualms about blasting stuff for two or three minutes, but the idea of food spinning round and round while waves of micro pass through it seems more like an hour in front of an X-ray machine than cooking. Which is silly. The fear of contamination by radiation from microwaves is baseless: the microwaves stop the minute the power is turned off and they are incapable of making either the food or the oven radioactive – unless, of course, your oven door has a faulty seal in which case microwaves can leak from it. It's sensible to check from time to time that the door closes properly, and if you have any doubt get it inspected by a technician.

On the same basis, don't stand with your face close to the oven watching your meal going round and round, however mesmerising. Your door probably isn't leaking, but what if it is? Be extra careful around a microwave if you have a pacemaker, as radiation can interfere with its functioning. And don't operate the microwave when it's empty, as the waves will have nothing to focus on, sparks will fly and you risk damaging the magnetron tube.

Microwave burns

The most harm you are likely to do yourself is a bad burn from steam that bursts from a microwaved dish when the cover is removed. If you are using cling wrap to cover food, puncture holes in it to release any build-up of steam and remove it with great care.

A further risk is scalding from drinking overheated liquids. This is especially pertinent to the heating of a baby's bottle, which is a perfectly safe thing to do provided you check the temperature of the milk on your wrist rather than in the baby's mouth.

Using plastic in a microwave

There is a slight risk of plastic migrating into food, especially fatty food, when it reaches a high temperature. Cling wrap shouldn't come into contact with the food in a microwave in any case: dishes are best covered with paper towel.

On the subject of dishes, many are labelled suitable for microwave use, but there's no legal standard. Plastic containers as a general rule (ice-cream containers especially, because they are flimsy and meltable) are less reliable than glass.

·········· SOME COOKING CHALLENGES ··········

A challenge for the designated cook can be anything from a recipe failure to flames in the frying pan. Those below have had to be addressed in our household and so, presumably, in many others.

Getting household members to eat vegetables

The sad truth is that not everyone grows to like vegetables. Especially those vegetables not cooked in fat. If this is a problem in your household, you can get around it in all sorts of ways:

- Sneak vegetables into curries, stir-fries or any stews which are predominantly spicy or aromatic. This is especially good for beans, spinach, red capsicum, carrot, pumpkin, sweet potato, cauliflower, zucchini (courgette), eggplant (aubergine) and mushrooms.

VEGETABLE SOUP

Soup is a great option for vegetable avoiders or picky eaters. You can get all five food groups into the same delicious dish. What follows is a very close relative of minestrone and includes as many vegetables as you can muster. It's a main meal for a medium-sized household of averagely hungry people.

Boil 1 cup of macaroni in a pan of salted water, cook until al dente, then drain. Meanwhile, soften 2 chopped onions in olive oil, add three rashers of thick bacon (chopped) but only if you like it, 3 cloves of garlic (crushed), 1 sliced carrot and 1 sliced red capsicum. Cook until browned. Add 2 x 400-gram (14 oz) tins of tomatoes and 4–6 cups of stock. After five minutes, add a handful of green beans, and after another five minutes add 1 cup of sliced cabbage. When the vegetables have softened (but not collapsed), add the cooked pasta and a 400-gram (14 oz) tin of cannellini or haricot beans (drained). Season with salt and pepper, flavour with a spoonful of pesto if you like it, and sprinkle with parmesan and some fresh basil before serving.

- Add them to a tomato-based pasta sauce (good for carrots, celery, zucchini, eggplant, rocket, red capsicum).

- Spread them about in fried rice (peas, red pepper, mushrooms, onions).

- Brush with oil and roast, grill or barbecue (red capsicum, eggplant, zucchini, pumpkin, sweet potato, onions). Serve as an accompaniment, as a sandwich filling, or with couscous or rice.

- Boil or steam them, puree them, flavour with salt, pepper and any complementary herbs or spices, dilute with water, stock and a dash of cream and call them soup (anything you like, really).

Cooking the perfect poached egg

Remove the egg from the fridge in advance to get it to as close to room temperature as possible. Crack it into a cup: if the white is runny (almost watery), forget it, as you need it to set immediately when added to the pan. I consulted a local egg farmer, who says freshness isn't the guarantee of albumen-rich whites. Runny whites can be a result of the hens' diet, so (though freshness should be a given) checking for set-ability is the more reliable indicator of a happy outcome.

If the egg white looks good, bring a deepish quantity of water to the boil in a saucepan, then turn it down to a simmer. Stir the water to create a small whirlpool, then slide in the egg. (Some people suggest adding vinegar to the water: this isn't essential in my experience, but a dash speeds up the setting process and keeps the whites white.) Cook until the white has set around the yolk in an oval package, then remove the egg carefully with a slotted spoon. Don't be tempted to cook more than two eggs at a time, because each addition changes the temperature of the water and poached eggs hate overcrowding.

If the above method doesn't work for you – if, for instance, the whites break up regardless, or they form a funny shape – try shallow-poaching eggs in a frying pan in just enough water to cover them. You won't get your perfect oval package, but you will get a poached egg. (If you're still not happy, try melting a little butter in a pan, breaking the egg/s into it, putting a lid on the pan and semi-steaming until set.)

Dressing a salad

Salad is nothing without dressing – not just green salad, any salad: pasta, rice, couscous, tomato. Here's a recipe for your basic vinaigrette, followed by a suggested variation.

Once you have the hang of varying, go for your life. Essential for both dressings is a decent oil: my preference is for extra-virgin olive oil.

The *simplest vinaigrette* is a combination of oil and wine vinegar – roughly in a ratio of four parts oil to one part vinegar, plus salt and pepper – but the ratio really is a matter of personal preference. To the basic mixture you can add crushed garlic, sugar and mustard to taste. You can either mix it in the salad bowl, shake in a screwtop jar or whisk in a bowl.

The fancier version requires 2 cloves of garlic, sea salt, 1 heaped teaspoon of raspberry jam, 1 heaped teaspoon of Dijon mustard, the juice of ½ lemon, 1 tablespoon of red wine vinegar, 4 tablespoons of virgin olive oil, and freshly ground pepper. Crush the garlic and grind to a paste with a pinch of sea salt. Mix in the jam, mustard and lemon juice, and whisk briskly until you have a thick, oily paste. Add the vinegar, then the olive oil, gradually mixing until you have a thick dressing. Add pepper to taste.

Making a decent gravy

'Jus' is currently more fashionable that gravy these days when it comes to sauces made from pan juices. To make it, pour excess fat from the pan after frying or roasting, leaving just the meat juices and any little bits of meat still hanging around in the pan as they add flavour. Pour in a hefty slug of white wine and cook over medium–high heat until the liquid is reduced to a cup or two of wondrous essence. Add a little water and any seasonings you like. It's simple, quick to make and the result is delicious.

For some tastes, however, this is a skimpy sauce. Those tastes prefer a gravy that is thick – well, thicker – rich and brown. As above, pour off excess fat (but in this case not all of it) and add a tablespoon or two (depending on the quantity of gravy required – it's worth making enough gravy for the next day's shepherd's or cottage pie from leftover meat) of plain flour to what remains. Brown the flour over a low heat, stirring to prevent sticking, and add salt to taste. When the flour is a good rich colour, slowly add water, whisking the whole time to deter lumps. Add a slug of wine and keep whisking. Check for flavour.

Crisping potatoes

Cut potatoes to the required size and parboil for 7–10 minutes (depending on the size of the pieces). Drain them well, then return them to the saucepan and toss with a tablespoon or two of oil, plus salt and pepper. My preference is then to roast them, in which case place fresh oil in a baking tray and preheat in the oven on the shelf above the meat. When the oil is hot, add the potatoes (they should sizzle when dropped in). Cook for about forty minutes, tossing every now and then to prevent sticking.

For sautéed potatoes, heat some oil in a frying pan and add the parboiled and drained potatoes. Cook, turning often, until the potatoes are soft inside, golden-brown outside and crisped all over.

Melting chocolate

There are three ways of doing this, all of which begin with breaking the chocolate into small pieces that you place in a heatproof bowl. You might then set the bowl (uncovered) over a saucepan of simmering water, put it in a preheated (110°C/230°F) oven, or microwave it at the highest setting for 15 seconds. Chocolate is sensitive to overheating and steam, which make it grainy, so remove it from the oven or the microwave before it has melted completely. The heat of the bowl will finish the job. Check the chocolate in the oven every minute or so; if microwaving, repeat the microwaving process if necessary, but only after a minute or so when you're sure melting hasn't occurred. If the chocolate does go grainy, add a little oil.

Adding flavour

Even recipes from books by the best cooks can occasionally end up tasting of nothing, which is seriously disappointing when it's flavour that makes food pleasurable. The taste sensations our palates recognise and we are attracted to, either separately or in a finely balanced combination, are sweet, sour, bitter, salt, umami (the Japanese word for savouriness, as in cheese and monosodium glutamate) and, most recently identified, fat. Our preferences are personal and some of us are infinitely more sensitive/discriminating than others, but the fact is that food which is truly disgusting for one person may well be seriously hideous for everyone, so it helps to train your palate. When you cook, taste as you go so you can adjust as required. If flavour is lacking, the dish may only need extra salt or pepper, something sweet (sugar, mango chutney, anything appropriate to the dish) or something sour (lemon juice, vinegar, wine).

Experiment with herbs and spices: garlic; fresh ginger (especially in Asian dishes); fresh green herbs like mint, basil, thyme, oregano, chives (especially in Italian or Thai dishes); aromatic spices such as coriander, cumin and cardamom (for Indian and Middle Eastern flavours); paprika, cayenne or chilli (for heat, according to taste). The possibilities and the combinations are endless. Four anchovies from a jar are a great alternative to salt in any manner of dishes, from koftas to stews.

Don't underestimate onions: not only do they add fine flavour to just about any savoury dish but (raw or cooked) they count as one of your five-a-day vegetables. They're very nutritious, containing vitamin C, calcium, iron, folate, magnesium and zinc.

Never be afraid of adding wine. Don't worry about the alcohol content (when including it in a dish that children will be eating, for example), because alcohol evaporates with cooking and all that's left is the flavour. With this in mind, don't add it at the end of the cooking process as a thinner – it needs to be cooked for at least ten minutes, no matter who's going to eat it.

Cooking perfect rice without the benefit of a rice-maker

This how I produce fluffy rice. About half an hour before you want to serve it, assuming you are feeding four, put 6 cups of water in a largish saucepan and add 1 cup of rice. Bring to the boil, uncovered, and simmer, keeping the flame low or it will boil over and leave a glutinous mess. When the rice is almost done (test a few grains: they should be resistant but not rock-hard), take the pan off the heat and put the lid on. When the rest of the meal is almost ready, check the rice again and Bob should be your uncle. If, however, it looks too wet or is too gluggy, strain the rice into a sieve, run it under cold water, tip it into a dish, cover with paper towel and place in microwave until hot. If you don't have a microwave, you can remove the nearly cooked rice from the heat, strain it under cold water, place it in a buttered dish, cover the dish and finish cooking it a conventional oven at a low to moderate heat. Brown rice takes longer to cook than white.

Fixing curdled or separated sauces

Curdling and separating tends to occur with emulsion sauces that contain eggs: hollandaise, béarnaise and custard (all cooked sauces) or mayonnaise (cold). Hollandaise and béarnaise both include egg yolks, vinegar or lemon juice, water and butter: the problem is getting these not-very-compatible elements to amalgamate happily.

The ingredients should be combined very slowly in a double boiler (or a bowl over a pan of simmering water) on low heat. Should the eggs begin to scramble, remove from the heat at once, add more lemon juice and whisk frantically. (A wire whisk is essential for all sauce-making because of its magic, lump-disintegrating qualities.) Should the sauce separate (fat from liquid) as you add the butter – which, for hollandaise and béarnaise, must be done so slowly that you may collapse from boredom in the process – remove the pan from the heat, add a little water, and again whisk like mad. For custard, which won't need lemon juice, add a little more cold cream or milk and whisk. If necessary, strain before serving.

Most such sauces suffer from heating too quickly, so it helps not just to remove it from the heat but, if necessary, to cool it rapidly by plunging the pan or bowl into iced water that comes about halfway up its sides. Then whisk and whisk.

A remedy for curdled mayonnaise, which clearly won't be caused by overheating, is to tip the failing version into clean bowl, add another egg and whisk again.

Combating cake disasters

According to the Australian *Women's Weekly* cookery gurus, many cake-making problems are related to oven temperature. If it's too hot, a cake might:

- shrink;
- develop a raised crust around the edge;
- brown on the outside, but stay runny inside;
- rise, but crack on the top;
- sink during cooking.

Undercooking, or cooking at too low a temperature, may cause the cake to:

- sink;
- shrink;
- wrinkle after cooking;
- remain pale and sticky on top;
- (with fruit cake) remain doughy after cooking.

If a sponge cake is flat and tough, the flour hasn't been folded properly into the mixture. A gentle circular motion is required.

Cleverly using leftovers

Turning yesterday's lunch or dinner into today's meal and tomorrow's stock eliminates waste and encourages true inventiveness in the kitchen. Culinary invention carries its risks, but the joy of a triumph makes it well worth the effort.

Most leftovers don't require modification from their original form. Pasta and rice dishes, soups, stews and curries need only careful storing and reheating. Some foods are worth deliberately cooking in greater quantities than required for a meal, with leftovers in mind. The trick is to use next day, not next week.

Suggestions for leftovers and/or surfeits:

- pasta, rice – salads;

- risotto/pilaf – rice balls;

- potatoes (steamed or boiled) – salads; fish, meat or vegetable cakes or balls; frittatas; shepherd's/cottage pie; fry-ups, such as bubble and squeak;

- other vegetables (steamed, roasted or boiled) – salads; puréed soups; frittatas; pizzas; savoury pastries like samosas;

- pulses (chickpeas, dried beans, etc.) – salads; soups; mashed for dips;

- fish – fish pie; fish cakes; fried rice (prawns);

- roast meat – shepherd's pie (lamb) or cottage pie (beef); salads;

- bread (stale) – breadcrumbs for toppings, coatings, stuffings, etc.; croutons;

- eggs – meringues, mousses (whites); mayonnaise, custards, ice-cream (yolks);

- cream or sour cream – pastry;

- yoghurt – ice-cream; cakes;

- milk – custard; sauces; scones and pancakes (sour milk).

REHEATING

A common mistake we make when reheating food is failing to bring it to the recommended temperature, which is 75°C (165°F) or steaming hot. This may be because we have never been familiar with the recommended temperature or we're just too hungry and tired to care. Warming food through, which is to say to any temperature between 5°C and 60°C (40°F and 140°F), just isn't good enough, as bacteria thrive in this danger zone; few will survive 75°C (165°F). Don't try to warm cold food by simply covering it in a hot sauce (gravy, say), as this will raise the temperature of the food just enough to thrill any lurking bacteria and then you'll be sorry.

COOKING WITH LEFTOVER WINE

The rule, according to experts, is never use for cooking any wine you wouldn't drink, but this is less about safety than about flavour. I have never stuck to it and though it's perfectly possible that sometimes a sauce or stew I've made has been a little more bitter than is desirable, no one has been rude enough to say so and I haven't noticed. The critical question, really, is when wine is beyond drinking. The answer? 'Not as soon as you'd expect.' Put wine in the fridge with its cork or cap in place and it will be drinkable for at least four days. What's more, if you transfer the wine from the bottle into a smaller screwtop bottle that you fill to the brim (to prevent further oxidising), it might last up to a month and still taste like wine. If old wine makes your food taste metallic, then it's too old.

Useful cooking conversions

OVEN TEMPERATURES

Recipes may describe oven temperatures in any one of four ways: in words (from Very slow to Very hot); in degrees Celsius or Fahrenheit, or as 'Gas Mark' 1 to 9. It's a total pain not to know what the equivalents are, so here goes. The verbal descriptions can vary, but those below are the most common:

° Celsius	° Fahrenheit	Description	Gas Mark
110–130	225–250	Very slow	¼–½
140–150	275–300	Slow	1–2
160–180	325–350	Moderate	3–4
190–200	375–400	Moderately hot	5–6
220–230	425–450	Hot	7–8
240	475	Very hot	9

MEASURING INGREDIENTS

Just as irritating is not knowing what a cup equals in grams or ounces, and in millilitres or fluid ounces; let alone what a 'stick' (a US measure for butter) weighs – the answer to which is that 1 stick equals 112 grams (4 ounces).

Cup and spoon equivalents are even more complicated, because their sizes vary between continents. For liquid measures, one Australian cup equals 250 ml, one UK cup is 284 ml and a US cup equals 237 ml, so it helps to know where your recipe comes from. (To be honest, there's not that much in it and the differences aren't usually critical). A US cup of butter or sugar, for example, is 250 grams or 8 ounces. A US cup of flour is 112 grams (4 ounces).

Spoon measures can also be a little elusive, but usually in Australia one spoon (teaspoon, tablespoon, any old spoon) means a level spoon; a large spoon means a heaped spoon. Again, though, just to confuse the issue further, the Australian and UK tablespoons are 20 ml, while an American tablespoon is 15 ml, so you have to be on the ball. In general, it's also handy to know that 3 teaspoons = 1 tablespoon; 4 tablespoons = ¼ cup.

The following charts are based on conversions from the US websites www.convert2cook.com and www.scienceofcooking.com:

Solid measures

Ounces (oz)	Pounds (lb)	Grams (g)	Kilograms (kg)
1		25	
1½		40	
2		50	
3		60	
3½		100	
4	¼	112	
5		150	
6		175	
7		200	
8	½	225	
9		250	
10		275	
12	¾	350	
16	1	450	
	1¼	575	
	1½	675	
	1¾	800	
32	2	900	

Ounces (oz)	Pounds (lb)	Grams (g)	Kilograms (kg)
	2¼	1000	1
	3		1.35
	4		1.8
	4½		2
	5		2.25
	6		2.75

Liquid measures

Spoons/cups	Fluid ounces (fl. oz)	Pints	Millilitres (ml)	Litres (l)
1 teaspoon	⅙		5	
2 teaspoons	¼		10	
1 tablespoon	½		15	
2 tablespoons	1		30	
4 tablespoons/ ¼ cup	2		60	
⅓ cup	2⅔		80	
½ cup	4		110	
⅔ cup	5		140	
¾ cup	6		170	
1 cup	8	½	250	
1¼ cups	10		280	
1½ cups	12		375	
2 cups	16	1	500	
2½ cups	20		560	
3 cups	24	1½	670	
3½ cups	28		780	
3¾ cups	30		840	
4 cups	32	2	900	
4½ cups	36		1000	1
5 cups	40			1.1
6 cups	48	3		1.4
8 cups	64			1.8

FEEDING CHILDREN

Here's the truth: some children are great eaters, others are picky; some are picky all their lives, some improve with age; great eaters can all of a sudden go picky on you and there seems to be nothing you can do about it. There will be people whose lifelong training is in the getting of children to eat properly and I bet their advice works a lot of the time. But only in extremis, in my view, would you take a child who eats only sausage and sweetcorn to an expert. As in all things with children, stages come and go and you don't have to treat every quirk of every stage.

It's a big responsibility, creating good eating habits, but the alternative is grim. Overweight kids with tooth decay aren't good advertisements for parenting, whatever the extenuating circumstances, and there aren't that many of them: only a world-war veteran who's been hiding in a cave to avoid capture could plead ignorance. Rule one for feeding kids is to eat well yourself. You know the elements of a balanced diet, and they're the same for your children. Identical, in fact. Keep things low in saturated fat, salt and sugar; high in complex carbs, vegetables and fruit; and provide respectable amounts of protein. Keep your own less-than-healthy treats to a minimum. Have mostly nourishing food in the house, offer it in the most tempting ways you can, and let your child eat it or not eat it, as the case may be.

Eight things to know about feeding kids

1. Toddlers can eat the same food as their parents, only much less of it. Go easy on fibre, because their systems can't handle too much of it.

2. Watch salt and sugar intake from the word go. If children don't get used to them, they won't miss them.

3. Watch the drinks: kids need milk and water – mostly water once they're on solids, and when they're thirsty that's what they'll drink unless you offer them sugary stuff instead. Small amounts of fruit juice (not 'fruit drinks') are fine, but even juice is high in fructose (fruit sugar). Soft drinks, sports drinks and 'vitamin' drinks are particularly harmful to young teeth because of their high acid content. If your child goes off water, offer it in a bottle or with a straw.

4. It's generally agreed that children up to the age of two require full-cream milk. From then on, they may be offered reduced-fat versions. But really, why would you? Unless your child has a serious weight problem and consumes buckets of milk every day, the amount of fat in full-cream milk (around 3.8 per cent) is relatively small while the taste differential is large.

5. Don't give toddlers uncooked eggs: there's a salmonella risk and an allergy risk – egg is the most common food allergen for very young children.

6. Avoid nuts for very small children, especially peanuts. There's an allergy risk and a risk of choking.

7. Limit snack foods, which are often high in saturated fat: read all labels diligently. Take advantage of after-school hunger by offering healthy food – I'm not talking steamed veg with lentils, but fruit or a wholemeal sandwich.

8. Adolescents may: a) eat a lot of rubbish; or b) eat next to nothing. The only way to deal with a) is to offer plenty of alternatives. You don't need to deal with b) unless you fear seriously disordered eating (in which case get professional advice).

Handling avoidance

Many, many children gag on anything green for a long time. Who knows why? Are they born with a gag-on-green reflex, or do they learn it? It's true that some green foods have a texture that isn't immediately palate-friendly – I'm thinking half-cooked pea, pointy bits of bean or sodden mass of spinach. Some children remain disgusted by the taste and texture of tomatoes or bananas or eggs all their lives. Really, all their lives! Maybe it's a survival instinct based on inherited memory or maybe it's not, but who cares? Understanding the dislike may help you accept it but won't change anything, so my advice is not to dwell. If the poor thing hates it, don't offer it. Move on. Offer different foods regularly in small amounts, insist they are tried, and if they're rejected wait for a while before offering them again. Don't sulk if the experiment fails and don't make children stay at the table once they've tried it.

Also, don't blame yourself if food goes uneaten: maybe you are a terrible cook, but I doubt it. Anyone can chop potatoes into chips, parboil them for 8 minutes, toss them in olive oil and bake them for half an hour. They look like chips, they are chips and they're nutritious and delicious. Maybe you will burn them as a matter of course. Even so, plenty of children have grown into healthy adults in homes where the cooking was less than gourmet. Just make sure that what you offer falls within the boundaries of healthy eating. There's nothing wrong with tuna or baked beans from a tin.

EATING NICELY

Food aside, you want mealtimes to be pleasant family experiences when a) you can chat and b) you can teach your children manners (oh yes!). There are rituals attached to eating which make children pleasant or unpleasant company at the table and these have nothing to do with how much or what they eat. The sooner they are learnt, the better.

I accept that what counts for me won't necessarily count for you, but the basics count for everyone. In order of importance:

- Don't stuff your mouth full of food.
- Don't chew with your mouth open.
- Don't talk with your mouth full.
- However you use a knife and fork, don't stick your elbows into your neighbour's face when cutting food.
- Don't start eating before everyone has been served.
- Don't leave the table until everyone has finished eating.
- Don't eat with your elbows on the table.

STAYING CALM

Confronted by an overly picky eater, you need to be firm, but you also need to stay calm. You need to know your child, and how long and how insistent 'firm' needs to be before you back off (which ought not be confused with giving in).

Try not to put a value on particular foods. 'Treating', or rewarding, kids by giving them sugary or junk food sets up all sorts of unhelpful precedents. I know it can be hard to avoid – you apply the policy at your place and it doesn't exist at their friends'. The trick is a sense of proportion: prohibition can be counter-productive. We had a jar from which our daughters were allowed two sweets a day, after dinner. None of them has a very sweet tooth (though this may be a fluke of nature). Do your best; try not to be obsessive.

Packed lunches

School lunches can be a total pain, because not only do you have to think of what to put in them, but once you've decided on the regulation sandwich, fruit, juice and a snack bar, the box can still come back with only the snack bar eaten. You take the snack bar out and then nothing gets eaten.

I'm in two minds about all this: either you try really hard to be adventurous with pasta salads, felafel and couscous which is lovely for your own sense of virtue, or you give them what you know they'll eat because it's more or less what all the other kids are eating. If your child's appetite is small, keep portions small – sandwiches cut into quarters and fruit into delicate slices.

In Australia, each state and territory offers guidelines for school lunches. In both Australia and the UK, most groups seem to agree that a lunchbox should contain the following:

- 1 portion of vegetables;
- 1 portion of fresh fruit;
- 1 portion of dairy (cheese, yoghurt, milk);
- 1 portion of protein (lean meat, fish, beans);
- 1 portion of starch (bread/roll, crackers, pasta, rice).

As yoghurt and milk mightn't fare that well in hot weather, use an insulated lunchbox or freeze yoghurt the night before (it will thaw during the morning).

The UK Food Standards Agency suggests that the school lunchbox protein portion may consist of nuts, but owing to the increasing incidence of nut (especially peanut) allergies in children, many schools discourage their inclusion in kids' lunches. The FSA also suggests great lunchbox menus for different age groups, for which they give nutritional values and a broad idea of cost. Prices clearly won't apply outside the UK, but you'll get an idea of their comparative value. Here are a couple of examples.

VERSION 1

- banana sandwich (wholemeal bread);
- tomato;
- hard-boiled egg;
- low-fat fruit yoghurt;
- box of raisins;
- semi-skimmed milk.

Total cost: 60 p

VERSION 2

- chicken and couscous salad (with spring onion, capsicum and cherry tomatoes);
- pear;
- banana-flavoured milk.

Total cost £1.20

A final thought. As soon as you can, let children pack their own lunches the night before.

12

DRINKING SENSIBLY

We might be able to survive for months without food, but if we don't drink we die within days, poisoned by our waste products. Lovely, I know, but between appreciating how much we should drink and dying for want of it are levels of dehydration, ranging from imperceptible to seriously damaging. Any level is best avoided, really, especially by those of us born before 1960, who mostly drink less than we should and are still wondering what made everyone else so thirsty. When, we ask ourselves, did it become essential to have about your person a large quantity of water, as if death for want of it was imminent, even though you are on a bus in town and it's raining?

The answer is that, somewhere along the track, someone decided we needed to drink eight glasses of water a day for perfect health, and the manufacturers of bottled water said, 'Fantastic!' It's in the region of right, but according to more recent research by authorities including Kidney Health Australia, if you're in good health the rule of thumb is to drink when you're thirsty, which will vary according to factors such as the weather and how physically active you are.

······ FLUIDS: HOW MUCH DO WE NEED? ······

The thing to remember is that we are hydrated not only by drinks but by food (especially fruit and vegetables) and by certain chemical reactions within the body itself. The World Health Organization advises that a 70-kg (11 st) man needs 2.5 litres (85 fl. oz) a day of fluid from both food and drink; a woman weighing 58 kg (9 st) needs 2.2 litres (74 fl. oz); and children from 10 kg (22 lb) need one litre (36 fl. oz). This broadly translates in liquid terms to between six and eight medium-sized glasses of something a day which don't need necessarily to be drunk. Water remains the recommended drink to quench thirst, but it can be fruit juice, tea, coffee – anything except booze – so no need to be gagging over your fourth glass of water: have another cup of tea or eat an orange. It's true there is caffeine in tea and coffee, but provided they're drunk in moderation at any given sitting, the levels aren't enough to counter the hydrating effects. And you can't beat an orange.

Signs of dehydration

Chronic under-drinkers tend to stop noticing when they are thirsty. Early signs of dehydration, which you can easily miss, include:

- severe thirst (which can feel normal);
- almost no desire to pee;
- dry mouth and lips;
- dry eyes;
- headache;
- tiredness;
- dizziness.

In more extreme cases, additional symptoms might be:

- severe cramps;
- loss of skin elasticity;
- clammy hands and feet;
- fainting;
- burning sensation in the stomach.

An important, but not infallible, indicator of dehydration is colour of your pee. Dark brown isn't good; clear and straw-coloured is great. Just keep an eye on it, and factor drinking regularly into your day even if it does make you pee more to begin with. Your bladder recovers from the shock and your trips to the loo soon return to normal.

Tap versus bottled water

As far as I'm concerned, there's no argument. Unless you're travelling in countries where the quality of the water is a known health hazard, there's no real reason to drink anything other than tap water. Not only is the cost of the bottled variety outrageous compared to tap in both Australia and the UK (over a hundred times more expensive, depending on where you live and what you buy), there is the huge cost to the environment of packaging, chilling and transporting bottled water. (A plastic bottle is reckoned to take up to 450 years to decompose, though which 450-year-old tip attendant told us that I don't know.)

Anyway, for what? In most cities there is little discernible difference between tap and bottled, as endless blind tastings have shown, and there is nothing to be gained nutritionally or health-wise from bottled water. What's more, the UK consumer organisation Which? found that once opened, if a bottle isn't kept in the fridge, bacteria levels in the water could increase. If you don't like the taste of your local tap water, try refrigerating it or invest in a filter system. One reassuring fact for bottled-water users: fear of plastic from the bottle contaminating the water is groundless because, according to a study conducted by *Choice* (Australia) in 2005, bottles used for water are either made from glass or polyethylene terephthalate (PET), so they rarely (if ever) contain plasticisers. As well, according to Cancer Research UK there is no evidence (despite the claims made) that re-using or freezing plastic water bottles (or leaving them in cars) causes cancer. It's not, however, a reason to reject tap water.

FLAVOURING YOUR WATER

If you hate the taste of water unadorned, you can always add mint or a squeeze of lime or lemon juice. If that doesn't do it for you, and you're loath to use industrial-strength cordials, the following home-made drinks are delicious.

Lemon squash

⊙ 2 lemons

⊙ 2 litres (4 pints) water

- 750 grams (1½ lb) sugar

- 50 grams (2 oz) citric acid

Peel the lemons and place the peel in a processor of some sort with 500 millilitres (1 pint) of the water, blitz for a minute, then strain. Pour mixture, plus the remaining water, into a saucepan, add the sugar and stir to dissolve, then bring to the boil. Squeeze the lemons, add the juice and the citric acid to the syrup, give it a good stir, then strain and bottle.

Keep it in the fridge, but it never stays there long enough to go off. The same goes for the recipe below, which is almost identical except it contains elderflowers and more sugar, and is steeped while the flavour develops.

Elderflower syrup

- 24 heads of elderflowers

- zest and juice of 2 lemons

- 2 litres (4 pints) water

- 1 kg (2¼ lb) sugar

- 50 grams (2 oz) citric acid

Place elderflower heads in the water with the lemon zest, bring to the boil and leave to stand overnight.

The next day, strain the liquid, add the sugar and bring to the boil. Add the lemon juice and citric acid, stir, strain again and bottle.

TEA AND COFFEE

Where would we be without them? I say we, but me – where would I be? I need coffee in the morning to get the day going and tea in the afternoon to relax before the final push. And both are fluids, even if we are constantly being alerted as to how much caffeine is healthy to drink. 'In moderation' is the favourite term of government health agencies and this seems to average around three cups of coffee and six cups of tea a day. Of greater concern might be how much sugar or full-fat milk or cream you add to those cups, which, as the lawyers say, is a matter for you.

A decent cup of tea

Australians drink 700 grams (25 oz) of tea per year, which is a lot, but the British drink more: around 2.1 kilos (5 lb). The preferred style is 'white with one [sugar]' and the preferred method of delivery is via teabag. Given that this usually involves dunking a teabag in a cup filled with water from a kettle which may have boiled a few minutes before, then jiggling the bag to get the colour right, it's pretty amazing that we do it as often as we do. The process is getting the least possible from the poor tea leaf.

What it suggests is that we buy and drink tea largely as a matter of habit and regardless of outcome because the ritual of making and drinking it is comforting in itself. Most of us choose teabags over loose-leaf tea in the interests of mess management, but then we must ask ourselves: what actually counts here – mess or a great cuppa? I personally hate a teabag, mostly because it never produces anything tasting like tea and what's in the bag looks like dust.

This turns out to be overly harsh. I sought the advice of David Thompson, renowned tea expert from Australian tea merchants Larsen and Thompson. He explained that what is actually in the bag are very small leaves, which produce quicker liquor (a technical term meaning faster brew) than large leaves and whose taste is designed not to offend. The large tea companies blend leaves from several countries (Kenya, Sri Lanka, India) from plantations which produce leaves all year round even though tea is a seasonal crop. Their leaves won't be of premium quality because the main criterion is price-acceptability (an increasing challenge as the amount paid to the tea farmers rightly rises), but they deliver a consistent flavour.

David Thompson's view is that if you are going to use a teabag, make the tea in a pot exactly as you would make tea from loose leaves, because the same four elements are critical. These are: the amount of tea; the amount of water; the temperature of the water; the time allowed for the tea to brew. To make great tea:

- Warm the pot so the water temperature isn't too dramatically reduced after being poured from the kettle.

- With black tea, allow approximately 2 grams (roughly 1 teaspoon or teabag) of tea per person. The exact quantity will depend on the size of the leaf: use a heaped teaspoon for full-leaf tea, and a level teaspoon for small or broken leaf – but anyway, none of this 'and one for the pot' business.

- Pour the water from the kettle (roughly 1 cup per person) while it's still boiling, because the temperature releases the tea's flavour.

- To maintain the temperature of the water for as long as possible, cover the pot in a tea cosy or a tea towel.

- Allow tea to brew in the pot for between three and five minutes before pouring.

If the water isn't boiling and if the tea isn't allowed to brew, the result is coloured water with virtually no flavour. This no doubt accounts for the 'white with one' habit: warm, sweet watery milk that has turned a brown colour might taste nicer than amber-coloured water with no flavour. To experience the true flavour of tea, give it a go without milk and sugar.

David Thompson recommends a test that might encourage you. He suggests we do this every time we open a new packet of tea (leaf or bags) because every batch is different, despite the tea manufacturers' claims. In any case, it will allow you to discover the strength of brew that suits your palate.

- Make a pot of tea for three people, following method above, using 3 teaspoons of tea leaves (or teabags if you must) and 3 cups of boiling water.

- Allow the tea to infuse for three minutes, then pour a third of the pot contents into a cup. Taste.

- Wait a minute, then pour another cup. Taste.

- Wait another minute and then pour the final cup. Taste.

- If you are going to add milk, add it last and gradually until you find the strength you like.

TYPES OF TEA

There are loads of teas, thousands if you include blends and flavoured versions, but there are four basic types: black, green, white and oolong.

Black teas (Assam, Darjeeling, Ceylon, etc.), which get their colour from a natural oxidation process, are those we associate with the everyday cup of tea. Increasingly popular are flavoured black teas, the most popular of which are probably Lapsang Souchong, a strongly flavoured smoky tea, and Earl Grey, whose flavour is achieved by having bergamot sprayed onto it after curing. Orange Pekoe, you might be interested to know, isn't a flavour, but a description of the size of the leaf.

Green tea, usually served in a glass, is produced from unoxidised leaves and is valued for its high concentration of polyphenols (antioxidants). The flavour is usually sweet and fragrant. It should not be prepared with boiling water: boil the water and allow it to cool before pouring over the leaves.

White tea is a luxury commodity. It's the least processed of teas, and is made from leaf buds that are hand-picked twice a year. It is mellow, and less bitter than green tea, with a grassy/floral flavour.

Oolong (meaning 'black dragon') is produced from semi-fermented leaves, and is a cross between green and black tea. It's widely appreciated for its benefits to digestion.

Like wine, tea quality is often defined by the growing region. And also as with wine, the best teas are expensive: the common or garden teas that most of us drink daily are like cask wines – nothing wrong with them, but they by no means deliver the commodity's full potential. If you like the taste of tea, experiment.

A decent cup of coffee

As far as I'm concerned, a rubbish cup of coffee in the morning can mar an otherwise perfect day. It's why I prefer to make my own, which I do in a percolator: after pouring, I add warm milk – this is what suits me.

Huge amounts of anxious consideration are given to what constitutes the best cup of coffee, but the best cup of coffee is only the one you like best and everyone has their preference. That said, I can't go as far as recommending instant coffee: typically, lower-grade coffee beans are used, which produce average-tasting coffee supported by massive advertising.

POSSUM MAGIC?

A little known property of Lapsang Souchong is its possum-deterrent quality. Make the brew as usual, cool it, and pour into a spray bottle. Spray it wherever you wish to deter a possum and, lo, the possum will be deterred (according to my sister's garden centre).

SOME FINER POINTS OF COFFEE-MAKING

I'm sharing these with you because, with the rise and rise of domestic espresso machines, imagining you are a barista is a common fantasy but according to real baristas, like Mark Hickman, whom I met on a plane, it's not so simple. You need to understand your machine, for a start. You need to read the instructions and follow them, but be prepared to experiment. You need to keep the handles clean and the water fresh. You need to know when things aren't going well.

Generally, espresso coffee takes around 25 seconds to be expressed. Temperature can affect the beans in the hopper: if the beans get hot, they expand and can sweat, which generally results in a decreased flow, so the grind itself needs to be adjusted. A finer grind will result in more densely packed coffee and a slower pour; a coarser grind will result in a quicker pour because the water faces less resistance as it works through the coffee. If coffee pours for too long, it can pick up a burnt and over-cooked flavour. If it pours too slowly and fails to extract enough oil from the coffee, its flavour is weak and thin, with no real aftertaste.

The milk is of great importance to both the flavour and the texture of a white espresso coffee. Overheating will burn the milk and so prevent it developing the smooth texture and creamy shininess that every skilled barista looks for. Baristas say the 'right' temperature is when you can't hold your fingers on the side of the jug for more than two to three seconds.

Tips

However you make your coffee, buy decent-quality beans. There's nothing wrong with pre-ground coffee if you can live with the gradual loss of flavour once the packet is opened, but investing in a good grinder if you don't have an espresso machine is, in my experience, worth every cent. Specialist shops ought to have fresher beans than supermarkets, but don't necessarily.

- Buy only enough for a week or two (you know how much you drink – my percolator takes four rounded scoops for four medium mugs), and keep in an airtight container, out of the light and at room temperature. (Refrigeration or freezing will extend the life of the coffee, but not the flavour. Coffee is porous and can absorb smells as well as moisture. Freezing may cause coffee beans to shrink and curl.)

WHY PLUNGER JUGS BREAK SO OFTEN

On four separate occasions in my kitchen, before I signed up for the percolator, I pressed down the plunger of a cafetière and the beaker shattered. Near-boiling water full of grains spewed across the benchtop and down into the drawers beneath it, then all over the floor and into my shoes. How can this be avoided?

● Don't place a heated plunger beaker directly on a cold surface, as it could crack.

● Don't force the plunger down when the coffee is brewing: wait until there is no resistance.

● Handle and store the beaker with the respect you'd accord any glassware, as even a hairline crack may cause it to fracture when filled.

● Beakers don't appreciate having the coffee stirred with a metal spoon. Use only plastic spoons.

● Some cafetières suffer from the beakers being too tight a fit in the metal frame, so when the glass of hot liquid expands, it's squeezed and shatters. Test your beaker for ease of removal before its first outing.

● **Grind the beans just before use. Follow the manufacturer's instructions to achieve the required texture. (Plungers, for instance, require a coarser grind than a drip filter or an espresso machine.)**

● **For plunger coffee, use very hot but not boiling water.**

Weak coffee is simply not worth making. Be generous with your coffee-to-water ratio. In a plunger or percolator, say, for every 110-ml (4-oz) serving cup use a rounded scoop of ground coffee. If you're using a metal percolator, don't remove it from heat until the perking has stopped.

THE HARD STUFF

Drinking alcohol sensibly is as pertinent to our health and happiness as eating properly, which means it pays to know safe drinking limits. If your happiness is improved by a decent drop, it also pays to know how to choose it, store it and serve it.

Safe drinking

Unsurprisingly, advice concerning safe levels of liquid refreshment is as confused by inconclusive science as the advice on food, and it's arguably more problematic because, like it or not, alcohol in excessive quantities is shocking for our health even though it's a legal substance and most people's drug of choice.

The amount of available research into exactly why alcohol has the long-term but apparently random effects it does is woeful. What we know for an absolute fact is scant. It makes most of us feel great to begin with, drunk eventually, hung-over as a result, alcoholic if we're prone to addiction, very ill if it damages our organs, then dead if we don't mend our ways.

The trouble for those of us who drink regularly is knowing when we're heading for trouble and when our ways need mending. The time frame is increasingly tight and the outcome increasingly sinister for a pastime that has given so much pleasure to so many since Adam was a boy. I, no question, associate alcohol with fun and relaxation, and to this end I drink at least five days out of seven. I stick more or less to the current guidelines on safe intake (see page 229), but if I'm out and about I forget them, which puts me at risk on several levels.

THE MILLION WOMEN STUDY

Oxford University's Million Women Study, which looked at the relationship between low–moderate levels of drinking among women in the UK and their risk of cancer, published a report in February 2009. The findings, widely reported in the press, were alarming to the point of incredible: just one alcoholic drink a day, whether it's wine, spirits or beer, 'causes an extra 7000 cancer cases – mostly breast cancer – in UK women each year'. It was the kind of study-speak that drives an ordinary householder crazy. What did it mean? Was every woman in the UK who had a drink a day bringing about another 7000 cases? Were the 7000 women who were getting the extra cancers drinking one a day, and if they were, what was everyone else drinking?

The study was based on the average alcohol consumption of 1.3 million middle-aged women attending breast-screening clinics between 1996 and 2001. Followed up seven years later, one in nineteen of them had been diagnosed with cancer. The more the women drank, the more likely they were to develop cancer.

It was unclear how the authors eliminated cancers caused by unknown agents, or fathomed the increased risk to individuals in percentage terms, but the message was clear. For every drink per day that we drink, the greater our risk of cancer.

The UK's NHS noted the strength of the study, but was disinclined to change its existing recommendations, which were for women to avoid binge-drinking and to consume no more than two to three units of alcohol per day. The arguments that ensued didn't clarify the matter. It became clear that there was no safe level for drinking for some people, but exactly who these people might be is a mystery. Variables include smoking, age (pre-menopausal women were at far greater risk of breast cancer than were post-menopausal) and genetic make-up.

In Australia in March 2009, the National Health and Medical Research Council (NHMRC) issued new guidelines. These noted that there is no level of drinking that can be guaranteed safe or without risk, but that if healthy men and women drink no more than two standard drinks a day they reduce their lifetime risk of harm from alcohol-related disease or injury. The US National Institute on Alcohol Abuse and Alcoholism advises that moderate drinking is two drinks a day for men and one drink a day for women.

So who and what to believe? The best advice, when weighing the impact of drinking on your health, would seem to be that you consider the following:

- How much do you enjoy drinking and why?

- Is your drinking within current guidelines?

- Do you smoke?

- Are you pre-menopausal?

- Do you (man or woman, because it applies to both) have a family history of breast cancer?

Finally, what is your attitude to risk-taking in general? In the end, that's what it comes down to. Drinking alcohol carries a risk and it's up to the individual to consider what it means to them – it's not dissimilar to travelling by car. If we're looking for some perspective, though, it's worth noting that smoking is reckoned by far to be the largest single cause of cancer and accounts for a third of all diagnosed cases; obesity and other diet-related factors are reckoned to account for another third, and alcohol, one-twentieth. If that's a case, I'm resting it.

BINGE DRINKING

This is not to be confused with going on a bender. A bender is a spree that can last days or weeks. Binge drinking is setting out to and succeeding in getting totally hammered in a very short space of time (a few hours) or, at least, drinking far more than is recommended.

According to the Australian Bureau of Statistics, about one in eight Australians drinks at a risky or high-risk level. 'Risky' is defined as seven or more standard drinks in one day for males and five or more for females, and 'high risk' as eleven or more standard drinks in one day for males and seven or more for females. In the UK, the 2007 General Household Survey revealed that 41 per cent of men drank more than four units, and 34 per cent of women drank more than three units, at least one day a week. Twenty-five per cent of men and 16 per cent of women reported binge drinking, defined as eight or more units for men and six or more for women, at least one day a week.

The trouble is that on a great night out, high-risk or binge drinking isn't all that hard to achieve. Why it should be avoided is succinctly summed up by the Royal College of Psychiatrists in the UK, who point out that:

⊙ Alcohol is a tranquilliser and it's addictive.

⊙ It skews your judgement – think road accidents, regretted sex, aggression, overspending.

⊙ Alcoholic poisoning can cause severe hangovers, gastritis, internal bleeding, unconsciousness and death.

⊙ Despite drunken euphoria, alcohol can cause depression.

⊙ It can lead to memory failure.

⊙ It can cause brain damage.

⊙ It can cause psychosis.

And if that's not enough, even moderate drinking can cause sleep disruption. Regular, immoderate levels of drinking are linked to a range of serious health problems including cancers, diabetes and cardiovascular, liver and mental diseases.

DRINKING GUIDELINES: 'UNIT' SIZES

The recommended maximum amount of alcohol we should drink, over one week, is fourteen units for women and twenty-one units for men. The size of a unit is shockingly smaller than you might imagine (pour water into a measuring jug and see for yourself). Below are those listed in Australia's NHMRC 2009 guidelines:

- One unit of wine is 100 ml; a standard glass of wine is 150 ml (1.5 units); there are 7.5 units to a bottle.

- Champagne served in a flute is roughly 150 ml and equals 1.4 units.

- One unit of spirits is 30 ml (2 tablespoons).

- One unit of fortified wine (port, sherry, etc.) is 50 ml.

- Beer units very according to country. In Australia, a low-strength stubbie (375 ml) is 0.8 unit; a mid-strength stubbie is one unit; and a full-strength stubbie is 1.4 units. In the UK, ½ pint (225 ml) of regular-strength beer, lager or cider constitutes one unit; the same quantity of 'export-strength' beer (Stella Artois, Heineken, etc.) is 1.25 units, and of extra-strong beer (Special Brew, Diamond White, etc.), it is 2.5 units.

- One 'standard' alcopop (spirit-based, premixed drinks such as Bacardi Breezer, etc.) is 1.7 units, but their alcohol content varies, so read the label.

Wine-glass sizes vary, of course, and one glass may hold as much as 200 ml. Wines also vary in strength, usually between 11 and 15 per cent alcohol, so it's worth acknowledging the glass size and checking the wine label.

MINIMISING THE RISKS

Since we're all agreed that too much alcohol is a bad thing for both our health and our wellbeing, we need to minimise the damage to both by embracing sensible drinking, which includes any or all of the following:

- Pace yourself. Aim for a maximum of one unit an hour and if this isn't always realistic, at least make every second drink a glass of water.

- Eat before you drink, or at least while you drink, preferably something that takes a while to digest, like pasta. (Eating slows your metabolism, so less alcohol is absorbed into the bloodstream.) Failing that, a glass of milk before you drink is said (but not by everyone) to line your stomach. Don't mix your drinks, not even wines. You're overloading your system with toxins.

- Keep carbonated drinks (like champagne, beer or mixers) to a minimum, because they deliver alcohol to the bloodstream faster.

- Have a couple of alcohol-free days every week, but especially after a relatively heavy session.

- Drink less if you have a small frame or aren't used to drinking.

- Drink less if you're a woman. You are likely to be smaller than the men you're with, and it counts. Women's physical characteristics make them prone to higher concentrations of alcohol in the blood, and to greater health risks at lower consumption levels.

Handling hangovers

Three in four of us get hangovers if we drink too much. They should be enough to put anyone off overdoing it, but they aren't. We say, 'Never again' and know it's a lie.

Typical symptoms are a thumping headache and nausea; at the very least, dire thirst, fatigue and a general feeling of malaise. For some people, a single drink is enough to do the damage, and the effects vary between individuals but, generally speaking, three to five drinks is enough to affect most women and five to six drinks to affect most men. Why we get them is (no surprise here) a matter for conjecture, but there are so many good reasons why alcohol might make us sick that it almost doesn't matter. The following have all been mooted:

- Alcohol is a diuretic and causes dehydration, which produces multiple hangover symptoms including headache, dry mouth and bloodshot eyes.

- As the body can't store alcohol, it's broken down by the liver and converted into a range of noxious by-products including the toxic compound acetaldehyde, which becomes acetate. This process takes hours; in the meantime the acetaldehyde accumulates in the bloodstream, delivering its poison to the brain, the gastrointestinal system and the central nervous system – which is why, when you are very hung-over indeed, you want to die.

- Blame is also attributed to chemicals in alcohol called congeners, which are more prevalent in darker-coloured drinks (rum, whisky) than light (vodka, gin), and sulfites in wines (especially reds), to which some of us are especially sensitive.

- Alcohol can trigger a drop in blood sugar, which can cause headaches and nausea.

- As it leaves the body, alcohol may cause short-term 'withdrawal' symptoms like those of a hangover.

There are as many theories about the best hangover cures as there are reasons to drink. Should you end up with one despite your best efforts, the following remedies are commonly recommended:

- Take paracetamol for headache – aspirin and ibuprofen aren't recommended if your stomach is upset.

- Drink lots of fluids (not a hair of the dog) – your whole system needs rehydration.

- Eat to steady your blood-sugar levels. The most experienced drinkers I know swear by a fry-up, and the science for this turns out to be sound: bacon and eggs contain amino acids, which among other things improve liver function. Your stomach, on the other hand, mightn't be so sure.

Alcohol and kilojoules

The precise effect of alcohol on our metabolism is uncertain. It's a curious thing just how many thin alcoholics there are, and you may think this is because alcoholics don't eat but this is apparently not the case. On the other hand, dieticians assure us that excessive drinking can make us put on weight for two reasons. First, alcohol is laden with kilojoules: in terms of energy content per gram of food, only fat contains more. But this doesn't seem to matter as much as the liver converting alcohol into acetate, which the body recognises as an immediate and effective source of energy which it uses as an alternative fuel to any fat on offer. The fat isn't used, therefore it's stored, so, as with high-fat foods, you are likely to put on weight if you drink a lot and don't burn off the extra kilojoules. Unless you are one of those people who stay thin whatever they eat or drink.

Benefits of alcohol

And so to the plus side – which, medically speaking, is kind of small. In fact, most of the latest findings are a little depressing. Or vague. Or both.

It's generally reckoned that the health-giving properties of alcohol have been overestimated and no one benefits much from any of it. The exceptions may be middle-aged men and post-menopausal women who drink just about nothing (maybe three or four units a week) and who, it's believed, may be afforded some protection against cardiovascular and cognitive disorders (such as dementia), especially if their tipple of choice is a tannic red wine rich in the antioxidant phytochemicals known as polyphenols. Even then, not everyone is of this opinion.

POLYPHENOLS

It is now pretty well acknowledged that to benefit from polyphenols you'd have to down thousands of litres of wine a day. (Please don't try this at home.) According to Professor Valerie Beral, lead author of the Million Women Study, the evidence for protection against heart disease is just not there. She is as scathing about 'the French Paradox', the frequently cited fluke of nature whereby the French eat loads of saturated fat but don't die young and in their squillions of heart disease. She says this has nothing to do with wine but everything to do with the amount of fish and fresh vegetables they eat.

The debate is ongoing (as is the debate about the effects of alcohol on the development of dementia and Alzheimer's disease), and my contribution is this. Alcohol is, in my case and I'm sure I speak for at least a few others, a stress-buster. I nearly always end a long, hard day with a drink and although my shoulders have crept up to my eyes and my back teeth are locked in a deathlike embrace, I relax. It may not be doing much for my heart, but it does a power of good for my wellbeing and my wellbeing must have some bearing on my general health. Or what?

ALCOHOL DEPENDENCE (ALCOHOLISM)

As is well documented, alcohol dependence is a health problem in both Australia and the UK. The consensus is that a person is alcohol-dependent if, over a twelve-month period, they show any of the following characteristics:

- inability to control their drinking (e.g. drinking for longer than intended);

- drinking taking priority over other commitments;

- increasing tolerance for alcohol (that is, needing to drink more to become intoxicated);

- memory blanks, when they can't remember what happened over a period of hours or days;

- failed attempts to reduce their drinking, despite health and/or social problems;

- withdrawal symptoms (e.g. shakes and sweating) if they go without alcohol.

If you or anyone in your household has a drinking problem, get help. This is, of course, easier said than done: to admit you have a serious problem means abandoning the crutch that you haven't necessarily even acknowledged. You may even have joked about it – drinking is a constant source of hilarity – but eyeballing the problem and dealing with it is no laughing matter. It takes courage and commitment.

Happily, there are respected organisations that help with alcohol addiction, offering a range of management and treatment options. In Australia, Lifeline, the 24-hour crisis support centre; in the UK, the national agency Alcohol Concern.

Buying wine

If we are going to limit our alcohol intake, it makes sense to make the most of what's sensible. Beer and spirit drinkers for the most part know what they're drinking and why – they might flip between one variety and another, but only serious connoisseurs are challenged by the choices available. Wine is a different matter: there are so many; they can be so different, and yet so similar; they can be rough, they can be sublime. Moderately serious wine drinkers have a rudimentary understanding of what's what. But the frivolous, among whom I include myself, know not much more than the names of a few popular whites, reds and sparklings. What follows is for anyone in this category.

The aim is to discover what you like at a price you can afford, which will, if you want it to, complement the food you're eating but isn't necessarily the same wine you've been buying for the last five years. Your first port of call should be the person behind the counter at the wine store, bottle shop or off-licence. Tell them what you want to pay, give them a rough idea of the wine you prefer and also what you need it for: as a table wine (when what you'll be eating is relevant) or for quaffing. The more you pay, clearly the greater your chance of finding something superior, but there are great-value wines for under $20 in Australia or £10 in the UK. Most staff know a little about their product – if they don't, only buy from them the stuff you've already tried and liked, then go elsewhere to expand your understanding. And go armed: read wine columns in newspapers and magazines, and ask about recommended wines in your price range.

As with cooking, there are many fine books out there to advise you but, for quick and easy reference, below is a short guide to the most popular varieties. There are two things worth noting before you memorise it. First, although the difference between new- and old-world wines remains distinct, it's diminishing as growers flit about the world learning from each other. (The new world, when it comes to wine, consists of Australia, New Zealand, Chile, Argentina, the USA, Uruguay and South Africa. The old world includes the wine-growing countries of Europe.)

The serious distinction that remains is that old-world wines are, for the most part, named after the regions in which the grapes are grown, while new-world wines tend to be identified by the grape variety. This means that anyone who drinks primarily new-world wines will eventually more or less know what to expect from a particular grape or blend of grapes. They might, however, remain flummoxed by the subtle variations in European wines whose influence is 'terroir' (a combination of the sod from which the grapevines have sprung, and the area's microclimate). A Sancerre, for example, is a sauvignon blanc from the place of that name at the east end of the Loire Valley. The French would argue that it's the Sancerre-ness of it that makes this sauvignon blanc different from any other. But just to confuse you, 'claret' (from the French word *clairet*) describes a full-bodied red from Graves in Bordeaux; the French don't use the word claret – it's a British thing – and presumably before long no one else will either.

Second, if you're matching wine to food, the criterion is weightiness (not to be confused with weight): the lighter the food, the lighter the wine. (The finest pairing I ever had was champagne with perfect potato roesti and fried eggs.) Colour-matching (red wine with red meat, etc.) is no longer the order of the day, since some whites can be heavier than some reds. And the same grape can produce different weights of wine: chardonnays, for example, are traditionally light, but some are medium- to full-bodied, so ask the retailer. You can learn a lot from reading the labels.

The list below is for medium-dry to dry wines, in order of weightiness from lightest to heaviest, compiled with a little help from *Wine Spectator* magazine's website, which notes that the ranking is open to dispute. It provides a pretty good overview, however.

WHITE WINE (FROM LIGHTEST TO HEAVIEST)

- Soave, orvieto classico, pinot gris/grigio
- Riesling
- Muscadet
- Champagne
- Chenin blanc
- French chardonnays (including chablis)
- Sauvignon blanc (also sometimes called fumé blanc)
- White bordeaux
- White burgundy
- Gewürztraminer
- Australian chardonnays

RED WINE (FROM LIGHTEST TO HEAVIEST)

- Valpolicella
- Beaujolais
- Dolcetto
- Rioja
- Pinot noir
- Burgundy
- Barbera
- Chianti classico
- Barbaresco
- Barolo
- Bordeaux
- Merlot
- Zinfandel
- Cabernet sauvignon
- Rhône, shiraz

As well as understanding how light or heavy a wine might be, it's useful to appreciate even vaguely what it might taste like. Labels often describe the weight and the aroma or bouquet as well as recommending food accompaniments. But even a small knowledge of wine types will point you in the right direction. (You will soon notice that descriptions of aroma for different wines can sound not so much similar as indistinguishable.) Also look at the weightiness and then taste the wines to discover the difference for yourself. With thanks to *The Australian Wine Guide* and others, below are loose descriptions of wine types most readily available to the householder.

WHITES

Chardonnay is light- to full-bodied (oaked is heavier than un-oaked and it's a mistake to assume it's always woody). The aroma is fruity or nutty (and may have overtones of mineral or cordite, so they say). Lighter versions are great with fish; the heavier ones, with chicken. It's very food-friendly, in any case.

Riesling is often dismissed as a sweet wine, but there are drier varieties and they should be tried; aroma can be citrus, floral or mineral. Of course it suits fish, but more importantly is a great partner to aromatic Asian food.

Sauvignon blanc has a fruity or grassy aroma, always with a dash of acidity. Again, great with fish but its perfect match, according to those with palates, is goat's cheese. I loathe goat's cheese, but aside from champagne, my favourite wine is a sauvignon blanc, which proves nothing except the diversity of palates whose expertise we are relying on.

Semillon (in Australia, best from the Hunter Valley) has a citrus, grassy or mineral aroma when young, honey with citrus when aged. In France, the grape is mostly used in the production of sweet wines, but in Australia it's often blended with sauvignon blanc for a light dry wine that's suited to seafood and poultry.

Pinot gris and pinot grigio are the same grape variety: *gris* is the French name; grigio, the Italian. It has a floral, peachy, nutty aroma. Try with chicken, fish or pasta.

Verdelho can be dry or sweet, so ask. The aroma is floral or grassy and complements chicken, pork or veal.

Rosé is a light and dry wine; its aroma may be raspberries or sometimes spicy. It can be mouth-numbingly sweet, so know before you buy it – or ask. It's a lovely accompaniment to anything that feels light and Mediterranean.

REDS

Merlot is midway between the light and the heavy reds with an aroma of plums and blackberry. It's great paired with veal, but is safe with any not-too-light/not-too-heavy meal.

Pinot noir grapes can be tricky to grow, so this variety can be pricey – but it's delicious and light. The aroma is cherry or truffle. It's great with salmon or sea bass, and with duck or lamb.

Cabernet sauvignon is a robust red with a fruity aroma but detectable tannin and acidity. It ages well and goes famously well with lamb.

Shiraz is the biggest of the red wines, with the aroma of pepper, plum and/or spices. Have it with the biggest meal you've got – hearty beef stew, barbecued steak, roast pork.

In the end, it's all a matter of personal preference and just to confuse you, any of the above reds and whites might be blended to produce something altogether different on your palate.

How do you know when wine is off?

The two things that most commonly ruin wine are cork taint and oxidation. You can tell one by smelling and the other by looking.

The incidence of corked wine has dropped significantly with the rise in screwtop bottles, but you still need to appreciate the problem. It's caused by the presence of a fungus called *trichloroanisole* (TCA) and you can detect it best by sniffing the cork if the smell of the wine has alarmed you. It's a kind of mouldy pong: Australian wine writer Matt Skinner calls it 'cardboard and mould', though he points out that not every corked wine generates much smell and it's in the nature of the fungus that the more you try to smell it, the less you can. Corked wine also tastes off – not so much mouldy as flat, and the longer the wine stands in the glass, the more obvious this taste will become. The trend towards screwtops takes care of the risk but since they are largely confined to new-world wines, by all means give anything old-world a good swirl and a sniff before sipping.

Oxidised white wine goes a golden-brown colour; oxidised red goes brown. The cause, clearly, is too much oxygen in the wine; the effect is wine that tastes like vinegar.

Wine glasses

There is increasing snobbery attached to the purchase of wine glasses, but wine buffs insist that a superior glass greatly improves the taste of its contents and what non-buff would disagree? The more you pay for your wine, the more worthwhile it is to invest in decent glasses. But you don't have to go mad.

You can survive on one style of superior glass, which should have a tapering bowl and a stem. Always hold the glass by the stem, as clutching the bowl will affect the wine's temperature. You can have different glasses for both light- and full-bodied red and white wines as well as sparkling and fortified wines, but most households manage with three: a champagne flute, a glass for whites and a slightly larger glass for reds.

Since good glasses are very delicate, they must be washed with care. Avoid overly scented detergents: wash each glass, rinse in cold water, drain on a tea towel, then polish with a clean cloth and stand the right way up in a cupboard.

That's enough about wine. On to even weightier matters.

PART 5

MANAGING
MONEY

THE MOST IMPORTANT THING to understand about your money is that the buck really does stop with you. There may be people in the world who care as much as you do about what you are worth, but should your assets and income dwindle to nothing, the problem is all yours. And should you lose track of what you have and learn too late in the day that others are making more from your money than you are, you only have yourself to blame.

Whatever your wealth, it pays to understand how to make what you have work best for you and for anyone else who might be depending on you. This means balancing your books and mastering the basics of saving, banking, borrowing, investing, spending and insurance, all of which are critical sooner or later to everyone not in a religious order. It doesn't mean conquering the All Ordinaries Index. It means making sense of the small print in terms and conditions you're going to swear you've understood, and wading through the jargon to get to the point. It means subscribing to an old-fashioned dictum that the best financial advisers agree is the core to successful money management: live within your means. The alternative could be a stress-induced heart attack and not living at all.

13

BUDGETS AND BANKING

$

For those of us who are spenders by nature, it's a constant and terrible shock to discover that every month we overspend by an amount that's insignificant on the face of it, but by the year's end is substantial. Our choices are to pretend we are solvent because we have endless lines of credit; to watch our bank balance disappear even as we're saying, 'But I haven't bought anything'; or to be master of our fortunes by managing our money prudently, which turns out to be a matter of willpower. This requires us to look at our current practices, to ask ourselves if they coincide with desirable practices and if they don't, why they don't. Then we can haul ourselves into line.

BEST MONEY MANAGEMENT

It starts with a goal: what you would like to achieve from your income over a given period. It might be as modest as living within your means or repaying a large debt, but it could include building a fund to live on while you study, saving a deposit on a property, or accumulating a nest egg for travel or retirement. However urgent it might seem, it needs to be realistic, and you achieve realism by a ruthless examination of your spending habits in relation to your income.

This exercise may already be central to your existence, but if it isn't, I can tell you from experience that closing your eyes and hoping for the best is useless. Don't kid yourself that it's all in your head. Your head arranges information as a matter of convenience and 'not enough money' is never a convenient thought. You need to get the numbers in front of you so you can see how they stack up. This means getting to grips with your daily, weekly, monthly, quarterly and annual cash flow. It's a painstaking process but, once done, you'll know where you stand in relation to your goal.

Your first step is to monitor the traffic of all money in and out of your household for a month, noting every transaction – whether it's in cash, on credit, by cheque, in person, online or by phone. Your aim is to establish how much you're spending, and on what, so keep receipts and a daily tally to be added up at the month's end. For the bigger picture, which includes bills that are paid yearly or quarterly and may not appear in a month chosen at random, you will have to examine a year's bank and credit-card statements: if you haven't kept them, track them online or order them from the bank or credit-card company. You can't leave out anything, no matter how incidental it seems.

You're looking for patterns: regular outgoings like rent, food, tax, petrol, fares, child care, electricity bills or gym membership; and irregular outgoings that turn out to be astonishingly regular, like takeaways, drinks at the pub, pharmaceuticals and clothes purchases. Patterns form the basis of a household budget: fixed income/ variable income; fixed spending and variable spending.

THE HOUSEHOLD BUDGET

Once you have the information at your fingertips, you can calculate each expense as a monthly outgoing and arrange the outgoings in some sort of order. The most practical way is to rank them according to importance to survival, so less essential items (drinks at the pub, trips to the cinema, haircuts) can be lost from the bottom in lean times.

There are loads of budget templates available online, so have a browse, or you could compile a basic one yourself. A good starting point is the kind of household expenditure statement that banks ask you to complete before they'll lend you anything. A very simple template such as the one below might work for you.

	Weekly	Monthly	Quarterly	Annually Average
INCOME				
Householder 1				
Salary				
Overtime/Bonuses				
Interest				
Gifts/Allowances				
Householder 2				
EXPENSES				
Tax				
Mortgage/rent				
Loans				
Credit card/s				
1				
2				
Services/Utilities				
Council rates				
Water				
Electricity				
Gas				
Telephone				
Land				
Mobile				
Internet access				
Household shopping				
Food/supermarket				

	Weekly	Monthly	Quarterly	Annually Average
Pharmacy				
Household insurances				
House				
Contents				
Life				
Car				
Registration				
Insurance				
Maintenance/repairs				
Medical				
GP/specialist				
Health insurance				
Optometry/glasses				
Pharmaceutical				
Scripts				
Cosmetics, etc.				
Clothing and shoes				
Member 1				
Member 2				
Member 3				
Member 4				
Laundry/dry-cleaning				
Travel				
Petrol				
Public transport				
Taxis				
Road tolls				
Alcohol/cigarettes				
Professional body/union expenses				
Children				
Child care				
Babysitting				

	Weekly	Monthly	Quarterly	Annually Average
Uniforms				
School/university fees				
Books and stationery				
Extras (sports, outings)				
Newspapers, magazines, subscriptions, books				
Haircuts				
Leisure				
Bars/cafes/restaurants/takeaways				
Movies/concerts/theatre				
Sports/hobbies [e.g. gym]				
Pay TV				
House and garden				
Repairs/maintenance				
Goods (e.g. plants, white goods)				
Holidays				
Presents				

How you apply your budget to the household will depend on the relationship of household members to each other, as well as the ages of its members. But I consulted a thrifty couple with two small children whose goal is to save as much as they can. They try to live off the husband's full-time income and save the wife's part-time income. When they stray outside their budget limits, they trim, mainly on eating out and holidays. Central to their saving is their approach to day-to-day expenses: each is given a fixed amount, and once it's spent they aren't allowed to withdraw more cash or put anything on credit card. This forces them to live within their means.

Reviewing your monthly finances

The point of the above exercise is to assess whether you have a shortfall or a surfeit at the end of every month, and then to address it. Addressing it is, of course, the tricky part, but it's essential because a monthly shortfall takes no time to become a monetary difficulty and a surfeit neglected is just plain wasteful.

SHORTFALLS

If you identify a shortfall, a series of uncomfortable questions will be required, to which fudged answers just won't do. Are you spending too much or earning too little? Is spending less more achievable than earning more? If it is, and usually it is, what can you live without and what do you absolutely need in order to live? Are outgoings properly prioritised or are they skewed (say, in favour of one member of the household at the expense of everyone else)?

On the basis of your answers, confront the problem and deal with it. No beating about the bush: adopt a position of radical frugality and make the necessary cuts. These may be as small as taking instead of buying lunch (doing this even two days a week could save you $900 or more a year). For most people, keeping credit-card spending in check (and paying it off every month so it doesn't incur interest charges) can make a big difference. (See also Chapter 14 for tips on saving.)

SURFEITS

Should you be in the happy position of scoring a surplus at the end of every month, ask yourself if it's being put to the best possible use. A cushion in the way of readily accessible emergency funds (generally recommended to be the equivalent of three to six months' pay) is desirable. But if there is still money left over, your choice might be to repay a mortgage early or to invest either in some kind of retirement fund or to enhance your income. If investing, you need to understand the options, risks and charges attached without letting greed get the better of you. (For more about investing, also see Chapter 14.)

SORTING OUT YOUR PRIORITIES

Before you consider saving, or upping your mortgage payments, these should be your priorities:

- Pay off or reduce any urgent debts. If you are struggling, try to arrange with the person or institution to whom you owe money a reasonable amount to repay each month.

- If you're self-employed, set aside money regularly to cover your tax; unpaid tax becomes a debt before you know it.

- Pay your credit card off in full each month, to avoid accruing interest charges.

Money by household type

It's a fundamental rule of money that the more we have, the more we want. The very least we need is enough to pay for essentials, so the question for all householders is how much is enough and what is essential. This will be determined by household type.

People *renting a shared house or flat* may have fewer responsibilities (no rates to pay, for one), but their obligations are no less pressing. The first is to ensure that income covers the rent and any agreed bills; the second is to take the future into account, which may seem unappealing but futures, however distant, do need considering. Unsurprisingly, regular failure to meet current obligations will tax the patience and good will of other household members. Even if they are prepared to take up the slack now and again, they are entitled to expel chronically indebted housemates. Failure to meet future obligations may not, on the other hand, feel risky right now, but futures have a way of rushing to meet you and credit-card debts, for example, must be paid eventually.

Single-person households are both worse off and better off than other households. They are worse off owing to the single nature of the household's income, but better off owing to the single nature of the household's priorities. The significance of each of these will depend entirely on the size of the income because it's a brutal fact that living alone costs more per head than living with others. Mortgages, rent, bills of all sorts, while not necessarily being substantially less than those of multi-person households, must be met from that one income. This can be challenging and stressful. With no second income to fall back on, it is crucial to have insurance cover for all critical contingencies (income, buildings and contents, etc.) and an emergency fund.

Above all, single householders must recognise that it's their spending habits that will determine their quality of life, so controlling outgoings is essential. Pensioners with fixed incomes have the least room for manoeuvre, especially if their income is substantially reduced (which it usually is), but even then cutting costs is possible. Help may be available from Centrelink in Australia or in the UK from the Pension Credit helpline.

Members of *multiple-income households* must reach a mutual understanding on expenditure – how much, on what and by whom – because arguments over money are uglier than scrapping over chores, neglect and loyalty. It's an enormous boon if everyone's approach is the same, but mostly it isn't; and, worse, everyone imagines their attitude to money is the correct one, even if it's mean or profligate in the opinion of others. The approach to joint expenditure must, therefore, be utterly pragmatic from day one. Get all cards (debit, credit, metaphorical) on the table so everyone knows what's what. Look at the ideal world; look at the real world. In an ideal world, each member of the household has access to money of their own as well as each other's for shared goods and services. But in the real world, given the cost of shared goods and services (housing, food, utilities, children), what's left for personal use might just about cover fares and lunches.

In an ideal world, when one member of a couple household earns all or the bulk of the income, sharing is negotiated without rancour. But 'What's mine is yours' doesn't work for everyone, especially when priorities differ. Accepting an occasional hand-out that's given with unexpressed but completely detectable resentment is disastrous for the poorer person. Likewise, forking out day after day for stuff that is, in the opinion of the better-off party, neither urgent nor useful, can strain the sunniest of relationships. My personal view is that in couple households – with or without children – where attitudes to money are poles apart, co-existence is possible only where incomes are equal and contributed equally to common expenses, with the remainder entirely the business of its possessor. It's up to you, poorer person: maintain your non-earning status only if you can stand the stress.

BANKING

Banks emerged as the bad guys fom the global financial meltdown of 2008–2010 and we may have much to resent about them, but like them or not we need them. The good news is that since, in addition to the big four in Australia and in the UK, there are a number of them, so we can shop around. This seems to go curiously against our grain: we might compare credit cards before committing, but we tend to stick with the bank we've always had, perhaps because the effort of swapping direct debits and other arrangements is too boring to contemplate. But it's actually easy. If you are fed up with your bank (too expensive, foul customer service), moving is no big deal providing your credit rating isn't appalling (see Chapter 15). The bank you are joining will do the hard work: all you have to do is cancel any automatic debits and credits attached to the account you are leaving before you switch.

The right bank arrangement

The right bank for you is the one that best suits your needs. And this may well be one of the smaller community banks, so don't overlook them when trawling possible homes for your money or a loan. (Some, like the Bendigo Bank in Australia, are committed to returning surplus profits to their members and working with their local communities.)

They all have endless screeds of information describing the huge range of products and services on offer, their schedules of fees and charges, and their terms and conditions. Your very first lesson in becoming money-literate is to read and digest these, even when they look totally indigestible. Scrutinise in particular their charges on overdrafts, interest paid on assorted accounts and the services available to you: internet banking, phone banking, automatic internal transfer of funds from one account to another, bill-paying, overseas transfers and so forth.

The greatest area of contention is fees and charges, so list what the demands on your account might be and hunt down the page on which the bank explains what it will charge you for them. There are websites that compare bank accounts, and credit cards and other loans, so it makes sense to use them and minimise the pain. (Check that the site has a financial licence and bear in mind that some commercial sites may be associated with particular financial institutions.)

Of far less consequence than banks' fees and charges are the sweeteners they offer, like free insurances which lull you into feeling secure but could well be inadequate or inappropriate for your actual needs. Always read the small print relating to any 'complimentary extras'.

WHICH ACCOUNT?

Whatever your circumstances, you need two basic accounts: an everyday account to cover regular/household expenses; and an account for savings that pays proper interest (yes, you do, even though you can't imagine how you can save a cent when you spend everything you earn, and sometimes more, every month).

Everyday/transaction accounts attract next to no interest (and, often, actually none at all). If you spend your entire income every month and constantly teeter on the edge of an overdraft, you need a current account with a competitively priced overdraft facility. If you save regularly, your best option is a low-cost, high-interest-paying account with access to funds when you want them. If, say, you want to use any regular surplus funds to reduce your mortgage, you can arrange an offset account where the interest earned on your savings is used to reduce the interest on your mortgage (either the monthly repayments or the principal).

In many cases, you can open a savings account with as little as a dollar or a pound – and the way to increase it is to put into it dollars and pounds either by direct debit from your transactional account (as per the savings plan attached to your new budget) or as and when you can manage it. Make it a point of honour never to touch these funds until you reach an agreed amount or after an agreed time.

Some high interest–paying accounts require you to commit your funds for a fixed term (term accounts), during which you won't have access to them anyway. Should your savings be substantial and/or you want ready access to them, think carefully before making a lengthy commitment (not least because interest rates could rise during the fixed term). These days, 'paperless' accounts (online or phone banking only) usually offer higher interest rates than standard savings accounts, and there are accounts that reward you with extra interest if you deposit money and make no withdrawals in any one month. Should you be part of a household couple, it makes sense to open a savings account in the name of the lower earner so that the interest earned is taxed at a lower rate.

It's easy to be baffled by the names of bank accounts. But all banks offer broadly the same products – they just call them different fancy things. For clarification, talk to the bank and/or read the brochures to see what's on offer and what the costs are, then decide whether it's right for you. To compare and contrast, it's not a bad idea to drop into branches of a selection of banks and consult the staff: you'll get a feel not only for each bank's competitiveness as regards fees, charges, scope of services and so on, but also for how they score on customer relations. If you can't be fagged to do the hard yards yourself, consult any of the websites that compare financial products but be aware that as information-gathering goes, they might lack the level of detail that you need.

JOINT ACCOUNTS

Joint accounts can be held in the names of any two people for whatever reason, but for the purposes of the household they're especially convenient for the payment of regular bills like rent or mortgage, rates, insurance and utilities.

With a joint account each signatory can contribute a fixed amount monthly to cover agreed outgoings, or both signatories can stick all their income into the account and draw from it at will. Should it be an everyday account, and assuming the

CONVERTING MONEY INTO FOREIGN CURRENCIES

Most householders at some stage have to convert funds from one currency to another, usually for an overseas trip or possibly because they have a second household in a different country. The question is how to get the best deal, and once more shopping around is essential. Even though converting money starts with the bank rates in the local currency, different companies offer different rates according to how clever they are in dealing.

The householder planning a trip looks at the exchange rates on offer and finds two amounts – 'bank buys' and 'bank sells' – which seems a little nuts when in any one transaction you are both buying foreign currency and selling local currency (or vice versa). The selling rate (when the bank is selling and you are buying) is always lower than the buy rate (when the bank is buying and you are selling). In other words, when you are purchasing foreign currency you will get the lower figure, and when you are changing foreign currency back to your own you will get the higher figure.

Tips

◉ Operate on the basis that changing foreign currency back to the local one gets you a better deal. To convert your own currency into another national currency (that's you selling and the bank buying), make the exchange abroad. To convert foreign currency back to your own currency (still selling), do so after you get home.

◉ Exchange rates vary from day to day and there is no guaranteed right time to sell. Watch the market for trends, but don't rely on them absolutely.

◉ Watch out for handling charges and commission on transactions, which can blow any clever manoeuvring on your part. You can buy online from a currency dealer (especially worthwhile if you are exchanging big amounts), or in person at a bank branch. Both Australia Post and the UK Post Office often give reasonable rates and they don't charge commission. Avoid exchanging at airports and Bureau de Change outlets, where rates are definitely less favourable.

◉ Using a foreign ATM to withdraw local currency can be costly. Not only can you get a poor rate of exchange, but you may be hit by additional charges. Check the terms with your bank before travelling.

household is living on a 'What's mine is ours' principle, you could organise regular payments from it by direct debit into a separate, joint savings account.

As you would expect from anything called joint, both signatories have equal liability for the account and equal access to it, although there may be instances where both signatures are required (to set up a direct debit, say). There is, of course, a risk that one account-holder will scarper with the loot, so it's a financial act of faith in as well as a commitment to each other, but a major plus is that, in the event of one account-holder dying, the other can have automatic access to the funds. On the other hand, should one of you be declared bankrupt the account may be frozen and the innocent party's credit record negatively affected. So, trusting though you may well be, keep an eye on your co-accountee's financial wellbeing and be prepared to jump ship in the event of the arrangement looking more risky than convenient.

14

SAVING, SPENDING LESS AND INVESTING

According to the financial experts I consulted, few of us have any real under-standing of the relationship between the money we earn and what we can achieve with it. This may be because achieving anything other than staying afloat seems to be so ludicrously out of the question; or it may be because the language of money (unit trusts, bonds, exchange, hedge funds, etc.) is so unfamiliar that we regard it as an irrelevance. But one way or another, we do need the money we earn to work properly for us and it's not such a mammoth undertaking.

There are three ways of accumulating funds from income: saving, spending less, and investing. If you get to grips with all three, you will be in control of your finances and not the other way round. Your household budget will sort out the micro-management, which is to say saving and spending less. Appreciating what we have, what we expect to have and what we need to achieve is central to the macro, which is to say our medium- and long-term prospects. For this we may need expert advice and there is plenty around.

Bank managers and accountants can help, but only to a certain extent. Bank managers have their own products to sell and not all accountants offer advice on day-to-day money management or investment. Each may well point you in the direction of a licensed financial adviser or planner, however.

In theory (so an actuary told me) financial advisers should be spoken of in the same breath as doctors, with whom we should have an intimate and long-term relationship from which we hope to derive security and comfort. But they aren't and we don't, because historically we view them as dodgy dealers who make a fortune from us by using information that's either compromised or freely available to anyone not too knackered to look for it.

Which isn't completely fair. There may be dodgy dealers and the traditional practice of financial planners receiving commission from companies they recommend certainly has a dodgy component. But commission in lieu of a fee is in the process if being outlawed in Australia and in the UK, and good financial advisers have the expertise to factor your income, your outgoings and your potential earnings into your hopes and expectations in the short, medium and long terms and to convert the lot into a written plan describing how these hopes and expectations can best be met. This is very helpful. They can offer advice on day-to-day spending, medium- and long-term spending, long-term saving and investing, as well as insurance, investments, pensions, superannuation (in Australia) and mortgages. The ever-changing superannuation rules can be confusing, so getting advice on this alone might well be worth the fee. It makes sense to consult an independent financial adviser the minute you commit yourself to a long-term domestic relationship with joint responsibility for bills and money planning, so you can plot a prudent strategy.

Trust and choosing a financial adviser

First, the trust issue: in both Australia and the UK, licensed financial advisers (or planners) are governed by law and they must also comply with the conditions laid down by their regulatory bodies – the Financial Services Authority (FSA) in the UK and the Australian Securities and Investment Commission (ASIC) in Australia.

Having established that the adviser you are considering is licensed by the FSA or ASIC (or is employed by a licence-holder), you should look for:

- proper financial qualifications (check the regulatory body's website for a list of qualified advisers);

- at least two years' experience in the financial-services industry;

- a reliable track record;

- easy accessibility (if it takes ages to arrange a meeting, forget it);

- independence;

- reasonable costs.

Ideally you'll be acting on personal recommendation from a long-standing client, but you and any adviser you choose need to get on with each other. The initial meeting is critical for establishing mutual respect as well as trust. You will want to know what they can do for you; they will need to know what you expect.

A licensed adviser must supply a document setting out information such as the services and financial products they offer, how they get paid (including any commissions, until these are finally phased out), and any interests or relationships that could influence their advice. The initial meeting is usually free and, if agreed, will result in a statement of advice or personal financial plan for a one-off cost (also to be agreed in advance).

When it comes to your personal plan, don't look for answers off the top of the adviser's head. Whose personal circumstances are that simple? You want a written plan, in plain English, which makes sense logically, and you want the advice to be independent and reasonably priced.

Fees

Until 2012, when commission-based fees will be banned in both Australia and the UK, financial advisers may:

- charge you a fee, which might be an hourly rate, project-based or an ongoing percentage of your investments;

- receive a commission, usually a percentage of the investment, from the product provider/s, which might include an initial commission as well as an annual (or 'trailing') commission that lasts for the term of the investment;

- charge you a fee and also earn commission.

Be very clear about what the adviser is earning, where the fee is coming from (they are obliged to tell you) and what you can expect to get in return.

It's increasingly less likely that your adviser's income will depend solely on commission. Both ASIC and the FSA acted because the potential conflict of interest was rarely in the client's favour. But clarify the position anyway. Should your adviser work for a large firm, he or she may not benefit directly from commissions, but if the firm itself receives the commission the advice can't be regarded as disinterested.

The same goes for recommendations of in-house products. Not all in-house products are to be sniffed at, but you want unencumbered comparisons and reassurance that what's on offer is the most appropriate solution for your needs. It stands to reason that the best-value financial arrangement you can have with an adviser is fee-based, but as things stand you may have to settle for paying her or him a percentage of the total value of any investments made on your behalf. The drawback with asset-based fees is that they aren't entirely disinterested. The planner might recommend, for instance, selling a property or drawing down equity from a property (from which asset they can take no percentage as a fee) to increase your investment in shares (from which they can).

SAVING

The key to effective saving is a realistic plan with or without the help of a planner – and the key to a realistic plan is attitude so no moaning and no self-pity. Granted, you need to have some quality of life and tomorrow you could be hit by a bus, but constantly reminding yourself that this is the case is a poor start, as is throwing yourself into a regime that's insanely harsh. You're aiming for firmness of intent and an achievable goal so you can watch your tiny acorn grow into something bigger (even marginally) or a mighty oak of debt tumble branch by branch.

Your starting point is to put money aside each week. If you save $100 a month in a bank account with a modest interest rate, say 3 per cent, at the end of a year you have the money you've saved plus the interest it's earned. Continue to save in that account, don't make any withdrawals for ten years, and you will earn interest on the savings and on the interest you've earned in previous years (this is compound interest). Before tax, after ten years you'll have a fund in the region of $14,000.

Save by spending less

Keeping household accounts is a great start: there's nothing like a notebook full of expenses to remind you of your profligacy and where it can be curbed. There are dozens of ways to cut everyday costs, both big and small, and all need to be considered.

THE BIGGER PICTURE

◉ Reassess your bank fees and other charges. Is your bank offering you best value for your money? Are you paying too much for your loans?

◉ If you're renting but hoping to buy, calculate the difference between your rent and the mortgage repayment you might be able to afford, and put the sum into a savings account.

◉ Reassess your insurance policies (personal, household). Are they good value for money? Do they suit your situation and needs? Are they essential? (See Chapter 16.)

◉ Dump your credit card and use only a debit card, so that you're paying as you go, not borrowing.

◉ Consult an accountant about minimising tax. Why pay more than you need to? It makes sense to know exactly what your allowances and obligations are and how best to go about claiming or meeting them.

◉ Compare utility and internet providers for the best deals. Most offer discounts if you make use of 'bundled' services (e.g. phone/s plus internet).

SMALL WAYS TO CUT COSTS

◉ Switch appliances off at the wall when not in use, to reduce power bills.

◉ Limit car use where possible. If driving is the only practical option, consider car pooling and shared school runs.

◉ Dump the gym. Get an exercise DVD, go for a walk, run or swim. If you need help to get motivated, a couple of sessions with a personal trainer is cheaper than most gym subscriptions.

◉ Limit eating out, takeaways and convenience foods. Cooking from scratch is miles cheaper, more nutritious and almost always tastes better.

- Stop buying coffees and lunches; make them at home and take them with you.

- Shop sensibly for food: plan a weekly menu, use a list, buy in bulk where practical, buy seasonal and look for specials (see Chapter 10).

RETHINK YOUR SHOPPING HABITS

Essential to our long-term happiness, whatever we may think, is buying according to need, not want. This, I appreciate, is a fine distinction when most of us actually need less than we have already (or think we must have), and when we rarely need top-of-the-range whatever we tell us ourselves about value for money.

Spending should be a matter of prioritising: as soon as you decide that you want something, ask yourself, 'Do I need it?' If the answer is yes, then ask, 'Do I need it to be this expensive?' Need, in case you are in any doubt, applies mostly to not going hungry, naked, without shelter or other fundamental creature comforts like soap and toilet paper.

Understanding how to consume modestly and sustainably is as useful as knowing how to invest wisely, but with the advent of easy credit and limitless aspirations, we've lost the knack. We can reclaim it by focusing on saving and there are huge savings to be made by the canny shopper, especially if you have access to the internet.

Top shopping tips

The following information was provided by the canniest shopper I know, Jo Foley, former UK newspaper and magazine editor, now a travel writer, whose expertise is breathtaking:

- Never buy in retail shops if you can avoid it. Sales can be excellent value, but online shopping is less hit-and-miss. If possible, investigate shops to find what you want, note the brand or make and the style/item number, then google the brand to find suppliers. Most prices are far lower than you'll find in stores (fewer overheads) and delivery can be heaps faster than many outlets manage. Check the delivery or shipping costs, however, if you live out of town, interstate or overseas. Stores with websites usually offer lower prices online, so check them out before buying.

- If you aren't sure whether prices offered online are good or bad, go to one of the price-comparison websites and check who's offering the best value. These sites exist for everything from domestic appliances to insurance policies, banks and energy suppliers.

● Use compare-prices websites for last-minute travel deals, but even if you aren't travelling last-minute, check the price on offer from airlines or hotels themselves as well as intermediaries such as booking agencies.

● If you're buying clothing and are prepared to accept a rough approximation of what you want, try one of the general fashion websites, which usually carry a range of brands. Most have detailed information on sizes but, even so, be prepared to have clothes altered if necessary (no change from shop buying, really).

● If you're reluctant to buy clothes online, buy vintage (which used to be called second-hand) from markets and charity shops. Some now have special racks of designer clothes where you can find great bargains, although anything with a label is usually given the reverence (and price) its pedigree deserves. You may not get a Chanel jacket for five bucks, but the price is likely to be in no more than three figures. (Let local vintage shops and market stall-holders know what you like and what you're looking for: you can telephone to find out if there has been a drop from somebody whose taste and size you share.)

● When buying 'in-store', pay cash for large items. Even the smartest shops will offer a discount for ready money. Ask to see the manager or department head and make your offer to him or her.

● If you're willing to accept less than perfect, you'll always get a bargain. Most large stores have special outlets for barely scratched fridges, slightly frayed rugs, or tables with a wonky leg, which can usually be easily fixed.

● Check the small ads in local papers for hotel and office sales. They're great sources of bargain lamps, beds, mattresses, bedside tables, desks and filing cabinets. Check the goods for wear and tear, then ignore the price tag and make an offer.

● Buy in bulk with friends or neighbours, from local 'cash-and-carry' or bulk warehouses – everything from cleaning products to pet food. If you don't know one and don't have access to online information, try the Yellow Pages.

● Buying stuff at auctions can be great value, but you need to do your homework beforehand – especially for big purchases like cars. (In the case of cars, study the details, dimensions and history, and take an expert with you if all you know is the colour you want.) View smaller purchases like tables, curtains or Grecian urns at least once prior to the auction, check the reserve price, decide what you're willing to pay and never go above that figure.

● Auctions are particularly good for art, antiques and jewellery. But buying gems and jewellery is often much cheaper if you're travelling to the place where they're sourced (South Africa and India, for instance, are both great for diamonds, which are mined in South Africa and cut in India; Sri Lanka is great for sapphires, topaz, aquamarine and garnets; South Sea pearls are cheaper in Australia than they are in the South Seas). You'll have to pay tax at customs on what you buy abroad.

INVESTING

Generally speaking, investing means taking a pile of money that isn't required for day-to-day living and placing it somewhere which offers a better return (percentage growth) than we can expect from bank accounts. It can be a precarious venture for the ill-informed and inexperienced; even the most experienced work on the basis that markets go down as well as up, and that a true picture is only achieved if you look at the long rather than short term. On the other hand, prudence, diligence, common sense, good advice and good luck can turn a modest nest egg into a fortune over a period of time. As well as the money market, there is the property market and the worlds of art and collectables to consider. It seriously pays to do your homework: read all the relevant publications (financial pages, property pages, art world magazines) so you are abreast of trends and values, and seek out people in the businesses for inside information.

Best advice when it comes to investment of any sort is to spread the risk – in other words, don't pile the lot into a single enterprise. When it comes to the money market, there are options ranging from 'gilts' (government bonds that pay a fixed rate of interest twice a year and are regarded as ideal for the conservative investor) to high-risk shares in companies whose value may double overnight or halve, depending on the stock market. Banks, brokers and financial planners can all offer advice on the different investment types – shares (literally, portions of a company to whose fortunes you are linking your own), property, fixed-interest investments, cash (the short-term money market) – but ultimately the choice is yours.

Your decision will be governed by the size of your investment pot, the amount you can afford to lose and your attitude to risk in general. Many planners will ask you to fill in a form that indicates your attitude to risk when it comes to your money, but this is daft. Risk isn't central to our needs. The amount of money we end up with is central to our needs, so bets must be hedged. Prudence, says an adviser I consulted, is diversification: investments should be spread between slow-growing and safe, slightly faster-growing and slightly less safe. If you have oodles of money and can afford to take hits, go high-risk by all means; otherwise forget it unless you don't mind recouping a big loss over time.

For most of us, the younger we are, the more risks we can take with the investments we choose; the later we start, the more prudent we must be.

Investing for retirement

The GFC caused confidence in the share market as a reliable source of retirement funds to wobble, but both superannuation schemes in Australia and pension schemes in the UK still offer great tax incentives. And whichever way you look at it you need to save so you have something to live on when you retire, to spare not just the state but anyone else on whom you might become a burden.

A government pension is available in the UK to everyone who has paid National Insurance contributions; in Australia, age pensions are means-tested. In both countries these provisions are, at best, modest. Therefore, after the family home our largest investment is likely to be, or in any case should be, in a fund to support us once we stop earning. This is most commonly via a superannuation scheme in Australia and a pension fund in the UK, though you may also choose to invest more directly – in, say, rental property that provides a regular income stream.

As critical as how we invest is how much we're going to need to be comfortable which is, of course, the length of a bit of string, but the rule of thumb is that we need 60 per cent of our pre-retirement disposable income. Should this be in the region of £40,000 or $80,000, you will need (very roughly, as it will vary according to the current economic climate) a fund worth about £600,000 in the UK and about $1.2 million in Australia. What this means in monthly budget terms depends on how old you are when you start to save. Another rule of thumb, however distant the prospect of retirement may seem, is to start sooner rather than later and, as with any investment, to spread your money between shares, cash and fixed interest (the return on cash and fixed-interest funds is modest, but safer in uncertain times). The danger with a solely shares-based fund is that, if the market collapses just before you are due to retire – and the fund collapses with it – your provision may be decimated. It's a tricky business, no denying it, not only because your future welfare depends on it but because you can only control the outcome to a certain extent, for example selecting, or moving your investment from, high-risk to low-risk funds.

Most of our retirement investments are tucked away in managed funds and dependent on the judgement of unknown people who are never going to be called to account. This hideous state of affairs is why self-managed funds are increasingly popular. Whether you should self-manage will depend on the amount of money you have to invest, the trust you have in yourself to master the market and develop an investment strategy, and the time you have available to manage your investments within the regulations laid down by the law. There is no training required for you to manage your own funds but, unless you are born with a gift for it, there should be. Consider undertaking the minimum training required for a financial planner (contact the regulatory bodies for advice), so you at least know as much as the next slightly informed person.

Both the share market and the property market, should you choose to invest there, carry risks; both need a steady nerve and a degree of expertise. If you hate the small print, if money bores you to sobs, if you can't even bear to think about it, get help.

Superannuation

In Australia, it is compulsory for employers to pay into a superannuation fund for all their permanent employees earning over a statutory minimum; employees may also contribute to the fund and it's a fine way to save, as you pay less tax on interest from superannuation than you do for other savings. The government may also make a matching co-contribution (currently to a maximum of $1000) when low- or middle-income earners contribute to their super.

In the case of the self-employed, there is currently no compulsion to contribute to a super fund, but if you own a company and have employees you may be required to make contributions on their behalf. Casual and part-time workers, as well as some self-employed, can fall through the superannuation net, so if you're in this situation, the onus is on you to make some provision for your future.

Your superannuation savings are available once you hit 60 and stop working (otherwise, at age 65), and in some other circumstances subject to various conditions. Generally you don't pay tax on your super when you cash it in, though the rules are complicated and (of course) some exceptions apply. Should you die before retirement, the fund will be left to your estate (or a named beneficiary, so it is vital that you specify your beneficiary in the policy documents), but with luck you will live to enjoy it by either withdrawing it as a lump sum (to pay off your mortgage, for instance) or reinvesting some or all of it to give yourself an income.

Anybody about to retire should consult a financial adviser for the full range of products available, and what might best suit your particular circumstances, but broadly you are looking at three (plus permutations). A lifetime pension provides a guaranteed income until you die and has the advantage of security but the disadvantages of zero flexibility, lower returns than other products, and dying when you do. A life-expectancy annuity is calculated according to the length of time you expect to live. You guess. Women, for example, are reckoned to live until they are 86, so their income is calculated on a 26-year payout period if they buy the annuity when they are 60. Another variation on the theme is the ever-popular allocated or account-based income stream (pension or annuity), favoured by four in five retirees. This enables you to withdraw money, including lump sums, as and when required (though you must make at least one withdrawal, for a set minimum amount, annually). Whatever is left in the account can be left to your estate when you die, although it may be precious little.

Pension schemes

In the UK, employees may or may not have access to company pension schemes. Companies aren't obliged to offer them and few do. But, as in Australia, you do need to make some provision for retirement. It doesn't have to be via a pension fund: you could choose to invest elsewhere (in property, collectables or the stock market), but pension funds have the value of being tax-effective and of producing a guaranteed regular income for life. From April 2011, it will no longer be compulsory to buy an annuity with a pension fund. Amounts can be drawn down according to need provided the pensioners can show they won't run out of cash. Pensions in the UK are taxable apart from 25 per cent of the fund which can be taken tax free on retirement.

IS A HOME AN INVESTMENT?

Whatever anyone says, the biggest investment most of us make is in the family home. This used not to be the case – the family home was once a place where the family lived until the last member died. But the extraordinary capital growth in residential property over the last forty years has changed everything. Not only has the cost of homes increased obscenely relative to earnings, but their value as personal or family assets has risen exponentially.

As a result, those who can afford to buy their own home now regard it as a nest egg: cash can be raised by swapping the property for something smaller and cheaper, or by accessing the equity (the difference between the property's worth and what is owed on it). Both options are handy, though they're not appropriate for everyone. You can downsize once too often and find yourself distressingly uncomfortable because you've moved into something that is just too modest for your needs; you can draw down once too often and find the debt attached to your home has replaced the security it offered.

So, as far as investments go, keep the importance of your home in perspective. You will always need somewhere to live. Buying beyond your means in the hope that you will end up with a socking-great profit down the track is dangerous. You can't predict the housing market even if history suggests a home is a relatively secure asset.

Investing in property

Investing in the rental (buy-to-let) market is attractive on two counts: one, it's less daunting and unfamiliar than the share market to investors who have bought and sold their own homes more than once or twice; two, bricks and mortar look so much more substantial than notional shares in a company run by executives who seem to take most of the profit into retirement with them. You can get your fingers burnt and tenants can be hugely annoying, but there are basic guidelines that make it manageable:

● **Don't expect too much. Returns on buy-to-let properties aren't that great, usually around 4 per cent, but if you add to this the property's capital growth over a proper period (at least five years) then the investment can become appealing.**

● Don't over-reach yourself. You need a hefty deposit (usually 25 per cent), as banks like to see the rent covering the mortgage repayments.

● You are buying to let, not buying to live in, so do your research. Check out rents and what they buy, in any area that interests you.

● Buy in an area where there is a healthy demand for rental.

● Don't charge top dollar. A little less will ensure lengthier tenancies and, with luck, tenants less likely to make undue trouble.

● Owning a rental property can be very tax-efficient, so get proper advice on what is claimable. Common mistakes made by investors include overstating claims for interest on loans when part of the loan has been used for something that has had nothing at all to do with the property, and claiming deductions for a period when the property has been used by friends or family.

15

BORROWING AND DEBT

36721910036BS120

There's borrowing for a purpose and there's sliding into debt. Both have become integral to the finances of most households, because somehow we've come to regard any line of credit as a plus and not an ongoing minus. By all means borrow if you must, but sliding into debt because you are chronically overspending is unacceptable. Understanding the distinction is central to money management.

Borrowing for something you need, like a house or a car, is considered acceptable debt. Borrowing to repay another debt is acceptable only if the interest rate on the second loan is lower than the interest rate on the original and your ultimate aim is to rid yourself of the debt completely. Most other borrowing needs to be carefully considered because we are trying here to live on what we have. The danger we place ourselves in (by living on what we borrow) is that we must then work so hard to earn enough to repay what we owe in order to own what we think we need that we end up too worried to enjoy it anyway. Having agreed that, we nearly all need to borrow some time and central to our borrowing potential is our rating.

About credit ratings

Credit ratings are, to a certain extent, notional. There is no actual score sitting in a repository somewhere to which banks and credit-card providers have access. Each institution has its own risk-scoring system, calculated on the basis of what's in your credit file and the information you supply when you apply for credit, be it a mortgage, personal loan or credit card.

Credit files are compiled by credit reference agencies like Veda Advantage in Australia and Experian in the UK. (Government money websites list the main agencies.) A credit file contains a list of every application for credit that you've made; your repayment history, as supplied by current and previous credit providers; your history of unpaid bills; and anything relevant about you that might be on the public record, like bankruptcies, directorships or court judgements. If you haven't sought credit for the last five years, you won't have a credit file. Information stays on your credit file for between one and six years, but be reassured: lenders are much more interested in your current situation than in anything historical.

Provided the file information is up-to-date and accurate, it's a reasonable basis from which a credit provider can decide how much (if anything) to lend you and at what interest rate. Oddly, the same information can cause one provider to make you an offer and another to turn you down. Your application will be taken more seriously the longer you've been in a job, the longer you've lived at the same address, if you own your own home, if you are middle-aged and if you are married. Unhappily, you may not be able to address any of these criteria as a matter of urgency.

You'll be refused credit if the provider judges you, according to their particular scoring system, to be a bad risk. (You might not be turned down outright, but be offered a lesser sum than you've applied for at a higher interest rate.) You're a bad risk if you have a consistently poor repayment record, a history of unpaid debts or poor money management (as in the case of a bankrupt) or if you aren't on the electoral roll (which is the usual check for proof of address). Should a rejection come as a surprise to you, it's advisable to apply to a credit rating agency for access to your file just in case:

- there has been some kind of clerical error;

- you have been the victim of credit-card fraud;

- someone has stolen your identity;

- the system has recorded multiple credit enquiries from you, which suggests to them that you are being frequently rejected (although all it might mean is that you are conducting a thorough research);

- you need to place yourself on the electoral roll.

It's a good idea to check your credit status occasionally anyway, with or without a dodgy call against you. Should you discover an error in your file, there are standard procedures for applying to have it corrected, initially via the lending institution. (Further information on this, and on making a complaint if you're not satisfied with the response, is available from the credit reference agencies.) The costs of seeing your file vary from agency to agency. In Australia, Veda Advantage currently charges $32.95; UK agencies charge no more than £2 for a basic (statutory) report, though your credit 'score' will cost more.

Home loans (mortgages)

For the average householder, a home loan is the biggest debt they will ever acquire. A rule of thumb from most financial advisers is to keep it modest. In straitened times you'd expect banks to be cautious about lending and to consider carefully the maximum amount an applicant might be able to repay relatively painlessly, but they don't necessarily. It's up to you to be circumspect: overestimating what you can pay back will place you under maximum financial stress. It's tempting to go for broke when interest rates are low, but interest rates don't stay low and before you know it they can balloon beyond recognition.

Decide for yourself what you can afford, if anything, then look for something in that price range. This may not seem an attractive proposition when your heart is set on blue-chip – or any old chip in tricky times – but your heart will count for nothing if you stress it to death. Take into account your life plan, your potential earnings, any potential future costs (such as children), and calculate what you might be able to afford in the way of mortgage repayments when you're earning less. If you're struggling to get into a property market which is increasingly beyond the reach of so many, you first need to get a decent deposit saved. Banks might lend up to 95 per cent of a property's value, but most like borrowers to have at least 10 per cent of the total value of a property before they will come to the party.

HOW TO GET A HOME LOAN

You can find a mortgage yourself or you can find a mortgage through a broker.

Using a broker

You might not want to use a broker, on the basis that it will cost you money you could save by doing it yourself, but as with all middlemen, the good ones are worth their weight in whatever currency is doing well on the day. They have the decided advantages of knowing the market and having some leverage with lenders who trust them to do their legwork for them, so they can advise you of your eligibility without you having to apply to a lender who might knock you back. This is a major plus for borderline cases. All knock-backs appear on your credit file and a horrible cycle can begin. Lenders each have their own scoring system, which means a third bank might lend to you where the first two wouldn't, but there is a strong possibility that, if you're borderline, the third will turn you down simply because the others did. Good brokers know how best to apply for a loan, and to whom.

If you decide to go the broker route, look for someone registered with a professional body (the Mortgage Industry Association of Australia or the National Association of Commerical Finance Brokers in the UK), who is experienced and, if at all possible, comes personally recommended. At your first meeting, establish whether they have special connections to any particular lenders, the range of choice they can offer you and how they expect to be paid. Currently, unless they agree to act on a fee basis, mortgage brokers charge their clients nothing, but all brokers must disclose how and what they will earn from the deal they are doing for you. Most are paid by commission (although this is under review) which, in Australia on a $100,000 loan, will be in the region of $700 upfront and then $6 a month for the life of the loan. For this you get, according to a broker with a 90 per cent personal referral rate, at least seventeen hours' work preparing your application. Like many brokers these days, much of his work comes via local banks who, he says, find it cheaper to refer clients to him than to process the loan application themselves. He considers it's in his interests to get the best possible deal for his clients from wherever he can. For him, a good reputation is everything.

Finding a mortgage yourself

Should you decide to go it alone, check out the comparison websites and keep abreast of current rates by reading the financial sections of newspapers and magazines. They may seem, in the first place, barely comprehensible, but the more you look the more you understand. Make sure you compare like with like: the annual percentage rate (APR) of the loan is the best indication of its actual cost.

Regardless of published rates, your own bank should be your first port of call. It will confirm, or not, your eligibility for a loan, tell you how much they might lend you, and explain the different mortgage products they can offer. If these aren't the best available, and you now know you're a reasonable proposition, go elsewhere.

As with any loan application, try to make yourself as attractive a borrower as possible. Check your credit rating well in advance of any application (see page 271) and take measures to improve it if necessary. Reduce the number of credit cards you have, to one if possible, make sure any existing debts are under control, and maintain a healthy repayment record for a good year in advance. In Australia it is increasingly important to show you have saved a deposit (in some kind of savings account). Lenders want to see you aren't completely reliant on other borrowing, gifts or government grants. Bear in mind there is no hard and fast rule for how much you might be offered. All lenders have their systems: as well as what's on your credit file, your earnings, household expenditure and your age, they will consider how much money you can contribute to the purchase. Even if your credit file looks ugly, should you only want to borrow half the value of the property, the risk you pose to the lender is immediately reduced. In Australia, should you not be an entirely attractive proposition on paper but the lender has faith in your ability to make the required repayments, you may be offered a 'low doc' (low documentation) loan for which you aren't required to produce the usual proofs of income. These might also be offered for speed of processing. But consider what strings, such as higher interest rates, are attached.

TYPES OF MORTGAGES

Don't be fooled by all the fancy names. The choice is simpler than it looks. There are repayment mortgages, there are interest-only mortgages, there are offset mortgages and there are reverse (or equity-release) mortgages.

Repayment mortgages are paid off, usually fortnightly or monthly, over a term of up to thirty years. Part of each repayment meets the interest you're being charged for the loan, which is calculated daily (usually). The rest reduces the balance.

Interest-only loans are more affordable since, as the name suggests, you are only paying the interest on the loan and nothing off the principal, but they are suitable only if you have some way of paying off the loan at the end of the agreed term. Banks are increasingly cautious about offering them without a hefty deposit and evidence that you have other assets to cover the debt.

Offset mortgages are linked to nominated everyday accounts. You pay interest only on the balance of your mortgage, less the amount in the nominated account, so if your mortgage is $150,000 and you have $25,000 in your nominated account, the interest is calculated on $125,000. You can choose either to reduce your mortgage repayments or to use overpayments to reduce the principal. Offset mortgages may also include a drawdown facility, which gives you the opportunity to borrow against the value of your property. If, for example, you have a mortgage which is 80 per cent of the value of your property, the bank may offer 10 per cent of the property's value at home-loan rates, to be drawn down when required.

Reverse (or equity-release) mortgages, which are similar in principle to a mortgage current account reserve, are available to (mostly older) people wanting to access some of the capital tied up in their home, to cover an expense or to live on. The closer to death you are the better, since you don't want to eat the entire house while you still need it. On the other hand, the scheme has definite advantages, so consult an adviser.

With every mortgage a whole range of conditions apply, which you should examine with a fine toothcomb before making any commitment. There may be hefty application fees or none; legal fees or none; valuation fees or none; penalties if you repay the mortgage early, or none; a large minimum deposit required; and/or a drawdown facility provided. Ask the lender to explain all the terms, then read every word of the bumph and note the salient points, because claiming later that you didn't know won't wash with anyone.

HOW TO SAVE MONEY ON YOUR MORTGAGE

● Reassess your mortgage from time to time – it's a competitive market. Check the loan features, fees, interest rates, terms and conditions; there are websites that will compare mortgages for you. Use a mortgage broker if you find the maze impossible to negotiate, though try to find one who isn't tied to one product but has access to several lenders.

● Make your repayments fortnightly (or even weekly, if you can) instead of monthly. As the amount of interest you owe is calculated daily, the more frequently you reduce the overall amount, the less interest you will fork out and you'll pay off the loan sooner. Read the small print of your loan agreement to make sure you won't be penalised for early repayment.

● Similarly, increase your repayments whenever you can, especially when interest rates are low. Small but regular overpayments can reduce the term of your mortgage by years. Over twenty-five years, say, paying even an extra $43 each month on a $250,000 mortgage will save you $17,000 in interest.

INTEREST RATES

Even more intricate than the choices you have about how you pay off your mortgage is the range of interest terms on offer. There is *variable*, which fluctuates according to the official (or bank base) rate and there is *fixed*, which remains the same for a specified period during which it cannot be repaid without penalty, though the period is rarely longer than five years.

A 'standard' variable rate is a specified percentage above the official rate. It can go up; it can go down. A 'discounted' rate means you pay an agreed percentage less than the standard rate, usually for a fixed period (two to three years, say). In the UK, a 'tracker' mortgage means the interest rate is guaranteed to stay at an agreed 'discounted' percentage above the Bank of England base rate. In Australia, tracker mortgages may be tied to the Reserve Bank rate or offer to undercut the standard variable rates of the 'Big Four' banks. A 'capped' rate means the variable rate will remain at an agreed percentage below the standard variable for a set time.

GUARANTOR MORTGAGES

In some circumstances, banks may ask for someone to guarantee your home loan. Should you be struggling, for instance, to get into the property market because lenders are multiplying your income by X and coming up with a Y, which will buy you a box under a bridge, you may consider asking a parent or relative to be your guarantor. If your lender uses the test of 'income multiples' to work out borrowing limits (your income multiplied by three, for example) you can also benefit from your guarantor's borrowing power. By combining your income with your guarantor's income, you can increase the size of mortgage available to you. With luck, it won't cost them a cent. Without luck, they may end up having to meet your mortgage payments. You and the guarantor should have some kind of agreement (preferably binding) that, in the event of your failing to make repayments regularly, the property can be sold and any debt to them repaid.

Overdrafts and personal loans

Banks will offer overdraft facilities and personal loans to anyone who meets their lending criteria, even if the borrower has no obvious collateral. The interest rates on both these forms of borrowing will vary, but are miles higher than those for home loans. If the loan required is temporary (for a matter of months rather than years), an overdraft might be preferable: the danger is that if you go over the agreed amount you can be slugged for unauthorised spending, which is costly.

Personal loans are useful for a single expensive purchase, like a car, or to consolidate a series of small debts. When borrowing to buy a car, do your homework. The car salesman will almost certainly offer you terms, but they won't necessarily be the most competitive. (Back to the internet and the financial pages for comparison charts on personal loans.) If you're consolidating small loans, do the maths carefully, factor in the number of repayments the new loan will require (the longer the agreement, the more interest repayments).

Credit cards

There's no denying the usefulness of credit cards. They eliminate the need for messy cash and they provide a free loan for up to eight weeks if you pay the bill in full each month. They can also spread the cost of an expensive item over a few months, which can be a godsend in an emergency. But how slippery is the slope that starts with a modest credit limit and a very attractive 'minimum payment due' date? Know this:

1. Credit cards are expensive: while interest rates vary, according to the competition and the state of the economy, the least you pay on purchases is a lot (compared to home loan or personal loan rates); the interest on cash advances is exorbitant and there may be no interest-free period.

2. The 'minimum payment' has nothing to do with reducing the debt: it just keeps you in there, potentially paying interest forever while the amount you owe keeps going up. Of the $46 billion or so Australians owed on credit cards early in 2010, 72 per cent was accounted for by accruing interest, so you won't feel lonely with your credit-card debt but you will feel poor – poorer and poorer – if you don't start reducing it. According to the financial pages of the *Sydney Morning Herald*, if your debt is $10,000 and you pay off only the minimum (which is around 2 per cent of the balance) each month, it will take sixty-two years and eight months to clear. If you can't pay your credit-card debt in full every month, at least pay as much as you can afford.

It always pays to shop for a better deal. Look at a price comparison website to see if you should take your custom elsewhere, or simply opt for a cheaper card from the same institution. There is a largish gap (up to 10 per cent) between the cheapest and the most expensive.

Many credit-card firms offer a 0 per cent interest introductory offer, which can last from six to fifteen months on balance transfers. The application fee will be between 2 per cent and 4 per cent, so should you be ducking from one card to the next, factor in the cost of moving and always read the terms and conditions. Dates for interest-free transfers, for instance, expire well before the 0 per cent period, and you can find yourself paying full whack on amounts you thought were included in the arrangement but were accessed outside the discounted period. (Remember not to apply for several cards at once or your credit file will register alarm bells.) Watch carefully for when the interest-free period expires and either pay off in full, move again, or take out a personal loan (invariably cheaper than a credit-card debt).

TRY DEBIT, NOT CREDIT

If credit, store and even loyalty cards – which may encourage you to spend more than you should – are your undoing, get rid of them all and use a debit card. The money is deducted directly from your bank account, so you know exactly what you've spent and the effect of the purchase on your budget.

Identity thieves can not only use your credit card but, with the right information stolen from your personal documents, they can also take out new passports in your name or apply for financial transactions in your name – buy or rent a property, buy or rent a car, even take out a mortgage. You may not discover the theft until legal action is taken against you to recover the debt.

To avoid stolen identity:

- Carry as few credit cards and important personal documents about with you as possible. If any are stolen, report the theft immediately to your credit organisations and to the police. Report loss of a passport at once to the appropriate government body.

- Never allow a trader to remove your debit or credit card from your sight.

- Clear your postbox daily or, if this isn't possible, lock it.

- Destroy (shred or burn) unwanted documents containing personal information, such as receipts, bills, bank statements, etc. Don't dump them in the rubbish, from where they can be retrieved.

- Take precautions against online fraud (see page 291).

- Check your credit card and bank statements regularly.

DEBT

We can fudge the issue all we like, but there is a difference between borrowing and debt even though both refer to money owed. Borrowing is embarked upon as a matter of choice with a plan for repayment; debt rarely is. You slide into debt because you haven't properly matched your income to your outgoings.

Stopping the rot

Debt can be both costly and stressful beyond belief, so urgent steps must be taken to get out of it. Your first is to acknowledge its size and scope and to factor into your monthly budget as much as you can to repay it.

Should you have more than one debt (credit card/s, overdraft, mobile phone), it may be wise to consolidate all of them into the cheapest-possible personal loan, over a time-frame that makes the repayments manageable. Try your bank first: explain your situation and see what they suggest. They will ask you to fill out a form setting out your earnings and outgoings, and if you can prove a regular income and scope for improvement they may help. The interest rate for any loan they offer is likely to be higher than the going rate because, let's face it, you're not looking too reliable. You still have rights, however: do insist on an opt-out clause so that you won't be penalised for repaying the loan early or switching to a less punitive arrangement down the track.

If your bank won't come to the party and your debts are out of control or on the way to being so, get help. Try to come to an agreement with your creditors (either on an informal basis or through the courts) to pay what you can when you can. If this is beyond you, get help from a financial counsellor. Some banks offer their services. Otherwise, in Australia, try the Australian Financial Counselling and Credit Reform Association (AFCCRA) or ASIC, or, failing those, welfare or charity services like Moneycare, run by the Salvation Army in Australia. In the UK you could get help from the Consumer Credit Counselling Service, which provides free and confidential advice for people in financial difficulties.

Should your financial hardship not be your fault but the result of illness, injury or job loss against which you are not insured, the state can and will provide. In Australia, your first port of call is Centrelink; in the UK it's the Department for Work and Pensions, the local Jobcentre or your local Citizen's Advice Bureau.

Bankruptcy

Bankruptcy is neither simple nor desirable. If you have serious ongoing and unmanageable debts, seek help as above. You can also get advice from a registered trustee or an 'insolvency practitioner'. Don't, under any circumstances, imagine you can protect yourself by transferring to anyone else assets you think might be seized, as anything transferred up to five years prior to bankruptcy may be considered, on the day of judgement, to be current assets.

WHY BECOME BANKRUPT?

The short answer, and the long, really, is to get creditors off your back. If you can't pay your debts, if your creditors won't give you any more time to pay and if you've exhausted all alternative ways to address the horror, you can choose to be made bankrupt.

More likely than voluntary bankruptcy, however, is that your creditors will apply to have you made bankrupt. To do this they need to show the court that you haven't repaid what you owe them (above a minimum of $2000 in Australia or £750 in the UK, as of 2009). Once you are bankrupt, unsecured creditors (anyone who can't repossess an item they've sold you or for which they've lent you money) must then stop pursuing you for further payment. Secured creditors (say, holders of the mortgage on your house or the bill of sale on your car) may still seek to recover their loss.

WHY IT'S BEST AVOIDED

Not only are the conditions horrible for the duration of a bankruptcy, but the black mark against you remains on the public record permanently. During bankruptcy, your affairs are placed in the hands of a trustee whose duty is to recover whatever money can be raised from the sale of your assets and by deductions from your income to meet your creditors' claims.

For a full list of the restrictions that apply to bankrupts, consult the Insolvency and Trustee Service Australia or the Insolvency Service in the UK. Among the conditions, as gleaned from ITSA, are possibly having to surrender your passport, being unable to continue employment in certain trades and professions, and having to inform some people (notably those you seek a loan from or have business dealings with) that you are a bankrupt.

It may be cold comfort, but certain assets cannot be sold by the trustee to pay creditors. These include necessary household furniture, personal effects, limited tools of trade, life insurance, superannuation policies and your primary means of transport (up to a prescribed value).

BEING DISCHARGED FROM BANKRUPTCY

Provided you abide by the conditions, bankruptcy is automatically discharged a specified time after you've been made bankrupt (three years and one day in Australia, one year in the UK), though it may be extended in some circumstances. It can be annulled (wiped out altogether) earlier if you pay off all your debts or reach an agreement with your creditors as to how you will do so, or you can satisfy the court that you should never have been declared bankrupt in the first place.

Whatever the degree of your indebtedness, once you've fixed on a solution that is viable, it's your bounden duty to start living within your means. This won't necessarily be easy: bad habits – mainly spending and borrowing more than you can afford – acquired early are hard to break, but really your only choice is to knuckle down or face a grim future.

16
RISK MANAGEMENT

The importance of protecting what you have grows in direct proportion to the devastation wreaked should you lose it. A zillionnaire might lose a zillion and not notice. A householder with a sizeable mortgage and three dependants can't afford to get run over; a householder with the usual financial commitments to everyday survival would struggle without earning for months. And none of us wants to find out the hard way, when it goes up in smoke, that our home is under-insured or not insured at all. So we'd better all cover our backs.

As I see it, there are three key elements to risk management for householders:

- living within your means;

- protecting yourself and your dependants from catastrophic loss with prudent insurance;

- making a will.

Living within your means has been dealt with in Chapters 14 and 15, so we'll move right along.

We all need insurance, whatever we think about it. You can regard insurance as a wager with a large company as to whether a specified unfavourable outcome will occur: you win the bet (get paid) if it does, but lose it (don't get paid) if it doesn't. Or you can regard insurance as risk management: you pay the company to absorb the risk that an unfavourable outcome will occur, and you get paid if it does; or the unfavourable outcome never eventuates and your 'loss' (a happy outcome) is limited to the premiums you've paid.

The latter view is favoured by the insurance industry and makes perfect sense. It's just not so palatable to people like me who've spent hundreds of thousands – over many years, it's true – on insurance of all sorts to protect the household from stuff that never happened. Sometimes we've paid for policies that turned out to offer no protection whatsoever. Once, an underwriter acting for the bank whose gold card I believed had insured us for travel said to us, as she turned down our claim, 'Never assume you are insured.' Which was upsetting, because that's exactly what most insured people do. I know we need insurance, but instead of appreciating it, I resent it. The resentment stems from my profound suspicion that no matter how reliable I am in my payments, something will fail me in the event of a claim – I won't meet the policy's terms and conditions – and this fear stems from the wriggle room built into the terms and conditions which idiot purchasers, such as myself, fail to note.

Protecting yourself from the people protecting you

Having consulted two highly regarded insurance brokers as well as a bank manager and an actuary, I now know that much in the insurance industry hinges on 'utmost good faith'. Insurance contracts are based on it. It's with the utmost good faith that you answer the enquiries an insurer makes so that they can establish the degree of risk you represent before they give you a quote. Should your honesty be in any way questionable – should you, for instance, not be entirely accurate about your claims history and should you end up having to make a claim – then, out the window goes any commitment of the company to good faith, and bye-bye cover. Of less import to the industry, it seems, is the utmost good faith with which you expect them to cough up should the worst occur.

So, buyer beware. There are two important caveats when it comes to placing your faith in a provider or a policy: first, understand the limits and the extent of the policy before you sign up, noting precisely what it does and doesn't cover; second, reread the terms and conditions during the cooling-off period, even if they are 100 pages long, because, sure enough, on page 37 at point 51, subsection Z, will be the bit that says you are covered for all circumstances except those in which you find yourself. Ignorance carries no weight in the event of a claim.

The alternative is to self-insure, which means making certain you have the funds to meet, from your own pocket, the costs of any disasters. This can make sense when the risk is small and the potential cost to you relatively low. But some disasters are so enormous that few of us can afford to meet their cost, so we have to offload the risk. Judicious offloading is what is required – but when, how much and to whom?

What type of insurance do you need?

The insurance industry describes itself in terms of three broad categories:

- *Life*. This includes life insurance, which usually covers you for an agreed term (e.g. to age 80), during which your dependants will be paid a lump sum in the event of your death. There is income protection (also called permanent health insurance in the UK), which replaces your earnings if you are unable to work owing to injury or disability, usually after a waiting period, typically of twelve months; critical illness (or trauma) insurance, which will pay a lump sum should you be diagnosed with a specified major illness or suffer a major accident; and there's total disability insurance, which pays a lump sum should the disability prevent you from working either in your own occupation or any occupation (depending on the terms you agree). You can also have payment protection insurance, which will cover your loan repayments for a given period of time should your income drop below an agreed level owing to accident, illness or unemployment (some mortgage lenders insist you have it before they agree to lend you anything).

- *General*. This includes household insurance (buildings and contents), travel insurance and car insurance.

- *Health*. This covers you for (all or mostly some of) the costs of hospitalisation and for treatment by specialists to whom you have been referred by a GP.

When deciding what type of insurance to buy, it makes sense to look at your life, at who and what is in it, and then decide which of these needs protecting. Consider whether the cost/risk ratio is tolerable and then research how best to arrange the kind of cover you want.

For example, should you be a single person in rented accommodation, with no dependants and no car but some debt – which means your obligation is chiefly to yourself – you might consider the following cover: a life insurance policy; income protection insurance that includes trauma cover; household contents cover, if you have valuable possessions; and health insurance. If your budget is tight, prioritise: contents cover may be more prudent than private health cover, and the life cover might be necessary only if you have a debt not covered by your assets and too large to be met by your next-of-kin (and with luck, you won't).

Should you, on the other hand, be part of a couple, with dependants and a large home and/or car loan, you need to consider the impact on your household if your income drops or stops owing to job loss, accident, sickness or death. The risk of any or all of these might be small, but it is there nonetheless and responsible householders should provide for it. Income protection is important in your circumstances (in Australia, it is offered by many superannuation funds, so check before you consider buying it separately). The alternative might be life insurance and some form of mortgage protection (though this usually provides cover for a very limited period). Ideally, you would arrange a parcel of cover (structured for the lowest possible cost) that includes income protection, life cover and some trauma insurance, and to arrange this you might need to get advice.

CAR INSURANCE

Since we're compelled by law to have basic motor insurance, you need to understand the scope of the cover you are buying. The basic legal requirement is for third party insurance: in Australia, this covers death or injury to a third party; in the UK, it covers death or injury to a third party and/or damage to their vehicle or property. In Australia, to be covered for damage you might cause to someone else's property (and any legal costs involved), you need separate, 'third party property' insurance. The UK and Australia also offer third party, fire and theft insurance, which covers damage your car does to other people's property, and also damage to your car caused by fire, or its loss through theft.

Comprehensive insurance is the most expensive car insurance, but it is also the most reassuring as it covers all the above as well as accidental damage to your vehicle. Premiums vary from company to company, and according to your personal circumstances which include your claims record (this can entitle you to a no-claims bonus); your driving record; your age and your gender; where you live; whether you have a garage; the age, make and model of the car; the number and age of additional drivers; and, with larger companies, whether you have other policies which entitle you to some kind of deduction for loyalty. You would imagine that car insurance is a straightforward matter and in many respects it is, but the small print is as critical here as anywhere else. Be very clear about what is excluded, the excess (the amount you agree to pay in the event of any claim), and whether you are insuring for 'agreed' or 'market' value.

PERSONAL INSURANCE BUGBEARS: TRAVEL AND CAR RENTAL

I appreciate these may not be of as much interest to other householders as they are to me, but I'd like to address travel and car rental insurance in more detail than they might appear to warrant because the aggravation they can cause is great. The policy documents for travel insurance, for instance, contain the most wriggle room of any insurance and can drive you (have driven me) to distraction. On the other hand, doing without it is foolhardy.

Travel insurance

When claims on travel-insurance policies are rejected, it's usually because (according to ASIC in Australia) the situation that has led to the claim is specifically excluded under the policy. In other words, the terms and conditions weren't read and thoroughly understood by the purchaser. This will be because the purchaser couldn't be fagged and trusted the policy to look after them.

One of the brokers whose advice I sought suggested that our expectations of what is covered by travel insurance are probably unrealistic. Generally speaking, it's 'catastrophic cover' designed to provide for us in the event of a death or lesser medical emergency. Lost luggage is an add-on. Insurers rarely pay out more than half the replacement value of lost luggage since, in the absence of receipts, there is no way of proving their value. There is no payout on jewellery or laptops placed in the hold, unless you've cleared placing them in the hold beforehand with the airline. Airlines, in any case, accept very limited liability for any loss. It can be increased (on request and for a fee) at check-in, according to an adviser with British Airways customer service.

Shopping around for the right policy is critical. Buying from a travel agent who is paid a handsome commission, for instance, may not be in your best interests. Relying on the cover from your credit card or bank most definitely isn't.

Car rental insurance

This is just as perplexing. A perfectly reasonable quote for the rental itself suddenly swells with the cost of insurance (taken out by the rental company with their insurers and passed on to you) and then with the optional cost of reducing the excess by paying a higher daily rental rate. You can't avoid the cost of the insurance, but only about half of us decide to take up the excess waiver option. I pay up and always call myself a coward for doing it. A good option is to have it included in your travel insurance (look under Car Rental Excess): it may be automatically included, but if not you can request it. Check all the conditions carefully for exclusions, like off-road travel or windscreen damage.

Choosing an insurer

There is plenty of information available online to inform our decisions about insurance. You just punch in your needs and scrutinise charts comparing policies and providers, though these are for the most part price- and not terms-and-conditions-based. Alternatively, you might use an insurance broker. Whichever path you choose, make sure you understand what's being offered, as apparently straightforward terms can mean different things to different providers.

USING AN INSURANCE BROKER

As is the case with financial planners, insurance brokers (who may call themselves 'risk advisers') are experts with whom you can and should have an ongoing relationship as your household's needs change. The main argument against them, again as with financial advisers, is that their fee (or commission) can seem inordinate – the latter can be as high as 25 per cent of the insurance premium. The best argument in their favour is the work they take off your hands, which is not just to find the best and best-priced policy for you but also to pursue claims on your behalf should the occasion arise. Your obligation to yourself here is to find an independent broker, which is to say one not attached to any specific provider (like a bank) or to in-house products which it is their job to sell regardless of their suitability. Ask around: word of mouth is always the best recommendation. Otherwise, check with the National Insurance Brokers Association in Australia or the British Insurance Brokers Association in the UK.

Brokers usually specialise in life, general or health insurance (as defined earlier), so that part of your selection process is a matter of horses for courses. Agree a meeting to discuss your needs, to hear suggestions and to decide for yourself whether this is a person with whom you can have an ongoing professional relationship. Discuss fees and commissions up-front and discuss independence up-front, since brokers are, to a certain extent, bound by laws of disclosure. A good broker can make comparisons on the basis of small print you may not easily understand or bother to decipher at all, can vouch for the terms being watertight, and will, in the event of a claim, be in your corner defending his or her integrity as well as your rights. If you can afford advice, take it. Life policies, owing to their comparative lack of wriggle room, are less likely than, say, household contents cover, to require defending in the event of a claim, but you are more likely to benefit from advice as to the best and most appropriate policy.

BUYING INSURANCE WITHOUT A BROKER

Should you decide to rely on your own counsel, pay particular attention to the following:

- The cheapest policy is by no means always the best. Scour the small print for conditions and exclusions, and clarify them with the provider if necessary.

- Don't under-insure on the basis of expense; place a proper value on the risk. Get the replacement cost of your house (as well as jewellery, art and other expensive possessions) assessed regularly by appropriate experts. The ASIC (Australia) and Financial Services Authority (UK) websites have calculators and excellent advice on making realistic evaluations.

- Try to maintain some kind of personal liability insurance in case you, say, whack someone in the head with a golf ball. Most buildings and contents insurance includes it, but check to make sure yours does.

Insurance disputes

Should you not have a broker to do battle for you, and you find yourself in a dispute with an insurer that can't be resolved, you have recourse to the financial ombudsman service. Bear in mind that the most common causes for dispute with insurance companies are:

- non-disclosed (by you) facts that may have a bearing on your claim, such as inadequate home security;

- exclusions by household insurers, such as the theft of goods from outside the building, theft without forced entry, or limits on the claimable value of jewellery;

● in car insurance, a whole raft of issues: market value (even when it's agreed on the policy); the size of the excess, though this too will have been agreed up-front; the option to choose your own repairer; and whether windscreen damage is covered, to name just a few.

Extended warranties

Retailers often try to persuade you to buy an extended warranty on the item you've purchased, which typically prolongs the manufacturer's warranty for up to five years. And because you don't really have any faith in whatever-it-is lasting longer than a year without giving trouble, you may be tempted. But it's needless, according to Choice, Australia's independent consumer advocate. First, all goods and services are implicitly covered, under the Trade Practices Act, by a statutory warranty. Second, extended warranties are invariably chock-full of exclusions. New rules to protect consumers' rights regarding extended warranties were introduced in the UK in 2005, but Australians must continue to be wary and look out for themselves. Before you commit, ask for a written explanation of the warranty and check with the office of consumer affairs or fair trading in your state to see if you are already covered by a statutory guarantee.

MAKING A WILL

It doesn't matter how ghoulish you find the idea, you should set out what you want to happen to your money and possessions when you die. If you don't, you'll be creating a mess for those you leave behind, causing them extra distress and possibly years of legal entanglement.

Should you die intestate (which is to say, without making a will) or should the will you leave be found to be invalid, your assets will be frozen, maybe for years, while an administrator decides who is entitled to what, according to the relevant law. This may not be the people you wanted or intended to provide for: your partner or dependants, should you have either, won't automatically get the lot. It will be distributed among eligible claimants according to some legally defined pecking order which begins with the closeness of blood ties between you. In the event of there being no legitimate claimants, the whole kit and caboodle goes to the government. So there. Do it.

Making a valid will is a simple enough process, though certain provisos apply:

AVOIDING ONLINE FRAUD

Buying and paying bills online is a scary prospect when your banking details are being shunted into the ether and are potentially accessible to all and sundry. The question for the householder is how risky it is, precisely, and what can be done to make it less so. It's worth bearing in mind, if you are ether-phobic, that it's not much more risky than buying by phone, dumping bank statements in your roadside rubbish bin or leaving mailed bank or credit-card statements in an unlocked letterbox.

The important thing to check when paying for anything online is that the site requesting the payment is secure. A locked padlock icon should be displayed and/or there should be 'https' (standing for HyperText Transfer Protocol Secure) in the address, which means the site encrypts the information you are sending and reassures your browser that the site is who it says it is ('http', without the 's', does not mean the site or page is secure). Banks, online sellers and payment agencies are constantly upgrading their security and monitoring systems to outwit fraudsters. Your responsibility is to be vigilant. Scammers can infiltrate your computer with spyware – often via junk emails or free download offers – which, if it contains a keylogger (a program that records all your keystrokes) can capture everything you key in and gives the scammer access to your pin numbers, account numbers and other personal or financial details. To protect yourself:

● Never download spam; if you open a junk email by mistake, never click on any links it contains.

● Be wary of anything that has been sent to you unsolicited.

● Always check a website's security.

● Never reply to any email requests for financial information or verification (account numbers, passwords), even if it appears to be from your bank or credit provider. Contact them for confirmation.

● You need to be over the age of eighteen.

● You need to be of sound mind and aware of the will's legal implications.

● You need to make it free from duress.

● You must sign it in the presence of witnesses (in the UK, beneficiaries or the spouses of beneficiaries cannot witness a will).

- You need to be aware of the extent of your assets and of the people who might reasonably expect you to provide for them.

- Your will needs to be made in writing (handwritten, printed or typed).

You need to keep your instructions up to date. If your circumstances change – if, for instance, you marry, divorce or have children, or one of your beneficiaries dies before you – you should change your will or make a new one. New, old, amended, whatever, your main concerns will be your assets, your beneficiaries and your executor/s.

- Your assets are anything and everything you own at the time you die – insurance policies, investments and valuable items of jewellery or art, as well as your house and what's in the bank. It's up to you to decide whether you want to make individual bequests. You can simply call it your estate and bequeath it as a job-lot to one person, or to be divided equally.

- Your beneficiaries are those you nominate to receive your assets. You can leave whatever you like to anyone, but it's always worth bearing in mind that a will can be challenged by friends or relatives who believe they should have been provided for and haven't been, or who believe they haven't been provided for fairly or adequately.

- Your executor is a person (or persons) you appoint to be responsible for any arrangements (including the funeral) after your death as well as to carry out your wishes as expressed in the will. This can be a burdensome task, so consider carefully who you nominate (and ask them first): you want someone robust enough to deal with any conflict, who can be relied upon to do the job with due diligence and diplomacy (so not likely to fall out with beneficiaries or any other executor). You can appoint a lawyer or accountant as your executor, but this will be expensive.

Other considerations

In Australia, it's vital that you note your wishes regarding any superannuation, not only in your will but also in the fund membership contract. If your nominated beneficiary needs to be changed (in the event, say, of divorce or a death) you must make appropriate amendment to the details.

In the UK, your assets will be liable for inheritance tax if they are valued above the current threshold as determined by HM Revenue and Customs.

Do you need a solicitor?

If your financial affairs are straightforward, you can draw up a will yourself. If properly completed, signed and witnessed, it will be legally valid. (DIY will kits or printed forms are available from post offices, newsagents and stationers, or online.) But for your peace of mind, it's worth getting a solicitor to do it for you. Apart from anything else, intention can be open to all sorts of interpretation in court. Banks, building societies and financial planners can also offer advice.

If you choose not to use a solicitor, the Public Trustee Office can, for a smaller fee, prepare a will for you and also act as an executor. (Using the Public Trustee is more common in Australia than the UK.) Some charities will draw up a will for you, free of charge, if you leave them something.

PART 6

WHERE AND HOW TO LIVE

WHERE WE LIVE depends in the first place on circumstance, in the second place on inclination, and in the third, on the amount of money we have to spend in relation to the number of people we need to house. After that, it's a matter of timing and luck, because what is actually available when we decide to move is anyone's guess and setting our heart on anything in particular is no guarantee we'll get it. Unless we're one of those freakily stubborn people as seen on TV saying, 'I wouldn't accept anything less and the ten-year wait was worth it.'

How we live is also dependent on what we can afford, but less so. Once we've accepted that it won't be in luxury, we still have endless choices to make. These are governed by taste, temperament, energy and the extent of any interest we have in our immediate environment. We can choose to maximise the potential of where we live by judicious improvements and vigilant maintenance; we can opt for maximum comfort within our budget; we can make environmentally friendly choices about everything from appliances to energy and water sources to the cars we drive. Or we can just not bother, which is our God-given right.

All such decisions are central to our happiness because home is a refuge, however humble, and in terms of what we do to it and how we live in it, it's an extension of ourselves. The world will recognise it as an extension of ourselves and when we ask ourselves if we care, mostly we say no but really we mean yes.

17

MOVING HOUSE

You move house for the following reasons: you need to get away from your parents; you've outgrown your flatmates; you can't afford where you are now or you can afford more; you've entered a new relationship; you're getting married; you're leaving a relationship; you're having a baby; you're having another baby; your babies have grown up and it's time to downsize or at least move on. Why you move will influence what you move to, as much as what you can afford to spend. Once those decisions have been made, the critical thing is *how* you move. The aim is to manage it with as little hysteria, slapping and stomping off as possible. The aim is to arrive at our destination tired but happy. The key to this is planning, which is essential regardless of how blighted we might be by luck.

Within our control are broad choices: rent or buy; city or suburbs; town or country; flat or house; new or old; large or small. Each has its own peculiarities, which are best recognised before the move rather than regretted after it, but as important are the overall considerations that must be made by all home-hunters whether we're renters or buyers, young or old, rich or poor. Moving house is notoriously stressful, but you can minimise the nightmare. Preparation is everything.

You might choose to rent in order to be unencumbered by debt or by the obligations that come with ownership (like maintenance); because you know the housing arrangement you're entering is going to be short-term or because you value the flexibility that renting offers. Most of us, however, rent because we can't afford to buy: rent is usually less than the mortgage payments on a comparable property. It's true that not everyone thinks property ownership is essential or even desirable, but the prevailing view is that rent is dead money and that gradually repaying a loan on a property you will one day own at least results in something solid for the money you've spent on housing over fifty-odd years. The waters are muddy, however.

Increasingly, home ownership has come to say something not only about status and stability but about canny investing, yet the cost of buying has soared way beyond its proper place in a household budget. It's crazy to borrow far more than we can afford in order to live somewhere so far beyond our means that it gives us minimal pleasure while causing us maximum pain. It's almost as depressing to find the only place you can afford to buy is a dump. This may not be an argument for renting until you die, but it is an argument for renting until you have a large enough deposit to buy something you want to live in. Depending on interest rates and the terms of an affordable mortgage, you might get more for your money if you rent, especially if the area in which you choose to live for convenience has purchase values that are through the roof. It can sometimes make sense to live in rented accommodation but buy an investment property in a cheaper part of town to get you into the property market at a level you can afford.

Renting

The move into rented accommodation isn't cheap. If you rent via an agency, you will have to pay a bond or deposit (typically between four and six weeks' rent) and a month's rent in advance. If the place is unfurnished or only partly furnished, you'll need enough money left over to buy whatever furniture and appliances aren't included in the rental. (In Australia, this will more than likely be everything except window coverings and an oven.) As well as the rent, tenants are, of course, responsible for all household bills they run up themselves (gas, electricity, phone); in the UK, tenants also pay council and water rates, which in Australia are paid by the landlord.

The obligations of both tenant and landlord are contained in a lease (or 'tenancy agreement') which can be written or verbal: all are covered by law (tenancy laws vary from state to state in Australia). A written agreement is in the interests of both tenant and landlord: in the event of a dispute, there can be no argument about what either party's expectations were. The lease or agreement stipulates the period of the tenancy, the size of the deposit or bond and who holds it, the rent (and the amount of rent required in advance), how the rent is to be paid, how and when rent can be increased, and how and when the agreement can be terminated. It also covers the obligations of both tenant and landlord, which are pretty much as you would expect: the tenant pays rent and respects the property; the landlord allows the tenant to enjoy the property in peace and safety, and is responsible for maintenance and repairs. As with all contracts, it's up to both parties to read and understand the details and to get advice if anything seems odd or unreasonable.

If you're a prospective tenant, no matter how desperate you are to secure the place, don't accept the unacceptable out of panic. Check that the oven works, the lights work, all wall and floor tiles are in place and not cracked, the doors and windows open and close, there are enough power points and phone outlets, the carpets are clean and there's no sign of damp. Make sure you get an agreement in writing about the condition of the property, signed by both you and the landlord (or the landlord's agent), noting obvious signs of dilapidation so you're not blamed for them at the end of the tenancy. A certain amount of wear and tear is expected, but tenants are required to leave the place in good order (no seriously stained carpets or holes in the walls) or have money deducted from their bond to restore good order. Disputed claims can be referred to a tribunal for arbitration. And don't imagine this isn't worth the trouble: tribunals view with sympathy tenants who are unfairly slugged for a big chunk of their bond/deposit.

Buying

Buying a property involves a clearly established, step-by-step process, any part of which can drive you to drink. To stay sane, you must be patient and you must keep your hopes and expectations firmly in check.

This is the usual order of play for buying a property by private treaty (meaning, not at auction, which is the favoured method of selling in Australia, especially when markets are keen):

⊙ Arrange finance in principle.

⊙ Arrange conveyancing, which is to say line up a conveyancer or buy a DIY conveyancing kit.

- Find a property.

- Make an offer.

- Negotiate.

- Pray that nothing goes wrong; you don't own the property until contracts are exchanged.

- Exchange signed contracts.

- Settle (complete the sale).

- Move in.

The process is only slightly different for buying at auction. Much of the legwork is done prior to the auction, for which you should be thoroughly prepared because there is no going back if you're the successful bidder. Contracts are signed on the day and you must fork out the deposit (usually 10 per cent of the purchase price). There is no cooling-off period.

A further word on the order of play: should you be both selling and buying (selling one property to fund the purchase of another), it's always wise to have a firm offer on the place you are selling before putting in an offer on the property you want to buy. Finding yourself committed to a purchase whose funds are dependent on a sale that could fall through invites trouble in the form of a bridging loan. A bridging loan is a headache from which you may never fully recover.

LOCATION

Where you want to live is dictated by:

- the kind of life you want for yourself, and how you see yourself in the grand scheme of things;

- convenience to work and anything else you value (like shops, good schools, open spaces, a church);

- acceptability of particular neighbourhoods (and neighbours) to your sensibilities;

- the sort of housing that doesn't repel you aesthetically.

That said, where you actually live at any given stage of your life is as likely to be determined by your financial situation and whether you are renting or buying.

The big picture is city or suburbs, town or country, and this can vary according to where you are in life and what the rest of the household wants. Just bear in mind that neighbourhoods tend to be tribal and that we all naturally gravitate towards our tribe, plus its shops and restaurants, for a very good reason. You can live beyond the tribe if you hate tribal but most of us only do so if we think an alien tribe's area is at the centre of an imminent property growth spurt. The same thought will have occurred to other members of your tribe and so you will force out the alien tribe and, pretty soon, prices will be beyond the reach of that alien tribe's children. This is called mobility and it's really only acceptable if it's upward and taking you with it which is oddly both selfish and sensible.

Usually, instinct directs us towards a location that offers familiarity and comfort. This is not to be confused with 'Location, location, location', the boring mantra of annoying real-estate agents. (As if we didn't know the risks of buying into landfill.) Housing, from their point of view, is a commodity that will sooner or later be traded. But it's not always that simple: if housing were a straightforward investment we would always buy something undervalued in the best part of town (or country), but this is a home we're purchasing, so we take the best we can get in the range available to us.

FLAT OR HOUSE?

Comparing them like for like, in terms of quality and space, a flat is likely to give you more for your money than a house. A three-bedroom house can be 30 per cent more expensive to buy than a three-bedroom flat in the same neighbourhood. A flat may offer less outside space to manage (which can be a plus) and greater security (definitely a plus), but there are downsides like common walls and parts and lack of privacy.

Design-wise, a flat is usually less forgiving than a house – a poorly laid-out flat is a nightmare and there's often not too much you can do about it. Clever design, however, can compensate for lack of space and here your choice is, in the first instance, between new and old. Older-style, smaller blocks tend to be high on charm and easier on expenses (no lifts or gyms in the basement), with larger floor areas, higher ceilings and better sound-proofing, but knocking down walls can be more challenging in terms of planning and being lift-free might become an issue. Modern flats are usually slicker in design and more likely to acknowledge the current vogue for cooking, eating and relaxing in the same large room, but they may not be as solidly built.

Houses usually offer a better range of outside space and freedom from noise above or below, enormous pluses for households with children. That said, we had two children very comfortably in a flat and when we moved, with the arrival of the third, we lost a great view, nicer rooms and a better neighbourhood, even though our new home was only a street away. It's always a trade-off, but flats are certainly worth considering when location is critical, funds are tight and the household is of a manageable size.

Buying a flat

Buying a flat is more complicated than buying a house and it's worth appreciating the nature of the complications when a house is also a possibility. When you buy a flat you're not buying the entire building, just a defined space within it. In Australia, a flat is usually bought under a 'strata title' scheme, where the shared parts of the block are managed by a corporation ('the body corporate') made up of all the owners in the building. All owners pay levies for day-to-day and long-term maintenance, repairs and other expenses.

Some older flats are sold under 'company title', where you buy shares in the company that owns the building and these entitle you to live there. This system is unwieldy and restrictive, and such flats are sold for anything up to a third less than comparable strata-title properties. As with any home purchase, you should have all the legalities (levies, restrictions and so on) checked by a conveyancer.

In the UK, the system of flat ownership is different: you buy a leasehold on the flat for anything up to 999 years (but more usually 125 years) from the freeholder who owns the building in perpetuity (or until it is sold on). Either a new lease is issued on purchase, or you buy the remaining term of the originally issued lease. The freeholder is responsible for the upkeep and maintenance of the common parts, which is funded by the annual ground rent (usually nominal) and service charges (sometimes astronomical) that are determined by the freeholder and paid by the leaseholder. It's increasingly common for leaseholders to join together and buy the freehold or commonhold of the property with other owners in the same building and take over responsibility for the upkeep and maintenance themselves. Management of the common parts is usually through an owners' company, which establishes a sinking fund, but small blocks might manage on an informal, ad-hoc basis. The precise arrangement needs to be fully explored by your conveyancer – and understood by you – prior to purchase. If you're buying off the plan in either country, check the number of luxury amenities included, like a gym or a pool, as they can send the levies through the roof.

PRODUCTIVE SEARCHING

To find the home you want, you are going to have to search systematically and relentlessly. It can pay off in days, but usually not. If you're stuck for a system, try the following:

- Narrow your focus to no more than three areas, by which I mean specific parts (a few blocks, say) in favoured districts.

- Get to know these areas inside out. Visit them at different times of the day and week, checking for noise, parking restrictions, industrial smells, wild animals, graffiti or anything else that might send you nuts if you lived there.

- Talk to as many estate agents as you can stand about zoning, local amenities, public transport, who's buying into the area, who is selling, how long properties are on the market. Read the local papers for the area's reputation: community events, mugging (and that they're not one and the same).

- Track property values on agents' websites and local property pages to get a feel for what's selling, what's not and what you might get with a cheeky offer.

- Look only at properties that have the minimum space (overall and in individual rooms) you need to fit your household and its essential paraphernalia (make a list of the essential paraphernalia and, if necessary, measure it). If your household is likely to expand within the next five years, take that into account as well.

When you find something you like, go back for second and third viewings at different times of the day and week. Don't be blinded by cosmetic improvements like paintwork and landscaping, but don't be overly concerned about flaws that can be cheaply or reasonably improved. The finish of the kitchen, for instance, isn't critical. Look at the real value: the elements of the property that can't be changed, or could be changed but only at vast expense – these include size, structure, layout, position, light, privacy, noise, outlook, outdoor space, local traffic, access. For maximum light, you want the garden or main living areas to face north in the southern hemisphere or south in the northern. If the property is built onto a slope, you are better off on the street's high side, to minimise the likelihood of being flooded in heavy rain.

Knowing what you now do about the property, compare its asking or estimated price with similar recently sold properties in the same area. Estate agents' websites sometimes include these, or look online and in newspapers and magazines for property price guides.

BEFORE YOU MAKE AN OFFER

Once you've found the property you want, you need an expert to confirm your worst fears or best hopes. If you're an old hand at property purchase, you might just need a trusted builder to give the place his considered opinion and combine this with your extensive local knowledge to calculate a sensible offer. If you're new to it, or the area is new to you, it makes sense to get building/structural and pest inspections (there are specialised services that offer these, often in one go: make sure they have professional indemnity insurance), and a land/property survey (by a certified surveyor). They will provide detailed reports, so you know exactly what you're getting.

The older the property, the more important this is: don't just rely on the mortgage valuation – this is meant for the bank, who needs to know they'll get their money back in the event of a forced sale. Be prepared for the details to be terrifying. Given the age of the property, there will always be disintegration of some sort. Not all of it is irreparable and most of it won't make or break the deal. You are looking for problems way beyond your ability to fix.

Be realistic about buying to renovate yourself. Only a few people should take on wrecks, and mostly these people are called builders. Falling-down houses are falling down for a reason: the level of repairs required will be profound and the cost could be huge; not only that, but a wreck might have some kind of restrictive conservation order on it and the paperwork can be shocking.

ORGANISING FINANCE

This will depend on how much the bank is prepared to lend you, but also – and more importantly – on what you think you can afford to repay, which isn't necessarily the same thing. It's wise (though not desperately helpful when your finances are borderline) to calculate the repayments with an interest rate that's 2 per cent higher than the one the bank offers, since getting caught short by fluctuations in the market is a horror.

SECOND IMPRESSIONS

If you like the idea of a property and it ticks boxes for space, area and overall acceptability, examine the general condition inside and outside, noting any shortfalls that might play a part in negotiations. You may be able to get the vendor to make repairs prior to purchase, or reduce the asking price. The things to focus on are:

- **roof and guttering** – Look for rust on downpipes, or downpipes not feeding into drains. Look at the condition of the roof (age, loose tiles, etc.).

- **walls** – Examine the brickwork for missing grouting and look for cracks, especially around windows, which are often a sign of movement in the building.

- **damp** – Even if you can't smell it, look for discoloured patches in the corners of ceilings or bubbling paintwork, both outside and in, especially in basement rooms and bathrooms. This could be a sign of poor construction, leaking gutters, faulty brickwork or an ongoing mystery problem which will destroy your marriage. Or it could be minor.

- **plumbing and wiring** – Be vigilant about inadequate or possibly faulty arrangements.

- **pest damage**.

Now you need to calculate the minimum you would need to make the property both habitable and pleasing, and factor this into the price you're willing to pay. A proper professional inspection done by an architectural or building service will include estimated repair costs.

The ins, outs, ifs and buts of home loans are covered in detail in Chapter 15. Once you know how much is on offer and you've met the lender's conditions (like saving the deposit) you can be more focused in your searching and researching. While you can't exceed the agreed amount, however tempted you are, this doesn't mean you should write off properties with an estimated or asking price marginally (but up to 20 per cent in a slow market) outside that figure. Just be disciplined: if the property's for sale, make an offer but be ready to walk away if it isn't accepted; if the place is being auctioned, set your maximum and stick to it on the day.

How much can you borrow?

There is no fixed formula for how much you will be lent, since one bank will consider you a safe bet and another won't, but generally speaking the decision will be based on your annual income. Some banks may lend only 75 per cent of the property value, others up to 95 per cent.

If you're a single income earner, you're likely to be offered something in the region of three times your yearly income. If you're part of a couple with two incomes, buying as joint tenants, both incomes will be taken into account; two friends buying together as tenants in common will be assessed separately and may be offered different amounts, with different terms and conditions. In the UK, the rough rule of thumb which banks may or may not adhere to is three and a half times the annual earnings of a single borrower; two and a half times the combined earnings of a couple, or possibly three and a half times the income of the greater earner plus a year's earnings of the lesser.

BUYING WITH OTHERS

If you are buying a property with one or more others (partner, friend, relative), you must decide up-front what your legal attachment will be to each other. You can be 'joint tenants' (you each own the whole property and are, to all intents and purposes, regarded as a single entity) or 'tenants in common' (with distinct and specified shares in the property). The deciding factor is your personal relationship: joint tenancy is most usually chosen by couples in a relationship who are establishing a long-term household together. Should one die, ownership of the property automatically passes to the survivor; should one default on a payment, the other is responsible for it.

Tenants in common can sell their share of the property if they so choose, and their share is part of their estate when they die.

Friends pooling their resources to buy together is an increasingly popular solution to the exorbitant cost of getting into the property market. It needs to be formalised: a solicitor will draw up a document to be signed and witnessed, covering what will happen if one owner wants to sell. The usual provision is that the first option to buy the share on sale goes to the co-purchaser, with the sale price established by an independent registered valuer.

ADDITIONAL COSTS

As well as the price of the property itself, you need to factor in a range of associated expenses, which are considerable. They include:

- **Stamp duty** (a government tax based on the price of the property), which is a killer. In Australia the scale varies from state to state, but according to the range you are buying in, it is a fixed amount plus a percentage. The percentage, at the time of writing, on a $500,000 purchase ranges from 3.5 per cent in Queensland to 6 per cent in Victoria. There are online calculators to help you through the maze. In the UK, it's a percentage only and the escalator starts at £125,000: you pay 1 per cent to £250,000, 3 per cent to £500,000 and 4 per cent above £500,000.

- **Mortgage costs** – loan application and establishment fees, mortgage protection insurance.

- **Conveyancing costs** – fee, plus extra expenses such as costs of searches, postage, etc. (commonly known as disbursements).

- **Valuation and inspections fees.**

- **Insurance** on the new property, for which the buyer is responsible (depending on state laws in Australia) once contracts are exchanged, when you assume a legal interest in the property.

- **Cost of the move.**

Conveyancing

Conveyancing is all the legal work attached to buying and selling a property. It includes the preparation, examination and exchange of contracts between the seller and buyer, and the buyer and mortgage lender; conducting title and other relevant searches, like development proposals that might affect the property, or any outstanding debts against it; arranging all exchanges of funds; the payment of stamp duty; overseeing the change of title with the Land Registry; the adjustment of the final settlement amount once all outstanding bills have been deducted; and finalising the settlement. It can be carried out by a solicitor or a licensed conveyancer, or you can do it yourself (DIY kits are available online).

The work isn't arduous, but if you do it yourself you won't have the protection of professional indemnity, and professional indemnity is not to be sniffed at when it comes to contracts. The advantage of professionals is that they take the strain and they know what they are doing; the disadvantage is that you pay for the privilege. Agree on the fee in advance and ask for a list of all related disbursements and additional fees (searches, transfers, etc.).

If you are both buying and selling, each transaction will be charged separately (the cost of buying is marginally lower). The seemingly plodding progress of the conveyancer can drive you up the wall, but there are efficient, accessible and reasonably priced firms out there, so ask around for recommendations.

SELLER'S INFORMATION ABOUT THE PROPERTY

The conveyancer will press the seller for information on anything that looks cloudy or uncertain. But in the first instance, the contract of sale (or vendor's statement) must document everything a buyer might need to know, including the title (evidence of who owns the property), plans and diagrams (drainage, etc.), easements and covenants, planning information, building approvals, council rates, and so on. In the UK, vendors must supply an Energy Performance Certificate (EPC) as well as all the info above though a Home Information Pack (HIP) is no longer obligatory. Sellers of leasehold properties will need to provide a copy of the lease, most recent service charge accounts and receipts, building insurance policy details and receipts, regulations made by the landlord or management company as well as memorandum and articles of the landlord or management company.

Making an offer

If the property is being sold privately, make a reasonable offer on the basis of everything you know (though always 'subject to contract', meaning unless your conveyancer finds a reason for you to withdraw). It certainly doesn't have to be the asking price, or even your best offer: it might be the asking price less whatever you think you'll have to spend immediately to get the property up to scratch, or less whatever you think brings it into line with its true value.

If your offer is rejected, you can increase it and keep on increasing it by small increments until you reach your maximum, where you stick. The seller's agent should let you know if anyone else is interested. If others are, you might have to act aggressively and decisively – forget the small increments, and get in there with the asking price to demonstrate that you are prepared to move quickly.

Once your offer is accepted you may be asked for a small (refundable) deposit, which doesn't guarantee your purchase but indicates to the seller that you are serious.

At any point between your offer being accepted and the exchange of contracts, you can be gazumped, which means that someone else can enter the picture, make a higher offer and do the deal. It's a bugger. Alternatively, you might be invited to enter a ghastly bidding war, which you should reject come what may. Your best offer stays your best offer.

THE CHAIN

The joy of buying or selling at auctions is that it avoids 'the chain'. Bidders will already have their finance in place and the deal is agreed and made on the day. When you are buying or selling by private treaty, the real nightmare may only begin after you've made an offer, especially if you are buying as well as selling and your purchase is dependent on your sale. It means there are at least three people in the chain, but there can be many more – with everyone depending on each other's sales to get to their own exchange of contracts.

You escape the dreaded chain only if you or your purchaser is a cash buyer who doesn't need to sell a property to finance the purchase. The best precaution you can take as a seller who is also buying is to instruct agents only to show your property to buyers who have already received an offer on anything they are selling. It's no guarantee, but it's a help.

Buying at auction

The most important piece of advice is to know your limit and stick to it. The seller, in consultation with the agent, will have fixed a reserve price (the lowest price they are prepared to accept) for the property. If the bidding doesn't reach the reserve, the property is passed in and the seller usually negotiates (in the first instance, at least) with the highest bidder. If it passes the reserve, the property is then sold at the fall of the hammer. You are then obliged to proceed with the purchase or lose your deposit.

Always do your homework before attending an auction. Have the contract checked by a lawyer or conveyancer, get a copy of the Bidder's Guide (the selling agent is legally required to provide this) and make sure you read it. Familiarise yourself with the procedure by attending a couple of auctions as a viewer: watch the agents and watch the clever bidders. Don't allow yourself to be 'talked up' by the agent. If at all possible, though this is often not an option in Australia, avoid buying at auction when the market is strong.

Selling your home is hideous because the process of uprooting, which has become central to your happiness, is way beyond your control. No matter how appealing your property is to you, it just might not be what anyone in the marketplace wants right now at that price. You can drop the price or you can redo the kitchen, but it mightn't help and you don't want a fire sale. Hordes of people (with luck) are going to traipse through the rooms you live in deciding if they could possibly live in them. Some will like it, some won't, and the best you can do is hope that at least one lot comes back, makes an offer that isn't insulting and doesn't haggle interminably because their inspection report finds a brick loose. Then you have to hope they don't find something they like better the day before the deal becomes binding.

TIPS FOR AUCTION DAY

I have had only miserable experiences with the auction process, once buying and once selling. We were hustled into the purchase by the vendor's agent, who withheld salient facts regarding the property (it flooded) from us. We were hustled into the sale, where a single bidder paid 15 per cent less for the property than he later confided he might have, had the agent agreed to negotiate with him beforehand. More fool me. Never be hustled.

Some dos and don'ts:

● If you think you might get too emotionally involved and blow your budget, have a buyer's agent or at least a trusted friend bid for you. (If using a buyer's agent, negotiate a flat fee rather than a percentage of the purchase price.)

● Bear in mind that the auctioneer is entitled to make a bid on behalf of the seller (but must make clear that this is a seller's bid).

● Don't be pressured by agents into making a bid before you want to. Make your bids strongly and quickly in small increments.

● If the bidding stops and yours was the last bid, be wary of agents asking you for your best price, getting the seller to reduce the reserve to meet it, then informing the auctioneer the property is now on the market and inviting further bids. Keep your own counsel. Whoever wins the day, one of you will end up paying more than you otherwise might have.

Even at best it's a nightmare, unless you truly don't care whether you sell your place this year, next year or the year after. The only way to keep your stress levels in check is to modify your expectations. The market does what the market does, however great your hopes might be. You may, however, improve your chances of a successful sale by observing the following:

- Find an estate agent you like and trust. Get as many as you can bear to view your property, value it and explain how they think they can sell it. You're looking for someone who knows the area inside out, who doesn't exaggerate the potential of your property, who talks sense about its presentation, understands its unique selling points and so has a clear marketing strategy. Check local real-estate boards to see who has greatest claim to the area and who is selling most.

- Negotiate terms with them. Fees will depend on whether you agree sole agency rights or whether you want to place the property with several agents at the same time. If the agency's marketing strategy is a good one, sole agency is perfectly OK for a limited (agreed) period. Also agree how the arrangement can be terminated (automatically at the end of the term, or by notice in writing). Agents' fees aren't governed by law, so there's no standard rate: it can be anything from 1 per cent (rock-bottom in the UK) to 3 per cent. Make sure you know what you're getting for your money (where and how the property will be advertised, and so on): cheapest isn't necessarily best.

- Be realistic. As when buying, you will have done your homework and know what comparable properties are selling for. Yours might be top-of-the-range or bottom, but there will be a range, so work within it. Listen to the agents: their valuations should be more or less within the same ballpark – if they aren't, consult several more until you get the picture. Ignore anyone wildly above or below the mean.

- If you have overcapitalised, which is to say spent more on your house than you can possibly get back, remember the pleasure you took in the improvements and let that be your reward.

- Prepare the paperwork. Find a conveyancer. In the UK, arrange your Homebuyers Information Pack: you can do it yourself, or purchase one (for roughly £500) from a specialised firm or through your estate agent. If you do it yourself, you will have to pay for the Energy Performance Certificate. Talk to the agent.

- Prepare your house. Know the market and your likely purchasers. On the basis that you will be selling within the tribe, but possibly to a younger or older member, eliminate anything that might obviously offend them. I don't know – gnomes, damp, unpruned trees.

- Be flexible about viewings. Open houses are all very well, but don't suit everyone.

- Keep a record of all conversations with conveyancers and agents (emailing confirmation of what you've been told is great).

- If an offer is made, be guided by the expert – experienced agents know how to negotiate – but be clear in your head the price below which you will not go.

Before you decide to sell at auction, check the current success rate. It's usual for only three in five properties to sell under the hammer. In keen times, auctions can inflate prices; in lean times, more than the usual number of properties can be passed in (not sell). You can actually sell prior to auction, at auction or post auction, and you can set a reserve price below which the property may not be sold. This figure isn't declared to potential buyers prior to the auction and only becomes clear if it isn't reached and the highest bidder is encouraged to meet it.

When selecting an agent, take into account the candidates' track records at auctions. Because the sale may be decided and become final on the day of the auction, as with buying, all paperwork, (including the terms for settling any existing mortgage you may have) must be in place. Your agent and conveyancer will advise you, but information is also available online from consumer and real-estate websites.

Preparing your property for sale

First impressions count. Give the market what it wants to see: maybe stylish; maybe practical. In any case, make it clean and habitable, light and friendly, a place that works.

- Declutter.

- If a room or exterior woodwork badly needs a coat of paint, give it one.

- Fix any leaking taps.

- Sort out your wardrobes and cupboards, because people do look inside them.

- Tart up your garden if it needs it. Planting an abundance of lavender, red geraniums, or white impatiens can work wonders.

- If you have a tiled courtyard, power-clean the tiles.

- Keep the place clean, really clean, and always tidy before an inspection.

- Eliminate any strange or unpleasant odours (drains, damp), but don't go overboard with heady candles or browning onions.

- Be willing to accept professional advice on presentation if buyer interest is lacklustre.

FINALISING THE DEAL

At auctions this occurs on the day, if the property is sold. Buying by private treaty is a more measured process, which is both good and bad. You avoid the dreaded chain at auction but you must have nerves of steel to bid only within your range.

Exchange of contracts

When buying or selling by private treaty, contracts are only exchanged when both you and the conveyancer are happy to proceed on the basis of all the reports and searches; both seller and buyer are happy; any mortgage offers are in; the deposit is in place; and you've agreed a settlement date. When the contracts are signed the deal becomes legally binding. If you drop out now you lose your deposit, although in some Australian states there is a three- to five-day cooling-off period. Don't drop out now unless something monumental has occurred. Breathe a huge sigh of relief, and get stuck into packing up and moving out (or preparing to do so if the settlement date is distant). This can be an orderly and calm process, if you still have orderly and calm in you.

Preparing to move

The minute you've exchanged contracts and fixed a settlement date, the die is cast. Don't pretend you can just book removalists and go. It's never so simple. First you must cull, and this begins with a serious look at every room with a hard heart and a beady eye (see Chapter 5). Get rid of everything you haven't used in years, will probably never use again and to which you have no sentimental attachment. This includes clothes, books, kitchen stuff, china, vases, empty boxes, gardening equipment, flower pots, ancient paperwork and most things in the bathroom cabinet.

If settlement is weeks away, book a removalist to take your goods from A to B; to pack your things at A and remove to B; or to pack your things at A, remove to B, and unpack. If you want the movers to pack and unpack, they will need one or more days on either side of the move in both your former and new homes. Unless their labelling is scrupulous and everything they pack has a precise designation, you need to be realistic about their input and whether those extra days are worth the extra cost.

If you choose to do the packing yourself, you will need many, many boxes. Removal people sell them or you can collect them from supermarkets and bottle shops. Pack them in your own time, if this is the route you choose, and continue to cull as you go. Label every box, before it leaves the house, by: a) designated room; and b) contents.

Completion (settlement)

Completion (settlement) takes place at a date agreed in the contract, usually four weeks after the exchange of contracts but any time that suits both buyer and seller (it can be on the same day as exchange of contracts). On the agreed date, the usual process is for the buyer (or the buyer's lender) to forward the balance of the purchase price to the vendor's conveyancer and for the buyer to receive the deeds and the keys to the property.

Should you be both buying and selling on the same day, your nerves will have been thoroughly racked because you will have had two processes to finalise, with twice as many steps to master. But hooray! By now, with luck, the removalists will be on the way and you will have organised the transfer of utilities and services (gas, water, rates, electricity, phone) and made sure that the seller has arranged final meter readings at your new home (the estate agent often organises this).

········ MOVING INTO YOUR NEW PLACE ········

How quickly you settle in will be a matter of temperament and energy. Most of us, in the early stages, tackle the most urgent mess – make the beds, hang our clothes, store the cutlery, pots and pans and china, put away food, stick essentials into the bathroom and laundry – then we take a breather.

This breather can last several years. During this time, we may be living with a room totally occupied by unemptied boxes containing books, family photos, paintings, lamps, additional china and glasses, toys, family games, out-of-season clothes and the rest of the towels and sheets, and we'll do without them until we badly need the room they are occupying. This raises the question: can we do without them permanently? Give the box contents four weeks to be missed and then read them the riot act: Find a place to be or leave home.

DOWNSIZING

Downsizing is one of life's great tests of character. When your children leave home, you need less space on the one hand, but enough room on the other for the whole family to be together in the event of a nuclear war or Christmas. We decided to swap the family house in town for a smaller house in town and a place in the country. I say 'in the country' – the town house was in London, the country house in Australia.

Life in the smaller house was a disaster from day one, mostly because I broke every one of the above rules, especially the culling one. The only way our stuff could be shoehorned into the smaller house was by stacking every room to the rafters. Then builders moved in to extend the place and though I put half our possessions into storage, the builders could still only do their extending if they moved like crabs. Then my husband and I caught flu and had to spent a week in bed, during which time the heaving mess downstairs became part of a nightmare which never went away. So we had to move. We swapped the smaller house for a flat, culled properly and made provision for stuff we loved but didn't need every day. There were two morals: don't swap large for small when you really want different; cull and label. Seriously.

18

GETTING THE PLACE STRAIGHT

The conditions in which we live describe us to the world. Not completely, obviously – the dark recesses are the dark recesses. But our slightly-less-than-basic instincts are reflected well and truly in our own four walls. Strangers walk in the door, they clock the colour scheme, the furniture, the smell of disinfectant or candles, the light, the space, the air, and they already know more about us than the taxman. This isn't an argument for getting your place up to scratch, because whose business is it if you are a stinky hoarder? No. The reason you keep your house in order is because it does wonders for your head and for your heart. This is true whether you've just moved in or whether you've lived in the same place for years, only vaguely noticing the decay.

House-proud doesn't have to mean barking. It can just mean quiet satisfaction with the way you've arranged things. This can extend from having the right number of rooms doing exactly what you want them to do while looking rather nice to living in a show house. I'm in no position to advise on the show house, but simple enhancements can be tackled by any old householder, however strapped for cash or time. All that's required is a will and a moderate understanding of light, space and air (as well as the significance of smells). According to design guru Terence Conran, flooding a room with natural light will make your heart sing. Even if you do nothing else, wash the curtains and clean the windows. On the other hand, the time might have come for you to rip the place apart and turn it into a home that works for you.

RENOVATING

A major renovation, by which I mean a serious reconstruction of one sort or another, is never undertaken lightly. It's most likely to be required when you move into a run-down place you already knew was too small or too shabby, or when your household expands and the choice is to move or improve. Improving can be so much easier and cheaper than moving. You can get a new kitchen for the cost of the stamp duty on the sale of your house, and a new bathroom for the estate agent's fees.

The question might arise as to how much of the work you can do yourself. Were it asked in our house the answer would be 'None', but that's us. Only you know how skilled you are, how much time you have, your level of commitment and the level of commitment of the friends you will be calling upon to help. Everyone else knows you'd have to score pretty high on all four counts to entertain the idea even vaguely, so the first rule of renovation is 'Don't kid yourself'. If you haven't already done so, live in the place for a while to see exactly what changes must be made, then calculate how much can be achieved, with the least disruption, for the money you have. If you need more rooms because all the others are spilling into the hallway, maybe you need to declutter and build storage (see Chapter 5). If you need more light, your problem may be as straightforward as the tunnel that is your hall, which could be fixed with a modest skylight. Look first for simplicity of action, then examine the likely effectiveness of anything so simple.

Most serious reconstruction needs council approval and this will involve the submission of plans and contracts. Since these requirements can change from year to year and are different from council to council, your very first step is a phone call to the local planning office to see what is required for the work you're considering. In the UK, both planning and building departments need to be consulted, so phone both. Next step is to get advice.

Which expert?

Who you need depends on the scope of the project and the amount of expert input you'd appreciate. If you know what you want but not how to achieve it, and you're talking big bucks, you really need an architect. If you know what you want and how to achieve it, but need plans for council approval and for your builder to work from, an architectural draughtsman to translate your ideas onto paper will fit the bill (and be cheaper). If council approval isn't required, you know what you want and you simply need to know if it's achievable and at what cost, talk to a builder. Talk to several builders.

For advice and information about choosing and working with architects and builders, contact the Royal Australian Institute of Architects (RAIA) or Royal Institute of British Architects (RIBA).

ARCHITECTS

Architects are costly, but if you have a serious problem with space, light or function, and originality of design is important to you, they are your best bet. Architects also advise on planning, construction, cost and building regulations, and they oversee the project to make sure that what you want to have happen is happening. Architects would argue that their ingenuity can save you money and their originality will add value to your property, and these are no mean considerations.

To find an architect that suits you, the usual rules apply:

- Ask around for recommendations.

- Talk to more than one candidate, and look at their work.

- Find someone whose speciality suits your problem.

- Make sure they are qualified, and registered with the relevant professional body.

- Be clear about fees (including the first consultation). They may suggest a flat fee, an hourly rate, or a percentage – which can be as high as 20 per cent of the final cost of the project. Also make sure you know what the fee covers.

ARCHITECTURAL DRAUGHTSPERSONS

An accomplished draughtsman or woman can be excellent value for money. Not only do they draw up plans to your specifications, but they often find simple yet cunning improvements to your vision. They will provide a site plan showing how your recon-structed building will look from various angles in relation to the buildings and gardens around it, and a floor plan specifying not only dimensions but also the materials to be used. Their plan will form the basis of your instructions to the builder.

Their fee should be agreed in advance (they may charge per hour) and you should discuss in an initial consultation exactly what you can expect for it. The best recommendations I ever had for draughtsmen came from builders, so if you have a builder in mind, ask him or her.

BUILDERS

A good builder can walk into a property, spot flaws that must be addressed, appreciate problems you've identified and have solutions for both. He (or she) will be able to cost the work required, work within a budget and a time-frame and have the flexibility to negotiate the changing circumstances and/or unforeseen difficulties which are the hallmark of renovations. You find these paragons only by asking around. Since the job is by its nature fraught, anyone who can be recommended with few reservations is worth considering. You will be looking for a problem-solver, a positive thinker with clear insights into buildings and how they work, and with access to a reliable and loyal team.

How to find a builder

⊙ Ask around for personal recommendations (three if possible).

⊙ If you can't get recommendations, ask for the names of local builders from trade associations (Federation of Master Builders in the UK or the Master Builders Association in Australia), then contact them and ask for references. Ask to see examples of their work.

⊙ Write a detailed specification of the work you want done. Trade associations have specification forms to make life easier. If you need help, consult an draughtsman who will write one for you (advisable on large jobs).

⊙ Specify preferred materials. Builders usually quote for the cheapest available.

⊙ Talk to the builders about your plans and assess their approach. Your problem-solver must have endless stamina and patience.

⊙ Ask only builders you like to quote for the job. Quotes should be separated into labour and materials for every step of the project (plastering, painting, wiring, etc.) and should include any GST or VAT payable.

⊙ Check the builder has appropriate insurance. Forget the 'home-owners' warranty' (Australia), which is currently compulsory but also toothless: the builder should have their own insurance against accident and faulty materials, and to guarantee the quality of the work.

⊙ Avoid changing your mind halfway through the job. Variations, as they are called, cost more money and cause delays as well as that funny look builders get before they shake their heads in disbelief.

⊙ Festering relationships with builders are disastrous. If the problem lingers, put it in writing. If it can't be resolved, get advice from offices of fair trading or consumer affairs.

Your approach to the work and workers

Both builders and architects are notoriously quick to take offence, possibly owing to their artistic natures or possibly because, over the years, their every job has entailed a degree of customer dissatisfaction that has taken years off their lives, or anyway miles off their tether. You need to establish a productive relationship with both.

THE BUILDING CONTRACT

You should have a contract with your builder. In Australia contracts between registered builders and owners are governed by legislation, which as usual differs from state to state, but you can get a standard contract from offices of fair trading or consumer affairs or the Master Builders Association in Australia, or from the Federation of Master Builders in the UK.

Things that should be included:

⊙ a payment schedule, which should be dependent on the completion of specified stages (a final 10 per cent should be withheld until final inspection);

⊙ who is responsible for inspections (in Australia, contact your local council; in the UK, both the planning and building departments of local authorities who have separate regulations);

⊙ start and finish dates (and any penalties that might be appropriate if a job is abandoned or unacceptably delayed);

⊙ extra terms, like the site being cleared at the end of the day and where materials can be stored.

Make sure you understand the contract: what is included in the price and what costs might change throughout the job. Contracts may be fixed-price (for a specified amount), although these will include clauses to protect builders from unforeseen expenses; or cost-plus, which are for recoverable costs plus the builder's profit (which is often not specified). Read every word and clarify anything you don't understand or find acceptable.

An architect may provide some sort of buffer between you and your builder, but if you're living in the property while it's being renovated, or if you are overseeing the project yourself, then sympathy for your builder is critical. I'd go so far as to say that a householder's relationship with their builder is as delicate as the most finely tuned marriage, so sensitivity is required from the word go. Jobs always cost them money; plans are never as simple as they looked when quoting; clients never stick to the brief; the cost of materials always rises mid-job; the tradesmen they use will always let them down eventually; and the weather never fails to interrupt their flow. In the interests of a happy home, you must respect their levels of stress and not overreact the minute you spot a flaw in the craftsmanship.

Develop a frank but friendly relationship: if you have concerns, ask questions before making accusations; if concerns become problems, ask for options before delivering an ultimatum. If the materials aren't those you asked for, the dimensions aren't those you agreed, the quality of the workmanship is less than perfect, or there are cigarette butts in the sink, mention it at once, but nicely. It's unusual for jobs to end on completely comfortable terms because there's always 'snagging', the resolving of last-minute details, and builders dislike last-minute details as much as the next busy person. Be firm but fair. You don't want to be staring at unfinished paintwork in the bathroom for the next ten years and cursing the person who refused to fix it just because he or she had had enough of you and you couldn't bear to complain.

REDESIGNING

This is another word for rearranging your home without having to rebuild it. You do this when the spaces available to you aren't delivering according to the need and expectations you have of them, either functionally or aesthetically.

To discover the root of your problem, if it isn't immediately apparent, examine the basics. All householders need spaces for sleeping, bathing, cooking, eating, laundry, entertaining and mooching about. Spaces for sleeping must generally incorporate a space for clothes and for dressing; spaces for bathing also need a space for dressing and body maintenance; spaces for cooking must also include the storage of food and possibly eating it; if a separate laundry isn't available, it may need to be housed in a cupboard in or off the bathroom or kitchen; living areas require enough space for all the things you, as an idiosyncratic household, do in the usual course of a day or week when you aren't sleeping, eating, working or bathing.

A simple exercise is to draw a plan of each room in your home, list the things you expect of it and decide where it's going wrong. If you move things about, will it be more effective? If you swap a bedroom for a living room or a study, do matters improve? If you replace heavy furniture with open shelves or with something less weighty (like cane or bamboo), will the tension go away? If light (the lack of it) is the problem, can it be resolved with mirrors, paler paintwork, bigger windows, or swapping heavy curtains for double-glazed windows hung with blinds or lighter curtains?

The possibilities for small improvements are endless. I've covered those that I have had to make with every house move I've ever made, which isn't to say there aren't dozens more. If you're stuck, a one-off consultation with an interior designer can solve a multitude of problems. Check the websites of anyone local or recommended, and look for a style that appeals to you, bearing in mind that taste isn't acquired with training – it's either yours or it's not.

Quick kitchen makeover

Kitchens can be instantly and vastly improved by changing cupboard doors, drawer fronts, door handles, the work surface and light fittings, none of which need cost a fortune. You can use tile paint on the splashback and you can smarten your white goods with fridge and appliance paint (available from hardware shops). If the bare bones make sense – which is to say, you have enough storage and work spaces, and the appliances are in the right place – then you need go no further.

Ideally, a triangle should be created by the sink, fridge and stove for maximum efficiency during cooking and cleaning up. The theory is that this minimises the number of steps the cook or cleaner-up must take, with each leg of the triangle being somewhere between one and three metres. If your kitchen just doesn't work and you can't afford a made-to-measure solution, loads of firms sell units off the peg for DIY assembly (and if you hate DIY assembly, loads of odd-job firms devote themselves exclusively to converting a flat pack into a five-storey building – google 'flat pack assembly' for your nearest).

Quick bathroom makeover

Bathrooms look miles worse than they are if there's damp above the shower and discoloured or loose grout between the tiles, and there's a build-up of soap in the shower or around the taps. Before chucking the baby out with the bathwater, give the room a decent clean (see Chapter 6) and address the damp issue (see Chapter 19).

If an old bath is handsome but stained, get it resurfaced. It's possible to do this yourself, but if you're not used to or even inclined to work with unfamiliar and hazardous chemicals in a small space, bring in an expert. If other fixtures and fittings are chipped, outdated or thoroughly clapped out, replace them. Provided you don't want to move them (which can be a plumbing nightmare), the cost doesn't have to be vast. You can take the opportunity to buy water-saving taps and showerheads.

Since this room is usually your smallest, space will be at a premium and clutter does it no favours. Minimalism is only averagely successful in a bathroom, even if it does look great in showrooms. We have to put our toothbrushes, shavers and spare toilet paper somewhere, so allow at least for a cabinet: either freestanding, or behind the mirror above the basin, below the basin in a vanity unit, or above the loo where it must be slim enough not to knock anyone in a hurry unconscious. Replace old and ineffective light fittings, and give the room a fresh coast of paint, including any tiles that are stained, horrible or need re-grouting anyway.

PAINTING

It's staggering how quickly painting, especially when combined with decluttering, can transform a room from Fagin's den to a sunroom. And all of us can do both if we try. I know it needs time and patience, but finding time and patience is nothing compared to living with gloom and despair.

Which colours to use doesn't warrant much discussion and too many alternatives will only put you off, so I'll keep it simple. Choose them to suit your interesting new mood: light colours brighten and soften a room; a ceiling lighter than the walls gives an impression of greater height, and vice versa; feature walls are a matter of taste, but can visually shorten a long skinny room. Three colours to a room is as much as any single space can stand, in my opinion, and if there are two they should ideally be different depths of the same colour.

The paint

What follows is the broad advice given by traditionalists. As with anything defined by taste, you can do what you like and the options stretch far beyond those described here. If you're planning to redecorate, it always pays to pick up a clutch of interior-design magazines to inform and inspire you, even if they do send you scurrying back to the good old ways.

The usual rule is a matte (flat) emulsion (water-based acrylic) paint for walls and ceilings, and tougher, enamel or gloss (traditionally oil-based, but now available in acrylic) for woodwork. Gloss can be shiny, less shiny or even less shiny: the less shiny versions are called semi-gloss, eggshell or satin. Generally speaking, the more imperfections there are in woodwork, the less shiny it should be. Semi-gloss paint is often recommended for bathroom and kitchen walls because it's easily washable and steam-resistant.

You will need an undercoat paint for new unpainted surfaces, for surfaces that have been painted in gloss and for dark colours that need covering. White emulsion is recommended because it's cheaper, and a paint that goes on pink and dries to white is better still, so that when you paint white over white you can see where you've been. You'll also need a primer for any woodwork, because it creates a flat and less porous surface on which to paint, and protects both the wood and the paint. Other than that, most surfaces require two coats of the chosen colour.

The quality of paint you buy is a matter of taste and cost. Some upmarket specialist shops offer a broader range of subtle colours, but generally speaking, most paint shops can colour-match anything and the finish is rarely obviously cheap or expensive. If your concern is avoiding the use of chemicals, eco-friendly paints (which have no volatile organic compounds) are available in both emulsion and gloss, though not necessarily on your doorstep. They are water-based and solvent-free, and so fume-free, and are more expensive than traditional paints but may well be worth the investment. Google 'eco-friendly paints' and the choice is yours.

HOW MUCH?

The paint store can advise on the amount of paint you're likely to need; but, roughly, 1 litre of paint covers an area of 14 square metres (150 square feet). To calculate the area of each room, multiply the height by the length by the width (or, for each wall, the height by the width). A room of, say, 4 metres by 4 metres will need about 2 litres for the walls and 1.2 litres for the ceiling. (You should increase the quantity by about 20 per cent if painting previously unpainted or very absorbent surfaces.)

Rollers, brushes and other equipment

As well as the paint you'll need the following basics:

- One or more paint rollers and several sleeves. The wider the diameter of the roller, the more coverage it will give; the thicker and fluffier the sleeve, the better it will hide imperfections. Sleeves come in natural or man-made fibres. Mohair sleeves can be used on textured walls; for a smoother finish, use a short-pile microfibre sleeve. Foam rollers are fine for smooth surfaces.

- One or two roller trays. Also invest in a pole for the roller (saves you scrambling up and down the ladder to refill the tray).

- Brushes for small surfaces and woodwork (at least one 74-mm/3-in brush); and for 'cutting in' – which is to say, painting a straight line along an edge, to avoid the abutting surface – at least one 37-mm/1½-in brush.

Other useful tools are:

- sheets to cover furniture and floors (not plastic sheets, which don't absorb spillage);

- lots of old cloths, for wiping up spills;

- masking tape;

- a surface filler for cracks and small holes, and/or a flexible sealant (usually acrylic) for gaps around windows, etc.; and a knife or spatula to apply it;

- sandpaper of different grades (the rougher the surface you are preparing, the coarser the grade you will need) and a dust mask;

- goggles;

- a stepladder.

Painting tips

Once equipped, you are ready to begin. Remove whatever you can from the room, then drag everything else into the middle and cover it with one or more old sheets. Cover the floor with sheets (or with newspaper if you've now run out of sheets). Take everything from the walls and windows, then use masking tape to cover areas that aren't intentionally to be painted in the wall colours: the edges of doorways, skirting boards, cornices, picture rails, windows, light fittings and switches and power points.

An option at this juncture is to apply a mist coat to the walls (one part white emulsion to one part water). This will reveal any imperfections in the surface, which you can then fill. Also at this stage fill any gaps around window frames and skirting boards, and sandpaper not only the filled areas but all the walls and woodwork. Finally, dust them down thoroughly with a clean, dry brush.

Now you can start the painting.

- Begin with the ceiling. (Wear goggles if you think paint might drip into your eyes, and some sort of head covering to avoid paint-speckled hair.) Methods are always open to argument, but the advice I had was first, to 'cut in' where the ceiling meets the wall. You hold a loaded brush with its edge tight to the junction, and paint a horizontal 5-centimetre (2-inch) strip all the way around the room. Then use a roller on a pole for the body of the ceiling: paint about a square metre at a time, overlapping each section as you go, zigzagging for maximum coverage and then blending the sections in when you've finished. You may need three coats for a perfect finish.

- Before painting the walls, use a small brush to cut in again, this time around the wall where it joins the ceiling, skirting boards, windows and door frames, as well as any light fittings and power points.

- To paint large expanses of walls, use a roller on a pole held at a 45° angle to the wall. Beginning with an upward stroke, paint the undercoat using zigzag diagonal strokes. The first of the colour coats should be horizontal strokes; the top coat should be painted vertically. Follow the manufacturer's instructions about the drying time needed between coats.

- Remember to remove any masking tape before the paint dries.

- Paint doors and windows last, using a small brush to apply a primer first if needed, then an undercoat (sometimes these are combined in a single product) and finally, the top coat. As you go, shield freshly painted walls with a strip of cardboard held at an angle between the edge of the wall and the trim.

- To store unused paint, replace the lid and leave the can upside down to stop a skin forming.

If there is a damp patch on a wall or ceiling, sort it out before you tackle the rest of the room. First, make sure the cause of the damp has been identified and rectified and that the area is now dry (see Chapter 19). Scrape away anything that looks like mould, then sand the area. Apply a coat or two of stain-block paint (from any paint shop) and then paint as per the above advice.

SANDING FLOORS

It's a job many of us would rather not – and, in many cases, just shouldn't – do ourselves, but it is doable and the results, even when not entirely perfect, can be miraculous. First, however, ask yourself:

- what condition the floorboards are in (are they thick enough to take sanding; are they covered in old glue, full of nails, half-rotten or mismatching, and so not worth the effort of sanding?);

- how handy you are with a heavy piece of machinery;

- what it would cost to employ a professional compared to what it would cost to hire sanding and edging machines as well as pay for the bits and pieces that go with them (sandpaper, dust mask, sealants, stains, etc.);

- whether you can stand the disruption, given that the whole process can take four or five days;

- whether sisal, coir or some other natural covering mightn't be a better option, as they are as stylish and long-wearing as timber, if not as allergy-friendly or as easy to clean if stained.

The cost

As a very rough guide, having a room professionally sanded costs £25–£50 a square metre in the UK and $20–$50 in Australia; DIY would cost about half that much. Sisal costs somewhere in the region of £35 (around $60) a square metre.

DIY sanding

Should you decide to have a go yourself, you will need two sanders, a heavy one for the main floor surface and a smaller one for the edges (the main machine will need two people to lift it). The following tips (while not comprehensive instructions) are from a floor-equipment hirer:

○ Seal the room and any electrical outlets and fittings before you start: fine dust spreads through the house like a mist from the marsh.

○ Sink any protruding nails (use a nail punch) below the boards' surface, as well as filling any gaps between the boards.

○ Make sure you attach the sandpaper tightly enough (consult the hirer as to the exact method when you collect the machines).

○ Wear a proper dust mask and goggles.

○ Do the edging first, then the main floor area.

○ Most floors need to be sanded three times with different grades of sandpaper, beginning with rough and ending with fine.

○ To avoid track marks, the first sanding should crisscross the room and subsequent ones should be along (up and down) the boards.

○ Keep the sander moving slowly and steadily: if you allow the machine to rest, it will continue to sand on the spot. For the same reason, tilt the machine so the sandpaper is not touching the floor when you turn around at the end of each run.

APPLYING VARNISH

Before applying varnish, dust the floor very thoroughly. It will need two or three coats of varnish and you should sand the floor lightly between coats. Follow the manufacturer's instructions for applying the varnish and for drying times.

FURNISHINGS

Not everyone furnishes their house with a view to style. Mostly a house is furnished according to needs that grow and change according to who's in residence. New householders begin with the basics according to budget; existing households are subject to periods of reorganisation as a result of bursts of energy, income or despair.

Out goes retro or shabby chic to be replaced by minimalism, which lasts as long as it takes for the household to return to its default position of cluttered.

Whenever you are furnishing or refurnishing, your two considerations are function – within the available space and according to the needs of the household – then style. Dumping a solid table for something glorious in glass won't work if children or clumsy adults will crash into it and brain themselves. If you're starting from scratch:

- Buy on a 'needs must' basis: that is, the basics first – and maybe also last if you like your spaces clear and uncluttered.

- Start with the main item in the room (bed, sofa or table), place it for light and convenience, then add subsidiary items. Balance the room with pieces of a similar scale: a large sofa needs another sofa or a pair of large occasional chairs opposite it.

- If you can, spend money on sofas and beds, because you want them to last and you want them to be comfortable. You can spend your life on them.

- Mix soft with solid. Wooden floors are served best by rugs and soft upholstery, and not too much more wood.

- Mix the heights of your furniture. Lamps provide good variation.

What you buy is up to you, but there are two things worth remembering. Identifying what you want in a shop and then buying it online can save a fortune. Buying from secondhand or charity shops, auctions and markets is well worth exploring: not only can you pick up bargains, but they are likely to be as stylish as any furniture fashionista could want and they won't be contributing to some huge pile of landfill.

I would like to suggest buying eco-friendly furniture, but in befriending one bit of eco you will be offending another. If it's not made from something that should never have been chopped down in the first place, its manufacture will be sure to have involved petrochemicals or it will have been shipped many miles at some exorbitant cost to the ozone layer. Try, where you can:

- to buy locally made;

- to buy organic upholstery and bedding (from organically grown cotton, for example);

- to shun endangered timbers and choose bamboo or rattan, or anything else un-endangered or climate-friendly.

HOUSE PLANTS

If your main rooms look lifeless and flat, a strategically placed house plant can make a monumental difference. Just don't let it die, because turning a room into a plant morgue is worse than it looking lifeless in the first place.

When it comes to deciding which plants, the first things to consider are the room's available light and typical temperature. Too much light and the leaves will scorch; too little and the plant can't produce enough food to survive. The temperature should be warm but even (somewhere between 18°C/65°F and 20°C/70°F). So look for a spot near a window but not on the sill (too cold in the winter and too hot in the summer) or near a radiator (too warm). A test for enough light is being able to see the plant's shadow on the wall behind on a sunny day.

Plant care

Tropical plants appreciate a spray of water each day, but house plants in general are more likely to be killed by kindness than by neglect, so don't overwater. (Leaves going brown from the tip is a sign of dryness.) Keep the soil moist but not sopping, and use luke-warm rather than cold water to avoid giving the plant heart failure. Water the pot in a tray, so the plant can slurp up any overflow.

Feed plants with something liquid containing potash when they are actively growing (spring and summer). Repot them when they seem seriously to have out-grown their current one. Water the plant and let it drain before repotting, and try to remember what potting mixture you used in the first pot because the plant would very much appreciate the same again.

HANGING PICTURES

Bare walls are depressing as are walls hung with plates and rugs and pictures of every sort, which bear down on you in a Temple of Doom kind of way, but you know what you like. On the other hand, you may not know how to arrange what you like to its best advantage. You can hammer a nail in any old place and whack up a picture, but you need first to avoid having it fall on your head or the head of a passing baby, and second to hang it where it can be seen to its best advantage.

Secure hanging

How you hang pictures depends both on whether the wall is solid or hollow (cavity) and on the weight of the picture. You will, in any case, need:

- a hammer;

- a pencil;

- a tape measure or ruler;

- a spirit level;

- two people, if possible and the pictures are heavy;

- picture hooks, if the pictures are small;

- a drill, if the pictures are large/heavy, plus plastic rawl (wall) plugs and screws for a solid wall, or spring toggles for a cavity wall.

Small to medium pictures can, by and large, be hung anywhere. To hang a heavy picture on a solid wall, drill a hole, insert a plug and then the screw. For a cavity wall, since plaster provides an unreliable fixing, make your fitting to a stud (vertical beam): to locate one, tap along the wall until the sound stops being hollow and is more of a thud (or buy a stud finder from the hardware store). With plasterboard, drill a hole and insert a spring toggle or similar fitting (the toggle springs out behind the plasterboard and so can't be wrenched out).

Arrangement

This will depend on how many pictures you have to hang, how much wall space is available to you and the effect you are going for. In my opinion, a small lonely picture on a large wall looks mad and a very large picture on a small wall terrifying. A cluster can form the focal point of a room or it can just mean that some gems get lost in a pretty ordinary crowd. Since what you rate as a gem is a matter for you, only you can decide which pictures deserve prominence and special lighting. That said, if you are talking serious artworks and you don't mind paying, specialist advice on hanging and even framing is available (search online for 'art hanging advice').

For DIY picture placement, consider the following guidelines:

- Match the arrangement to the shape of the available space.

- Equal-sized pictures work best side by side, unless you are hanging in a vertical rectangle (when one on top of the other works better, especially if pictures are smallish).

- Take into account what else is on the wall – light switches, lamps, windows – and don't argue with them,

- Pictures are best hung at eye level.

- When hanging pictures beside stairs, follow the angle of the banister.

Having decided where you want to hang your picture or pictures, measure distances between the pictures and any obvious boundaries like walls and doors and floors. If you are hanging several pictures in a group, make a plan on a piece of paper, noting the measurements between each and between the boundaries of the allocated space. Make pencil marks on the wall if the arrangement is in any way intricate (more than two), starting with the central picture and moving outwards or upwards according to the layout.

To place the fitting accurately, enlist a helper if you can to hold the picture up to the wall, in the space assigned to it. Agree between you that there are no pipes or wires behind it (so, it should not be not directly above light fittings, power points or any rough patches that might suggest pipes). Now take hold of the picture wire and make a pencil mark on the wall at a spot roughly two-thirds of the way up the picture. Put in a temporary fitting (a couple of nails if necessary) and hang the picture, with the second person ready to catch it if it drops. Stand back, adjust the position if necessary, then install the appropriate fitting. Test the picture is straight, using a spirit level, adjust again and then stand back. Under no circumstances should you hit the second person with the hammer at this point in time. This method has been tried and tested in our household more times than I care to remember.

19

HOUSEHOLD MAINTENANCE

Looking after the structure that is your home is critical for many reasons, even if you do prefer a relaxed approach to property. What begins as mild wear and tear can become neglect without notice, and neglect will lead to dilapidation. Dilapidation causes emergencies and emergencies cost time, money and comfort. So keep the light bulbs working, the gutters in order, the drains clear, the paintwork up to scratch and the lawns mowed. Attend to the dripping taps and the sticking doors. Ignoring them may not lead to the place falling down, but they will cause a sagging of the spirits in everyone but the most transcended.

Having said that, I'm not going to overwhelm you with technical drawings and overly complicated instructions. I've confined the scope of this chapter to the very least householders who aren't too cack-handed might be expected to master in order to keep misery at bay. It's for those like me who have a minimum commitment to maintenance, because frankly there's always something better to do, but have come to appreciate that it can't be ignored and it isn't so hard once you understand it.

DIY OR GET HELP?

For any electrical or plumbing job that's more technical than changing a light bulb or possibly unblocking the sink, it's worth getting expert (or at least experienced) help. Not only can attempting to solve it yourself complicate matters needlessly, but it can kill you (for which reason, certain jobs must by law be done by qualified tradespeople in Australia, and/or approved by a building inspector in the UK). This isn't to suggest you are next to useless, just that you are almost certainly time-poor and ill-equipped and probably not very interested.

Finding tradespeople you can trust (not only to do the job but also to turn up at all in a crisis) isn't always easy, but make a point of hunting them down and cherishing them. Ask friends and neighbours for greatly respected locals, but if you're truly stuck, look in the Yellow Pages or online for someone registered with a trade organisation.

REGULAR INSPECTIONS

Regardless of your usefulness (or otherwise) with tools, there is a simple task for which all householders can and must be responsible. This is to be vigilant, to recognise a problem when you smell or see it, and to be able to conduct an informed conversation with any expert summoned to help, who might try to blind you with science. Infinitely better, though, is to avoid the problem in the first place.

On the basis that prevention is better than cure, keep a beady eye on the trouble spots. For peace of mind, get your wiring checked by an electrician and your gas fittings by a plumber regularly; every couple of years, get in a pest inspector to look for anything gnawing into the timbers or making nests in the eaves. But every single year, it pays to make regular maintenance checks yourself.

This means checking the place from top to bottom, starting with the roof and ending with whatever is under the house, or starting with ceilings and ending with floors if you're in a flat. Begin with a preventive clearing of the drains by pouring some kind of cleanser down them to clear any build-up of grease. (To be even more preventive, avoid pouring fat down them in the first place.) You are looking for any sign of decay, collapse, damp or damage: discoloured or peeling paintwork, rotting or broken timbers, chipped glass, cracks or gaps around windows and doors, missing flyscreens, missing or non-functioning light bulbs, dripping taps, leaking showerheads, crumbling plaster – anything that suggests a problem in the offing. The offing is soon enough for a problem to be tackled, and nowhere is this more evident that in the case of damp.

INDOORS

Damp

Damp is harrowing. I appreciate that its effects can be felt both indoors and outdoors, but damp indoors is marginally more upsetting. It not only smells disheartening and produces mould on your walls, in your wardrobes and on your clothes, but it can be a health hazard ridiculously difficult to treat. The usual causes are less-than-vigilant maintenance, poor construction or dodgy plumbing.

IDENTIFYING IT

There's a limit to the amount that you, as a non-expert, can do to remedy the problem once it's occurred, but you can recognise it when you see it and act quickly. If you spot a damp patch in an unlikely place (in the middle of a ceiling, for example, as opposed to on the bathroom floor), you're probably looking at a leak from a rogue central-heating or water pipe, a poor seal around a bath or shower upstairs, or a badly plumbed-in appliance.

But it could be *penetrating damp* which is to say that water has found a way in through some kind of gap in an external wall and travelled along a joist to pool where it wants to (as it did once in a kitchen of ours). You need a plumber to conduct a proper search (as ours did). Penetrating damp can also be caused by faulty downpipes, broken guttering, missing grout in brickwork, missing roof tiles, or any number of structural flaws a good builder can locate.

Rising damp, on the other hand, which starts at the base of walls, can often be spotted as bubbling or stained plaster around skirting boards. It is usually caused by a failure of an existing damp-proof course, the lack of a damp-proof course, or a deterioration in the building's substructure, possibly as a result of movement. But there may be other causes so get advice from a firm specialising in the treatment of damp. Rising damp is commonly remedied by the installation of a new damp-proof course (an injection of chemicals into the walls, which creates a membrane above which the damp can't travel). Whoever does the job should guarantee their work, because you'll need paperwork as proof should you ever sell your house.

There's also damp caused by *poor ventilation*, which sounds harmless enough when ensuring proper air circulation is as simple as opening doors and windows (always air the bathroom even if it has an extractor fan). Something may, though, be blocking the flow of air through or under the house, or preventing the release of moisture from a room, and this needs investigating. Or the problem can be profound and structural, so it's worth getting a damp-proofer to confirm your diagnosis and to fix the problem. With luck, the cause will be obvious and the right tradesperson will be able to fix it without fuss or undue cost: the solutions can be as straightforward as fans in the bathroom and kitchen, or air vents in or below affected rooms.

But here's the thing. It might have been avoided if you'd spotted the problem early.

Plumbing

Most plumbing problems are related to blockages and, as per the above, the best you can do is take preventive measures. The simplest is to fit sinks and drains with strainers to filter tea leaves, coffee dregs, remains of meals, and hair before they get the chance to congeal into such an unpalatable ball that the trap in the drain just gives up and goes home. They're available in supermarkets and hardware stores, and cost next-to nothing compared to the trouble they're avoiding. Even easier in theory, but so much less simple in practice, is to respect the limitations of drains and sinks and toilets in the first place: so no oil, fat, grease or remains of meals down the kitchen sink and no disposable nappies, sanitary towels, newspaper or too much toilet paper down the loo.

UNBLOCKING A TOILET OR DRAIN

You know your drain or sewer is blocked when it backs up or overflows. In the case of drains, the overflow may be outside but it's never a pretty sight. Neither gagging nor panicking is helpful.

Critical to unblocking a toilet is where and what the blockage is. Usually it's in the pan itself and this is good news: all you may have to do is clear out whatever you can see (you *can* do this: look away, and wear thick rubber gloves). To remove what you can't see but isn't far away, use a drain plunger and apply heartily. This will with luck dislodge any further accessible blockage. You can use a sink plunger from your toolbox or a special-purpose toilet plunger (a flexible augur), but you may not have or ever want to have one of these, in which case use an old mop with a plastic bag tied around the head. Plunge it in and out of the pan to create maximum suction, then remove debris and throw into the pan a handful of bicarbonate of soda, half a cupful of vinegar followed by a couple of saucepanfuls of boiling water. The chemical alternative to this is caustic soda diluted according to the manufacturer's instructions, though this is generally recommended as a last resort only. If this doesn't work, you can try carefully easing a wire around the bend, though you risk pushing the problem further into the system. If you know where the drain inspection cover is, lift it to check for signs of obstruction; anything obvious can be hooked out with a wire coathanger. When all else fails, call an emergency plumber: get a quote and then call another plumber to make sure the first quote was reasonable.

Drains require roughly the same treatment as toilets, in roughly the following order: sink plunger; wire coathanger; soda and vinegar (or other drain-cleaning product); boiling water; expert. The problem may be caused by tree roots, subsidence, or elderly pipes that have collapsed. These can only be detected by a camera fed into the system by someone who knows what they are doing. Again, get several quotes: drain unblockers are notoriously expensive.

Sinks not draining are treated similarly to drains and loos, though between the plunger and the wire coathanger you might try dismantling the pipe beneath the sink in case the blockage is immediately below. Even if the sink is full of water, put the plug in it. Put a bucket underneath the pipe from the sink (it may be in a cupboard), unscrew the pipe and let water gush into the bucket. Test for blockages with the wire coathanger, then proceed as if for drains.

DRIPPING TAPS

fig. 1   *fig. 2*   *fig. 3*

Dripping taps are torture, we know for a fact. The fault can be the washer, which is replaced with relative ease, so everyone says. The more I looked into it, the plainer it became that there are more taps than you can poke a stick at and the problem isn't always the washer. Unless yours is obligingly easy to dismantle and if you are as handy as I am (minus handy), no amount of step-by-step guiding will help. Under those circumstances, should, for instance, your tap be a ceramic-disc tap where the problem is likely to be cartridge (not washer) based, get someone who knows what they're doing to sort it out for you. I can advise on the faulty washer in a regular tap as illustrated, however.

You need a new washer (if you don't know the exact size, you may have to remove the old one, match it and then replace it), your spanner (adjustable), screwdriver (adjustable heads), wire wool and a cloth. Before you do anything else, turn off your water supply (the stopcock is usually in the kitchen, under the sink) or, if the tap has an isolating valve, turn that off. Put a plug in the sink to stop anything falling down it while you're working, then turn on the tap to get rid of any water already in the system – if it gushes, you haven't completely disconnected the water supply. Remove the tap handle, either with a spanner or by releasing the screw (with a screwdriver) beneath the hot or cold indicator disc or any other fancy disc on top of the tap and then pulling. (You will want to stop now, but you can't.) Within the body of the tap you will see a nut. Holding fast to the tap to stop it turning, unscrew the nut with the spanner. This releases the stem of the tap from the body of the tap.

The offending washer is attached to the base of the stem. It may be held in place by another nut, which you should carefully remove. Ease off the washer, give the tap stem a good going-over with the wire wool, wipe it with a cloth, replace the washer with a new one, reassemble the tap. Should the tap continue to drip because it's a valve seat matter after all, call in an expert because you will now be very tired and probably pretty cross.

Sticking doors

You can live with a door that never closes, but it's annoying and not ideal during a house fire. The problem may be caused by too many coats of paint, by humidity swelling the wood or by the door sagging as a result of building movement. Unless the interference is minor and can be resolved with a quick adjustment of the door hinges or sandpapering of the sticking point, you need more than the average toolkit to tackle it. You need a sander or a plane, and possibly a workbench.

Your first step is to fathom where the sticking is occurring. If it's where the door meets the door frame, tightening the screws in hinges may help. For any other sticking edge, mark the offending point with a ruler and pencil. Try wedging the door open and addressing (with a plane or sander) the surface that's sticking; if that fails, you'll need to remove the door, clamp it to a work surface and then attack it with a plane, either along the wood grain at an angle of 45° or, if planing the top or bottom of the door, working from each end towards the centre to avoid the wood splintering. You'll then need to prime the surface of the door, paint it and rehang it. If humidity is an ongoing issue, you might want to sand the door all over and apply a wood preservative before priming and painting.

Electrics

As with plumbing, the householder's main responsibility towards electrics is vigilance. Regardless of your level of interest, it really is important to familiarise yourself with the fusebox (also now known as the consumer unit): first, where it is, and then how it works. It's usually somewhere near the electricity meter; its function is to distribute electrical current to the various circuits designated for lights, appliances (like hot water) and power points. Upgraded safety mechanisms – a circuit breaker (or MCB, miniature circuit breaker) and a safety switch (or RCD, residual current device), replacing old-fashioned fuses contained in the consumer unit – are now mandatory for any electrical installation (new wiring, any form of upgrading or rewiring, even a new power point).

LEARN TO LOVE YOUR FUSEBOX

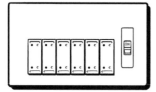 

The circuit breaker functions pretty much as the old fuses do (which is to say that, in the event of an overload, malfunction or short-circuit, the fuse wire melts, which shuts the circuit down), switching off the power to the affected circuit. Unlike the fuse, which self-destructs, the MCB can be reset immediately with the flick of a trip switch on the panel in the fusebox. The safety switch, or RCB, offers extra protection, shutting down power in a circuit within 0.03 seconds if it detects a problem that poses a risk to personal safety. Once the source of the problem has been identified, you can reset the switch.

Circuit breakers and safety switches will forestall most major electrical problems, but should lights flicker, points give off a fishy smell (usually caused by overheating) or the power to anything fail for reasons that remain a mystery, you must call in an electrician to sort it out. In your regular inspection, check for frayed and badly positioned cables (too close to water or heat sources, or under everyone's feet). Should the worst occur and an appliance catch fire, don't sling water at it: disconnect it, switch the power off at the fusebox and then try to put out the fire using your fire extinguisher or a blanket. If that fails, dial the emergency services and get out of the house.

Changing a fuse

If you have an old-style fusebox and a fuse blows, the wires can be replaced but it's infinitely preferable for you to replace the fuses with circuit breakers and a safety switch. If this isn't immediately possible and you have no experience with fuse wire, consult a qualified electrician. This isn't the place for a crash course in electrics. The experienced will already know that rewireable fuses have a piece of special-purpose wire running between two screws and that the amperage (amount of electrical charge) of the wires depends on the demands of the circuit (8 amps are generally used for lights), and like must always be replaced with like. The inexperienced need only know the phone number of their electrician.

The same applies if a fuse goes in an appliance. First you need to know why (before examining the appliance, disconnect it from the power source): read the manufacturer's instructions for specific advice, by all means, but if the problem is anything more complicated than an element in need of cleaning and you don't know your way around electrics, call in a qualified service person. In Australia, modern appliance plugs don't contain fuses: protection is provided by the main consumer unit (either via fuses or, with luck, via MCBs and an RDC). In the UK, most new appliances come with moulded plugs containing a cartridge fuse: to repair it, you disconnect the appliance from the power source, lever out the cartridge with a small screwdriver and replace the fuse (making sure you replace it with a fuse of the same rating). To change the fuse in a traditional plug, unscrew the back of the plug with a screwdriver (thank God you have one). There before you will be three different-coloured wires and a fuse which looks like a tiny bullet: unscrew the screw holding it in place, take it to the shop, buy an identical one to replace it and screw it back into place. When you do so, try not to upset the wires.

Power surges

The next most important device to insure against appliance meltdown in the house-hold is a surge diverter (or surge protection device), which, as I know you've guessed, protects against a power surge: an unexpected and uncontrolled increase in the voltage to an electrical circuit, which can cause appliances to fail without warning – especially grim when you're working on a computer. Depending on the path of the surge, it can take out more than one appliance (in our house, for example, the satellite dish and the television) in one big hit. The cause might be lightning, your switching another large appliance on or off, or the power company switching grids – the trigger doesn't really matter, but you do need to protect your household, as a surge can permanently damage delicate electronic equipment. You can buy surge protectors for individual appliances, but by far the best bet is to get an electrician to advise you on what's best fitted where and how to protect the whole house.

What to do when the power goes down

Blackout, power outage, power failure – call it what you will, your heart sinks when everything stops. The first step, however, is simple: see if the problem is throughout the house or confined to a single circuit, bearing in mind that electrical circuitry in old houses can be a bit random and a light in the hallway may go off at the same time as the toaster in the kitchen.

A faulty appliance or a circuit overload can trip just a single circuit or the main circuit. Check your fusebox and confront the buttons that control each circuit (lights, power sockets, appliances such as ovens, hot water). Any switch that has tripped will be pointing in the opposite direction to the others. If possible, identify the cause, usually a faulty appliance, and unplug it from the power source, then flick the tripped switch back into place. If you can't identify a cause of the circuit failure, check with your neighbours to see if they're affected or call the local energy provider. If the area is suffering from a power outage, the energy company will give you some kind of indication of the problem and when it is likely to be resolved.

If no one is aware of a local problem and you can't narrow down the trouble to a specific appliance, you'll need an electrician. You should turn off any appliances (computers, kitchen equipment) you were using when the power failed, but not (if you have any choice in the matter) anything that's usually on all the time (like fridges and hot-water systems). If the fridge and freezer have gone off, keep their doors closed, dig out the torches, candles and battery-run lanterns you've set aside for just such a situation, and sit tight until help arrives.

BEGINNER'S GUIDE TO CHANGING A LIGHT BULB

You may laugh, but there are people who can't know how to do it, otherwise they would. First, switch the light off; then remove the shade if there is one. When the bulb is cool enough to handle, remove it: it will be either a bayonet fitting, which is removed by gently unclipping its two tiny arms (locating pins) from the holder and pulling it to remove; or a screw fitting, which is removed by gently pushing the lamp into the socket and then twisting anticlockwise to remove. Either way, don't hold the thing too tightly or it will crumble in your hand. Should this happen, stick half a potato into what's left of the bulb and use this to remove it.

Place a new bulb into the socket and either insert the locating pins into the slots and twist to secure, or, in the case of a screw fitting, turn it gently clockwise. Be very careful to replace the bulb with one of appropriate wattage: sticking a 150-watt bulb into a socket designed for 60 watts is likely to blow the fitting, which can cause a fire.

If you feel confident about working at heights, check your insurance cover before you even think about putting up the ladder. And stick to the following:

- Never use an extension ladder (or any ladder, if it can be avoided) outdoors on a wet or windy day.

- Place the ladder on very firm, level ground. If possible, secure it at the base and at the top; if the situation is at all precarious, get someone to stand at the base.

- Wear rubber-soled shoes to give you maximum grip.

- Take up only the minimum equipment, so you have maximum balance. For the same reason, especially on an extension ladder, minimise your movements and avoid leaning in any direction.

- Never use the top rung of a stepladder or the highest two rungs of an extension ladder.

OUTDOORS

Those of you with no outdoor space might be deluded into imagining there is no outside maintenance. There will be. Even if you aren't responsible for its deficiencies, you may be their victim, so attention is required, even from you. There are drains as described above, and there are gutters and downpipes. Problems once noticed should be addressed immediately, if not by you, then by whoever is responsible.

Cleaning gutters

Gutters can become clogged with twigs and leaves, so need to be cleared regularly. Not only can they increase a property's vulnerability to passing bushfires in fire-prone areas, but blocked gutters will eventually stop the free flow of rainwater to the drains and cause an overflow. The upshot can be penetrating damp and, worse, gutters pulled away from their moorings so even more damp.

Clearing gutters is an easy enough job, but access is the difficulty. It may require you to work from a very tall ladder or from a sloping rooftop and my advice – should you be anything other than a person familiar with working on roofs or up tall ladders – is forget it. Hire someone who is. If you can reach your gutters with a stepladder, then go ahead by all means, but with care: wear gloves, remove anything large with your hands, scoop out the rest with a trowel and drop it all directly to the ground (you can clean up the mess later). Now place mesh across the opening of the downpipes to prevent anything huge being flushed down them, and blast the gutter with a jet of water from the garden hose.

Lawnmowers

An overgrown lawn is an eyesore, and an ongoing battle with the lawnmower won't help. If you have a fuel-powered mower, you need to love it and not take things personally if it won't start. Be patient. Make sure everything that should be switched on is switched on. Check the fuel: if there is some but it's ancient (in a two-stroke mower, this means older than three months), replace it. You should also check the fuel line, the air filter and the spark plug, but if these are a mystery to you and you can't find the manufacturer's instructions, accept the inevitable and take the thing to a mower shop. Get it checked by someone who knows what they are doing, if necessary buy a new mower, then go home and mow the lawn. Before you do so, clear the lawn of rocks and debris, adjust the blade height according to the time of year (keep grass longer in the summer for water retention). When you've finished, rake up any clippings which, if left, can produce mould.

CAR MAINTENANCE

It's true that not all households have cars and that car maintenance isn't strictly speaking central to household maintenance, but a household's function can collapse with the failure of a car (and potentially, more catastrophically than it can from the failure of a drain), so maintain yours if you have one.

Toolkit for the car

You need one for the same reason that you need a kit for the house: one day you will need something in it. At the very least, carry with you at all times:

- owner's manual;

- jump (jumper) leads, in case of a flat battery (plus a surge-protection device for cars with a computerised engine system);

- a spare tyre in good condition;

- a first-aid kit;

- a torch;

- a fire extinguisher (some cars come with one already installed);

- lubricant (for loosening nuts and bolts);

- rope;

- blanket;

- maps.

Looking after your car

brake system alert

seat belt reminder

anti-lock break system warning light

open doors indicator

warning light

battery warning

front air bags

fuel notification

The minute you have possession of a car, familiarise yourself with the signs on the dashboard – they are there to keep you informed. Never ignore warning lights. If you're mid-journey when the light appears, stop: persevering could cause critical damage. The oil light means no oil pressure (not necessarily no oil); if the battery picture lights up, it means the battery isn't being charged properly, for any of several possible reasons, so get help.

The NRMA (National Roads and Motorists' Association) recommends the following basic measures for car maintenance:

- Check the manual to see what maintenance is advised for your particular make and model, and abide by it.

- Change the oil as recommended, or at least every 10,000 kilometres (6,000 miles). To check the oil level, turn the engine off and insert the (clean) dipstick while the engine is still warm. (If you don't know where the dipstick is, check the manual.)

- Get the car serviced every six months or so (the manual and/or your mechanic should record the appropriate intervals and level of service required). At every service, the mechanic should check the fluid in the battery, the automatic transmission and the power steering.

- Radiator coolant should be changed every two years, but occasionally, when the engine is cold, remove the radiator cap and check the level to see if it needs topping up. Also feel the hoses when they're cold: if they're hard, or soft and swollen, they need to be changed.

- Keep battery terminals greased with Vaseline to form a protective coating.

- Regularly check their pressure when the tyres are cold (the appropriate pressure will be noted somewhere in the car – in the glovebox, on the fuel cap or beside the driver's door). Also check for minimum tread: this is 15 mm (around ¾ in) on any part of the tyre surface that comes into contact with the road.

- Check the play in the steering wheel with the engine off: maximum desirable is 50 mm (about 2 in).

- Keep a spare tyre that's in good working order.

- Regularly check that all lights (head, rear, indicator) are working.

- Clear windscreen-wiper blades from time to time, by running your finger and thumb along them.

- Keep windscreen-washer bottle topped up with clean water and the right amount of cleanser (not household detergent).

- Keep the car washed and polished to prevent rusting.

Changing a tyre

It's the same as with a light bulb: everyone who uses one should be able to change it. I speak for myself, obviously, when I say who can be bothered when someone else can do it for you? But there will come a time when there's no someone else to do it for you, so you need to know how to do it yourself even if information of this sort shuts your brain down. The following instructions are as easy to digest as I can make them, especially as you might be on a busy freeway when it happens.

○ Secure the car: engine off and handbrake on; wedge a brick or a lump of wood under the wheel diagonally opposite the problem one; if necessary, put the hazard lights on.

○ Remove the car jack, wheel brace and spare tyre (usually found under the carpet in the boot).

○ Fix the jack to the car – not easy, I know. Get onto your knees and look for notches under the car to which the jack can be attached. If you can't identify them, get off your knees and look through the manual for drawings to guide you. Once the jack is in place, turn the handle to take some of the weight off the flat tyre.

○ Now place the wheel brace on one of the wheel nuts and turn anticlockwise until it gives. Loosen each of the nuts in turn. If any are too tight, use your foot on the brace, for extra leverage.

○ Wind the jack handle to lift the car to a height that will allow the wheel rim to carry an inflated tyre.

○ Remove the wheel nuts and lift the wheel from the car. If it's stuck, the NRMA suggests putting one of the nuts back on, tightening it and then giving the wheel a good kick. This will make you feel better and with any luck will loosen the rust that's causing the problem.

○ Place the spare tyre against the axle/support, lining up the holes so you can lift the new wheel directly into place.

○ Starting with the bottom nut, insert them all and give a few turns by hand, then tighten them further with the wheel brace (though not so they will never again budge tight).

○ Unwind the jack until the car is sitting on the new wheel, then remove the jack.

○ With straight arm and back, use the wheel brace to tighten the nuts for the last time (use body weight, the NRMA says).

○ Replace the tools and the flat tyre in the boot.

When the battery is flat

There are many reasons a car won't start. It could be out of fuel and your fuel gauge isn't working; you might have driven through water and flooded the engine; there may be some kind of system failure (say, with the immobiliser not recognising the ignition key you are using). But if the engine gasps and dies, or makes no sound other than a pathetic click when you turn the ignition key, the battery is probably flat. Check the lights on the dashboard: are they dim? Turn on the windscreen wipers: are they barely moving? If yes, it's the battery.

The obvious answer is to jump-start your car by connecting its battery to another battery – but it's not always the best answer. If your car is a manual, you might be able to push-start it. If it has electronic ignition, or on inspection you find the battery is leaking or looks damaged, jump-starting it is out of the question. But it's a procedure all drivers should master.

First, find a car with a healthy battery the same voltage as yours (it's a rare car battery that isn't 12.6 volts). Remove from your own body any clothing (loose scarf, tie) that could get caught in the engine, or anything metal (watch, ring) that could cause a massive spark if it came into contact with a battery post. Make sure both cars are parked with handbrakes on and ignition off. The vehicles mustn't touch, as this can cause sparks or, at worst, an explosion. The UK's Automobile Association (AA) suggests the following step-by-step method:

⦿ Use the red (positive) jump lead to connect the positive (+ sign) terminal of the donor vehicle's battery to the positive terminal of the flat battery.

⦿ Then use the black (negative) lead to connect the negative terminal of the good battery to a suitable earthing point (meaning any bit of accessible metal that's away from the battery and fuel system) on the engine or chassis of the non-functioning vehicle.

⦿ When both leads are connected, start the engine of the donor car and allow it to run for a few minutes. Then, with that engine still running, switch on your car's ignition – it should now start. Leave both engines running at a fast idle for ten minutes: do not remove the jump leads while the engines are running, as this can cause serious damage to the electronics on either car. (If the jump leads get hot, switch off both engines and allow the leads to cool before restarting the process.)

● Once your engine has been going for ten minutes, turn off the ignition in both cars and then disconnect the leads in reverse order: black (negative) first, then the red (positive). Be careful not to touch the clips against each other or against the car body.

● Finally, try to restart your car using its own battery power. If it won't start, this could indicate a more serious problem with the charging or ignition system, which will need investigating by a professional.

20

LIVING SAFELY AND SUSTAINABLY

How we live includes the obligations we have both to our household's safety and to the safety of the planet. The former requires us to render our immediate surroundings as hazard-free as we can, if not on our own account then in the interests of visitors. The latter requires us to do as little damage to the atmosphere as we can within our surroundings, if not for our own sake then for the sake of future generations (though I accept they aren't of interest to everyone). Since most steps to save the planet also improve the health of our immediate environment, there's actually nothing to lose.

Life within any four walls will always contain an element of danger, if only because it's lived between floor and ceiling. Sooner or later, someone will want to leave the floor to do something on the ceiling, and lo – a peril! We can, however, take measures to avoid the falls and collisions, burns and scalds, poisoning, cuts and other physical pitfalls that dog domestic life. Most accidents are attributed to carelessness, but the problem is much more likely to be failure of brain. If recognising a hazard after the event is easy as pie, how come it's so hard to identify in advance? Safety measures are the answer. It stands to reason that sharp objects should always be kept in a place of safety: knives in blocks, for example, and scissors out of the reach of children. You'd think precautions against every other hazard would be as obvious, but they're not or accident and emergency wards would be places of peace and quiet. What follows are simple guidelines for identifying avoidable household mishaps.

Falls and collisions

More than half of all accidental injuries in the home are caused by falls: children falling downstairs or out of windows; householders with uncertain balance falling when getting out of the bath or shower, or slipping on a wet surface; householders tripping over loose cables, carpets or generally uneven surfaces; and householders falling off chairs they've stood on to get something from a high shelf. We also damage ourselves needlessly by colliding with bits of furniture. This is because we don't look where we're going and also because we place furniture unrealistically and sometimes move it and forget that we have. If it sounds stupid, it's because it is. So as part of your regular household inspection or as required:

- Childproof stairs and windows with guards and locks.

- Keep furniture of all sorts away from windows that can be opened by small children who climb to reach them.

- Buy the household a low set of steps, so chairs or ill-advised balancing isn't an option.

- Store heavy items within reach, not four feet above your head.

- Fix rails to baths or showers if any household member's balance is unsteady.

- Put non-slip mats in the bath and shower.

- Keep carpet in good order, especially on stairs. Trim frayed edges.

- Make sure stairs are well lit and have switches at both top and bottom.

- Wear sensible shoes around the house.

- Arrange furniture sensibly to provide free and unimpeded access from one room to another, in and out of every room, and around awkward items with sharp edges.

- Keep floors free of clutter, especially in hallways.

- Don't carry large loads about the house: they obscure vision and upset balance.

- Move perilous items if and when you see them.

- Secure appliance cables and wires in a bunch and store away (under desks, in cupboards or behind shelving) from well-trodden paths about the house.

- Avoid polishing floors too highly.

- Buy non-slip underlay for rugs.

- If you do feel yourself falling, relax, allow yourself to drop, then roll as if you were in a motorbike race.

Burns

There's burning yourself on a hot appliance and there's getting burnt in a fire. To avoid the former, use oven mitts when transferring pans into or from the oven. Also, move slowly and cautiously about the kitchen because clumsiness and an open flame or a scorching hotplate are just not compatible.

House fires are terrifying and mostly avoidable. As precautionary measures, buy a small fire extinguisher and a fire blanket, and place them somewhere obvious and accessible; install a smoke detector between the bedrooms and the rest of the house, and on each level of your house. Smoke alarms can be wired in or battery-operated; wired-in units are mandatory in all new homes in Australia. To avoid setting the alarm off every time you burn the toast, either install a 'toast-proof' version specially designed for kitchens or fit it a sensible distance from the stove. (If the alarm does go off and you're sure it's false, open a window and stand underneath the detector waving a tea towel to disperse the smoke.) Check the batteries regularly and don't switch the thing off because the noise drives you mad.

Statistically, smokers are less likely than non-smokers to install an alarm, which is insanity when cigarettes, matches and lighters are among the biggest causes of house fires. The following are other prudent precautions against fire:

○ Never leave a deep-fryer (or any pan containing fat) unattended. Never fill it more than one-third full or let it overheat. If the contents of a pan catch fire, turn off the power or heat at once, then smother the pan with a damp tea towel or use your fire extinguisher or blanket; never throw water on it. Make oven chips.

○ Always use a fireguard in front of an open fire.

○ Never overload a power point, even if it isn't easily managed. A 13-amp socket connected to a 240-volt circuit has a capacity of 3120 watts (you multiply the two numbers). Most appliances display their wattage: just add up the wattage of the appliances connected to the same socket and stay within range.

○ If any appliance cables or leads are frayed, replace them.

○ Be wary when using candles – even tealights, small though they are, can generate enough heat to melt plastic. Always extinguish candles when you leave the house or go to bed.

○ Regularly clean the lint filter of your tumble dryer; a build-up of lint can produce a blockage which may cause the dryer to overheat and increase the risk of a fire.

○ Plan an exit route from your house in the event of a fire, as smoke can fill the place very quickly. Cover your face with a damp cloth, stay low to the ground and don't try to save anything inanimate.

○ Always keep house and car keys in an obvious and accessible place, for a quick exit.

Scalds

Carelessness is a significant factor in most scalds, which, not surprisingly, are the results of spills, of drinking liquid way too hot, or of immersing ourselves in water that's far too hot. We need to develop good habits, like running cold water before the hot in a shower, bath or sink; using cordless kettles; and keeping boiling pans at the back of the stove with their handles pointing away from the room so they can't be easily knocked. Never offer small children a hot drink without testing the temperature first, and always shake a baby's bottle and test a few drops on the inside of your arm before offering it. If there are small children in your household, consider installing a guard around the stove.

Poisoning

The most common causes of household poisoning after food are swallowing toxic substances or inhaling dangerous levels of carbon monoxide. As far as the first goes, you can protect household members by labelling all hazardous substances (cleaners, solvents, pesticides) not plainly identified by the manufacturer, and by storing medicines, cleaners and garden products in secure cupboards well out of the reach of children.

Carbon monoxide, which is colourless and odourless, is produced by poor combustion and in homes is usually associated with faulty fuel-burning (gas, oil, wood) appliances and/or the flues attached to them. Even though deaths from carbon monoxide poisoning are rare, it accounts for most accidental household poisoning so be alert. Carbon-monoxide alarms are available from hardware shops, but even if you have one you should take ordinary precautions.

● Since most deaths in fires are from breathing poisonous smoke and not burning, evacuate quickly even if the flames seem contained.

● Have gas appliances and their flues checked regularly. A gas flame on your stove turning from blue to yellow or orange might indicate a build-up of carbon monoxide. Get urgent advice from a qualified plumber.

● Make sure rooms where fuel-burning appliances are used are properly ventilated. Never block vents (flues from gas appliances, and chimneys to open fires). In the event of a gas leak, open windows, turn the appliance off and, if possible, turn the gas off at the mains. Avoid switching lights on or off, using electrical appliances, smoking or lighting a match since any of the above could trigger an explosion.

Symptoms of carbon monoxide poisoning, which can appear within an hour or two of exposure, include drowsiness, headaches and dizziness, and can easily be mistaken for the onset of flu. Distinguishing one from the other might only be possible with the help of a carbon-monoxide detector (alarm), so every home with an appliance requiring a flue should have one. The most obvious clues are more than one person experiencing symptoms at the same time and the symptoms disappearing when you leave the house.

In the garden

Utterly avoidable accidents occur in the garden, possibly because we feel relaxed and less than vigilant out in the open air, or possibly because we're ignorant. The following advice, from the UK's Royal Society for the Prevention of Accidents (whose thankless task has been to warn us of the inevitable for the last ninety years) takes both possibilities into account:

⊙ Be vigilant with all garden tools. Wear protective gear when using power tools, and always switch them off before working on them or the minute they're not in use.

⊙ Always wear sturdy shoes to protect against sharp objects and falling objects and for better balance.

⊙ Never pour petrol on a bonfire or barbecue.

⊙ Know your poisonous plants.

⊙ Respect wet slippery surfaces (tiles, lawns). They represent a major risk to life and limb.

SWIMMING POOLS

⊙ Always supervise children around pools and ponds.

⊙ Check current local regulations covering safety standards for any water features, and make sure you comply.

⊙ Be vigilant about closing swimming-pool gates.

⊙ Secure fencing is critical, even if in your area it isn't compulsory. Keep it well maintained.

Climate change is indisputable. It has been shown to the satisfaction of most people that humanity has contributed to the process (maybe it hasn't been shown to your satisfaction, but this isn't the place to argue the toss), and that what householders must do to moderate its dire effects is use less energy and do less of anything that directly or indirectly produces greenhouse gases such as carbon dioxide (CO_2). This presumes an understanding of the consequences, immediate and far-reaching, of our acts but why wouldn't we make it our business to understand them when failing to is likely to be catastrophic.

The argument that anything a householder might do will count for nothing because the problem is so vast simply doesn't wash. Australians per person are among the highest polluters in the world (4.5 times the global average). Households generate nearly one-fifth of Australia's CO_2 emissions. According to the World Wildlife Fund, if all Australian households cut their emissions by 5 per cent the national total would be reduced by 1 per cent. In the UK, it's reckoned that around 40 per cent of CO_2 emissions are caused by things we embrace as individual householders (car and air travel, air-conditioning and central heating being among the worst offenders). UK households generate 28 per cent of the nation's CO_2 emissions. Industry, which globally is responsible for much of the rest, ultimately must listen to the consumer.

This gives us two fronts on which to act: at home and in the marketplace. We can shop and eat with an eye to sustainability, but the most significant changes we can make are to more energy-efficient sources of domestic power, and in our choice of appliances and transport. It's true that the options aren't always clear-cut and that a saving to the environment here is often made at an expense to the environment over there, but the solution is to keep it simple: make adjustments where the effect is as clear as it can be, and pray that millions of profligate householders the world over are doing exactly the same thing.

Household power

Most of us power our homes with gas and electricity derived from non-renewable energy sources like coal and oil. An average Australian household uses 6579 kilowatt hours of electricity (a kilowatt hour being 1000 kilowatts per hour) per year and a UK household uses 4700. Our more sustainable options are to convert to other energy sources (solar, wind and arguably wood) that are renewable, reliable and pollution-free and/or to limit our use of non-renewable energy, which is for many of us a more realistic option. To encourage us to embrace sustainable options, local and government authorities both in Australia and in the UK offer a range of incentives (such as grants, rebates and credits) to householders to install solar panels, wind turbines, insulation and solar-powered hot-water systems. What's on offer from governments changes year by year, so check what's current from the relevant departments if you're looking at energy-efficiency options.

THE ALTERNATIVES
Solar power

The basic principle of solar energy is using the sun's light to generate electricity. To this end, photovoltaic panels are installed on the external wall of your property or part of your roof that captures most sunlight. They convert it into an electrical current, which is stored in a large battery: the current is directed into your house and any surplus can be fed into the local grid (for which you get paid).

Central to whether solar makes sense for you is how much sun your property attracts and how many panels you need to install to make it viable. A rule of thumb is that 100–150 watts of electricity can be generated per square metre area of panel. (To convert watts to usage, got to www.wavemaker.co.uk.) As well as being endlessly renewable, solar energy needs no fuel and produces no pollution (aside from the manufacture and transport of the required parts); it is an excellent power source in remote areas where mains power is often not available or is prohibitively expensive; and it saves you money eventually, even though the initial outlay can be on the hefty side.

If you're considering solar, arrange a site visit from an installer. Given that the market is increasingly competitive, it makes sense to get more than one opinion and to have the proposed system (cost, size, how it works, the suitability of your site, rebates process) explained to you in detail and on paper.

Solar hot water

Having hot water on tap accounts for up 50 per cent of a household's energy use, so replacing your conventional system would seem to be a fine aim. Solar hot-water systems use the sun's energy to heat water that runs through tubes (usually on your roof) and is then captured in a rooftop tank. They're usually used in conjunction with conventional water heating, which kicks in if there hasn't been sufficient sunlight, though recent technology is infinitely more efficient at using what sun it can get.

Cost can be an issue, so get several quotes, investigate rebates and examine your electricity bill minutely to see how long it might take to recoup your outlay. Factor in the help you are giving to the environment. It may not seem so valuable in the short term, but if you earn your initial investment back over, say, seven years, how pleased will you be with yourself? Very, I am thinking.

Wind power

Wind turbines are somewhat less realistic than solar power for most of us, owing to the size of the equipment and the availability of wind – but the figures are impressive. Where a 2-kilowatt domestic solar system can produce 1500 kilowatt-hours per year in the UK, a 1.5-kilowatt wind turbine will, on average, produce two and a half times as many. However, they function best away from built-up areas and where the average wind speed is 5 metres per second (10 miles an hour). Size-wise, the rotor diameter even of a small turbine may be up to 11 metres, and generally speaking, the turbine should be taller than any obstruction within 10–20 metres. In a clear space, think 'as tall as a telegraph pole', which leads me to ask: Do you have space in your grounds for a tower as tall as a telegraph pole? Do you want a tower as tall as a telegraph pole in your grounds? Will your neighbours and/or local council like the idea of a mast as tall as a telegraph pole in your grounds? These and other issues, such as cost-efficiency, are a little daunting, but as with solar power, government grants are available. In any event, get proper advice from a selection of installers.

General energy-saving practices

Even if you aren't in a position to harness the sun and wind to save the planet, you can adopt simple energy-saving practices:

- Insulate your home, especially the roof cavity, through which up to half the heat generated internally may be lost from a building. Since a further third is lost through wall cavities, they should also be tackled: this can be done from the outside and takes next to no time. Insulation also reduces cooling costs by 30 per cent. (Grants and rebates may be available.)

- Lag your hot-water pipes, especially if they're outside the house.

- Eliminate draughts which can add 25 per cent to your heating bill. Use simple fabric snakes to block draughts under doors, install brush sealants to draught-proof windows and doors, and for good measure, whack up heavy curtains.

- Choose ceiling fans over air-conditioners: they use less electricity than air-conditioners and can be used in winter to keep the heat from rising.

- Turn off lights that aren't needed. If a 100-watt bulb is using 100 watts of electricity an hour and if that bulb is lighting an empty room, think of the waste.

- Heat and cool only those rooms that are in use. Use timers and thermostats.

- Burning gas emits about 25 per cent of the carbon dioxide generated by burning coal (maybe less), so gas appliances trump electric ones.

- Never leave appliances on standby: they account for 5–10 per cent of household electricity use, and even turning just one off at the wall will spare the environment 45 kilograms of CO_2 per year.

- Test your fridge seal by closing the door over a piece of paper, leaving half of it sticking out. If you can pull the paper out easily, the hinge may need adjustment or the seal may need replacing.

- Don't place your fridge next to your oven or cram it too close to the wall. They need air to circulate behind them.

- Small appliances like rice cookers and microwaves use less electricity than oven or stove-top cooking.

- Only heat as much water as you need each time you use your kettle.

HEATING AND COOLING

The conventional fuels available to most households for heating are gas, oil and electricity, and of these gas is the most energy-efficient.

In the UK, where most houses have combined heating and hot-water systems, the boiler can account for 60 per cent of household carbon emissions. Currently the most energy-efficient system is a condensing boiler (which produces extra heat by converting steam to water), for which government grants may be available. In Australia, where the majority of houses are not centrally heated (although ducted heating is increasingly popular), options that don't require substantial initial outlay are open fires, slow-combustion fires, portable electric heaters and gas heaters. Wood-burning open fires, if the wood is from a sustainable source, can be emission-neutral though possibly polluting and not terribly efficient (most of the heat goes directly up the chimney); slow-combustion fires offer about 65 per cent heat efficiency. Electric heaters, especially oil-filled models, may be relatively cheap to purchase but can be hellishly expensive to run in both cash and carbon-emission terms. Flued gas heaters are preferable because they are cheaper to run and generally more eco-friendly.

Most Australian households rely on some form of cooling in the hotter months. If fans don't do it for you, a reverse-cycle air conditioner, which also provides heating, is a reasonably efficient solution, comparable, say, to a flued gas heater. For both heating and cooling products, government information and advice are available; check the energy rating before you go shopping.

LIGHTING

Incandescent bulbs are being phased out in both Australia and the UK in favour of more energy-efficient alternatives like compact fluorescent lamps (CFLs) and infra-red coating (IRC) and micro-fluoro lamps, which can replace costly and energy-intensive halogen downlights. It's estimated that the exchange will reduce average household emissions by 4 per cent.

Not only do CFLs use less electricity than incandescent lamps, but they last up to ten times longer. Despite fears that they would only emit the horrible white light we associate with not-at-all-cosy, they come in a range that includes warm, cool and daylight, which is a relief. A 35-watt IRC lamp provides the same amount of light as a 50-watt halogen lamp and has a much longer life, so swapping reduces your energy consumption by about a third.

APPLIANCES

Who can afford to replace appliances before they actually give up the ghost? On the other hand, if you're running something especially decrepit which is costly both to your pocket and to the environment, then think about it: inefficiency cancels out premature purchase.

Appliance manufacturers have become more energy-conscious, not least because they must rate each product according to its energy efficiency. It's worth appreciating which appliances in general are the great energy-gluggers, however, so you can use them with greater restraint. The larger the appliance, the more energy it consumes, so always buy to suit your needs rather than the space available. According to Energy Australia, energy consumption per year by common appliances in the average household – which, I appreciate, might not be yours – is as follows:

- air-conditioner – 1750 kilowatt-hours;

- electric kettle – 108;

- hot-water system – 3500;

- microwave oven – 100;

- pool filter – 2000;

- refrigerator – 600;

- tumble dryer – 370;

- wall oven – 350;

- washing machine – 350.

Recycling appliances

When you are buying a replacement appliance (or phone or computer, for that matter), ask the retailer if they have a recycling service. Some retailers have recycling bins for appliance accessories such as batteries and printer cartridges, and in both Australia and the UK most appliance retailers will dispose of unwanted larger appliances, though

ENERGY RATINGS

Both Australia and the UK have mandatory requirements for energy-efficiency labelling on appliances.

The Australian system is colour- and star-based. Red represents energy consumption, and blue, water use; the more stars (to a maximum of six), the more energy-efficient the product.

The UK system operates on the EU's A–G rating system, with fridges and freezers having an extended scale to include A+ and A++. In addition, the most energy-efficient products carry an 'Energy Saving Recommended' label (as judged by the Energy Saving Trust) so you can quickly identify commended products.

some may charge a small fee. If your old appliance is in reasonable working order, you could try selling it on eBay or via a recycling service (look online); some Australian states operate fridge buy-back schemes. Otherwise call your local council, scrap-dealer or charity shop, who may take your unwanted stuff off your hands for nothing.

Water

Australia may be one of the driest countries on earth, but it's one of the most profligate water consumers. Accurate statistics are hard to locate but the broad picture suggests that although we are increasingly water-aware, the average Australian household uses anything from 350 to 500 litres per person per day (compared to 150 litres a day in the UK and 66 litres a day used by two in three people the world over). Only 5–10 litres a day are required for basic survival: for drinking or used in cooking. The rest we use for showers/baths, laundry, washing dishes, flushing toilets and, when water restrictions permit, topping up pools, cleaning cars and watering lawns or gardens. We could get pretty close to halving our water use if we thought more carefully about how much to use and on what.

WATER-SAVING TIPS:

◉ Consider installing a rainwater tank to catch water from the roof. Even if you can't drink it, it may be fine for showering/bathing and flushing. Check local regulations.

◉ In any case, install some kind of butt to catch rainwater for use in the garden, and use mulch to reduce the need for watering.

◉ Install a dual-flush toilet (four in five Australian households already have, so get on with it).

◉ Check water-use ratings of appliances (dishwashers, washing machines) and fittings (showerheads, taps) and buy accordingly. A front-loading washing machine uses less energy and less water than a top-loader; a 3-star showerhead can reduce water use by 50 per cent.

◉ Use less hot water: heating it accounts for 16 per cent of household CO_2 emissions. Spending a minute less in the shower each day will save 180 kilograms of emissions each year.

◉ Fix leaking taps: a month of dripping can fill 10 bathtubs; fixing a dripping hot-water tap will save 100 kilograms of CO_2 emissions each year.

● Use grey water from the bathroom, laundry and kitchen for your garden or pots.

Transport

This is a vexed area when so many of us are dependent on getting from A to B as quickly and as comfortably as possible and old habits die exceedingly hard. A serious change in attitude requires something only marginally short of communal brain surgery but these are points to be considered:

● The simplest step we can take is to walk or cycle where possible, given that the average carbon emission from new cars is 175 grams per kilometre driven. Walking or cycling may mean leaving home earlier and getting back later, but think of the sense of virtue and previously unknown levels of fitness you will enjoy.

● The next-best thing is to use public transport when available. Get right across the timetables and learn to love thy neighbour whose face is an inch from yours.

● If you're a city-dweller, consider giving up your car and instead renting one when needed, from a car-sharing company like GoGet in Australia and Streetcar in the UK. Once joined up, you can pick up cars from designated spots at very reasonable rates. Petrol, insurance and repair costs are met by the company; in London the congestion charge, and in Australia your road tolls, are also covered.

● Car pooling makes sense for neighbours heading regularly in the same direction. It takes tolerance and organisation, but these can't be beyond the scope of the average householder without access to public transport, can they?

● Shop online.

● Don't buy a car larger than you need, and opt for the low-fuel, low-emission option.

● Choose rail over air travel. A simple example: a train trip from London to Paris emits 15 kilos of CO_2; an air trip, 115 kilos.

Growing your own food

Gardening is a whole separate life for the householder and there are many fine books and organisations available for guidance. The point here is to encourage even the least green-fingered householder to make a bit of an effort in the direction of sustainability. Apart from anything else it means you can have food so locally grown that you may only have to roll out of bed to harvest it, and it tastes much better than anything that's travelled for days to get to the shops. Also, imagine the joy when you eat what you've grown in the full knowledge that you haven't allowed a living thing to die from neglect.

Even if you have no garden, you will have a balcony or sunny window ledge that can accommodate crops like tomatoes, carrots, potatoes, salad leaves and herbs. And if you don't, you may well have access to a community-operated neighbourhood garden where local residents can rent and plant a plot. You mightn't watch gardening programs, flick through gardening books or read gardening tips in the newspaper, but you can pick up a pot or two and see what happens, for the heck of it.

For novices:

- You'll need one or more pots, tubs or other containers, a bag or two of decent potting mix and some plant food/fertiliser to give your plants a healthy start.

- Choose pots between 30 cm and 40 cm deep and as wide as your space allows, plus basins to sit them in that will catch excess water.

- Good drainage is very important: the containers should have two or three holes in the bottom, and a layer of rock or terracotta fragments beneath the potting mix.

- Place your pots in a spot that offers full sun for most or at least part of the day.

- If you want to start with something more ambitious than basil, try greens of all sorts: they're quick-growing and you get a high turnover because they can be planted close together. If you're more ambitious and have a balcony as well as a sunny window ledge, consider dwarf varieties of fruit trees.

- Plant your chosen seeds or seedlings according to the manufacturer's or garden centre's instructions. Water in well.

◉ Some herbs are seasonal: basil, for instance, is a summer herb and an annual (which is to say that once it's over for the year, it really is over). Rosemary, on the other hand, goes on and on and on.

◉ Potted vegetables need regular watering and feeding, but not overkill. Let the soil almost dry out between waterings (stick your fingers in to check) and try to avoid wetting the leaves. Feed every few weeks with a liquid plant food.

There are so many experts out there, I hesitate to recommend anyone but you can't really beat the public broadcasters (the ABC and the BBC) for accessibility.

PART 7

LOOKING AFTER YOURSELF

THE BRUTAL TRUTH, Householder, is that we are born and then we die, and that in between, if we want to get the best out of life, we must look after ourselves. Not to the exclusion of all others, or at the expense of anyone else, but because we'd like our bodies to serve us well for as long as possible. Treated properly, a regular body can last a hundred years, which is probably long enough.

Of course, when it comes to longevity there are things to consider other than our own healthy inclinations. There are genes which bestow on us unusual strengths or weaknesses; there are crippling diseases into whose path we might inadvertently wander; and there are freaky accidents over which we have limited control. This may lead you to think that no amount of jogging uphill drinking probiotics is going to help, so what's the point? But quality of life is the point: not just yours, but the quality of life of other household members, which will be horribly diminished if you fail to take the usual precautions concerning your physical wellbeing.

As for looking good: why would you choose not to? Why have listless and prematurely aged skin, or dirty and badly cut hair, or bad teeth or chipped nails when you don't have to? Your body doesn't have to be a temple, just a personal expression of respect for life, however ugly it can be at times. Keep fit, stay well and look good, out of respect. It's hard to know the order in which these conditions occur, but clearly if we're fit we stand a better chance of staying healthy and looking good. On the other hand, since none of the three actually guarantees any of the others, it makes sense to consider them separately and in order of importance as it occurs to me.

21

LOOKING
GOOD

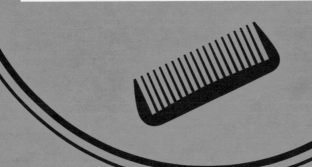

Appearances are known to be deceptive, and when it comes to personal grooming this is undoubtedly a good thing. Even if you are feeling less than groomed within, looking groomed without enables you to face the world with a heartening degree of composure. The world will see a composed person; it will hand back to you an image of a composed person; and pretty soon you will be feeling like a composed person. Never underestimate the value of composure when its opposite is unhinged.

You don't need an expert to tell you the four essential elements of looking good – and I'm not talking clothes because they've been addressed elsewhere. They are the same for everyone, however old, however rich, however delighted by their lack of vanity:

- skin;

- hair;

- teeth;

- posture.

I appreciate that we can fall short in any of these respects owing to poor health or unlucky genes, but it's our obligation to do our best with what we have and not to abandon any of them as a lost cause. Each needs to be attended to on a regular basis. The cost can be anything from next-to-nothing to a small fortune annually, and this will be determined by both where you place your faith and the depth of your pocket – except possibly in the case of teeth (you can be unlucky with teeth, so watch them).

As with anything to do with household management, preventive measures are your best bet. Simple skin and hair care, obsessively regular dental care and due attention to posture from the minute you're old enough to look in a mirror and think, 'Yuk!' are critical.

Your skin is a pretty good indication of your state of health, but this isn't to say that every healthy person on the planet has the skin they should have. Eat well, sleep well, exercise and drink plenty of water, by all means. But you still need to follow a proper maintenance regime: clean your skin morning and night; moisturise it morning and night; protect it from the sun. It's a simple insurance to avoid sag and to ensure hydration and protection, so don't skimp. And don't think sticking your face under the shower will do the trick: turning your face or chest up to the shower spray for a prolonged battering by hot water can lead to broken capillaries – and who willingly embraces the horror of broken capillaries on the face and chest?

Like it or not, a decent skin-care regime requires the application of assorted unguents and these need explaining because there are just so many of them. There are billions and billions of products for every conceivable skin-care procedure and they are so constantly improved and enhanced that you can only wonder how pathetic they must have been in the first place.

Which products?

A cleanser, a moisturiser and a sunblock are essential. But what about the rest? Below is a selection suggested by Zoe Foster (former beauty director of *Harper's Bazaar*), aimed at improving and maintaining skins of all types and ages. You may choose not to embrace all or even many of them, but at least your choice will be informed.

> ● A *soap-free cleanser* (wipe- or wash-off, and non-penetrative). Cleansers are preferable to soaps because most soaps upset the skin's pH levels (acid/alkali balance) which, if disrupted, can cause irritation. They can be foaming or creamy or gel-like: as you approach 30, you should switch from a foam cleanser to a creamier one. If you have dry skin or wear foundation all day, try a cleansing oil.

> ● A *toner*. This is to wet your skin and prepare it for a moisturiser, in the same way that wetting a sponge prepares it for Jif or any other cleaning product. You don't need anything fancy: a herbal spritz will do it.

> ● A decent *moisturiser* (one for day and one for night, to moisturise you while you sleep). Buy according to skin type, and possibly choose a day cream that's combined with a sunscreen.

● *Sun protection*. This is the key both to anti-ageing and to comfort. It should be provided by a daily moisturiser with a broad-spectrum SPF which you apply all year round regardless of cloud cover. SPF stands for 'sun-protection factor' and is intended to indicate the length of time you can stay in the sun without burning, but actually it doesn't. An SP30 sunscreen doesn't double the protection offered by SPF15: SPF15 filters out about 93 per cent of the UVB rays, SPF30 about 97 per cent, and SPF50 about 98 per cent, so there's not much difference beyond SP30. In any case, they all lose effectiveness over time; best advice is to reapply every few hours. Broad-spectrum (which is to say that it protects against both UVB and UVA rays) is more important than a high SPF. UVB rays are said to be more carcinogenic than UVA, but exposure to both places you at risk. So you're looking for a SPF30 broad-spectrum product, possibly with add-ons like vitamins A, B, C and E, or AHAs (alpha hydroxy acids, better known as fruit acids, which remove fine lines and improve skin texture).

● An *eye cream or gel*. This isn't essential, but it is desirable: the area around the eyes is the first to age, owing to its paucity of oil glands, and requires constant hydration (which means every day).

● A face *serum*, which is applied underneath a moisturiser or, if you like, instead of a moisturiser. Zoe Foster advises that serums are to moisturising creams what a glass of tequila is to a glass of wine. They are super-nourishing and very targeted, so look for what you need – anti-ageing, rehydrating, calming, etc. Or buy rosehip oil, which is rich in vitamin C and an infinitely cheaper alternative.

● *Exfoliators* for body and face, which remove the sad bits on the surface. They are best applied to, and removed from, dry skin because water ruins the abrasion process.

● *Hand and body lotions* should be applied every day after a shower. Palmer's provide great low-cost options. Hands show age as much as the face and for the same reason should be protected with sunscreen.

● *Fake tan* is infinitely less harmful than suntan (even one acquired in a solarium) and so much easier to apply, and less smelly, than it used to be. It needs to be maintained, however, to avoid uneven fading, which means regular exfoliation and reapplication.

ORDER OF PLAY

The order of product play varies between day and night, but basically it's: cleanse, exfoliate, tone then apply serum and/or moisturiser (either a night cream or a day cream). Bear in mind that the face stops at the breast or chest, wherever it happens to lie, so cleansing, moisturising and protecting should extend well below the neck.

If you're going to apply make-up, you can prepare your skin with primer, a relatively new product that is supposed to ensure a smoother, longer-lasting application. If you are taking make-up off, you can use an oil-based pre-cleanser before the actual cleanse, but really this is only necessary if you've been wearing an awful lot of foundation.

MORE ON SUNSCREENS

Sun damage can be anything from premature wrinkles or uneven pigmentation to melanomas, which are potentially fatal skin cancers. You need protecting from all of it. Apart from staying out of the sun and covering up, you need to apply sunscreen liberally. Most people skimp to the tune of 50 per cent. According to Australia's Cancer Council, the face, neck and ears – ears are easily neglected – need half a teaspoon; every exposed limb needs a teaspoon each. If your skin is fully exposed for long periods, you need to reapply every couple of hours.

MORE ON EXFOLIATION

It's easily overlooked. Exfoliating your body should be a once-a-week exercise or, in the case of skin that's very dry or has been fake-tanned, twice a week. Before exfoliating your face, take a good look at the ingredients in other products you're using: you don't need both a scrub and a peel, and many moisturisers and some sunscreens also contain AHAs (which are chemical peels). Scrubs, so you know, should have small, soft, round beads: anything too harsh can cause minute tears in the skin.

VALUE FOR MONEY

You don't need to buy top-of-the-range. You can easily assemble a complete and effective face- and body-care range for under $100 (£50). Well-publicised studies show that cheaper alternatives like Olay and Boots are as likely, or even more likely, to deliver on their promises than those that cost an entire pay packet. It's true that top-of-the-range tends to include ingredients which may be rare or highly concentrated, but dermatologists remain unimpressed – in fact, they tend to be scathing about the claims made for expensive skin-care. If you're going to spend big, spend it on serums, which are more likely to give you your money's worth.

ABOUT INGREDIENTS

According to the skin-care industry, there are two kinds of customer: those who buy to feed their skin (non-chemical) and those who want something that works. The former read the labels on products – whose ingredients generally sound like poisons, even if they're not – and run screaming to the organic counters. The second group, if they read the labels at all, decide that the industry must be well aware of consumer suspicion and so product-testing must be rigorous. But it's not really.

There is every reason to study the labels: we might not have actual allergic reactions, but all sorts of unpleasant things – like formaldehyde (a potential carcinogen which is commonly found in shampoos) – lurk within the gorgeously packaged tubes and bottles and their long-term effects may not be known. When the science is either inconclusive or unrecognised by the industry, many consumers tend just to hope for the best. It's difficult to say categorically which ingredients should be avoided, but common chemical additives that are known skin irritants/allergens include sodium lauryl sulphate (detergent), parabens (preservative), formaldehyde and phthalates (softeners).

Organic and mineral products are excellent for sensitive skins: mineral products (containing zinc or titanium oxide) were originally invented to speed healing after surgery or burns, and were found to be so effective they were adopted by the cosmetics industry. But if you're not sensitive and only mildly concerned, then at least read the labels so that you know you're buying a product that suits you. Peptides, ceramides, retinol and AHAs, for instance, have all been shown to help reverse signs of ageing. Ceramides are lipids (fats) that help the skin's water-retention capacity and render it plump and juicy. Peptides (short chains of amino acids that can boost production of collagen and hyaluronic acid) are shown to be very effective in reducing wrinkles. They're one of the most sought-after and expensive anti-ageing ingredients. Retinol, retinoic acid (prescription only) and retinyl palmitate are all forms of vitamin A, which stimulates the production of collagen and elastin; it can cause irritation in sensitive skins, but is reckoned to be highly effective in reducing fine lines and wrinkles. If your concern is more to protect and prevent, look for antioxidants.

Acne

Acne has nothing to do with poor diet or hygiene. It's a result of testosterone (a naturally occurring hormone in men and women) alerting the sebaceous glands to do their job more diligently than is required – which is to say, produce more sebum than the skin requires to remain supple. The excessive sebum clogs the pores through which it's excreted, and also the pores through which hairs grow: this can produce blackheads, whiteheads or, if you're unlucky, inflamed spots and larger cysts. There are any number of over-the-counter treatments for mild cases of acne, and they are certainly worth combining with a regime of gentle cleansing using appropriate products (ask a pharmacist) in the first instance, but get medical advice if the problem lasts more than a couple of months.

SQUEEZING SPOTS

Just don't. Beauticians perform 'extractions' after steaming, by gently applying pressure to clogged pores, but this isn't the same as squeezing spots. You're just as likely to force the bacteria further into the skin, aggravate the inflammation and cause scarring. Even when the spot looks as if it needs your help, it truly doesn't: it wants to be left alone to explode in private and it certainly doesn't want to turn into anything longer-lasting.

Anti-ageing

Australians of all ages, genders and dispositions spend hundreds of millions of dollars a year on non-surgical cosmetic procedures designed to make them look younger/better. The effects are open to question and to make them less so, new treatments are constantly being developed. Current fave is botox, which is fine if you decide that botulism injected into the skin is preferable to wrinkles and furrows (and plenty of dermatologists agree it is).

There are also dermal fillers of all sorts (cowhide, you will be pleased to know, has been replaced in general favour by hyaluronic acid, which contains no animal product) and the list of other anti-ageing products grows by the day. While they may effectively plump out those lines from your nose to your chin, or the crevice between your brows, their remnants can stay under the skin and, over time, cause an unevenness to the face, so they should only ever be used sparingly. Repeated injections into the same area every few months can cause irreversible scarring and lumpiness, so why would you? Given the randomness of results and the ever-widening scope of both surgical and non-surgical treatments, it really is essential to get advice from properly accredited and recommended practitioners (either a dermatologist or plastic surgeon).

Make-up

Nowhere more than on the face does less equal enough already. If your skin is up to scratch (which it will be if you follow the recommended skin-care regime), heavy cover just shouldn't be essential. Even if you love your foundation more than you hate the look on people's faces that says, 'She's wearing too much', at least give your skin a break now and then. Try a spell on a high-SPF tinted moisturiser; otherwise, there are a few high-quality, (certified) organic foundations which are perfectly fine to wear every day for years on end, owing to the presence of skin-friendly minerals, so hunt them down.

Other than foundation, what make-up you wear will depend on your mood, inclination and what's current. Whatever your choice, learn to apply it properly and in moderation (no matter how profound your five o'clock shadow, if you have one). A seriously stocked make-up bag will contain:

- foundation (liquid, cream or powder, or a liquid-to-powder combination);

- a concealer (creamy and illuminating for under the eyes and something thicker and waxier for covering blemishes;

- mascara;

- blush and/or bronzer (with a good-quality brush);

- eyeliner (such as kohl) and an eyeshadow palette (preferably with day and night shades);

- one rosy-nude lip product (gloss, balm, lipstick – the key word is 'nude', meaning barely coloured) and one more vibrant lipstick that works well with your skin tone.

As you get older, the product requirements won't change much but the textures and colours will. For example, a powder foundation accentuates lines and wrinkles, so switching to a light-diffusing liquid version is a smart move.

HAIR CARE

Hair should be clean, shiny and free from matting, which is not to be confused with fashionable tangles. Fashionable tangles should be abandoned the minute anyone asks if you have a bus pass. Other than that, hair should be well cut, so everyone needs a good hairdresser. This isn't just someone you like; it's someone who understands just how very weird your hair can be and is prepared to be as interested in this as you are over a long period, possibly for life. He or she needs to keep a precise record of when and how you change hair colour, because every change affects its structure and what we can't have is undermined structure leading to brittle, lifeless hair that breaks when you brush it.

That said, you need to take the same sort of responsibility for your hair as you do for your skin.

● Shampoo regularly according to need, so not necessarily daily, however shiny you think your hair needs to look. There may be plenty of gentle shampoos designed for everyday use but excessive shampooing can strip your hair of its natural oils. You can avoid daily shampooing by using a dry shampoo that absorbs surface dirt and oil.

● Apply only a small amount of shampoo and shampoo twice, especially if you use products (like mousse or spray). The first shampoo gets rid of product; the second cleans the hair.

- Always use a conditioner. Massage it in the palms of your hand before applying it to the hair shaft (stop before the roots). Conditioner coats and protects the cuticle (the outermost layer of hair) and prevents the build-up of static electricity that causes frizz. Coat well, comb it through, leave for the recommended time, and rinse.

- The final rinse should be in cold water.

- Comb wet hair; brush dry hair.

- Use a high-protein, nourishing mask now and then, especially if you use a hairdryer or other heated appliances.

- Shampoos don't lose their effectiveness with repeated use, but repeated use of the same product may alter the chemical balance of your hair, so it makes sense to change brands every couple of months. If the quality of your hair deteriorates, change to a product targeted to its new condition (dry, oily, permed, coloured, etc.).

- Don't have your hair coloured more often than every six weeks.

Hair removal

When it comes to inconvenient body parts, there's nothing more unwanted than hair on a bad day. This is my personal view and, I appreciate, not necessarily the view of anyone who regards hair as a political statement, luscious adornment, or nothing to be too fussed about. Not head hair, obviously – face, leg, chest, back, shoulders, upper arm, underarm, bikini line and any other hair that isn't head. Stubble is acceptable only on a male chin – and even then it's not always as acceptable as the male with stubble on his chin thinks, regardless of whose design it is. Solutions include:

- Shaving (legs, armpits): it costs next to nothing but the hair grows back quickly, the resulting stubble is unimpressive, and less than skilful scraping can cause a rash or bleeding.

- Plucking (face): it's cheap and efficient, provided your eyesight is good, but it's time-consuming.

- Waxing (face, legs, armpits, bikini line, back, upper arms): removes the hair from the under-skin follicle; the hair takes four to six weeks to grow back and becomes progressively finer. But it can hurt and, since it's best done at a salon, finding the time can mean it doesn't happen until far beyond the due date.

- Depilatory creams (legs, bikini line, upper lip) dissolve the hair shaft at the surface of the skin. They're quick, cheap and painless, but they can cause possible skin irritation, there's a relatively quick regrowth, and the process is both messy and smelly.

- Laser (anywhere on the body) involves pulsed beams of highly concentrated light applied after the area has been numbed by a local anaesthetic. It's permanent, though it may take between four and six sessions, but it's expensive and may cause skin darkening and blistering.

Nail care

Caring for your nails is as essential as washing your hair. If you can't manage a total manicure or pedicure, at least keep nails clean and short. You can turn it into an event if you like, but the basic process couldn't be simpler:

- Remove any nail polish with a cotton pad and nail-polish remover, soak your hands and/or feet for a few minutes in warm soapy water and pat them dry. Clean the nails, either with a nail file or nail brush. Use a pumice stone on your feet to get rid of hard skin.

- Shape your nails with a double-sided emery board using light strokes. For a manicure, treat your stronger hand first (using your weaker hand): begin with the thumb, then go to the little finger and move inwards. Use two or three short strokes followed by a single long stroke to smooth the edges.

- Apply a softener to your cuticles. Give it a minute to work, then return your hands to clean soapy water to soak.

- Use a cotton bud to push back the cuticles. Gently and carefully clip anything obvious.

- Massage your hands with hand lotion.

- If you are using nail polish apply a base coat, taking care not to overload the brush. Use three light strokes from bottom to top on each nail: begin with a stroke lengthways along the middle, then another on either side. Allow to dry and then apply two coats of polish, allowing each to dry before applying the next one. Clean up any messy edges with a cotton bud dipped in nail polish remover. (For a pedicure, before applying polish, roll a tissue into a long strand and wind it in and out of your toes to separate them so they don't smudge each other.)

Unless you are blessed with astonishing teeth genes, neglect will cause them eventually to fall out owing to decay and/or gum disease. Then you will not only have trouble eating but you'll look toothless and, I'm sorry, this is just not groomed. Between growing teeth and losing the lot lies a choice: regular dental care or poor dental care. It won't be yours to begin with, it will be a parental matter, but the minute you can grab control of it you should and, once you have, bear in mind that neglect encompasses a poor dental health regime, too much sugar in your diet, lack of calcium and magnesium in your diet, and smoking.

A good dental health regime includes maintaining oral hygiene by, at the very least, brushing twice a day, flossing every second day (minimum), annual check-ups and annual visits to the hygienist (who may also be your dentist) for scaling and polishing. It may include fillings (which are never fun), extractions, crowns, bridges and implants, but ultimately you will know that your mouth is a healthy place, that you aren't harbouring infections that will lead to mystery illnesses or heart disease and that when you smile, people won't sigh with disappointment. Your smile doesn't have to be two rows of perfectly even white teeth. It just has to be clean and have the regulation number of teeth in it.

The point of all the brushing and flossing is to avoid a build-up of plaque, which is a fancy name for a sticky layer of bacteria. The bacteria feed off sugar and produce acid; the acid causes tooth decay. A build-up of plaque can also cause an inflammation of the gums known as gingivitis, where the plaque hardens to form calculus, the gums loosen, the irritation spreads to the bone, the gum and the bone shrink and, blow me, the teeth fall out. If you don't feel a bit sick by now, I don't know why because I definitely do. The good news is that plaque build-up is reversible, and preventable by regular scaling.

So:

⊙ Brush your teeth before breakfast and before you go to bed, but not within an hour of eating. (Your mouth needs time to neutralise the acid caused by eating: brushing immediately afterwards can cause the enamel to wear away.)

⊙ Use a small-headed toothbrush (I prefer an electric one), placed at a 45° angle to the gum. Use small circular movements.

- Clean every tooth back, front and top, and the sides of back teeth. When you get to the front teeth, tilt the brush vertically and continue with the small circular movements. Clean around the gum line.

- Brush for two minutes if you can manage without gagging or drowning.

- Dentists recommend brushing your tongue to remove bacteria.

- Floss – ask your dentist to show you how.

- Use a fluoride toothpaste and use a mouthwash.

- Go to the dentist once a year and get your teeth scaled to remove any build-up of calculus, and polished to remove any stains.

POSTURE

Good posture not only makes you look lively, healthy, optimistic and confident, but it prevents unnecessary strain on your body and reduces the risk of injury and of joint pain owing to wear and tear.

Bad posture makes you look uncomfortable and prone to pain in the neck, back, shoulders, face, feet and legs, and it's increasingly linked to poor health in ways that aren't immediately obvious. In August 2007, a report in the magazine *New Scientist* suggested that hours hunched over a computer, especially a laptop, can raise your blood pressure owing to increased pressure on the neck muscles. Slouching, the very reason your mother told you to sit or stand up straight, causes the ribcage to fall forward. This restricts the movement of the diaphragm and upsets your breathing; it also forces the stomach closer to the oesophagus, which is terrible for reflux. There are plenty of reasons for carrying ourselves properly and if we haven't been, we can start now.

Check your posture and see how you stand. The three natural curves of your body – the neck, the upper back and the lower back – need to be in balanced alignment.

fig. 1

fig. 2

Stand facing a mirror, with your feet about shoulder-width apart, then check that your head is straight (not dropping to one side), your shoulders and hips are level, your knees are facing straight ahead and your weight is evenly distributed on both feet and neither more to the front nor more to the back. Rock back and forth on your feet until you find the correct balance.

Now turn side-on and see if your head is erect, your chin slightly tucked in (not sticking out), your shoulders in line with your ears (not up around your ears but dropped and probably pulled back a bit), your tummy slightly tucked in towards your navel, the curve in your lower back only slight, and your knees relaxed and not locked. If your posture is out of kilter, you may need help, certainly in the first instance, to discover exactly what is causing you to move, sit and stand the way you do. You can get a diagnosis from a physiotherapist, an osteopath or a chiropractor; then you can go to classes (pilates, yoga, Alexander Technique to name just some) to improve matters. I tried the three mentioned and even though each had something to offer, pilates suited me best, so you might need to experiment.

The following tips for your general consideration are from a combination of disciplines:

- Aim to lengthen and broaden your trunk and allow your shoulder blades to slide down from your shoulders. Imagine you are being pulled towards the ceiling by a string attached to your head.

- Standing up straight doesn't mean rigid; think tall. Soften your knees, keep your weight evenly distributed as above, pull your tummy in (navel to back) and lift your pelvic floor.

- Most problems come from the neck, because we stick out our chins and tilt our heads back. If you drop your chin and pull it back, your spine naturally lengthens.

- Don't cross your legs when sitting.

- Wear high heels only for special occasions.

For more on exercises to improve posture and core strength, see Chapter 22.

Workstations and poor posture

I have a build-up of muscle across my shoulders which will soon be a dowager's hump if I don't spend less time at a computer. I'm having physiotherapy and going to classes of all sorts, but I suspect in the end I'll be reduced to camouflaging it with bad behaviour and clothes too young for me. I know, after all I've said ... But it's not too late for you.

When sitting for long periods at a desk, keep your neck long, your shoulders down, your thighs supported and your feet firmly on the floor. (If you mostly use a laptop, get a separate keyboard and mouse so you can have the screen at eye level.) Make sure your lower back is supported, and also make sure you get up and walk around every half hour or so. Also, avoid resting your chin on your hands: there's a serious risk you will force your head back and compress your neck muscles. Alter your chair height, if needed, to make it uncomfortable to reach the desk. Every time you stop to think, drop your chin. (If you never stop to think, pull the screen slightly towards you, which forces you to lengthen your neck.)

THE ALEXANDER TECHNIQUE

The Alexander Technique, which aims to rid the body of unnecessary tension and make you more aware of how you are using your body, includes an exercise so easy you can't believe it's an exercise. Lie on the floor with your feet on the floor and your knees bent. You will have arranged beneath your head a book or enough books to prevent your head from tilting back. Rest your hands on your chest and allow your back to sink into the floor. Stay there for between ten and twenty minutes. It's a great reminder of how your body wants to be.

22

KEEPING FIT, STAYING WELL

Fitness is no guarantee of good health, as we know from the number of stories that begin 'He was the fittest man I knew' and end 'If only he'd been insured'. They would seem to imply that fitness as a life goal is overrated, so first we need to wrestle with notions of fitness and health, because the stupidest thing we can do is ignore one at the expense of the other. Fitness is to health as giving up smoking and wearing protection during sex with strangers are to living: it won't necessarily stop you getting ill or even dropping dead unexpectedly, but it will greatly shore up your defences.

Exercise (the route to fitness, as argued here) not only keeps your weight down, but it reduces blood pressure, lessens the risk of diabetes, stroke, heart disease, some cancers, joint pain and osteoporosis, relieves symptoms of stress, depression and anxiety, and improves your looks – which make it a kind of miracle. And because fit people look after themselves, as well as taking regular exercise they watch what they eat. Since exercise and diet (as well as giving up smoking and wearing protection during sex with strangers) are our chief weapons against disease and premature death, it stands to reason that the fitter you are, the more likely you are to be healthy.

Therefore we should abide by warnings to take exercise, eat sensibly, not smoke, wear sunscreen, and use protection during sex with strangers in the exactly the same way that we observe the 'Fasten seatbelts' sign in planes during turbulence. Some idiots won't, of course, and there's nothing we can do about them except hope that they don't land on us when the plane plummets.

What is fitness anyway, you will be asking. Being able to totter for a bus without turning blue? Being able to move most of your limbs in most directions with moderate ease? Maybe. Sports professionals reckon its key elements are stamina, suppleness, strength, speed and skill – but that's them. Householders wanting to achieve the bare minimum could and should pursue the sort of regime advocated by health professionals: aerobic exercise, strength training, stretching and building core strength, which includes balance training.

Aerobic exercise

Aerobic (cardiovascular) exercise forces you to breathe harder and faster, which makes your heart, lungs and blood vessels pump blood more efficiently around your body. It's the lynchpin of good health, so if you do nothing else you should take thirty minutes of moderate exercise (which makes you get slightly sweaty and out of breath) five days a week. Walking is great. If you're pretty fit and in your thirties or forties, you should be able to walk about one and a half kilometres (a rough mile) in fifteen minutes; if you're in your fifties or sixties, maybe twenty minutes. If you're nowhere near that pace, start slowly over half the distance, fast enough to get slightly out of breath, and work up from there. If you hate walking, do whatever it takes: cycle, jog, swim, dance, vacuum. Just do it for thirty minutes five days a week.

RULES FOR EXERCISING SENSIBLY

● Have a medical check (heart, blood pressure, etc.) before embarking on any ambitious exercise program.

● Know your limits and know when to stop. If you feel light-headed, dizzy, lose colour, or feel cold and clammy, stop at once. If you feel a sharp pain in any joint (or any part of the body, come to that), stop. If your heartbeat and breathing are uncomfortable, stop. Get advice.

● Increase the challenge slowly. The aim is to improve your fitness sensibly not stress your body alarmingly. If you feel fatigued, rest before continuing.

● Avoid dehydration: sip water during and after a long exercise session.

● If you're exercising hard, have something to eat within half an hour of finishing to sort out your sugar levels.

● To maintain a useful regime, set aside a time each day and stick to it.

Strength training

Strengthening your muscles stops them atrophying – or, anyway, stops the steady decline to weakness, inefficiency and pathos. It's simple enough: equip yourself with hand-held weights or resistance bands, some advice from a fitness instructor or physiotherapist about the right way to use them, and exercise regularly forever, not just for a few minutes now and again for a couple of weeks. Otherwise, try a few push-ups (for arms, upper body), abdominal crunches (yes, abs) and leg squats (thighs, bottom).

HOW TO DO A PUSH-UP

Push-ups, performed properly and regularly, strengthen the biceps and triceps, and tone the muscles in the upper chest, shoulders and back as well as core muscles in the abdomen. This will be why the armed services swear by them.

fig. 1   fig. 2   fig. 3

1. Start lying face-down on the floor with your arms bent and your hands flat to the ground, parallel to your shoulders.

2. Tighten your abdominal muscles slightly to protect your back. Push your upper body from the floor so you are supporting it with your arms and also, if you like, with your knees. Keep your back straight.

3. Repeat for as many times up to ten as you can manage. Rest for thirty seconds, then do another burst. Don't go nuts. You might only be able to manage groups of two to begin with. Once you are stronger, you can leave your knees out of the equation and balance your weight on your arms and toes – back straight, abs tight, head in line with your spine.

Stretching, building core strength, and balance training

Stretching improves your range of movement and relieves tension. Developing your core muscles (the ones in your abdomen, middle and lower back, buttocks, pelvis and thighs) improves posture and protects your back, which is now subjected to less strain. If your core muscles are sorted, you have better balance, but additional balance training is helpful if you're inclined to fall over.

Yoga and pilates classes address these exercises to a greater or lesser extent (depending on the class), so try a weekly attendance at whichever suits your needs and inclinations. If you hate classes but have a routine okayed by a professional muscle and limb person, go for it: just remember to warm up before you start – five minutes gentle jogging on the spot, if nothing else.

A SIMPLE YOGA EXERCISE – WELL, TWO REALLY

One of our daughters is a yoga teacher and her posture is the envy of all. She stands and moves effortlessly, and betrays no sign of a hump anywhere in her neck and shoulder region, which just goes to prove that good practice can defeat poor genes. Her two recommended poses are the tree pose, which aligns your body and your feet and improves balance, and the half-dog pose, which to my mind is easier because it gives you a wall to hang onto.

Tree pose

1. Stand with your feet underneath your hips and parallel to each other. Shift your weight slightly onto the left foot, keeping the inner foot firm to the floor, and bend your right knee.

2. Reach down with your right hand and clasp your right ankle. Draw your right foot up and place the sole against your inner left thigh; if possible, press your right heel into your inner left groin, toes pointing toward the floor. The centre of your pelvis should be directly over the left foot. Rest your hands on the top rim of your pelvis, making sure your pelvis is in a neutral position (neither forward nor back), with the top rim parallel to the floor. Lengthen your tailbone toward the floor. Firmly press the sole of your right foot against your left inner thigh and resist with the outer left leg.

3. Press your hands together in prayer pose at heart level, or lift and stretch your hands above head (which is preferable). Gaze softly at a fixed point in

front of you on the floor about a metre or so away. Stay for thirty to sixty seconds. Step back to the starting position with an exhalation and repeat for the same length of time with the legs reversed.

fig. 1

fig. 2

fig. 3

Half-dog pose

1. Face the wall and stand about a metre from it. Place your hands on the wall, shoulder-width apart and at about the level of your chest. Your head and neck should be in a line with your torso and your ears parallel to your arms.

2. Exhale and bend forward from the hips so that your legs stay parallel to the wall and your torso becomes more perpendicular to the floor. Inhale, and press your hands into the wall even more (your arms should now be almost parallel to the floor).

3. Exhale, push your hips back and elongate your spine while keeping the normal shape of the back. Inhale and raise your torso upward. Exhale and allow the torso to sink. Make sure that you have a curve at the lower back. If you don't have it, raise your arms up until you do feel the curve. (If you feel that the position is too stressful on your lumbar vertebrae, bend your knees.)

4. Your torso should now be at 90°. However, as you feel more comfortable you can walk your hands slowly down the wall, always bending from the hips and making sure that you are not stressing your spine.

fig. 1

fig. 2

There's a school of thought that says what you don't know can't hurt you, but this is so transparently untrue when it comes to health that I can't believe anyone actually says it out loud. It mightn't hurt you while you don't know about it, but when it does hurt you, you know about it and had you known about it earlier it mightn't have hurt you now or ever.

Have regular medical check-ups. If you haven't been to the doctor in years because you haven't been sick, you have no way of knowing whether your cholesterol or blood pressure is through the roof, you have underlying heart disease, or the mole on your leg is a melanoma, because none of these necessarily produces symptoms. See your doctor at least once a year so he or she can keep tabs on you, especially if you are over 45, smoke and are overweight by the standards described below. Blood-pressure and cholesterol checks, tests for skin, prostate, breast and cervical cancer, and for diabetes, are all part of the monitoring process. Your doctor can refer you for further tests (for heart, lung and liver function, and just about any other physical and mental matter), if necessary – and frankly, why wouldn't you go the whole hog when any dummy knows it's early intervention that saves lives.

Blood pressure

Your blood pressure is recorded as two numbers, one over the other, as in 125/83. The upper number indicates the 'systolic' pressure (pressure in the arteries as the heart squeezes out blood during each beat); the lower number indicates the 'diastolic' pressure (as the heart relaxes before the next beat).

Neither of these measures is constant: your blood pressure varies according to the amount of stress your heart is under, from exertion, anxiety, fear or excitement. The most reliable reading is taken when you are relaxed and sitting or lying down. Normal blood pressure is 120/80; at this level, our risk of a heart attack or stroke is low. Anything under 140/90 is okay, but actually is higher than desirable; if it stays over either 140 (top) or 90 (bottom) for any length of time (weeks), your blood pressure is high and needs controlling. Blood pressure can rise with age for a combination of reasons and, since we are all ageing, you are placing yourself at risk if you:

◉ eat too much salt;

◉ don't eat enough fruit and vegetables;

- are overweight;

- smoke;

- don't exercise;

- drink more than the recommended amounts of alcohol.

Your risk will also be increased if there's a family tendency to high blood pressure, but take heart: you can control your blood pressure by sticking to the above rules and, if necessary, taking the tablets. Blood-pressure medication is very effective.

Cholesterol

Cholesterol (which is fatty, waxy stuff produced by the liver) isn't all bad. Our bodies need a certain amount of it to coat cells, insulate nerve fibres and make hormones – but they don't need a lot.

There are two types of cholesterol: high-density lipoprotein (HDL, aka the good one) and low-density lipoprotein (LDL, aka the bad one). When cholesterol is delivered to your arteries, the good version shunts the bad one back to the liver, which disposes of it. If there isn't enough good to tackle large quantities of bad, fat builds up in your arteries and you're ripe for coronary heart disease. Recommended levels of cholesterol, measured in millimoles per litre, are below 5.4 for anyone without heart disease or below 4.0 for anyone with. Ideally your HDL cholesterol should be above 1.0 and your LDL cholesterol between 2.1 and 4.0.

... AND TRIGLYCERIDES

Triglycerides are also fats produced by the liver and stored by the body as fat when it's having to deal with too many calories. A blood test to measure your cholesterol also measures your triglyceride levels. High levels (over 2.0) combined with high LDL put you at even greater risk of heart disease, and of inflammation of the pancreas, which, when chronic, can cause all sorts of unpleasant complications.

LOWERING CHOLESTEROL AND TRIGLYCERIDE LEVELS

It's mostly a matter of exercise (as above) and diet (take a look at Chapter 9). If you can't be fagged altering your life drastically, at least:

- eat (much) less saturated fat and opt instead for mono- or polyunsaturated fats;

- include more fibre in your diet;

- eat more oily fish;

- reduce the amount of sugar in your diet;

- watch your weight.

When weight is a health hazard

Name thirty fat people over 80. If you want to live beyond the regulation three score years and ten, plus the further ten which is average, get your weight under control.

YOUR BMI

The most commonly used indicator of healthy body weight is the unforgiving body mass index (BMI), which calculates body fat by using a height-to-weight ratio. Its reliability fails only in the case of athletes (so, athletes, you can skip the test); and it doesn't apply to people aged 19 or below, whose results are interpreted differently.

It's simply enough calculated. First weigh yourself and then measure your height. The arithmetic is easy if you have a calculator (and half an hour to spare while you get it all wrong to begin with). In metrics, you multiply your height in metres by itself and divide it into your weight in kilos. Under the imperial system, you multiply your height in inches by itself, divide it into your weight in pounds, and multiply the total by 703. (I don't care why you multiply it by 703 and nor should you or we'll all turn to comfort eating.) So: for someone who weighs 63.5 kilos (10 stone or 140 lbs) and is 1.676 metres (5ft 6 or 66 inches) tall, the sum in metrics is 63.5 ÷ 1.676 x 1.676 (that is, 63.5 ÷ 2.8) and the answer is 22.6. In imperial, the sum is 140 ÷ 66 x 66, multiplied by 703 (that is, 140 ÷ 4356 x 703) and the answer 22.59. I tell you this just so you understand the principle. Use the table below.

If your BMI is between 25 and 29.9, doctors would classify you as overweight. If it's 30 or higher, they would regard you as obese. Either way, you probably need to address the amount you eat and drink (and I'm not talking water here).

YOUR WAIST

Your waist measurement is increasingly regarded as an even more significant determinant of susceptibility to disease than your BMI is. Excess fat around the stomach greatly increases the risk not only of heart disease but also of Type 2 diabetes (because deep abdominal fat can lead to insulin resistance). The good news is that it's

BMI CHART

Weight in kilograms

Height in centimetres	45	48	50	53	55	58	60	63	65	68	70	73	75	78	80	82.5	85	87.5	90
145.0	21.4	22.6	23.8	25.0	26.2	27.3	28.5	29.7	30.9	32.1	33.3	34.5	36.7	36.9	38.0	39.2	40.4	41.6	42.8
147.5	20.7	21.8	23.0	24.1	25.3	26.4	27.6	28.7	29.9	31.0	32.2	33.3	34.5	35.6	36.8	37.9	39.1	40.2	41.4
150.0	20.0	21.1	22.2	23.3	24.4	25.6	26.7	27.8	28.9	30.0	31.1	32.2	33.3	34.4	35.6	36.7	37.8	38.9	40.0
152.5	19.3	20.4	21.5	22.6	23.6	24.7	25.8	26.9	27.9	29.0	30.1	31.2	32.2	33.3	34.4	35.5	36.5	37.6	38.7
156.0	18.7	19.8	20.8	21.9	22.9	23.9	25.0	26.0	27.1	28.1	29.1	30.2	31.2	32.3	33.3	34.3	35.4	36.4	37.5
157.5	18.1	19.1	20.2	21.2	22.2	23.2	24.2	25.2	26.2	27.2	28.2	29.2	30.2	31.2	32.2	33.3	34.3	35.3	36.3
160.0	17.6	18.6	19.5	20.5	21.5	22.5	23.4	24.4	25.4	26.4	27.3	28.3	29.3	30.3	31.3	32.2	33.2	34.2	35.2
162.5	17.0	18.0	18.9	19.9	20.8	21.8	22.7	23.7	24.6	25.6	26.5	27.5	28.4	29.3	30.3	31.2	32.2	33.1	34.1
165.0	16.5	17.4	18.4	19.3	20.2	21.1	22.0	23.0	23.9	24.8	25.7	26.6	27.5	28.5	29.4	30.3	31.2	32.1	33.1
167.5	16.0	16.9	17.8	18.7	19.6	20.5	21.4	22.3	23.2	24.1	24.9	25.8	26.7	27.6	28.5	29.4	30.3	31.2	32.1
170.0	15.6	16.4	17.3	18.2	19.0	19.9	20.8	21.6	22.5	23.4	24.2	25.1	26.0	26.8	27.7	28.5	29.4	30.3	31.1
172.5	15.1	16.0	16.8	17.6	18.5	19.3	20.2	21.0	21.8	22.7	23.5	24.4	25.2	26.0	26.9	27.7	28.6	29.4	30.2
175.0	14.7	15.5	16.3	17.1	18.0	18.8	19.6	20.4	21.2	22.0	22.9	23.7	24.5	25.3	26.1	26.9	27.8	28.6	29.4
177.5	14.3	15.1	15.9	16.7	17.5	18.3	19.0	19.8	20.6	21.4	22.2	23.0	23.8	24.6	25.4	26.2	27.0	27.8	28.6
180.0	13.9	14.7	15.4	16.2	17.0	17.7	18.5	19.3	20.1	20.8	21.6	22.4	23.1	23.9	24.7	25.5	26.2	27.0	27.8
182.5	13.5	14.3	15.0	15.8	16.5	17.3	18.0	18.8	19.5	20.3	21.0	21.8	22.5	23.3	24.0	24.8	25.5	26.3	27.0
185.0	13.1	13.9	14.6	15.3	16.1	16.8	17.5	18.3	19.0	19.7	20.5	21.2	21.9	22.6	23.4	24.1	24.8	25.6	26.3
187.5	12.8	13.5	14.2	14.9	15.6	16.4	17.1	17.8	18.5	19.2	19.9	20.6	21.3	22.0	22.8	23.5	24.2	24.9	25.6
190.0	12.5	13.2	13.9	14.5	15.2	15.9	16.6	17.3	18.0	18.7	19.4	20.1	20.8	21.5	22.2	22.9	23.5	24.2	24.9

■ **Underweight** ■ **Normal** ■ **Overweight** ■ **Obesity**

infinitely easier to measure. (Your waist, in case you can no longer find it, is located just above your navel.)

To reduce the risk of health problems, it's recommended that a man's waist circumference be less than 102 centimetres (40 inches) and a woman's less than 88 centimetres (35 inches).

If your BMI or body shape is an issue for you, have your cholesterol and blood pressure checked regularly and address your calorie intake.

KILOJOULES/CALORIES

It's a simple, if cruel, fact that if we take in more kilojoules or calories (units of energy) than we burn, the surplus will be stored as fat, and fat is what does the damage. It's a less simple, but maybe even harsher, fact that high-kilojoule foods aren't necessarily those we immediately recognise as unhealthy, which is why it pays to read the labels and note the energy count per serve. Calorie-counting is a dreary exercise, but you need a rough idea of your intake. The Australian Department of Health and Ageing and the UK NHS agree very broadly:

- Men aged between 19 and 50 need about 10,500 kilojoules (2500 calories) a day; and women of the same age about 8400 (2000).

- Children (up to age eighteen) need more energy; older people, less.

- Tall people generally need more kilojoules than short ones do.

- Athletes and people who are physically active need more than those whose lives are mostly sedentary.

Health supplements

Mostly you shouldn't need them, as your diet ought to contain all the vitamins, minerals and trace elements you need. This isn't necessarily true if you're pregnant, elderly, vegetarian or vegan, or if your health is in some way compromised by chronic or acute illness, in which case you may find yourself needing more nutrients than your diet can naturally provide. Don't self-diagnose – ask a health professional.

Loads of people, including myself, swear by fish-oil supplements to reduce joint pain; echinacea and vitamin C at the first sign of a cold; and vitamin Bs of all sorts to relieve a hangover. There are scientific studies that show I'm deluded and others that show I'm not, so it's really a case of whatever works for you, but in any case the rules of moderation and common sense apply. Should you be taking supplements, store them in a sealed container in the fridge. Take them during the day, after a meal – never on an empty stomach, mostly because they will fail to be absorbed and quickly pass through the system, but also because it may cause nausea or a burning sensation in the stomach.

PROBIOTICS

Probiotics are live, good-for-you bacteria that live in your gut (along with the less beneficial types). If your diet is fibre-rich, you're likely to have enough probiotics in your system. But supplements are available (in tablet form, or via some yoghurt or fermented-milk drinks), by which many people place great store. This remains something of an act of faith, but there is a growing body of evidence which suggests that regular users of probiotic products get sick less often than those who don't use them, that they can aid digestion and help in the treatment of yeast infections, irritable bowel syndrome and childhood eczema (we have what we believe to be walking proof of this in our household).

Allergies and intolerances

There is a significant difference between one and the other. An allergy can cause anything from itching and sneezing (which can be treated by antihistamines) to anaphylactic shock (a severe, occasionally fatal, reaction whose symptoms may include acute breathing difficulty and low blood pressure, and which is usually treated with adrenaline). The smallest amount of exposure to the allergen will cause the reaction and anyone with a severe allergy and considered to be at risk should have a management plan (which might include carrying an epipen for emergency adrenaline treatment) and be eternally vigilant.

Intolerances are miles more common and require a much larger exposure to create a reaction. Usually they are the result of sensitivity to certain foods – most commonly milk, yeast and gluten – and symptoms may include nausea, diarrhoea, flushing or a plain old pain in the stomach. If you have what might be allergic reactions or an ongoing undiagnosed gut problem, see a doctor for a proper diagnosis rather than self-treating.

•••••••••••••••• WORK/LIFE BALANCE ••••••••••••••••

The most common afflictions of householders in industrialised countries are exhaustion and stress, and for many of us these are ongoing. Because we have skewed notions of our physical and mental capacity, we mightn't even recognise the signs: we go about our business quietly pleased with our ability to be superhuman, congratulating ourselves on our fine response to pressure. On we charge, tackling the world and everything it throws at us, until something – a job change, a family crisis, a house move – happens, we call upon reserves of energy to deal with it and, oh no, don't have any. The result mightn't be catastrophic, but it won't be fun.

We are biologically programmed to respond to moments of extreme fear (an immediate threat or stressor) by releasing large amounts of hormones, adrenaline most notably, that prepare us for fighting or fleeing. The danger passes and the hormone levels return to normal. If we produce a constant stream of fear-induced hormones to deal with constant stress, and don't take enough time out to allow our bodies to return to normal, we will exhaust ourselves, get all sorts of illnesses and our organs will fail. Yep, they will. Maybe not at once, but in the fullness of time, so it pays both to learn to recognise excessive stress and to learn, or remind ourselves, how to relax.

Signs of stress

Your nearest and dearest might simply have come to regard you as a pain in the neck rather than a stressed person, but if you tick most of the boxes below, you may regard them as warning signs:

- increased irritability;
- constant anxiety;
- super-sensitivity;
- irrational moods;
- loss of concentration;
- loss of sex drive;
- heart palpitations;
- over-eating and under-eating;
- relying on alcohol in order to relax;
- pain all over the place but especially in the back, neck and shoulders;
- insomnia, or waking at 4 am super-alert;
- indigestion;
- missed periods;
- nausea.

I could go on, but these are the most common symptoms and most of us will be familiar with many of them. The best remedies, according to those in the know, are regular aerobic exercise (which addresses the balance of hormones between fear-control and feel-good), mental down-time (your choice, but yoga is excellent), proper sleep and proper breathing.

If you're feeling overly and unmanageably stressed, get help both for the symptoms and for the cause. The cause may well be less easy to remedy than the symptoms, but it certainly needs to be addressed one way or another (even if it is just a strategy for dealing with the fact that the problem won't go away).

How much sleep we need

Your sleep needs vary according to your age, lifestyle and biological clock, and you're probably getting enough sleep if you're not tired or functioning below par during the day. Adults are generally reckoned to need seven or eight hours' sleep a night. Children need more: newborns sleep up to eighteen hours a day; children under five, between ten and twelve hours a day; and school-age children at least nine hours a night. Older people say they need less and maybe they do, but it's possible they just get less because they don't get enough exercise, are in discomfort or their sleep is more easily disturbed. At the other end of the spectrum, there is some suggestion that regularly sleeping too long (more than nine hours a night) is as unhealthy as a lack of sleep.

LACK OF SLEEP

There are two broad sleep types – REM (rapid eye movement) sleep and non-REM sleep – and we need enough of both to feel we have slept well. REM periods, which are scattered, typically account for around a quarter of an adult's total sleep. This means we have to sleep long enough, uninterrupted, to enter both critical stages.

Snoring or sleep-apnoea sufferers can feel sleep-deprived, as can new mothers. The rest of us might be sleepless for short periods, owing to anxiety, jetlag, work, or babies in the house, and even these will affect our performance. But chronic lack of sleep (whose causes may be physiological or psychological) not only results in ongoing fatigue, poor memory and concentration, but it can also lead to depression and further anxiety. We can catch up on modest amounts of lost sleep by daytime naps, which according to current science, should not last more than an hour or sleeping in at weekends. Neither will help a long-term sleep debt, however, in which case you should seek medical advice.

If you're prone to occasional sleeplessness, you could try the following:

- aerobic exercise, but not too close to bedtime as it can stimulate rather than soothe you;

- a bath;

- some kind of meditative activity to still your mind (even a book that bores you to sobs, though resist sobbing);

- a warm drink just before bed – a small one or you'll be up all night peeing;

- no TV in the bedroom and nothing on the radio to irritate or enrage you;

- a comfortable bed;

- room temperature on the low side rather than warm;

- visualising a positive activity to remove negative thoughts;

- breathing properly, through the nose (which has defence mechanisms to prevent impurities and excessively cold air entering the body).

BREATHING PROPERLY

I know: it's in out, in out. But there's also waking in the night and having no breathing pattern (in our household, anyway); there's sitting at a computer holding your breath; and there's racing through the day with breathing so shallow and quick that you don't take in sufficient oxygen or expel sufficient carbon dioxide. You know the dangers of failing to expel carbon dioxide from your system. (Yes, you do – toxic build-up.)

Oxygen purifies the bloodstream and is essential for the brain, nerves, glands and other internal organs to function properly. If your brain is consistently starved of oxygen, yogic thinking has it that you will become mentally sluggish, harbour negative thoughts and ultimately become depressed, which makes sense. But we can reprogram ourselves. Yoga regards proper breathing as the cornerstone to good health, and what follows is a simple yogic breathing technique.

The full yoga breath (Pranayama)

This is best learnt lying on your back with your eyes closed and your body relaxed, which can take a minute or so to achieve:

- Breathe in and out naturally through your nose, noticing your abdomen rise and fall. Keep your breath even and deepen the breathing. On the in-breath, allow your abdomen to rise as far as it will go, then on the out-breath let it drop completely. Repeat for twenty breaths, then return to normal breathing.

- Repeat the exercise, this time focusing on your chest. On the in-breath, allow your ribcage to lift and expand; as you breathe out, let your lungs subside completely. Keep your abdomen still, and move only your chest. Do this for twenty breaths.

● Now combine both steps. As you inhale, fill first your abdomen and then your chest. Exhale, allowing first your chest and then your abdomen to drop completely. Continue for twenty breaths. This is full yogic breathing.

You're not going to master this technique in a single session, or even in a few, but you are embracing the pattern: full inhalations from the abdomen to the chest and full exhalation from the chest to the abdomen – without strain and in a continuous, smooth wave.

Observe all the above and you will feel better, not just because you are showing your body respect, but because you are proving to yourself that you can take on a serious self-improvement challenge and meet it. Hurray!

23

FIRST AID

Every householder needs a grasp of basic first aid in order to deal with illness and accidents around the home without panicking. Taking a St John Ambulance course to provide perspective and instil confidence should be obligatory, but since it isn't I can only advise you to make time to do one. Their websites also have information and advice on all sorts of problems, from allergic reactions to resuscitation techniques. The following is very basic information only but sometimes, that is better than nothing.

Much as I adore self-diagnosis, it really is only advisable in the case of very minor, non-alarming symptoms, like a runny nose and sore throat, which last for no more than twenty-four hours. The information that follows is only a rough guide: common sense must prevail. To access common sense do a first aid course.

Symptoms

Apart from being in pain and generally feeling rotten, there are other clues as to how sick you or a member of your household might be. They include raised temperature, abnormal pulse, rashes, disorientation, whimpering (especially from a child and at night), abnormal sleepiness or listlessness, blurred vision, as well as disturbances of the stomach. When it comes to children, you really can't afford to ignore any such symptoms for any length of time because they don't necessarily explain pain well. A raised temperature for more than twenty-four hours, for example, needs medical advice. In conjunction with a rash, disorientation and/or whimpering, it needs immediate advice. Err on the side of caution with patients of all ages. It's better to be called panicking than negligent.

TEMPERATURE

If your temperature is higher than normal, normal being anywhere between 36.5°C and 37.2°C (97.7–99°F), you have a fever. This usually means your body is trying to ward off an infection or illness of some sort but since body temperature can rise and fall quickly and since it can vary from one part of the day to the next, you should double-check by taking it again half an hour after the first reading. Fevers aren't themselves dangerous, but are sound indicators of the seriousness of whatever illness or infection is lurking.

Temperature can be measured by a thermometer placed under the tongue, under the arm, on the forehead, in the ear or in the rectum. Most usually for adults, the temperature is taken under the tongue or in the armpit, where the thermometer is placed and left for a couple of minutes. Under the arm is regarded as less reliable and will register a lower temperature than in the mouth by about 0.5°C (0.9°F). A temperature taken within ten minutes of eating anything hot or cold will also be unreliable if you are putting the thermometer in your mouth, for obvious reasons. All households, it goes without saying, should have a thermometer. There is a range to choose from.

● *Digital thermometers* are the most costly but also the most accurate. They usually register the temperature within seconds. *Digital infrared* or *laser thermometers* can register a temperature without touching the body and are most commonly used to register the core body temperature via the ear (so are ideal for babies and extremely ill patients).

● *Thermometer strips* are placed on the forehead and read skin temperature rather than core body temperature, so they're not brilliantly accurate. They will, however, give you a rough idea (normal, high or low), which is usually all you need for children (on whom they are mostly used). Be careful not to put your hands across the sensor pad when you're holding the strip in place, or you'll blow the whole exercise.

● Old-fashioned *mercury thermometers* are best avoided. They're usually made of glass and can break easily, spilling the mercury, which indicates the temperature and is poisonous. If this is all you've got, shake it to return the mercury to a base reading and then leave it under the tongue for two minutes or in the armpit for four minutes. If you're taking a child's temperature, don't risk placing it in his or her mouth and never leave it unattended.

Febrile convulsions

One in twenty children aged up to five years old (but usually between six months and three years) may suffer a febrile convulsion as the result of a rapid increase in temperature. Usually it's one-off and lasts no more than six minutes, during which the child's body will become stiff, their limbs will twitch and they will lose consciousness. It looks terrifying but there are rarely any after-effects. Lower the child's temperature with paracetamol, by sponging them down and removing hot bedclothes, but inform your GP and get medical advice for whatever is causing the temperature. Get medical advice anyway if a baby's temperature is higher than 38°C (100.4°F) (under three months) or over 39°C (102.2°F) (under six months).

PULSE

A pulse is the thumping rhythm you can detect in a vein or artery as your heart pumps blood through your system. A normal adult 'resting' pulse is between 60 and 90 beats per minute. The 'normal' rate varies according to age and to activity and fitness levels: a child's pulse is faster than an adult's (a newborn baby's will be between 100 and 160 per minute); older people commonly have a slower pulse, as do athletes. A raised pulse rate may be an indicator of infection, disease, internal bleeding or dehydration. A radically lowered pulse, especially when combined with symptoms like coldness, clamminess and shortness of breath, in anyone not obviously an athlete, should be treated as an emergency.

You can feel a pulse in the neck, behind the knee and on the inside of the elbow, but the underside of the wrist, beneath the thumb, is most commonly used because it's usually most accessible. To take a pulse:

- Place your index and middle fingers over the chosen vein.

- Apply light pressure until you feel a pulse (having to hunt for it doesn't mean death is imminent), then count the number of beats in thirty seconds (use the second hand on your watch) and multiply by two to get the rate per minute. You may notice irregularities of rhythm, but your main concern is the number of beats. In case you think it doesn't have much relevance, you might like to know that it was a raised pulse which alerted our household to the fact that my husband was bleeding internally and in need of 7 pints (nearly 4 litres) of blood.

Painkillers

The miracles painkillers work in terms of pain relief and diagnosis never fail to amaze me; nor does the number of times householders fail to resort to them. If you have pain, however much you've been raised to grin and bear it, however sacred and unused to drugs your body might be, paracetamol or ibuprofen (not to be taken without advice if you suffer from stomach ulcers or asthma) will usually provide almost instant relief. This will not only make you feel better, but it will help determine the pain's seriousness. If the pain disappears altogether and permanently, you can forget it. If the pain grows steadily worse, or continues for more than forty-eight hours, you need help. Stick to recommended doses, however. Overuse can cause liver and kidney damage.

········ ACCIDENTS AND EMERGENCIES ········

Most household accidents are comparatively minor and can be treated at home with band-aids (cuts), arnica (bruising), a cold compress (strains, minor burns) and a mild painkiller, if required, for comfort. Should the damage be more serious, the measures we take might be to save a life or to stabilise a condition that requires medical attention.

Your first concern is recognising an emergency when you see it. They are best described as urgent and alarming – in this context, medical – situations beyond your scope and control. For the most part, you can trust your instinct as well as your eyes and ears: sudden and severe pain; loss of consciousness; loss of blood; immobility; unusual distress or pallor after an accident; snake bites; spider bites; babies arriving.

Over-reacting isn't the worst thing you can do when you are alarmed. Get help: call an emergency service – in Australia, dial 000; in the UK, dial 999. From a mobile, 112 is an emergency number in most countries. As you make the call, rehearse directions to wherever you are and how best to describe the condition of the patient. You may be in a panic, but being vague or inarticulate will waste valuable time.

Because you need to act quickly, you should also be able to recognise the symptoms of a heart attack and a stroke.

Heart attack

The American Heart Association explains that some heart attacks are sudden and of such intensity that you get the picture at once, but many begin slowly with mild pain and discomfort and take everyone by surprise. The symptoms to look for include:

- Discomfort in the centre of the chest, which lasts more than a few minutes or goes away and then comes back. Patients may describe it as uncomfortable pressure, squeezing, fullness or pain.

- Discomfort in other areas of the upper body. Symptoms can include pain or discomfort in one or both arms, the back, neck, jaw or stomach.

- Shortness of breath with or without chest discomfort.

Other signs may include breaking out in a cold sweat, nausea or lightheadedness.

Stroke

There are dramatic and immediate tests to determine whether someone has had a stroke, the effects of which can be immeasurably improved with urgent treatment (that is, within three hours). Think STR: get the patient to Smile, Talk (speak a simple sentence, such as 'Today is Sunday') and Raise their arms above their heads. Difficulty in accomplishing any of these actions should alert you to the possibility of a stroke and the need for urgent medical attention. You can also ask the patient to stick out their tongue: the tongue falling to one side is another stroke indicator.

Shock

Shock can affect victims of any accidents or emergencies and it must be treated. The victim will be cold and clammy, pale, breathing fast, yawning and sighing. They may have a rapid weak pulse and they may lose consciousness. Don't offer hot sweet tea or alcohol – in fact, give the patient nothing to eat or drink. Lay them down, cover them to keep them warm, and give constant reassurance until an ambulance arrives.

Choking

First, calm everyone down, especially the person who is choking.

FOR VICTIMS AGED 12 MONTHS PLUS

If they're having difficulty breathing, encourage them to try; if they are spluttering, get them to breathe through their nose. If something is caught in their throat, encourage them to cough; if you can see the obstruction, remove it carefully. In adults, it's reasonable to sweep the mouth with your finger to locate the obstruction but it's extremely dangerous to attempt this on children and infants because you risk pushing the object further into the airway.

fig. 1   *fig. 2*   *fig. 3*   *fig. 4*

If the victim can't speak, cry, breathe or cough, you need to act fast because there's a danger of the brain being starved of oxygen. Bend them forwards and, using the heel of your hand, give five sharp blows to their back, between the shoulder blades. If this doesn't work, you need to administer chest thrusts: to do this, place one hand on the person's back and another on the breastbone, and give slow and deliberate thrusts upwards. Check the mouth for signs of the obstruction. Repeat the cycle of five back blows and five chest thrusts, three times, then call an ambulance.

This procedure is similar to, but not the same as, the Heimlich manoeuvre, which has lost favour owing to it being so poorly performed by people trying to help but getting it wrong. Heimlich recommended abdominal (not chest) thrusts but these are now frowned upon by St John Ambulance owing to the damage they can inadvertently cause to the sternum, liver, stomach, oesophagus, bowel and spleen, especially in children. I was going to include it – who wouldn't want to master a technique that saved the lives of the late President Ronald Reagan and Elizabeth Taylor, for which so many people are grateful? But I can't. Perform it if you've been trained to do it, otherwise, don't.

FOR BABIES UNDER 12 MONTHS OLD

If the victim is an infant, St John Ambulance advises first placing the baby face-down along your forearm with its head towards your wrist and your arm at a downward angle. Using the heel of your hand, hit the baby firmly on the back, then check its mouth (do not finger-sweep the mouth). If this doesn't work, turn the baby onto its back and give up to five chest thrusts, using just two fingers, about a finger's breadth below the nipple line. If the obstruction hasn't cleared after three cycles, call an ambulance but keep going until help arrives.

Poisoning

You might suspect that a household member has been poisoned if a small child is standing in the kitchen with a bottle of poisonous something in their hand or when anyone of any age is showing symptoms that include pains in the stomach, nausea, shortness of breath, sleepiness, blurred vision, strange-smelling breath, blueness around the lips, or loss of consciousness.

Do not attempt to make the victim vomit. If the symptoms are so far mild, call the Poisons Information Hotline in Australia (13 11 26) or the National Poisons Information Service in the UK (0845 8920111). If the victim is displaying any of the symptoms mentioned above, don't hang about. Call an ambulance, and while you wait try to identify the poison. You're looking for any suspect container: for prescription medication; insecticides and herbicides; animal bait; bleaches and other cleaning products; paints and thinners; any petrol derivatives, even perfume or cosmetics. You might also be looking for plants, snakes or spiders.

SNAKE BITES

Gone are the days when you applied a tourniquet, cut the bite and sucked out the poison. Don't attempt any such treatments and don't wash the bite, as any traces of venom will help identify the type of snake. You need urgent medical assistance, but in the first instance:

- Apply a pressure bandage to the site, wherever it is, marking the position of the bite on the bandage. If the bite is on an arm or leg, wrap the bandage the full length of the limb.

- Keep the bandage firmly in place until medical help arrives: the pressure limits the spread of the venom.

- Keep the victim as still and calm as possible. If you can, apply a splint to the area of the bite to immobilise it. Don't, under any circumstances, let the victim move about: if transport is needed, carry the victim to it.

- If possible, identify the type of snake.

SPIDER BITES

In Australia, the most venomous spider bites are from funnelwebs and redbacks. The treatment is different for each, but in both cases seek medical help urgently (dial 000 from a landline, or 112 from a mobile). Antivenoms are available in most hospitals and are extremely effective, so the aim is to get to a hospital fast.

The symptoms of poisonous spider bites can be deeply unpleasant. They hurt like mad. The patient will be sick, weak, maybe numb, and have a pain in the stomach; they may have trouble breathing. They can also sweat profusely and produce a lot of saliva as the body reacts to the venom. A bite by any large black spider should be treated as a suspected funnelweb bite until it is proved to be otherwise.

A funnelweb bite is treated similarly to snake bite: apply a pressure bandage to the bite immediately, immobilise the area and reassure the patient. The bandage must not be removed by anyone other than a medical practitioner.

In the case of redbacks and other spiders, there may be swelling in the area of the bite, even though the puncture itself might not be easy to see. The venom of these spiders moves more slowly than that of a funnelweb, so a pressure bandage is not required (and, in the case of redbacks certainly, will only aggravate the pain): instead, apply an ice pack to the bite to reduce the swelling. Get medical attention as soon as possible.

OTHER BITING THINGS

The list could go on and on, but I'll confine myself to those most commonly encountered by members of our household.

Ticks (found on the humid east coast of Australia) attach themselves to you or your clothing if you brush against a tick-harbouring tree or bush. They feed on the blood of animals (including humans). Their toxin, released when they bite you, may produce no symptoms at all, but in susceptible individuals they can trigger a severe allergic reaction and occasionally paralysis; grass ticks can cause an itch. Always check household members for ticks after walks in the bush or bushy gardens where ticks are known to live (look especially in the hair and behind the ears, where they can be missed), but, better still, dress appropriately in long sleeves, long pants and a wide-brimmed hat. There are many suggestions for tick removal, but the current favourite is to use a pair of pointed tweezers, applied as close to the victim's skin and the tick's head as possible. Grasp and then pull with a steady pressure. Applying methylated spirits is not advisable, as it will only cause the tick to gag and release more toxins. If the area is painful after the tick has been removed, apply ice to reduce any swelling and use an antihistamine cream.

Wasp and bee stings should also be removed with tweezers. Don't squeeze, or the poison will spread beneath the skin. The same treatment applies as for ticks: apply ice to reduce swelling and follow with an antihistamine cream. Should you develop an allergy to stings, consult your doctor (who will prescribe emergency treatment) and carry a card identifying you as an allergy sufferer.

Jellyfish stings are caused by the nematocysts (the stinging bit) releasing toxins and leaving red weals across the affected area, so treatment involves neutralising the nematocysts and this is currently best achieved with vinegar: soak the affected area for fifteen minutes. If you have no vinegar, use seawater – fresh water will only make matters worse, as will ice, as will rubbing. If there are still tentacles attached to the affected area, remove them in sea water, wearing gloves if you have them but with anything available to protect your hands otherwise.

Vinegar is no longer advised for the treatment of *bluebottle stings*: immersion in hot water for at least twenty minutes is considered to be more effective.

Burns and scalds

Burns are graded (first degree, second degree or third degree) according to how many layers of skin are lost. First-degree burns that cover only a very small area of the body can be treated as minor, which means they can be treated at home. If they cover an area larger than a postage stamp, they require urgent medical attention. For home treatment, you will be treating redness, possibly swelling and pain.

Your first priority, whether the burn is serious or not, is to remove the victim from danger. If they are on fire, the rule is 'Stop, drop and roll', which means grab the person, who may be running, force them to the ground and roll them over the ground to extinguish the flames. If possible between grabbing and dropping, wrap the victim in a heavy fabric – a woollen coat is ideal to extinguish flames. Then run cold water across the burn (or submerge it in cold water) for ten minutes. If this isn't an option, apply a cold compress to the area for at least five minutes (twenty minutes in the case of chemical burns). Remove any jewellery, if you can, and cover the burn with clean, non-fluffy material to protect it from infection. (Gauze or cloth, a clean plastic bag or cling wrap all make good dressings, according to St John's Ambulance.) Because burns can really hurt, give the victim a painkiller; if they can in any way be called extensive, call an ambulance. The following advice applies for all burns:

- Never apply fat.

- Don't put ice directly on the burn.

- Never apply an adhesive bandage.

- Never touch the burnt or scalded area.

- Never attempt to remove anything sticking to burnt skin.

- Never attempt to pop blisters.

- If the burn is anything other than minor, you may need to treat shock as well as the burn.

SUNBURN

Sunburn damages the skin, causes premature ageing and places the sufferer at greater risk of cancer owing to the absorption if UV radiation. If that's not a case against tanning, I don't know what is. What's more, it may take only fifteen minutes in Australia to get burnt, so prevention is definitely the answer:

- Stay out of direct sunlight between 10 am and 2 pm.

- Wear protective clothing.

- Wear a sunscreen.

Should you be severely sunburnt, with blistering, headaches and nausea, get medical help. For mild and moderate cases, take a cool (not cold) shower and apply a soothing cream recommended by a pharmacist. Drink plenty of fluids: the Cancer Council of New South Wales suggests these not be iced (which can cause a chill), but simply cool and plentiful.

HOW TO GIVE CPR (CARDIOPULMONARY RESUSCITATION)

The aim of CPR is to get blood circulating and oxygen to the brain when a person's heart has stopped beating as a result of an injury, accident or illness. Having established the victim isn't breathing, you need to act quickly. There are enough oxygen reserves in the blood for three to five minutes only, after which a person becomes brain-dead. Ring for an ambulance and perform CPR while you wait.

The following instructions are based on British Red Cross guidelines. But really, everyone should do a course, so a trained instructor can confirm that we have it right.

- Kneel alongside the person and ensure the airway is open by tilting their head back with one hand and lifting the chin with the other.

- Place your mouth over the victim's mouth, making a seal. Breathe twice into their mouth, for one second each breath (these are called rescue breaths). Breathe slowly to ensure the air reaches the lungs: if it does, the victim's chest will rise slightly; if it doesn't, reposition the victim's head and try again. If this fails, begin chest compressions, as follows.

- Place your hands on top of each other and place them in the centre of the victim's chest (on the breastbone) in line with the nipples. Push straight down on the chest, with your elbows locked. You are aiming for a compression of 50 millimetres or 2 inches. Perform 100 compressions per minute. Allow the chest to rise again completely after each, and after thirty give two rescue breaths. Repeat this cycle until help arrives.

Electric shock

The most common threat of electric shock to household members is from faulty appliances, faulty household wiring, lightning strike, downed power lines, and electrical appliances coming into contact with water (in a swimming pool, bathroom, laundry or kitchen). Symptoms of electric shock are burns where the electric current enters and leaves the body, cardiac arrest, loss of consciousness, difficulty breathing, and weak pulse.

Do not, under any circumstances, touch the victim before you have switched off the power. If this isn't immediately possible, push away the source of the current with a wooden broomstick (nothing damp or metallic); to protect yourself, stand on a dry non-conducting surface such as a piece of cardboard or a rubber or plastic mat. If the victim is conscious and breathing, treat any obvious burns. Otherwise, call an ambulance and if necessary begin CPR (cardiopulmonary resuscitation). If you don't know how to do it, the ambulance operator will advise you.

Fractures, sprains and strains

It can be hard to tell the difference between one and another, but treat the injury as a fracture if you're not sure. Signs of a fracture include pain, swelling, loss of normal movement and power, tenderness and bruising. If a fracture is obvious, immobilise the limb with a splint held in place by a bandage attached above and below the fracture (don't attempt to straighten it). The size and nature of the splint will depend on the size of the limb and what's available: in the case of a child's arm, a wooden spoon might do it.

Sprains and strains also need medical attention, if only to confirm your diagnosis. Although their symptoms are the same – pain, swelling, tenderness and bruising – they are different injuries. A sprain is an overstretched or torn ligament (the fibrous tissue that connects bones), while a strain is an injury to muscles or tendons that connect the muscles to the bones. If medical attention is not immediately available, your key is 'RICE':

- Rest the injured limb.

- Ice (wrapped in a wet cloth) should be applied to the injury for fifteen minutes every two hours for the first twenty-four hours, then every four hours for another twenty-four hours. (A pack of frozen vegetables will do.)

- Compress the injured area by wrapping it (firmly but not too tightly) in a stretch bandage.

- Elevate the sprained or strained part (keep it raised above the level of your heart if possible).

BLEEDING

Bleeding can be totally alarming, but isn't usually as serious as it looks. Most cuts and grazes can be treated at home. Your first job is to stop the bleeding by applying pressure (anything from a bandage to a towel, depending on the size and severity) to the wound. If damage is to a limb, elevate it. Apply the pressure until the bleeding has stopped, clean the wound under running water, gently dry it, then cover it with a sterile dressing. The NHS (UK) advises against using antiseptic, which can slow the healing process.

If the wound is deep and/or you can't stop the bleeding, get urgent medical help. If the wound swells, causes undue pain or looks infected, or if redness radiates from it, it needs treatment from a doctor or nearest casualty department.

PART 8

DEALING
WITH
CATASTROPHES

YOU CAN PLAN, you can be prudent, you can fill your life with love and serenity, you can lead a blameless existence, but you can't escape outrageous fortune because that's the way of things.

Distress, disappointments and terrible frights assail all householders at some time or other. You can limit the damage by understanding the nature and scope of the crisis, and this is achieved with clear thinking and a basic knowledge of its likely implications. From these can be extracted a strategy for coping. You might not be able to embrace it immediately owing to extreme shock, temperament failure or an important physical encumbrance like unconsciousness, but having information at your fingertips is reassuring sooner or later. I'm providing it mostly in bullet points for clarity and easy recollection, and with luck to pre-empt wrangling and argument on the day because this exactly what you don't need. Of course, there is more to it all than is explained here, but the following should make possible an informed first response, which might be as much as we can hope for under the circumstances.

24

CRISES
OF
ALL SORTS

The point about crises is that at their peak they require action, and action is best managed without emotion. This, I hope, forgives the direct, practical and very basic nature of the advice that follows, even when the subject is a life that appears to be in danger or ruins or is fraught with uncertainty.

WHAT TO DO IN THE EVENT OF A NATURAL DISASTER

In anticipation of any natural catastrophe, every household needs an emergency kit or, at the very least, a list of essentials to leave the house with the household if you need to evacuate. How far ahead of the anticipated natural catastrophe you gather it all together is up to you but at least know where everything is. It should include:

- at least one powerful torch with batteries;

- first-aid kit and manual;

- Swiss Army knife or similar multipurpose pocket tool;

- supply of essential medication/s, to be reviewed annually for relevance and expiry dates;

- battery-powered radio;

- telephone not dependent on electricity supply (so, a mobile or a phone wired into the system);

- masking tape (to seal doors and windows in the event of fire or chemical explosion);

- basic food supplies including non-perishables that don't need cooking (tinned beans, tuna, etc., with tin-opener), bottled water, water-purification tablets;

- matches and candles;

- whistle to attract attention;

- thermal blanket;

- insect repellent;

- spare house and car keys;

- portable hard drive or USB stick containing essentials from computer;

- critical documents (or certified copies): passports; insurance; wills; birth and marriage certificates; bank and credit-card details; investments; deeds to house, or mortgage documents;

- enough petrol in the car at all times to make a safe getaway.

If you need to evacuate your home:

- turn off the electricity and gas;
- close all doors and windows;
- take your mobile phone and your emergency kit;
- lock the house.

If there's a fire

In the event of a bushfire you will, with luck, have a fire plan you can implement in accordance with local conditions. In any case, put on protective clothing (wool or cotton that covers your entire body, so including hat and gloves), as well as sturdy shoes, protective glasses, and a soaked cotton mask or towel across your face. If you have time before leaving:

- block gaps around doors and windows with damp towels;
- remove blinds and curtains from windows, and pull furniture to the centre of the room;
- put sentimental items in a garbage bag and take it with you.

If the building is surrounded by fire, don't evacuate.

- Call the fire brigade – never assume someone else has.
- Put out spot fires should embers enter the house.
- Drink plenty of water.

In the event of a fire that has started inside the house, you almost certainly won't have time for most of the above. You need to evacuate with all speed. Cover your face as recommended, stay close to the ground, and call the fire brigade once you are safe.

If there's a flood

If you are evacuating during a flood, behave as for a fire but your clothing should be warm and waterproof.

- If you have time, get as much furniture off the floor as you can and pile electrical items on top of it.

- If you are surrounded by flood, never evacuate, or attempt to drive through it. Make your way to the highest, driest part of the building and try to attract attention.

- Don't drive or wade through drains, culverts or any water above knee height.

If there's an earthquake

Owing to the suddenness with which they occur, there may be little you can do other than take the most basic evasive action, but even evasive action is best managed without panicking.

- If you are inside when the quake hits, keep clear of windows, chimneys and overhead lights or fans. If evacuating from a tall building, don't take the lift.

- If you are outside, head for clear space to reduce the risk from falling trees or structures.

- Watch for fallen powerlines.

- Expect aftershocks.

If there's a cyclone

You will have been warned of the cyclone's approach, but keep listening (on your battery radio if necessary) for news of its progress.

- Disconnect all electrical appliances.

- Drag mattresses and a strong table to the strongest part of the building (cellar, internal hallway, bathroom). Keep your emergency kit with you.

- If the building starts to collapse, take shelter under the mattress, under the table.

····· WHAT TO DO WHEN SOMEONE DIES ·····

Usually, when someone dies in your presence, the death is expected, you will be among the next of kin and you will already have vaguely considered what must be done next. If the death isn't in a hospital, call an ambulance and, if appropriate, your GP. (Clearly, if the death is of a stranger and you are in the street, your GP won't be the person to call.)

Once the medical emergency is over, there's an apparently endless list of matters to be attended to. Pace yourself. There is a clear order of play, which helps:

○ If the deceased is your next of kin, discuss with the medical authorities any preferences he or she may have had concerning organ donation.

○ Double-check that death has actually occurred and there is no possible way in which life could be restored. It's what you'd want before your heart was removed.

○ The death certificate is usually issued by the doctor who pronounces the person dead. (If an autopsy or coronial enquiry is required, the certificate won't be provided until afterwards.) You need a death certificate before you can register the death or arrange a funeral.

○ If the deceased hasn't already organised one, you will need to find a funeral director (undertaker), who can arrange for removal of the body, register the death and organise the funeral. If you've never used one before, phone a couple and ask what they can arrange and how much they will charge. He or she will visit you to discuss arrangements. These will include choosing a coffin. This will be ghastly. Don't be cajoled into accepting anything weird or more extravagant than you really want. You will know best the wishes of the deceased and if you don't, you're better placed than a stranger to guess.

○ Try to keep the peace with siblings or other concerned parties at this stage, even though you are very sad and bad-tempered and they are irritating (or vice versa). Honour the dead person with tolerance and patience even if it feels unfamiliar.

○ To register the death, if you are doing this yourself, go to the Registry of Births, Deaths and Marriages (registry office). This must by law be done within seven days in Australia (five days in the UK). You can also apply online. It's advisable to buy several copies of the death certificate, because it will be required by anyone likely to need proof that the deceased really is no longer alive, like insurance companies, banks, post offices and so on.

◉ In addition to family and friends, notify any or all of the following (if applicable) immediately:

* minister of religion;

* employer/school;

* bank/s and credit-card companies;

* solicitor;

* accountant;

* executor/s of will, if known;

* health professionals who may have attended the deceased prior to the death.

◉ As soon as possible, locate the following:

* will;

* birth and marriage certificates;

* insurance policies;

* mortgage details, property deeds or rental agreement;

* tax reference number;

* (in the UK) NHS and National Insurance numbers;

* pension or superannuation documents.

◉ When you are ready, notify the following:

* insurance companies;

* landlord;

* social security;

* pension provider or superannuation fund;

* mortgage provider;

* utility companies;

* hire-purchase companies.

- In due course, you will also need to inform any clubs or organisations (such as a union) the deceased belonged to; the tax office; the local council; vehicle registration and licensing bodies; the electoral office.

- Unless you have no fond memories, don't clear the dead person's clothes and personal effects immediately. Moving on is essential, but doing so gradually rather than in haste is easier on the heart.

- Get the deceased removed from mailing lists by writing to the Australian Direct Marketing Association: ADMA, Reply Paid 38, PO Box 464, Kings Cross NSW 1340; or in the UK to the Mail Preference Service (MPS) at FREEPOST 29 LON20771, London W1E 0ZT.

- If you are grieving, go easy on yourself. Don't underestimate the horror of bereavement. It can be exhausting and make you a bit mad. You may suffer from poor judgement, short-term memory loss and erratic energy. Get help if you need it (friends and family won't necessarily be enough) and cling to it no matter how proud you are.

·········· WHAT TO DO IF YOU WANT TO ··········
GET MARRIED

This might not feel like a crisis, but it's pretty well certain to become one sooner or later. Second thoughts are inevitable, and the longer the delay between agreeing to marry and marrying, the colder the feet you're likely to get. Even the most lavish weddings can be organised in a month, so unless you have seriously good reasons for a long engagement (war, illness), avoid it and don't dither about the details – plough on in all but extreme circumstances, even those involving your in-laws or your mother.

To marry you must be aged over eighteen (over sixteen if you have parental consent). In Australia you may not marry an ancestor, a descendant, a brother or sister, a half-brother or -sister, or an adoptive brother or sister. In the UK, the combinations are far more nuanced, so get a comprehensive list from a citizens' advice bureau if you're in any doubt. Once you are sure you are legally entitled to marry:

- Decide where to hold the ceremony. You can get married in any religious building registered for marriage; in a registry office (associated with the Registry of Births, Deaths and Marriages); at any venue with the appropriate licence in the UK – check with the registry office. In Australia you can marry pretty much wherever you choose.

⊙ Unless you are marrying in a registry office, you need to find an authorised (government-registered) celebrant, whether church or civil. Unless you have a favoured church or celebrant, go online for local possibilities and visit them before deciding.

⊙ In Australia you must give the celebrant at least one month's (and no more than eighteen months') written notice of the proposed marriage (your celebrant can provide the necessary form). The celebrant will also need to see your birth certificates, evidence that any prior marriage has been dissolved (by death or divorce), and/or a passport if you were born overseas. The notice time can be shortened under certain pressing circumstances, which include legal proceedings, job- or travel-related matters, and illness. Apply to the Registry of Births, Deaths and Marriages.

⊙ In the UK, for a civil marriage you must give between fifteen days' and twelve months' notice, in person, at a Register Office and you both must have lived in that registration district for seven days immediately prior to the wedding. If you are not marrying at a Register Office, you will be given a certificate authorising the marriage, which you pass on to the celebrant. For marriages within the Church of England or of Wales, banns (notice of your intention to marry) are read from the pulpit on three consecutive weeks prior to the marriage. The banns may also be read in a Catholic church but they won't count legally. With a Catholic marriage (as with anything other than Church of England or Church of Wales ceremonies), you need an authorising certificate from a Register Office.

⊙ You need two witnesses, who must be over the age of eighteen.

⊙ In Australia same-sex marriages aren't legally recognised, but commitment ceremonies are; in the UK, same-sex couples can register a civil partnership (the process is similar to a civil marriage).

⊙ Civil marriages are less formal in style than church marriages, but both include the pronouncement that the contract you are entering into voluntarily is for life. As in a court of law, life doesn't necessarily mean life. At least one in three couples eventually claim reduced sentences owing to unreasonable or incompatible behaviour.

● Deciding guests, budgets and the style of reception is best negotiated in a flak jacket. (It's a metaphor: who wants to to get married in a flak jacket?) Marriage is a minefield and planning a wedding is a very good example of the strains your union must endure, so acquiring a metaphoric flak jacket at this early stage is no bad thing.

·········· WHAT TO DO IF YOU WANT TO ·········· GET DIVORCED

Most people want to get divorced once they are married. The mood usually passes, but sometimes it doesn't and then we have heartache. Deciding to end a commitment which was made with joy is always poignant, no matter how relieved one or both parties might be when it's finally all over. Amid the distress, you cling to practicalities.

● In Australia only one of you has to want the divorce and the only grounds are that you have lived separately for twelve months and there's no hope of reconciliation; the court isn't interested in why. In the UK, the court will grant you a divorce if the judge agrees the marriage has broken down irretrievably, for one or more of the following reasons: adultery, unreasonable behaviour, desertion for at least two years, living separately for two years if you both agree to divorce, or living separately for five years if there is no agreement to divorce. As far as the law is concerned you can live separately under the one roof, but affidavits testifying to the separateness must be provided.

● You, your spouse or the two of you together can complete a divorce application (known in the UK as Form D8) – this can be done online – which you file with the Family Court. There is a fee, which is reviewed every two years. The hearing is usually two months after the application is filed.

● If the court approves the application for divorce, a decree nisi (interim) is issued on the spot. In Australia, a decree absolute (final) is granted a month later; in the UK, it is granted after six weeks.

● A divorce involves not only the termination of the marriage but also division of any property and assets and an arrangement for custody of any children. In Australia, a divorce hearing does not settle disputes over property or children. These matters can be settled by agreement and filed with the court, or you can request that the court consider them separately.

Before a decree nisi is granted in the UK, the judge will check that all arrangements concerning children's welfare and money matters are agreed or being resolved.

⦿ You can manage without a solicitor in cases where everyone is in agreement about everything, but this is an emotionally taxing time and highly experienced professionals are best equipped to guide you through it (even if their fees do contribute to the emotional toll). You will certainly need a lawyer if the divorce or any of the terms of the divorce (property settlement, arrangements for children) are to be contested; it is always advisable when substantial assets are at stake. Finding a good divorce lawyer is most likely through personal recommendation but do your research. Ask friends of friends of friends, if necessary; taking the time to find the right person for the job is essential, however low you feel. You are looking for efficiency, reasonable fees, energy and understanding.

⦿ If there are children under the age of eighteen, one of you must attend the hearing and a divorce will only be granted if the court is happy with arrangements for the welfare of the children. If there are no children under eighteen, you may request not to attend court.

⦿ Friends can be remarkably uneasy about lining themselves up with one partner against another, regardless of the circumstances, so you can find yourself curiously and sadly unsupported. There are organisations which help if you need them, like Relationships Australia and Relate in the UK.

De facto and gay relationships

If your de facto or same-sex relationship is ending, you can apply to the Family Court or the Federal Magistrates Court to settle disputes about children and financial matters. You need to apply within two years of the relationship breakdown for financial orders. For de facto relationships to be recognised by the courts, the following are taken into account:

⦿ the length of the relationship;

⦿ the degree of commitment;

⦿ whether the relationship was sexual;

- if it involved financial dependence/support;

- if it involved joint ownership of property and/or joint care and support of children.

·· WHAT TO DO IF YOU CAN'T HAVE A BABY ··

Technically, doctors don't regard you as infertile until you've been having unprotected sex regularly for two years and have failed to conceive. A large proportion of infertility conditions can be treated, especially in couples aged under thirty-five. Fertility drugs can trigger egg production in much the same way as the body's own hormones; surgery can reverse sterilisation (sometimes), clear blocked fallopian tubes (sometimes), and retrieve sperm for use in fertility treatment. Simpler still, though not to be relied on, stress reduction and healthier living can sometimes do the trick.

- Since both men and women can be infertile, if you are concerned about your failure to conceive you should both consult your GP, preferably together. You may then be referred to a specialist for treatment – either hormonal or surgical.

- For information about infertility and the options available to you, see Chapter 3. Other useful resources include the Infertility Network UK and Patient UK, the Australian and New Zealand Infertility Counsellors Association and the Australian Infertility Support Group.

- For advice on surrogacy, for which you need an iron will and an infinite capacity to cope with frustration and stress, get in touch with the Infertility Treatment Authority in Australia or the National Adoption and Surrogacy Centre in the UK.

···· IF YOU'RE CONSIDERING ADOPTING ····

In Australia, you will be subject to the rules of the state you live in. In the UK, regulations are administered by the local authority adoption services. But very broadly:

- To adopt a child, you must be over eighteen in Australia (where an upper age limit also applies; it's calculated according to the age difference between you and any child you would like to adopt), and over twenty-one in the UK.

- You must be in a stable marriage or de facto relationship (in Australia the de facto relationship must have existed for at least three years). Same-sex couples in some Australian states can adopt if the relinquishing parent/s agree. In the UK, both same sex-couples and single parents may apply to adopt.

- The applying couple must meet a number of conditions, such as citizenship, financial security, ability to meet the personal and cultural needs of the child, and the age of other children in your family (if applicable), to name just a few. In Australia you must not be pregnant or undertaking fertility treatment at the time an adopted child is placed with you.

- The application and placement processes typically take between five and seven years in Australia and around three years in the UK.

- Adopting from abroad will be subject to the rules of the country where the child is born.

·· WHAT TO DO IF YOU SENSE LATE-ONSET ·· SEXUAL REORIENTATION

No cause for alarm. It doesn't mean you've been in denial all your life. Whether you've been straight and now think you're gay, or the other way round, all you are experiencing is a change, which may prove to be temporary, intermittent or permanent. But even if you have been in denial all your life, so what?

- Get counselling if the development is upsetting, confusing or has the potential to cause misery to an existing partner or family member. Try Relationships Australia or, in the UK, Relate or the British Association for Sexual and Relationship Therapy.

- Should you not be in an existing relationship, come out to your family and friends if this relieves the stress of secrecy and deceit. Otherwise, it's no one else's business.

- If you are in an existing relationship and your new feelings are overwhelming, honesty with your existing partner is only fair.

• Don't take unnecessary risks in the first flush of your newly discovered sexuality. On the other hand, don't be paralysed by anxiety: if you aren't attracted to anyone in particular or don't know how to make a first approach, join a gender-appropriate social group until you find your nerve.

··············· BRUSHES WITH THE LAW ···············

Litigation (whether it's You v Another or Another v You) is to be avoided, because it is criminally expensive. Only the very rich and the poor (who can claim legal aid or may be eligible for pro bono legal representation) can afford to go to court.

• If you are neither very rich nor entitled to legal aid, the usual reasons for going to court are to defend yourself against a serious criminal or civil charge or to reclaim a serious amount of money – so steer clear of the former and explore other avenues first in the case of the latter.

• Be aware that the former includes such apparently innocent ventures such as dashing off angry letters to a person in authority concerning a third party about whom you are insulting. They can construed as defamatory and you may be sued.

• Most disputes involving money are referred to mediation bodies in the first instance. Mediation is compulsory in probate disputes in Australia. Consumer claims are referred to consumer claims tribunals, where you either win or run out of strength. You may require legal advice for employment-related issues (if, say, you're given the boot), but mediation will be your first port of call.

• Should you pursue a claim to the bitter end, be very sure that the risk of failure is worth both the battle, the point of principle and the cost.

• If litigation is unavoidable, you need a good lawyer, preferably with experience and expertise in relevant cases, to advise you so do your research. You need a solicitor in the first instance; should the matter go to court, you will also need a barrister (whom the solicitor will brief). Get to grips with the law as it applies to your case; it saves expensive time going over and over the basics with your lawyer.

FINDING A LAWYER

This is clearly a relationship that requires careful handling. Because the legal process is so expensive and potentially upsetting, you need a solicitor who won't unnecessarily (or carelessly) tax your time or your pocket or contribute to your stress levels. Even in urgent situations, explore the options carefully and thoughtfully.

- A personal recommendation is best, but you may not know anyone who has experienced your current difficulty. Go online and look for lawyers with expertise in the relevant area of law and match them to where you live.

- If this doesn't help, approach the Law Society. It won't recommend a lawyer but can provide a selection which ideally won't include anyone hopeless.

- Once you have identified a few possible firms or individual solicitors from either of the above sources, phone them. Explain your situation and ask them if they will take on your case. Use this conversation to get a sense of them and their approach: you need to like your lawyer and you need a frank speaker.

- Ask what their rates and fees are. (A good firm will initially give you five to ten minutes' free assessment by phone.) A lawyer who is coy about fees is a cause for alarm: request a rough estimate of the total cost to you, or a range into which the charges might fall plus an explanation of the major variables and any possible extras. Ask if they offer a 'no win, no fee' arrangement. The Law Society can provide approximate rates to help you make a comparison.

- Before you commit yourself, ask for a cost agreement, which you should read thoroughly. This should include not only the solicitor's fees, but also the possible cost should the case go to court and a barrister be required. Ask about anything you don't understand.

CRIME AND THE HOUSEHOLDER

Strictly speaking, the following crises are as likely to occur outside the home as inside, but on the basis that anyone can get arrested, witness a crime or want to make a citizen's arrest in what will, under the circumstances, be the discomfort of their own home, I have included them.

What to do if you are arrested

○ Don't try to escape. Remain calm. Be aware of your rights: the police must identify themselves as police and tell you why they are arresting you; they may not detain you for more than four hours without a special warrant; you may contact (or request the police do so for you) a relative, friend or lawyer.

○ You're not legally required to say anything (unless the scene is a car crash, in which case you are obliged to give specific information to the police), so say nothing. That is, *nothing*. No matter how innocent you are or how innocent the remark, anything and everything is on the record and can be used as evidence.

○ Be polite, no matter how outraged you feel.

○ If a solicitor attends, listen to their advice until you have excellent reason to think it's bad.

What to do if you witness a crime

○ Don't try to be a hero. Don't draw attention to yourself.

○ Phone 000 (in Australia), 999 (in the UK), or 112 from a mobile. Ask for both police and ambulance. They will want your exact location, the nature of the crime, and your name and number (though you aren't obliged to give these).

○ Use your mobile phone to photograph the scene, concentrating on the people and any vehicle involved.

○ Write down relevant details: where, how and by whom the crime was committed. Physical descriptions of those involved should include height, build, hair colour and length, and clothes.

○ If you can't write them down, commit the details to memory and write them down as soon as possible. Eyewitnesses' memories are notoriously unreliable.

○ When the immediate danger has passed, offer what help you can to the victim/s.

○ In police interviews or in court, tell the truth exactly as you recall it. If you aren't sure, say so.

How to make a citizen's arrest

○ You can make a citizen's arrest if you have reasonable grounds for believing an offence that is punishable by imprisonment has been or is in the process of being committed. 'Reasonable grounds' means that you have direct evidence. (In the UK, it must be an offence that would be tried at the Crown Court, so not a kid kicking your car but someone robbing your safe.) If you aren't sure, note the details, report it to the police and let them do the arresting (I know – not the same). If you make a wrongful arrest, you could be sued for defamation.

○ Having made the arrest, inform the person why you are arresting them without making a direct accusation. Say, 'I am detaining you because ... I have good reason to believe you burnt my house down.'

○ You may only use reasonable force to defend yourself or to prevent the offender escaping. Otherwise you could be sued for assault.

○ Don't risk your personal safety.

○ Call the police or have someone else call the police, and hand the arrested person over.

What to do if you're the victim of a crime

○ If you are alone and at home and you are threatened by an intruder, hide or run. If neither is possible, offer no resistance unless you are in immediate danger, in which case do what you must to defend yourself.

○ If you (and/or any member of the household) are threatened with physical harm, hand over your valuables.

○ Call the police as soon as possible.

○ Make an immediate note of the details as if you were a witness to the crime.

○ Seek victim support. You may be entitled to compensation but first you may very well need help with the shock.

What to do if you're in a car crash

Crashes, as we all know, can occur anywhere – even immediately outside your own home – and the usual rules apply:

- Turn on your hazard lights.

- Get out of the car only if it's safe to do so, otherwise stay there (seat-belted) until assistance arrives. In an emergency, dial 112 from your mobile and ask for police and ambulance.

- If possible, and it mostly is, take a note of the other driver's name, licence details, insurance company, the date, the time, the road and weather conditions. Make a quick diagram of the crash scene – the direction in which the cars were travelling, the number of passengers and who was sitting where.

- Report the crash to the police if:

  * anyone is injured;

  * a vehicle needs towing;

  * there is damage to property other than the cars involved;

  * a driver refuses to provide relevant details or if you suspect drink or drugs are involved.

- Police will want to know where you are (provide landmarks if you don't know exactly); how many vehicles are involved; the extent and nature of any injuries, as far as you can tell; whether the road is blocked; if there's any debris on the road.

- Don't admit liability or make a statement of any kind to anyone other than the police.

WHAT TO DO IF YOU'RE MADE REDUNDANT

Losing your job owing to company restructuring can be a huge body blow. Unlike sacking, when protocols exist that include warnings, redundancy can be sudden because companies can close down overnight. Almost inevitably there will have been rumours, and even though rumours often turn out to be scaremongering, it is always worth noting the rumbles and covering your back. If you think you could be made redundant, take stock of your financial circumstances sooner rather than later. Consider eliminating unnecessary expenses, and if possible save the equivalent of three months' salary to tide you over (see Chapter 14).

In Australia, all employees who have more than twelve months' continuous service for an employer whose workforce numbers more than fifteen are entitled to some kind of redundancy or severance pay. (In the UK, it's two years.) Check your entitlements at Fair Work Australia or, in the UK, with the Redundancy Payment Offices. (You may not be entitled to redundancy pay, for instance, if you are offered another job in the company and turn it down.) Other than that:

○ Don't regard any redundancy payment as a windfall: you may need it to live on.

○ If you think you've been treated unfairly and the company's human resources department isn't much help, you can apply to the Fair Work Ombudsman in Australia or an employment tribunal in the UK.

○ Redundancy isn't personal: stay positive. Don't whinge about your ex-employer to anyone other than your immediate household and even they will lose sympathy after a few weeks.

○ When it comes to looking for a new job, don't accept any old thing in haste. Apply yourself diligently – it's a nine-to-five, five-days-a-week task; apply for positions you know you can fill well. Use all your contacts to check the market for openings that might suit you. Sharpen your CV: it's your calling card and needs to be as impressive as possible. Imagine the questions an employer might ask and prepare intelligent and well-considered answers (which aren't lies).

○ If joblessness goes on and on, keep fit and do voluntary work using the skills you'd bring to a paid job. Seek careers advice.

·········· WHAT TO DO ABOUT TROUBLED ·········· HOUSEHOLD MEMBERS

However badly we want our lives to be normal, circumstances will arise to make it less so or even completely not so. The most challenging are those related to the mental stability of a household member. Unless the member is you, you will almost certainly not be able to do much about their circumstances; you do, however, need to take control of your own. In the short term, if necessary, make sure any children are safe. Make sure you are safe.

If a household member has an addiction problem

This could be a problem with alcohol, prescription drugs or recreational drugs. In terms of the havoc each can wreak on a household, there's not that much difference. Negative though it sounds for other household members, your first step towards improving the situation is accepting that you can't help until the person concerned appreciates they have a serious problem. After that:

- Accept that keeping the household together may not be best. It may contribute to masking the problem for the person concerned as well as the outside world.

- Recognise when the circumstances are unmanageable and either leave or ban the unfortunate person from the household. Bringing the misery to a climax may be in their best interests as well as those of other family members.

- Get help from family members who don't live with you, from friends or, if that's impossible, from outside agencies like Family Drug Support in Australia, Families Anonymous in the UK or Alcoholics Anonymous in either country.

If a household member is violent

Violence can be psychological, physical, sexual, emotional or even economic, and can affect household members of any age. Within families it often becomes a pattern and a habit. Recognise when it's happening and accept you are not to blame. Maintaining the appearance of normality only worsens matters.

- Never underestimate the danger you or other household members may be in. Physical attacks can be unprovoked and vicious, even if they are immediately regretted.

- Notify the police.

- If you or any children are in immediate physical danger, leave the house. You will need help and support, so confide in a friend or other family member or, if that's not possible, an advice agency.

- If the violent person is your partner, you can apply for a court order that protects your right to live in the family home (advice groups will help).

- Helpful telephone numbers: Violence Against Women (1800 200 526), Relationships Australia (1300 364 277), Mensline Australia (1300 78 99 78); English National Domestic Violence (0808 2000 24).

If a household member is depressed

It's reckoned that two in three of us will suffer from depression and everyone in Australia and the UK will be affected at some point in their lives by their own, or someone else's. It can be frightening and debilitating both for the sufferer and for those living with them.

There is, of course, a distinction to be made between unhappiness as the result of miserable circumstances, depression as the result of difficult circumstances which passes with time (a matter of weeks) but may require treatment, and severe depression which may recur for no obvious reason and does require treatment. Telling one from the other isn't always easy, but being unable to function normally is the critical symptom. Get proper advice and don't rest until the advice is actually helpful – it's shameful to say so, but much of it just isn't. Within the household:

- Acknowledge the problem, even if the depressed person can't or won't.

- Don't expect the depressed person to snap out of it. It's futile: they need help in the way of medication and/or therapy. Talking also often helps, even if relentless negativity does test the patience of the listener.

- Be patient and non-judgemental, but understand your limits. You can't banish the depression even if you can solve immediate problems, which you will be repeatedly required to do.

- Develop strategies for self-preservation. Establish boundaries: your life cannot be concerned solely with making things right for the depressed person. Get advice for yourself if you need it.

- Your response will be mirrored by any children in the household, so you need to take a loving, firm and decisive lead. Depression can be survived: a sense of perspective and strength of purpose is required and we all have both at our fingertips.

If a household member has a mid-life crisis

Its existence is mostly anecdotal, but it stands to reason. Everyone aged between thirty-five and seventy will one day question the point of their existence. It constitutes a crisis because it will become a positive turning point – and if it doesn't, it should.

- Most important, if you are living with someone else's mid-life crisis, keep it in perspective even when your feelings are murderous. It's not your crisis; it's theirs.

- Identify the trigger. It may be a parent's death, a friend's death, children leaving home, job loss, a physical reminder of ageing and life running out.

- Examine the nature of the upset, which may be:

  * loss of looks;

  * a sense that you or the person in crisis married the wrong person;

  * dissatisfaction with current professional and financial circumstances;

  * a sense of failure, of disgust that this is all there is;

  * a loss of purpose or direction;

  * a sense of being trapped in a life that you/they never wanted;

  * serious fear of illness and death.

Clarify why the trigger has caused the upset it has, then banish it; move on. That is the ideal, even if it isn't always so simple. It may take months of negotiation, so negotiate but not for the rest of your life. At this stage of the game, a positive outcome for everyone is essential. A mid-life crisis can feel like depression and maybe it is. A chat with your GP might be helpful, but drugs are rarely the answer. The crisis is depressing because its driving force is dissatisfaction. This is what needs to be addressed.

The aim, whatever our household, however old we are, is to live happily ever after. Never forget it. The trick is to identify happiness when we have it and to pursue it when we haven't. It doesn't have to be hugely ambitious. I can't describe yours, only mine, and for me it's a profound acceptance that, even if everything isn't right in the world as defined by my household and its extensions, it's as good as it can be under the circumstances.

A little order, a little planning and a vague comprehension of how to tackle the everyday challenges bring clarity, and clarity it turns out, does no harm at all.

I spoke to hundreds of people, read millions of printed words and scanned several thousand websites in the course of researching this book, for both information and perspective. I am extremely grateful to the people listed under Main Interviews below for their advice, which was given freely and patiently, and I would like to acknowledge the contribution of the listed websites, several of which I used as a reference throughout. (I would like to have acknowledged more of each, but the lists would have filled another book.) If I've left out anyone who would like to included (or included anyone who'd rather not be), I'm more than happy to correct the situation on the website, whattodoabouteverything.com, and in any future editions of the book.

Note: All website references were correct at the time of writing. Some UK government references may have changed owing to the proposed amalgamation of some services due to others having been disbanded.

Part 1 The happy household

PUBLICATIONS

'2006 Census Tables', *2006 Census of Population and Housing Australia (2068.0)*, Canberra, ACT, Australian Bureau of Statistics (ABS), 2007

Jim Bennett and Mike Dixon, *Single person households and social policy: looking forwards*, York, Joseph Rowntree Foundation, 2006. Retrieved from: www.jrf.org.uk/sites/files/jrf/bennett-9781859354759.pdf

Darian Clark, 'The Lone Person Household Demographic: Trends and Implications', *Australian Social Policy 2002–03*, Canberra, ACT, Department of Families, Community Services, n.d. Retrieved from: www.facs.gov.au/about/publicationsarticles/research/austsocialpolicy/

'Consensus views arising from the 56th Study Group: *Reproductive Ageing*', Susan Bewley, William Ledger and Dimitrios Nikolaou, eds, Reproductive Ageing, London, Royal College of Obstetricians and Gynaecologists Press, 2009, pp.353–6. Retrieved from: www.rcog.org.uk/files/rcog-corp/uploaded-files/ReproductiveAgeingConsensus0609.pdf

David de Vaus, *Diversity and Change in Australian Families: Statistical Profiles,* Melbourne, Australian Institute of Family Studies, 2004. Retrieved from: www.aifs.gov.au/institute/pubs/diversity/main.html

Alfred Michael Dockery, 'Measuring the "real" cost of children: A net wealth approach', *Australian Policy Online*, Melbourne, Institute of Social Research, Swinburne University of Technology, 12 March 2009. Retrieved from: www.apo.org.au/research/measuring-real-cost-children-net-wealth-approach

Donna Dunning, *Introduction to Type and Communication*, Palo Alto, CA, CPP Inc., 2003

Families, Incomes and Jobs, vols 1–4: Statistical Reports of the Hilda Survey, Melbourne, Melbourne Institute of Applied Economic and Social Research, 2006–2009. Retrieved from: www.melbourneinstitute.com/hilda/statreport.html

Sue Heath and Elizabeth Cleaver, *Young, Free and Single? Twenty-somethings and Household Change*, Houndmills, Basingstoke, Hampshire, Palgrave Macmillan, 2003

Household and Family Projections, Australia, 2001 to 2026 (3236.0), Canberra, ACT, Australian Bureau of Statistics, 2004

'Households and Living Space' *40% House Report*, chapter 3, Oxford, Environmental Change Institute, Oxford University, 2006. Retrieved from: www.eci.ox.ac.uk/research/energy/downloads/40house/chapter03.pdf

Damian Killen and Danica Murphy, *Introduction to Type and Conflict*, Palo Alto, CA, CPP Inc, 2003

'Lifetime marriage and divorce trends', *Australian Social Trends 2007* (4102.0), Canberra, ACT, Australian Bureau of Statistics

'Living Arrangements: Future living arrangements', *Australian Social Trends 2001* (4102.0), Canberra, ACT, Australian Bureau of Statistics

'New report busts myth that kids are costing more', *AMP Media release*, 11 December 2007, Sydney, AMP Financial Services. Retrieved from: http://media.amp.com.au

'One-parent families', *Australian Social Trends 2007* (4102.0), Canberra, ACT, Australian Bureau of Statistics

RCOG Statement on Later Maternal Age, London, Royal College of Obstetricians and Gynaecologists, 15 June 2009. Retrieved from: www.rcog.org.uk/what-we-do/campaigning-and-opinions/statement/rcog-statement-later-maternal-age

'Recent increases in Australia's fertility', *Australian Social Trends 2007* (4102.0), Canberra, ACT, Australian Bureau of Statistics, 2007

Elly Robinson and Robyn Parker, 'Prevention and early intervention in strengthening families and relationships: Challenges and implications', *AFRC Issues No. 2*, 2008, Australian Institute of Family Studies. Retrieved from: www.aifs.gov.au/afrc/pubs/issues/issues2.html

A. Taylor, 'ABC of subfertility: extent of the problem', *British Medical Journal*, v327 n7412, 2003, pp.434–6

Jessica Woodroffe, *Not having it all: how motherhood reduces women's pay and employment prospects*, London, Fawcett Society, July 2009. Retrieved from: www.fawcettsociety. org.uk/documents/NotHavingItAll.pdf

Working Tax Credit: Help with the Costs of Childcare, London, HM Revenue and Customs, 2010. Retrieved from: www.hmrc.gov.uk/leaflets/wtc5.pdf

MAIN WEBSITES
AUSTRALIA
Australian Bureau of Statistics: www.abs.gov.au

Australian College of Midwives: www.midwives.org.au

BabyCentre: www.babycentre.com.au

Careforkids.com.au: www.careforkids.com.au

UK
BBC Parenting: www.bbc.co.uk/parenting

Healthywomen.org.uk: www.healthywomen.org.uk

Human Fertilisation and Embryology Authority: www.hfea.gov.uk

National Health Service (NHS): www.nhs.uk

MAIN INTERVIEWS
Dr Debra Kennedy, Royal Hospital for Women in Sydney

Mary McGuinness, Institute for Type Development

Lixia Qu, Australian Institute of Family Studies

Part 2 Organising time and space
PUBLICATIONS
Canadian National Occupancy Standard, Canadian Mortgage and Housing Corporation. Retrieved from: www2.stats.govt.nz

Stephen R. Covey, *7 Habits of Highly Effective People*. Retrieved from: www.stephencovey.com/7habits/7habits.php

Rosemary Crompton and Clare Lyonette, 'Who Does the Housework: the division of labour within the home', A. Park et al., *British Social Attitudes: the 24th Report*, London, Sage Publications, 2008. Retrieved from: www.download-it.org

Josh Fear, 'Stuff happens: unused things cluttering up our homes', *Research Paper No. 52*, Australia Institute, 2008. Retrieved from: www.tai.org.au/index.php?q=node%2F19&pubid=491&act=display

Peter Walsh, *It's All Too Much*, Pymble, New South Wales, Simon & Schuster, 2009

Work and family responsibilities through life, Melbourne, Australian Institute of Family Studies, 2008. Retrieved from: www.aifs.gov.au/institute/pubs/snapshots/ssbrochure08/ssbrochure08.pdf

MAIN INTERVIEWS

Peter Bliss, Business is Bliss

Glenda Hamilton, Perfectly Organised

Lauren Hill/Michelle Dockary, 3 Little Words

Clare McPhee, Organise Your Life

Karen Perkins, Clear and Clutterfree

Susanne Thiebe, Less Mess

Narelle Todd, time and space management consultant

Part 3 Household chores

PUBLICATIONS

Dry Cleaning, New South Wales Office of Fair Trading. Retrieved from: www.fairtrading.nsw.gov.au/Consumers/Buying_services/Dry_cleaning.html

Hygiene Code for the Private Household: based on the Dutch situation, Netherlands Nutrition Centre, 1999. Retrieved from www.nutricion.org/publicaciones/pdf/hygiene_codehouses.pdf

Home Hygiene, Prevention of Infection in the Home: a training resource for carers and their trainers, Community Infection Control Nurses Network and International Scientific Forum on Home Hygiene, n.d. Retrieved from: www.nhs.uk/Livewell/homehygiene/Documents/ICNA-TRAINING-RESOURCE-BOOKLET%5B1%5D.pdf

Shannon Lush and Jennifer Fleming, *Spotless: room-by-room solutions to domestic disasters*, Sydney, ABC Books, 2005

MAIN WEBSITES

AUSTRALIA

Dial an Angel: www.dialanangel.com

Drycleaning Institute of Australia: www.drycleanersweb.com.au

MAIN INTERVIEWS

Bega Commercial Cleaning Service

Betty Egan, cleaning whiz

David Ellis, lecturer on laundering and textiles, Ultimo College, New South Wales

Footwear Repairers Institute of New South Wales

Kim Ford, launderer

Gordon Kilcorn, launderer

Andrew Lyle, launderer

Natures Organics

Shirley Naylor (ed.), National Drycleaner and Laundry Magazine

The Observatory Hotel, Sydney

Pins 'n' Needles, craft and quilting suppliers, Merimbula

Mark Tillson, folding genius

The Wolseley Restaurant, London

Part 4 Feeding the household

PUBLICATIONS

Stephanie Alexander, *The Cook's Companion*, Camberwell, Vic., Viking/Lantern, 1996

Australian Guide to Healthy Eating, Canberra, ACT, Department of Health and Aging, 2008. Retrieved from: www.health.gov.au/internet/main/publishing.nsf/content/health-pubhlth-strateg-food-guide-index.htm

Rachel L. Batterham et al., 'PYY modulation of cortical and hypothalamic brain areas predicts feeding behaviour in humans', *Nature* v450,n7166, 1 November 2007, pp. 106–109. Retrieved from: www.nature.com

Maggie Beer, *Maggie's Harvest*, Camberwell, Vic., Lantern, 2007

Carbohydrates in human nutrition: report of a joint FAO/WHO expert consultation, Rome, 14–18 April 1997, Rome, World Health Organization: Food and Agriculture Organization of the United Nations, 1998. Retrieved from: http://books.google.com/books?printsec=frontcover&vid=ISBN9251041148&vid=ISBN9251041148&vid=LCCN98210561#

Diet or exercise? New study finds sugar is important in obesity, London, Medical Research Council, 7 August 2007. Retrieved from: www.mrc.ac.uk/Newspublications/News/MRC003902

Environmental Impact of Food Production and Consumption: a research report completed for the Department of Environment Food and Rural Affairs. Manchester Business School,

University of Manchester, 2006. Retrieved from: www.heartland.org/custom/semod_policybot/pdf/20893.pdf

Healthy Eating Pyramid, Department of Nutrition, Harvard School of Public Health. Retrieved from: www.nutritionsource.org

'How to choose your eggs wisely', *Choose Wisely: an initiative of the RSPCA*. Retrieved from: www.choosewisely.org.au/choosing-eggs.htm

Dr Rob Hicks, *Food Poisoning*, BBC Health (online). Retrieved from: www.bbc.co.uk/health/physical_health/conditions/foodpoisoning1.shtml

Sarah Hills, *Further evidence backs traffic light food label scheme*, Health Promotion International, Oxford University Press, 6 April 2009. Retrieved from: www.foodnavigator.com/content/view/print/242340

P. Kristiansen et al., *Australian Organic Market Report 2008*, commissioned by the Biological Farmers of Australia, 2008. Retrieved from: www.bfa.com.au/index.asp?Sec_ID=259

Nutritional requirements, The Merck Manuals Online Medical Library. Retrieved from: www.merck.com/mmhe/sec12/ch152/ch152g.html

Jamie Oliver, *Cook with Jamie*, London, Michael Joseph, 2006

Protein and Amino Acid Requirements in Human Nutrition: Report of a Joint Who/FAO/UNU Expert Consultation, Rome, World Health Organization, 2007. Retrieved from: http://books.google.com/books?id=In2RQAAACAAJ&dq=Protein+and+Amino+Acid+Requirements+in+Human+Nutrition:+Report+of+a+Joint+Who/Fao/unu+Expert+Consultation&hl=en&ei=93x_TOi_NoqEvAPasazDBA&sa=X&oi=book_result&ct=result&resnum=1&ved=0CCsQ6AEwAA

Matt Skinner, *Thirsty Work*, London, Mitchell Beazley, 2005

Storing & Preserving: Keeping Food Safe At Home, Minnesota Department of Health. Retrieved from: www.health.state.mn.us/foodsafety/store

'A Triumph of Marketing – Pay for bottled water if you like the taste, but don't kid yourself it's healthier than tap water.' *Choice*, July 2005. Retrieved from: www.choice.com.au

MAIN WEBSITES
AUSTRALIA
ABC Health and Wellbeing: www.abc.net.au/health

Australian Chicken Meat Federation: www.chicken.org

Australian Egg Corporation: www.aecl.org

Choice: www.choice.com.au

Commonwealth Scientific and Industrial Research Organisation (CSIRO): www.csiro.au

Fishline: fishline@sydneyfishmarket.com.au

Food Science Australia: www.foodscience.csiro.au

Food Standards Australia New Zealand: www.foodstandards.gov.au

Safe Food Australia: info@safefood.net.au

National Health and Medical Research Council Australia: www.nhmrc.gov.au

Nutrient Reference Values (nutrient reference values): www.nrv.gov.au

UK

ACT ON CO2: http://actonco2.direct.gov.uk/home.html

BUPA: www.bupa.co.uk/health_information

Cancer Research UK: www.cancerresearchuk.org

Eatwell (Food Standards Agency): www.eatwell.gov.uk

Fish for Thought: www.fishforthought.co.uk

Love Food Hate Waste: www.lovefoodhatewaste.com/static/about_food_waste

Million Women Study: www.millionwomenstudy.org

National Health Service: www.nhs.uk

Royal College of Psychiatrists: www.rcpsych.ac.uk

Soil Association UK: www.soilassociation.org

The Tea Council: www.tea.co.uk

Tea Palace : www.teapalace.co.uk

US

Olive Oil Source: www.oliveoilsource.com

United States Department of Agriculture (USDA): www.usda.gov/wps/portal.usda.usdahome

University of California San Francisco Benioff Children's Hospital: www.ucsfbenioffchildrens.org

MAIN INTERVIEWS

Carol and Brian Ahern, free-range egg farmers

Allergy Unit, Royal Prince Alfred Hospital, Sydney

Glen Baker, Little Bottler, Pambula, New South Wales

Donna Cameron, supermarket manager

David Goodall, Goodalls Butcher, Merimbula, New South Wales

Mark Hickman, former barista

Manny's Market, Merimbula

Stan Soroka, Pelagic Fish Processors Pty Ltd, Eden, New South Wales

David Thomson, Larsen and Thompson tea merchants

Part 5 Managing money

PUBLICATIONS

'Chance to Slash Mortgage', *Sun Herald*, 7 September 2008, p.2

'Golden Opportunity', Lesley Parker, *Sydney Morning Herald* and *The Age* (online): Retrieved from: www.moneymanager.com.au/articles/2008/06/02/1212258 735870.html

'Wealth in home of owner occupier households', *Australian Social Trends 2007* (No. 4102.0), Australian Bureau of Statistics, Canberra, ACT

MAIN WEBSITES

AUSTRALIA

Australian Securities and Investments Commission (ASIC): www.asic.gov.au

Australian Securities and Investments Commission: www.fido.gov.au

Choice: www.choice.com.au

Financial Planning Association: www.fpa.asn.au

Insolvency and Trustee Service Australia: www.itsa.gov.au

Money Management: www.moneymanagement.com.au

New South Wales Trustee and Guardian: www.pt.nsw.gov.au

UK

British Airways Customer Services: www.contacthelp.com/directory/ British+Airways?ListingID=97

Directgov: www.direct.gov.uk

—— Money, tax and benefits: www.direct.gov.uk/en/MoneyTaxAndBenefits/index.htm

—— Shares, unit trusts, investment trusts: www.direct.gov.uk/en/

Financial Services Authority: www.fsa.gov.uk

Home Office: www.homeoffice.gov.uk

Money made clear: www.moneymadeclear.org.uk

Money Week: www.moneyweek.com

This Is Money: www.thisismoney.co.uk

MAIN INTERVIEWS

Katrina Aked, family budgets

Brock Halliday, Brock Halliday Pty Ltd

Bernie Heffernan, mortgage broker

David Keaveney, risk adviser, Stem Financial

Glenese Keaveney, financial planner, Centric Wealth Advisers Limited

Stuart Rodger, actuary

Kim Stevenson, Bendigo Bank, Pambula, New South Wales

Tony Sykes, Westcourt General Insurance Brokers

Part 6 Where and how to live

PUBLICATION

Terence Conran and Stafford Cliff, *Terence Conran's Inspiration*, London, Octopus
  Publishing Group, 2008

MAIN WEBSITES

AUSTRALIA

Department of the Environment, Water, Heritage and the Arts:
  www.environment.gov.au

Australian Institute of Architects: www.architecture.com.au

Energy Matters: www.energymatters.com.au

Energy Safe Victoria: www.esv.vic.gov.au

NRMA (National Roads and Motorists Association): www.openroad.com.au

New South Wales Office of Fair Trading: www.fairtrading.nsw.gov.au

Real Estate Institute of South Australia: www.reisa.com.au

Royal Life Saving: www.royallifesaving.com.au

Strataman: www.strataman.com.au

Urban Ecology Australia: www.urbanecology.org.au

UK

Child Accident Prevention Trust: www.capt.org.uk

Directgov: www.directgov.uk

The Electricity Guide: www.electricityguide.org.uk

Energy Saving Trust: www.energysavingtrust.org.uk

The Gas Guide: www.gas-guide.org.uk

Renewable UK (formerly British Wind Energy Association): www.bwea.com

Royal Institute of British Architects: www.architecture.com

Royal Society for the Prevention of Accidents: www.rospa.com

US

Data 360: www.data360.org

MAIN INTERVIEWS

Al Clark, electrician

Debbie Heron, Chris Wilson Real Estate, Eden, New South Wales

Part 7 Looking after yourself

PUBLICATIONS

R.E.B. Watson et al., 'Cosmetic "anti-ageing" product improves photoaged skin: a double-blind, randomized controlled trial' *British Journal of Dermatology*, v161 issue2, August 2009 pp.419–26. Retrieved from: http://onlinelibrary.wiley.com/doi/10.1111/bjd.2009.161.issue-2/issuetoc

'Bad posture can raise your blood pressure', *New Scientist*, issue 2616, 11August 2007, p.17. Retrieved from: www.newscientist.com/article/mg19526165.500-bad-posture-could-raise-your-blood-pressure.html

MAIN WEBSITES

AUSTRALIA

Department of Health and Ageing: www.health.gov.au

Australian Heart Foundation: www.heartfoundation.org.au

Australian Society of Plastic Surgeons: www.plasticsurgery.org.au

Cancer Council: www.cancer.org.au

New South Wales Department of Health: www.health.nsw.gov.au

St John's Ambulance: www.stjohns.org.au

UK

Association of the British Pharmaceutical Industry: www.abpi.org.uk

Blood Pressure Association: www.bpassoc.org.uk

BUPA: www.bupa.co.uk

Child Accident Prevention Trust: www.capt.org.uk

Economic & Social Research Council: www.esrcsocietytoday.ac.uk

Food Standards Agency: www.food.gov.uk

National Poisons Information Service: www.npis.org

NHS (National Health Service): www.nhs.uk

Patient UK: www.patient.co.uk

Portable Appliance Testing Information: www.pat-testing.info

Royal Society for the Prevention of Accidents: www.rospa.com

St John's Ambulance: www.sja.org.uk

US

American Heart Association: www.heart.org

Health and Yoga: www.healthandyoga.com

Living the Fit Life: www.livinthefitlife.com

Mayo Clinic: www.mayoclinic.com

MAIN INTERVIEWS

Zoe Foster, editor-at-large, Primped

Don Reed, GP

Part 8 Dealing with catastrophes

MAIN WEBSITES

AUSTRALIA

Australian Federal Police: www.afp.gov.au

Attorney General's Department: www.ag.gov.au/

Centrelink: www.centrelink.gov.au

Fair Work: www.fairwork.gov.au

Family Law Courts: www.familylawcourts.gov.au/

Gay and Lesbian Counselling and Community Services of Australia: www.glccs.org.au

Legal Services Commission of South Australia: www.lsc.sa.gov.au/

UK

British Association of Sexual and Relationship Therapy: www.basrt.org.uk

Directgov: www.direct.gov.uk

Her Majesty's Courts Service (HMCS): www.hmcs.gov.uk

Home Office: www.homeoffice.gov.uk

Human Fertilisation and Embryology Authority: www.hfea.gov.uk/

US

UK Health Care (Kentucky, US): www.ukhealthcare.uky.edu/

MAIN INTERVIEWS

Jim Hinkley, retired police officer

Dominic Wilson, solicitor

USEFUL WEBSITES

The composite Australian government website www.australia.gov.au has useful information and links for all sorts of matters that affect householders, including buying/renting, money, health, child care, relationships, and much more. The UK equivalent is www.direct.gov.uk.

Note: All website references were correct at the time of writing. Some UK government references may have changed owing to the proposed amalgamation of some services due to others having been disbanded.

Part 1 The happy household

CHAPTER 1 UNDERSTANDING THE HOUSEHOLD

Personality types
www.myersbriggs.org;
www.innerworks.ca/enneagram.htm;
www.healthymindconcepts.com

CHAPTER 3 ADDING CHILDREN TO THE HOUSEHOLD

General information
www.bbc.co.uk/parenting;
www.careforkids.com.au

Financial implications
www.familyassist.gov.au; www.taxpayer.com.au; www.ato.gov.au; www.hmrc.gov.uk (HM Revenue and Customs)

Conception, pregnancy and childbirth
www.healthinsite.gov.au; www.babycenter.com.au; www.bubhub.com.au; www.womens-health.co.uk; www.nhs.uk (National Health Service); www.babycentre.co.uk

Fertility treatment
www.fertilityplus.org; www.hfea.gov.uk (Human Fertilisation and Embryology Authority); www.ivf.com.au

Doulas
www.findadoula.com.au; www.doula.org.uk

Child care
www.ncac.gov.au (National Childcare Accreditation Council); www.careforkids.com.au; www.childcarelink.gov.uk

Part 2 Organising time and space

CHAPTER 4 TIME MANAGEMENT

Self-motivation
pauschlastlecturetranscript.pdf (wwwrandypausch.com); www.goal-setting-guide.com; www.businessisbliss.com.au

CHAPTER 5 SPACE MANAGEMENT

www.cluttergone.co.uk; Narelletodd.com; www.organised.net.au; www.lessmess.com.au; www.organizeyourlife.com.au; www.clutterfree.com.au; www.3littlewords.com.au

Part 3 Household chores

CHAPTER 6 CLEANING

Hospital corners
GMCAonline: Hospital Corners
youtube.com

Pests
www.howtogetridofstuff.com/pest
control; www.doyourownpestcontrol.
com; www.pestcontrol.org.au

Cleaning the office
www.computerhope.com

Getting someone to clean for you
www.ato.gov.au; www.hmrc.gov.uk

CHAPTER 7 LAUNDRY

Ironing
www.garmentcare.info

CHAPTER 8 CLOTHES CARE AND MAINTENANCE

Fabric and clothes care
www.geocities.com/garmentshop;
YouTube: how to fold a tshirt fast

Part 4 Feeding the household

General information
www.health.gov.au; www.nhmrc.gov.au;
www.foodscience.csiro.au;
www.food.gov.uk

CHAPTER 9 EATING PROPERLY

Balancing the diet
www.healthyfoodguide.com.au; www.
eatwell.gov.uk; www.hsph.harvard.edu/
nutritionsource/what-should-you-eat/
pyramid/index.html; www.bhf.org.au

How much to eat
www.guysandstthomas.nhs.uk;
www.lovefoodhatewaste.com/
perfect_portions

CHAPTER 10 BUYING AND STORING FOOD

Planning the shop
www.lovefoodhatewaste.com;
www.getgreen.com.au

Understanding food labels and additives
www.food.gov.uk/multimedia/pdfs/elist_
numbers.pdf; www.foodstandards.gov.au;
www.nhs.uk

Food for foodies
www.finefoodworld.co.uk; www.
pongcheese.co.uk; www.smellycheese.
com.au; www.gourmetshopper.com.au

Organic and sustainable food
www.organicguide.com (covers
the UK as well as Australia); www.
organicfooddirectory.com.au; www.
fountainhead.com.au; www.greenpeace.
org.uk; debateyourplate.com

Buying fish
www.amcs.org.au (Australian Marine
Conservation Society); or mcsuk.org
(UK equivalent); www.sydneyfishmarket.
com.au

Green tips for cooking
www.countryenergy.com.au

Feeding children
parentsjury.org.au;
www.kidsandnutrition.co.uk

CHAPTER 12 DRINKING SENSIBLY
Safe drinking
www.nhmrc.gov.au (National Health and
Medical Research Council); or www.
dh.gov.uk (Department of Health)

Problem drinking
www.lifeline.org.au; www.aa.org.au
(Alcoholics Anonymous); or www.
alcoholics-anonymous.org.uk

Buying wine
www.winespectator.com; www.majestic.
co.uk; www.winecompanion.com.au

Part 5 Managing money
**General Information (banking,
debt, savings, investment etc):**
Australia: www.fsa.gov.au (Financial
Services Authority); www.asic.gov.au
(Australian Securities and Investments
Commission, regulatory body); www.
fido.gov.au (ASIC financial tips and
information); www.fos.org.au (Financial
Ombudsman Service;)

UK: www.fsa.gov.uk (Financial Services
Authority); www.consumerdirect.
gov.uk (consumer advice);
www.moneymadeclear.fsa.gov.uk
(FSA financial tips and tools);
www.hmrc.gov.uk (HM Revenues and

Customs); www.financialplanning.org.
uk (Institute of Financial Planning
information and tips)

CHAPTER 13 BUDGETS AND BANKING
Budgeting
www.understandingmoney.gov.au; or
www.moneymadeclear.fsa.gov.uk

Comparing banks
www.money-au.com.au; or
www.moneysupermarket.com

Exchange rates
www.comparetravelmoney.co.uk;
www.rba.gov.au (Reserve Bank)

CHAPTER 14 SAVING, SPENDING LESS AND INVESTING
Financial advisors
www.findanadviser.org; www.fpa.asn.au
(Financial Planning Association);
www.centricwealth.com.au (financial
and investment advice)

**Investment properties
('buy-to-let')**
www.ato.gov.au or www.hmrc.gov.uk
(HM Revenues and Customs)

Clothes shopping online
www.asos.com

CHAPTER 15 BORROWING AND DEBT
Credit ratings
www.mycreditfile.com.au; www.
vedaadvantage.com; www.experian.co.uk

Debt

www.moneymadeclear.fsa.gov.uk; www.cccs.co.uk (Consumer Credit Counselling Service); www.salvos.org.au/need-help/financial-troubles; www.centrelink.gov.au

Identity theft

www.identitytheft.org.uk; www.fco.gov.uk/knowbeforeyougo (Foreign and Commonwealth Office); www.fsa.gov.uk (Financial Services Authority); www.crimeprevention.gov.au; www.ag.gov.au (Attorney General's Department); www.ftc.gov/bcp/edu/microsites/idtheft/consumers/about-identity-theft (US Federal Trade Commission);

CHAPTER 16 RISK MANAGEMENT

Making a will

www.lawsociety.org.uk; www.ageconcern.org.uk; www.courtfunds.gov.uk; www.australianprobate.com; www.statetrustees.com.au; www.seniors.gov.au; www.publictrustee.wa.gov.au (WA – google your own state or territory)

Insurance

www.cclcnsw.org.au (Consumer Credit Legal Centre of NSW – free advice); www.insuranceadvice.com.au; www.fos.org.au (Financial Ombudsman Service); www.financial-ombudsman.org.uk; www.westcourtgeneral.com.au (Westcourt General Insurance Brokers)

Part 6 Where and how to live

CHAPTER 17 MOVING HOUSE

Tenancy agreements

www.tenancyagreementservice.co.uk; www.rentalagreementsdiy.com.au; www.lawdepot.com

Buying a home

www.home.co.uk; www.homepriceguide.com.au; www.primelocation.com/uk-property

DIY conveyancing

www.diyconveyance.co.uk; www.diyconveyancingkit.net.au; www.landreg.gov.uk or www.landsearch.net/australia (land titles); www.adviceguide.org.uk (Citizens Advice Bureaux)

CHAPTER 18 GETTING THE PLACE STRAIGHT

Finding an architect or builder

www.designsonproperty.co.uk;www.fmb.org.uk/find-a-builder/free-contracts; www.architecture.com.au (Australian Institute of Architects); www.architecture.com (Royal Institute of British Architects); www.masterbuilders.com.au (Australian Master Builders Association); www.fmb.org.uk (UK Federation of Master Builders)

Repair and maintenance costs

www.archicentre.com.au (Institute of Architects advisory service); www.reao.com.au (Real Estate Australia Online)

Painting

www.naturalpaint.com.au or www.auro.co.uk (natural paints); www.highwayhardware.com.au or www.homecareessentials.co.uk (appliance paints)

Picture hanging

www.artperfect.com.au; www.art-install.co.uk

Plant care

www.kew.org (Royal Botanic Gardens Kew, UK); www.abc.net.au/gardening (Gardening Australia)

CHAPTER 19 HOUSEHOLD MAINTENANCE

Finding a tradesperson

www.serviceseeking.com.au; www.myhammer.co.uk

Car maintenance

www.mynrma.com.au (NRMA); www.theaa.com (UK Automobile Association)

CHAPTER 20 LIVING SAFELY AND SUSTAINABLY

Safety outdoors

www.childsafetyaustralia.com.au; www.kew.org/science or www.healthinsite.gov.au (poisonous plants)

Solar power/grants

www.uk-energy-saving.com/government_solar_power_grants.html; www.energymatters.com.au/government-rebates

Energy saving/appliances

www.energysavingtrust.org.uk; www.energyrating.gov.au; www.recycle.co.uk; www.adpost.com/au/appliances; www.fridgebuyback.com.au www.thegreendirectory.com.au/green-business/recycling-and-waste

Water saving

www.waterrating.gov.au; www.water-effiencylabel.org.uk

Part 7 Looking after yourself

CHAPTER 21 LOOKING GOOD

Skin care

www. primped.com.au; www.safersolutions.org.au (skin sensitivity); www.beautybible.com; shop.cancercouncil.com.au; www.safecosmetics.org

Teeth

www.bupa.co.uk (fact sheet); www.ada.org.au (Australian Dental Association); www.worldwidehealth.com

Posture

www.octagonclininc.co.uk; www.stat.org.uk (Society of Teachers of the Alexander Technique); www.ergonomics.com.au; www.yogajournal.com or www.findyoga.com.au (prenatal); www.lucyskelton.co.uk

CHAPTER 22 KEEPING FIT, STAYING WELL

General information

www.healthinsite.gov.au; www.health.gov.au; www.nhsdirect.nhs.uk

Blood pressure
www.bpassoc.org.uk (UK Blood Pressure Association); www.heartfoundation.org.au

Cholesterol
www.theonlineclinic.co.uk; www.daa.asn.au (Dietitians Association of Australia)

Weight/BMI
www.freebmicalculator.net/bmi-chart.php; www.mydr.com.au

First aid
www.stjohns.org.au; www.sja.org.uk; www.redcross.org.au; www.redcrossfirstaidtraining.co.uk

Poisoning
www.rch.org.au (Royal Childrens Hospital); www.childsafetyaustralia.com.au; www.npis.org (UK National Poisons Information Service); in Australia, google 'poison information centres' for state and territory centres; www.outback-australia-travel-secrets.com (snakes and spiders)

Part 8 Dealing with catastrophes
Natural disasters
www.news.bbc.co.uk/weather; www.bom.gov.au/weather

When someone dies
www.australia.gov.au/life-events; www.grief.org.au; www.ato.gov.au; www.directgov.uk; www.hmrc.gov.uk (HM Revenue and Customs)

If you want to get married
www.australia.gov.au/life-events; www.ag.gov.au (Attorney General's Department); www.adviceguide.org.uk

If you want to get divorced
www.divorceaid.co.uk; www.relationships.com.au.

Infertility
www.infertilitynetworkuk.com; www.patient.co.uk; www.anzica.org (Australian and New Zealand Infertility Counsellors Association): www.nor.com.au (Australian Infertility Support Group); www.patient.co.uk; www.ita.org.au (Infertility Treatment Authority, www.fertilitysociety.com.au or www.uksurrogatefamiliesonline.co.uk (surrogacy)

Coming out
www.ukgaynews.org.uk; www.comingout.com.au; www.relationships.com.au; www.relate.org.uk; www.basrt.org.uk (British Association for Sexual and relationship Therapy)

Finding a lawyer
www.lawsociety.com.au or www.lawsociety.org.uk; by state in Australia (e.g. www.legalaid.vic.gov.au) or www.communitylegaladvice.org.uk (free legal aid)

If you're the victim of a crime
www.victimsupport.org.au; www.victimsupport.org.uk

If you're made redundant

www.fairwork.gov.au (Fair Work
Online); www.direct.gov.uk;
www.employmenttribunals.gov.uk

Addiction problems

www.adca.org.au (Alcohol and Other
Drugs Council of Australia);
www.lifeline.org.au; www.aa.org.au; www.
al-anon.alateen.org/australia (for young
people); helpline@alcoholics-anonymous.
org.uk; www.al-anonuk.org.uk

Depression/Mental health

www.au.reachout.com (Reach Out
Australia); www.sane.org.uk

spider bites, 410

spouses, living with, 18–20

sprains, 414–15

stain removal, 95–6, 108–9

stainless steel, 92

stepchildren, 48–9

sticking doors, 341

stings, 411

stolen identity, 279

storage, 69–70, 73, 124–31, 180–91

store cupboards, 161–2, 181–3

strains, 414–15

stress, 398

strokes, 407

studies *see* offices

sugar, 145–6, 182, 183

sunburn, 412–13

superannuation, 265–6

supplements (health), 396

sustainable living, 359–68

swimming pools, 358

symptoms of illness, 404–6

T-shirts, folding, 128–9, **128**, **129**

taps, dripping, 340–1, **340**

tea (drink), 221–4

teeth, 382

temperature (body), 404–5

ticks, 411

tidying, 67–70, 79–81

timetables, 55–60

toilets, unblocking, 339–40

toolboxes, 337, 346–7

toys, 72

transport, energy-saving, 366

travel insurance, 287

trousers, 114, **114**, 135

tumble-dryers, 109–10

tyres, changing, 348–9

unblocking toilets and drains, 339–40

unit sizes (alcohol), 229–30

use-by dates, 167

vegetable soup, 202

vegetables, 152–3, 178–9, 183, 186, 189, 202–3

victims of crime, 434

violence, 437–8

waist measurements, 394–5

warranties, extended, 290

washing clothes, 103–9

washing machines, 103–6

washing up, 89–91

wasp stings, 411

waste, household *see* garbage

water (drinking), 220–1

water saving, 365–6

weekly timetables, 55–60

weevils, 93–4

weight (body), 394–6

wills, 290–3

wind power, 361

wine, 209, 234–9

wine glasses, 239

witnessing a crime, 433

wool, 108

work/life balance, 397–401

working from home, 62